Financial Mathematics for Actuaries

Second Edition

Financial Mathematics for Actuaries

Second Edition

Wai-Sum Chan *The Chinese University of Hong Kong, Hong Kong*
Yiu-Kuen Tse *Singapore Management University, Singapore*

World Scientific

NEW JERSEY · LONDON · SINGAPORE · BEIJING · SHANGHAI · HONG KONG · TAIPEI · CHENNAI · TOKYO

Published by

World Scientific Publishing Co. Pte. Ltd.

5 Toh Tuck Link, Singapore 596224

USA office: 27 Warren Street, Suite 401-402, Hackensack, NJ 07601

UK office: 57 Shelton Street, Covent Garden, London WC2H 9HE

British Library Cataloguing-in-Publication Data

A catalogue record for this book is available from the British Library.

FINANCIAL MATHEMATICS FOR ACTUARIES
Second Edition

ISBN 978-981-3224-66-7
ISBN 978-981-3224-67-4 (pbk)

Desk Editor: Shreya Gopi

Typeset by Stallion Press
Email: enquiries@stallionpress.com

Printed in Singapore

To Bonnie, Nikki and Kevin
for their continuously compounded rate of support

Wai-Sum Chan

To Vicky, Germaine, Gerald and Gemma
for their unyielding forbearance

Yiu-Kuen Tse

About the Authors

Wai-Sum Chan, PhD, FSA, HonFIA, CERA, graduated from the Chinese University of Hong Kong with a major in Accounting and a minor in Statistics. He pursued a doctorate in Applied Statistics at the Fox School of Business Management, Temple University (Philadelphia, USA), receiving his PhD in 1989. He qualified as a Fellow of the Society of Actuaries in 1995 and Chartered Enterprise Risk Analyst in 2008. He was conferred an Honorary Fellow by the Institute and Faculty of Actuaries in 2014. Dr Chan held teaching and research posts at the National University of Singapore, the University of Waterloo and the University of Hong Kong before his present appointment as Professor of Finance at the Chinese University of Hong Kong. Dr Chan's research interests include Health Care Financing, Actuarial Modeling and Financial Econometrics. He has had over 100 scientific articles published in scholarly journals. Dr Chan has been teaching financial and actuarial courses since 1992.

Yiu-Kuen Tse, PhD, FSA, graduated from the University of Hong Kong, majoring in Economics and Statistics. He obtained his MSc in Statistics and PhD in Econometrics from the London School of Economics. He has been a Fellow of the Society of Actuaries since 1993. Dr Tse's research interests are in Empirical Finance and Financial Econometrics. He is Professor of Economics at the School of Economics, Singapore Management University. He has published extensively in scholarly journals and is the author of the book *Nonlife Actuarial Models: Theory, Methods and Evaluation*. Dr Tse teaches undergraduate Actuarial Science and is also involved in many executive training programs.

Preface to the Second Edition

A good understanding of the fundamental concepts of financial mathematics is essential for the evaluation of any financial product and instrument. Mastering concepts of present and future values of streams of cash flows under different interest rate environments is core for actuaries and financial economists. It is with these perspectives in mind that we write this textbook.

This book covers the body of knowledge required by the Society of Actuaries (SOA) for its Financial Mathematics (FM) Exam. In this second edition, we expand the book to include topics introduced by the SOA in the FM Exam from 2017 onwards. In particular, in Chapter 3 we include the coverage of interest rate swaps. We also add a chapter on the determination of the rates of interest of various financial securities. Some institutional aspects of interest rate policies and the economic management of Central Banks are also discussed in this chapter.

This book also has a chapter on stochastic interest rate models. Students studying for the Institute and Faculty of Actuaries Exam CT1 will also find this book suitable for the preparation of the exam.

It is our hope that students in an undergraduate course on financial mathematics for actuaries will find this book useful. This book contains numerous examples and exercises, some of which are adapted from previous SOA FM Exams. We believe it is also useful for students preparing for the actuarial professional exams through self-study.

Users of this book are assumed to have prior knowledge of high school algebra and college level introductory calculus. An appendix on the preview of mathematics and statistics is included for the benefits of students who require a quick revision or occasional reference.

We continue to provide teaching aids to support instructors using this book for teaching. Instructors who wish to obtain the instructors' manual for the solutions of the exercises and/or the slides for use in lectures may write to the publisher at: customercare@wspc.com.

Wai-Sum Chan, PhD FSA CERA
Department of Finance
Chinese University of Hong Kong

Yiu-Kuen Tse, PhD FSA
School of Economics
Singapore Management University

Contents

List of Mathematical Symbols

Symbol	Meaning
$a_{\overline{n}\rvert}$	same as $a_{\overline{n}\rvert i}$ when the rate of interest is understood
$a_{\overline{n}\rvert i}$	present value of an annuity-immediate
$_{q\rvert}a_{\overline{n}\rvert i}$	present value of a q-period deferred annuity-immediate
$a_{\overline{\infty}\rvert}$	present value of a perpetuity-immediate
$a_{\overline{n}\rvert}^{(m)}$	same as $a_{\overline{n}\rvert i}^{(m)}$ when the rate of interest is understood
$a_{\overline{n}\rvert i}^{(m)}$	present value of an mn-payment annuity-immediate with m payments per interest-conversion period
$_{q\rvert}a_{\overline{n}\rvert i}^{(m)}$	present value of a q-period deferred, mn-payment annuity-immediate with m payments per interest-conversion period
$\ddot{a}_{\overline{n}\rvert}$	same as $\ddot{a}_{\overline{n}\rvert i}$ when the rate of interest is understood
$\ddot{a}_{\overline{n}\rvert i}$	present value of an annuity-due
$_{q\rvert}\ddot{a}_{\overline{n}\rvert i}$	present value of a q-period deferred annuity-due
$\ddot{a}_{\overline{\infty}\rvert}$	present value of a perpetuity-due
$\ddot{a}_{\overline{n}\rvert}^{(m)}$	same as $\ddot{a}_{\overline{n}\rvert i}^{(m)}$ when the rate of interest is understood
$\ddot{a}_{\overline{n}\rvert i}^{(m)}$	present value of an mn-payment annuity-due with m payments per interest-conversion period
$_{q\rvert}\ddot{a}_{\overline{n}\rvert i}^{(m)}$	present value of a q-period deferred, mn-payment annuity-due with m payments per interest-conversion period
$\bar{a}_{\overline{n}\rvert}$	present value of a continuous annuity
$_{q\rvert}\bar{a}_{\overline{n}\rvert}$	present value of a q-period deferred continuous annuity
$a(t)$	accumulation function at time t
$a_t(\tau)$	accumulation function for a forward payment due at time t
$A(t)$	amount function at time t

Symbol	Meaning
B_j^A	fund value after transaction at time t_j
B_j^B	fund value before transaction at time t_j
d	rate of discount
$d^{(m)}$	nominal rate of discount payable m times a year
δ	constant force of interest
$\delta(t)$	force of interest at time t
D	Macaulay duration
D^*	modified duration
D_F	Fisher-Weil duration
$(Da)_{\overline{n}|}$	present value of a decreasing annuity-immediate
$(D\ddot{a})_{\overline{n}|}$	present value of a decreasing annuity-due
$(D\bar{a})_{\overline{n}|}$	present value of a decreasing continuous annuity
$(\bar{D}\bar{a})_{\overline{n}|}$	present value of a continuously decreasing continuous annuity
$(Ds)_{\overline{n}|}$	future value of a decreasing annuity-immediate
$(D\ddot{s})_{\overline{n}|}$	future value of a decreasing annuity-due
$(D\bar{s})_{\overline{n}|}$	future value of a decreasing continuous annuity
$(\bar{D}\bar{s})_{\overline{n}|}$	future value of a continuously decreasing continuous annuity
i	constant annual effective rate of interest
i_H	one-year holding yield
i_P	par yield of a bond
i_t^Y	investment-year credit rate at year t
$i(t)$	annual effective rate of interest for year t
$i(t, t+n)$	annual effective rate of interest in the period t to $t+n$
i_t^F	forward rate of interest
$i_{t,\tau}^F$	annualized forward rate of interest over τ periods from t to $t+\tau$
i_t^S	spot rate of interest
$_t i_\tau^S$	the spot rate of interest applicable to period t to $t+\tau$
$I(t)$	interest incurred in period t

Symbol   Meaning

$(Ia)_{\overline{n}\rvert}$	present value of an increasing annuity-immediate
$(I\ddot{a})_{\overline{n}\rvert}$	present value of an increasing annuity-due
$(I\bar{a})_{\overline{n}\rvert}$	present value of an increasing continuous annuity
$(\bar{I}\bar{a})_{\overline{n}\rvert}$	present value of a continuously increasing continuous annuity
$(Is)_{\overline{n}\rvert}$	future value of an increasing annuity-immediate
$(I\ddot{s})_{\overline{n}\rvert}$	future value of an increasing annuity-due
$(I\bar{s})_{\overline{n}\rvert}$	future value of an increasing continuous annuity
$(\bar{I}\bar{s})_{\overline{n}\rvert}$	future value of a continuously increasing continuous annuity
$r^{(m)}$	nominal rate of interest payable m times a year
$\bar{r}$	continuously compounded rate of interest
r_I	rate of inflation
r_N	nominal rate of interest
r_R	real rate of interest
R_A	arithmetic mean rate of return
R_B	interest rate for borrowing
R_D	one-period DWRR (dollar-weighted rate of return)
R_G	geometric mean rate of return
R_L	interest rate for lending
R_P	rate of return for a portfolio
R_S	swap rate of an interest rate swap
R_T	one-period TWRR (time-weighted rate of return)
$s_{\overline{n}\rvert}$	same as $s_{\overline{n}\rvert i}$ when the rate of interest is understood
$s_{\overline{n}\rvert i}$	future value of an annuity-immediate
$_{q\rvert}s_{\overline{n}\rvert i}$	future value of a q-period deferred annuity-immediate
$s_{\overline{n}\rvert}^{(m)}$	same as $s_{\overline{n}\rvert i}^{(m)}$ when the rate of interest is understood
$s_{\overline{n}\rvert i}^{(m)}$	future value of an mn-payment annuity-immediate with m payments per interest-conversion period

Symbol   Meaning

$_{q\lvert}s_{\overline{n}\rvert i}^{(m)}$	future value of an q-period deferred, mn-payment annuity-immediate with m payments per interest-conversion period
$\ddot{s}_{\overline{n}\rvert}$	same as $\ddot{s}_{\overline{n}\rvert i}$ when the rate of interest is understood
$\ddot{s}_{\overline{n}\rvert i}$	future value of an annuity-due
$_{q\lvert}\ddot{s}_{\overline{n}\rvert i}$	future value of a q-period deferred annuity-due
$\ddot{s}_{\overline{n}\rvert}^{(m)}$	same as $\ddot{s}_{\overline{n}\rvert i}^{(m)}$ when the rate of interest is understood
$\ddot{s}_{\overline{n}\rvert i}^{(m)}$	future value of an mn-payment annuity-due with m payments per interest-conversion period
$_{q\lvert}\ddot{s}_{\overline{n}\rvert i}^{(m)}$	future value of a q-period deferred, mn-payment annuity-due with m payments per interest-conversion period
$\bar{s}_{\overline{n}\rvert}$	present value of a continuous annuity
$_{q\lvert}\bar{s}_{\overline{n}\rvert}$	present value of a q-period deferred continuous annuity
v	discount factor
$v(t)$	present value of 1 to be paid at time t

1 Interest Accumulation and Time Value of Money

From time to time we are faced with problems of making financial decisions. These may involve anything from borrowing a loan from a bank to purchase a house or a car; or investing money in bonds, stocks or other securities. To a large extent, intelligent wealth management means borrowing and investing wisely.

Financial decision making should take into account the **time value of money**. It is not difficult to see that a dollar received today is worth more than a dollar received one year later. The time value of money depends critically on how interest is calculated. For example, the frequency at which the interest is compounded may be an important factor in determining the cost of a loan.

In this chapter, we discuss the basic principles in the calculation of interest, including the simple- and compound-interest methods, the frequencies of compounding, the effective rate of interest and rate of discount, and the present and future values of a single payment.

1.1   Accumulation Function and Amount Function

Many financial transactions involve lending and borrowing. The sum of money borrowed is called the **principal**. To compensate the lender for the loss of use of the principal during the loan period the borrower pays the lender an amount of **interest**. At the end of the loan period the borrower pays the lender the **accumulated amount**, which is equal to the sum of the principal plus interest.

We denote $A(t)$ as the accumulated amount at time t, called the **amount function**. Hence, $A(0)$ is the initial principal and

$$I(t) = A(t) - A(t-1) \tag{1.1}$$

is the interest incurred from time $t-1$ to time t, namely, in the tth period. For the special case of an initial principal of 1 unit, we denote the accumulated amount at time t by $a(t)$, which is called the **accumulation function**. Thus, if the initial principal is $A(0) = k$, then

$$A(t) = k \times a(t).$$

This assumes that the same accumulation function is used for the amount function irrespective of the initial principal.

1.2   Simple and Compound Interest

Equation (1.1) shows that the growth of the accumulated amount depends on the way the interest is calculated, and vice versa. While theoretically there are numerous ways of calculating the interest, there are two methods which are commonly used in practice. These are the **simple-interest method** and the **compound-interest method**.

For the simple-interest method, the interest earned over a period of time is proportional to the length of the period. Thus the interest incurred from time 0 to time t, for a principal of 1 unit, is $r \times t$, where r is the constant of proportion called the **rate of interest**. Hence the accumulation function for the simple-interest method is

$$a(t) = 1 + rt, \qquad \text{for } t \geq 0, \qquad (1.2)$$

and

$$A(t) = A(0)a(t) = A(0)(1 + rt), \qquad \text{for } t \geq 0. \qquad (1.3)$$

In general the rate of interest may be quoted for any period of time (such as a month or a year). In practice, however, the most commonly used base is the year, in which case the term **annual rate of interest** is used. In what follows we shall maintain this assumption, unless stated otherwise.

Example 1.1: A person borrows $2,000 for 3 years at simple interest. The rate of interest is 8% per annum. What are the interest charges for year 1 and 2? What is the accumulated amount at the end of year 3?

Solution: The interest charges for year 1 and 2 are both equal to

$$2,000 \times 0.08 = \$160.$$

The accumulated amount at the end of year 3 is

$$2,000 \, (1 + 0.08 \times 3) = \$2,480.$$

For the compound-interest method, the accumulated amount over a period of time is the principal for the next period. Thus, a principal of 1 unit accumulates to $1 + r$ units at the end of the year, which becomes the principal for the second year. Continuing this process, the accumulation function becomes

$$a(t) = (1 + r)^t, \qquad \text{for } t = 0, 1, 2, \cdots, \qquad (1.4)$$

and the amount function is

$$A(t) = A(0)a(t) = A(0)(1 + r)^t, \qquad \text{for } t = 0, 1, 2, \cdots. \qquad (1.5)$$

Two remarks are noted. First, for the compound-interest method the accumulated amount at the end of a year becomes the principal for the following year.

This is in contrast to the simple-interest method, for which the principal remains unchanged through time. Second, while (1.2) and (1.3) apply for $t \geq 0$, (1.4) and (1.5) hold only for integral $t \geq 0$. As we shall see below, there are alternative ways to define the accumulation function for the compound-interest method when t is not an integer.

Example 1.2:   Solve the problem in Example 1.1 using the compound-interest method.

Solution: The interest for year 1 is

$$2,000 \times 0.08 = \$160.$$

For year 2 the principal is

$$2,000 + 160 = \$2,160,$$

so that the interest for the year is

$$2,160 \times 0.08 = \$172.80.$$

The accumulated amount at the end of year 3 is

$$2,000 \, (1 + 0.08)^3 = \$2,519.42.$$

Compounding has the effect of generating a larger accumulated amount. The effect is especially significant when the rate of interest is high. Table 1.1 shows two samples of the accumulated amounts under simple- and compound-interest methods. It can be seen that when the interest rate is high, compounding the interest induces the principal to grow much faster than the simple-interest method.

With compound interest at 10%, it takes less than 8 years to double the investment. With simple interest at the same rate it takes 10 years to get the same result. Over a 20-year period, an investment with compound interest at 10% will grow 6.73 times. Over a 50-year period, the principal will grow by a phenomenal 117.39 times. When the interest rate is higher the effect of compounding will be even more dramatic.

Table 1.1: Accumulated amount for a principal of $100

| Year | 5% interest | | 10% interest | |
	Simple interest ($)	Compound interest ($)	Simple interest ($)	Compound interest ($)
1	105.00	105.00	110.00	110.00
2	110.00	110.25	120.00	121.00
3	115.00	115.76	130.00	133.10
4	120.00	121.55	140.00	146.41
5	125.00	127.63	150.00	161.05
6	130.00	134.01	160.00	177.16
7	135.00	140.71	170.00	194.87
8	140.00	147.75	180.00	214.36
9	145.00	155.13	190.00	235.79
10	150.00	162.89	200.00	259.37

1.3 Frequency of Compounding

Although the rate of interest is often quoted in annual term, the interest accrued to an investment is often paid more frequently than once a year. For example, a savings account may pay interest at 3% per year, where the interest is credited monthly. In this case, 3% is called the nominal rate of interest payable 12 times a year. As we shall see, the **frequency of interest payment** (also called the **frequency of compounding**) makes an important difference to the accumulated amount and the total interest earned. Thus, it is important to define the rate of interest accurately.

To emphasize the importance of the frequency of compounding we use $r^{(m)}$ to denote the **nominal rate of interest payable m times a year**. Thus, m is the frequency of compounding per year and $\frac{1}{m}$ year is the **compounding period** or **conversion period**.

Let t (in years) be an integer multiple of $\frac{1}{m}$, i.e., tm is an integer representing the number of interest-conversion periods over t years. The interest earned over the next $\frac{1}{m}$ year, from time t to $t + \frac{1}{m}$, is

$$a(t) \times r^{(m)} \times \frac{1}{m} = \frac{a(t)r^{(m)}}{m}, \qquad \text{for } t = 0, \frac{1}{m}, \frac{2}{m}, \cdots .$$

Thus, the accumulated amount at time $t + \frac{1}{m}$ is

$$a\left(t + \frac{1}{m}\right) = a(t) + \frac{a(t)r^{(m)}}{m} = a(t)\left[1 + \frac{r^{(m)}}{m}\right], \qquad \text{for } t = 0, \frac{1}{m}, \frac{2}{m}, \cdots .$$

By recursive substitution, we conclude

$$a(t) = \left[1 + \frac{r^{(m)}}{m}\right]^{mt}, \qquad \text{for } t = 0, \frac{1}{m}, \frac{2}{m}, \cdots , \qquad (1.6)$$

and hence

$$A(t) = A(0)\left[1 + \frac{r^{(m)}}{m}\right]^{mt}, \qquad \text{for } t = 0, \frac{1}{m}, \frac{2}{m}, \cdots . \qquad (1.7)$$

Example 1.3:   A person deposits \$1,000 into a savings account that earns 3% interest payable monthly. How much interest will be credited in the first month? What is the accumulated amount at the end of the first month?

Solution: The rate of interest over one month is

$$0.03 \times \frac{1}{12} = 0.25\%,$$

so that the interest earned over one month is

$$1,000 \times 0.0025 = \$2.50,$$

and the accumulated amount after one month is

$$1,000 + 2.50 = \$1,002.50.$$

Example 1.4: \$1,000 is deposited into a savings account that pays 3% interest with monthly compounding. What is the accumulated amount after two and a half years? What is the amount of interest earned over this period?

Solution: The investment interval is 30 months. Thus, using (1.7), the accumulated amount is

$$1,000\left[1 + \frac{0.03}{12}\right]^{30} = \$1,077.78.$$

The amount of interest earned over this period is

$$1,077.78 - 1,000 = \$77.78.$$

Example 1.5: Solve the problem in Example 1.4, assuming that the interest is paid quarterly.

Solution: The investment interval is now 10 quarters. With $m = 4$, the accumulated amount is

$$1,000 \left[1 + \frac{0.03}{4} \right]^{10} = \$1,077.58,$$

and the amount of interest earned is $77.58.

When the loan period is not an integer multiple of the compounding period (i.e., tm is not an integer), care must be taken to define the way interest is calculated over the fraction of the compounding period. Two methods may be considered. First, we may extend (1.6) and (1.7) to apply to any $tm \geq 0$ (not necessarily an integer). Second, we may compute the accumulated value over the largest integral interest-conversion period using (1.7) and then apply the simple-interest method to the remaining fraction of the conversion period. The example below illustrates these two methods.

Example 1.6: What is the accumulated amount for a principal of $100 after 25 months if the nominal rate of interest is 4% compounded quarterly?

Solution: The accumulation period is $\frac{25}{3} = 8.33$ quarters. Using the first method, the accumulated amount is

$$100 \left[1 + \frac{0.04}{4} \right]^{8.33} = \$108.64.$$

Using the second method the accumulated amount after 24 months (8 quarters) is

$$100 \left[1 + \frac{0.04}{4} \right]^{8} = \$108.29,$$

so that the accumulated amount after 25 months is

$$108.29 \left[1 + 0.04 \times \frac{1}{12} \right] = 108.65.$$

It can be shown that the second method provides a larger accumulation function for any non-integer $tm > 0$ (see Exercise 1.41). As the first method is easier to apply, we shall adopt it to calculate the accumulated value over a non-integral compounding period, unless otherwise stated.

At the same nominal rate of interest, the more frequent the interest is paid, the faster the accumulated amount grows. For example, assuming the nominal rate of interest to be 5% and the principal to be $1,000, the accumulated amounts after 1 year under several different compounding frequencies are given in Table 1.2.

Note that when the compounding frequency m increases, the accumulated amount tends to a limit. Let $\bar{r}$ denote the nominal rate of interest for which compounding is made over infinitely small intervals (i.e., $m \to \infty$ so that $\bar{r} = r^{(\infty)}$). We call this compounding scheme **continuous compounding**. For practical purposes, daily compounding is very close to continuous compounding.

From the well-known limit theorem (see Appendix A.1) that

$$\lim_{m \to \infty} \left[1 + \frac{\bar{r}}{m}\right]^m = e^{\bar{r}} \tag{1.8}$$

for any constant $\bar{r}$, we conclude that, for continuous compounding, the accumulation function (see (1.6)) is

$$a(t) = \lim_{m \to \infty} \left[1 + \frac{\bar{r}}{m}\right]^{mt} = \left[\lim_{m \to \infty} \left(1 + \frac{\bar{r}}{m}\right)^m\right]^t = e^{\bar{r}t}. \tag{1.9}$$

We call $\bar{r}$ the **continuously compounded rate of interest**. Equation (1.9) provides the accumulation function of the continuously compounding scheme at nominal rate of interest $\bar{r}$.

Table 1.2: Accumulated amount for a principal of $1,000 with nominal interest rate of 5% per annum

Frequency of interest payment	m	Accumulated amount ($)
Yearly	1	1,050.00
Quarterly	4	1,050.95
Monthly	12	1,051.16
Daily	365	1,051.27

1.4 Effective Rate of Interest

As Table 1.2 shows, the accumulated amount depends on the compounding frequency. Hence, comparing two investment schemes by just referring to their nominal rates of interest without taking into account their compounding frequencies may be misleading. Different investment schemes must be compared on a common basis. To this end, the measure called the **effective rate of interest** is often used. The annual effective rate of interest for year t, denoted by $i(t)$, is the ratio of the amount of interest earned in a year, from time $t - 1$ to time t, to the accumulated amount at the beginning of the year (i.e., at time $t - 1$). It can be calculated by the following formula

$$i(t) = \frac{I(t)}{A(t-1)} = \frac{A(t) - A(t-1)}{A(t-1)} = \frac{a(t) - a(t-1)}{a(t-1)}. \qquad (1.10)$$

For the simple-interest method, we have

$$i(t) = \frac{(1+rt) - (1+r(t-1))}{1 + r(t-1)} = \frac{r}{1 + r(t-1)},$$

which decreases when t increases.

For the compound-interest method with annual compounding (i.e., $m = 1$), we have (denoting $r^{(1)} = r$)

$$i(t) = \frac{(1+r)^t - (1+r)^{t-1}}{(1+r)^{t-1}} = r,$$

which is the nominal rate of interest and does not vary with t. When m-compounding is used, the effective rate of interest is

$$i(t) = \frac{\left[1 + \frac{r^{(m)}}{m}\right]^{tm} - \left[1 + \frac{r^{(m)}}{m}\right]^{(t-1)m}}{\left[1 + \frac{r^{(m)}}{m}\right]^{(t-1)m}} = \left[1 + \frac{r^{(m)}}{m}\right]^m - 1, \qquad (1.11)$$

which again does not vary with t. Note that when $m > 1$,

$$\left[1 + \frac{r^{(m)}}{m}\right]^m - 1 > r^{(m)},$$

so that the effective rate of interest is larger than the nominal rate of interest.

For continuous compounding, we have

$$i(t) = \frac{\exp(\bar{r}t) - \exp[\bar{r}(t-1)]}{\exp[\bar{r}(t-1)]} = e^{\bar{r}} - 1, \tag{1.12}$$

which again does not vary with t.

As the effective rate of interest for the compound-interest method does not vary with t, we shall simplify the notation and denote $i \equiv i(t)$, which is given by (1.11) or (1.12). The effective rate of interest shows how much interest is earned in one year with a 1-unit investment. It is an appropriate *standardized* measure to compare interest-accumulation schemes with different compounding frequencies and nominal rates of interest.

Example 1.7: Consider two investment schemes A and B. Scheme A offers 12% interest with annual compounding. Scheme B offers 11.5% interest with monthly compounding. Calculate the effective rates of interest of the two investments. Which scheme would you choose?

Solution: The effective rate of interest of Scheme A is equal to its nominal rate of interest, i.e., 12%. The effective rate of interest of Scheme B is

$$\left[1 + \frac{0.115}{12} \right]^{12} - 1 = 12.13\%.$$

Although Scheme A has a higher nominal rate of interest, Scheme B offers a higher effective rate of interest. Hence, while an investment of $100 in Scheme A will generate an interest of $12 after one year, a similar investment in Scheme B will generate an interest of $12.13 over the same period. Thus, Scheme B is preferred.

■

Another advantage of the effective rate of interest is that, for investments that extend beyond one year, the calculation of the accumulated amount can be based on the effective rate without reference to the nominal rate.

Example 1.8: For the investment schemes in Example 1.7, calculate the accumulated amount after 10 years on a principal of $1,000.

Solution: The accumulated amount after 10 years for Scheme A is

$$1,000 (1 + 0.12)^{10} = \$3,105.85,$$

and that for Scheme B is

$$1,000 (1 + 0.1213)^{10} = \$3,142.09.$$

Note that in the above example, the accumulated amount of Scheme B is calculated without making use of its nominal rate.

■

Example 1.9: Solve the problem in Example 1.8 for an investment horizon of 12 years and 3 months.

Solution: The time frame of the investment is 12.25 years. Thus, the accumulated amount for Scheme A is

$$1,000\,(1.12)^{12.25} = \$4,007.94,$$

and that for Scheme B is

$$1,000\,(1.1213)^{12.25} = \$4,065.30.$$

Note that the calculation of the accumulated amount of Scheme B is done without using the fact that its compounding frequency is monthly. Indeed, the use of the effective rate of interest enables us to treat all investments *as if* the interest is credited only once a year and the compounding formula (1.4) is used for any $t \geq 0$, with the nominal rate r replaced by the effective rate i.

While $i(t)$ defined in (1.10) is a 1-period effective rate, the concept can be generalized to a n-period effective rate. Let us denote $i(t, t+n)$ as the annual effective rate of interest in the period t to $t+n$, for an integer $n > 1$. Thus, the amount $a(t)$ at time t compounded annually at the rate of $i(t, t+n)$ per year accumulates to $a(t+n)$ at time $t+n$, where

$$a(t+n) = a(t)[1 + i(t, t+n)]^n, \tag{1.13}$$

from which we obtain[1]

$$i(t, t+n) = \left[\frac{a(t+n)}{a(t)}\right]^{\frac{1}{n}} - 1. \tag{1.14}$$

We now consider investment intervals shorter than one year. Suppose $\Delta t < 1$, the effective rate of interest in the period t to $t + \Delta t$, denoted by $i(t, t+\Delta t)$ can be defined as

$$i(t, t+\Delta t) = \frac{a(t+\Delta t) - a(t)}{a(t)}. \tag{1.15}$$

Note that this is an effective rate over a period of $\Delta t < 1$ and is *not annualized*.

Example 1.10: Let the accumulation function be $a(t) = 0.01t^2 + 0.1t + 1$. Compute the annual effective rate of interest for the first 2 years and for the next 3 years. What is the effective rate of interest for the second half of year 3?

---

[1]We may use this formula to compute the annualized effective rate of interest over any investment horizon of $n > 1$, which is not necessarily an integer.

Solution: We have

$$a(2) = 0.01(2)^2 + 0.1(2) + 1 = 1.24,$$

and similarly $a(5) = 1.75$. Thus, from (1.14) the annual effective rate of interest over the first 2 years is

$$i(0,2) = \left[\frac{a(2)}{a(0)}\right]^{\frac{1}{2}} - 1 = (1.24)^{0.5} - 1 = 11.36\%,$$

and the annual effective rate of interest over the next 3 years is

$$i(2,5) = \left[\frac{a(5)}{a(2)}\right]^{\frac{1}{3}} - 1 = \left[\frac{1.75}{1.24}\right]^{\frac{1}{3}} - 1 = 12.17\%.$$

To compute the effective rate of interest for the second half of year 3, we note that $a(2.5) = 1.3125$ and $a(3) = 1.39$, so that the answer is

$$i(2.5,3) = \frac{a(3) - a(2.5)}{a(2.5)} = \frac{1.39 - 1.3125}{1.3125} = 5.90\%.$$

Note that this is an effective rate of interest over a half-year period. In contrast, $i(0,2)$ and $i(2,5)$ are annualized effective rates over a period of 2 years and 3 years, respectively.

1.5 Rates of Discount

So far we have assumed that the interest of a loan or investment is paid at the end of the period. There are, however, many financial transactions for which the interest is paid or deducted up-front. Indeed, a popular way of raising a short-term loan is to sell a financial security at a price less than the face value. Upon the maturity of the loan, the face value is repaid. For example, a Treasury Bill is a discount instrument.

For a discount security, the shortfall between the sale price and the face value is called the **discount** and it represents the interest of the loan. In such cases the **nominal principal (face value)** has to be adjusted to take account of the interest deducted. This adjustment will affect the rate of interest, as opposed to the **rate of discount** that is quoted. Thus, if the lender of a loan requires the interest, which is calculated at the quoted annual rate of discount, to be deducted from the principal at the time the proceed is released, and if the loan period is one year, the **effective principal** of the loan after the interest is deducted is

Effective principal = Nominal principal × (1 − Rate of discount).

Note that the effective principal is $A(0)$ and the nominal principal is $A(1)$. If the quoted rate of discount is d, we have

$$A(0) = A(1)(1 - d), \qquad (1.16)$$

and

$$I(1) = A(1) - A(0) = A(1)d.$$

While the rate of discount is often quoted for such securities, it is important to compare it against the equivalent effective rate of interest i over the period of the discount instrument, which is given by

$$i = \frac{A(1) - A(0)}{A(0)} = \frac{A(1)d}{A(1)(1 - d)} = \frac{d}{1 - d}, \qquad (1.17)$$

from which we have

$$d = \frac{i}{1 + i}.$$

Combining (1.4) and (1.17), we can see that

$$\begin{aligned} a(t) &= (1 + i)^t \\ &= \left[1 + \frac{d}{1 - d} \right]^t \\ &= (1 - d)^{-t}, \end{aligned}$$

which is the accumulated value of 1 at time t at the rate of discount d.

It should be noted that the effective rate of interest i is always higher than the rate of discount d. For example, if the rate of discount is 6% and the redemption of the security is to be made after 1 year, the effective rate of interest is

$$\frac{0.06}{1 - 0.06} = 6.38\%.$$

When the loan period is less than 1 year, we should first calculate the rate of interest over the period of the loan and then calculate the effective rate of interest using the principle of compounding. Thus, suppose the period of loan is $\frac{1}{m}$ of a year, we denote the **nominal rate of discount**, which is the discount quoted in annual term for the $\frac{1}{m}$-year instrument, by $d^{(m)}$. As the face value is to be repaid $\frac{1}{m}$ of a year later, the nominal principal is $A\left(\frac{1}{m}\right)$ and the interest deducted is

$$I\left(\frac{1}{m}\right) = A\left(\frac{1}{m}\right) \times d^{(m)} \times \frac{1}{m},$$

so that the effective principal is

$$A(0) = A\left(\frac{1}{m}\right) - I\left(\frac{1}{m}\right) = A\left(\frac{1}{m}\right)\left[1 - \frac{d^{(m)}}{m}\right],$$

from which we obtain the rate of interest charged over the $\frac{1}{m}$-year period as

$$\frac{A\left(\frac{1}{m}\right) - A(0)}{A(0)} = \frac{\dfrac{d^{(m)}}{m}}{1 - \dfrac{d^{(m)}}{m}} = \frac{d^{(m)}}{m - d^{(m)}}.$$

Hence, the **annualized equivalent nominal rate of interest** is

$$r^{(m)} = m \times \frac{d^{(m)}}{m - d^{(m)}} = \frac{d^{(m)}}{1 - \dfrac{d^{(m)}}{m}}, \tag{1.18}$$

and the annual effective rate of interest is

$$i = \left[1 + \frac{r^{(m)}}{m}\right]^m - 1 = \left[1 + \frac{d^{(m)}}{m - d^{(m)}}\right]^m - 1 = \left[1 - \frac{d^{(m)}}{m}\right]^{-m} - 1. \tag{1.19}$$

As Treasury Bills that mature in less than a year are discount instruments, their effective rates should be computed in the above manner.

To compute the accumulation function $a(t)$ for a discount instrument with maturity of $\frac{1}{m}$ year ($m > 1$), we observe, from (1.19), that

$$\begin{aligned} a(t) &= (1 + i)^t \\ &= \left[1 - \frac{d^{(m)}}{m}\right]^{-mt}, \qquad \text{for } t = 0, \frac{1}{m}, \frac{2}{m}, \cdots. \end{aligned} \tag{1.20}$$

Furthermore, from (1.19) we have

$$1 - \frac{d^{(m)}}{m} = (1 + i)^{-\frac{1}{m}}, \tag{1.21}$$

so that from (1.18) we conclude

$$r^{(m)} = (1 + i)^{\frac{1}{m}} d^{(m)}. \tag{1.22}$$

For a discount security with a loan period longer than one year, (1.16) can be modified to

$$A(0) = A(t)(1 - dt), \qquad 1 < t,$$

provided $dt < 1$. Hence, we have

$$A(t) = \frac{A(0)}{1 - dt}, \qquad dt < 1 < t,$$

and

$$a(t) = \frac{1}{1 - dt}, \qquad dt < 1 < t, \tag{1.23}$$

which is the accumulation function for simple discount for $dt < 1 < t$.

Example 1.11: The discount rate of a 3-month Treasury Bill is 6% per annum. What is the annual effective rate of interest? What is the accumulated value of 1 in 2 years?

Solution: The rate of interest charged for the 3-month period is

$$\frac{0.06 \times \dfrac{1}{4}}{1 - 0.06 \times \dfrac{1}{4}} \;=\; 1.52\%.$$

Therefore, the equivalent nominal rate of interest compounded quarterly is

$$4 \times 0.0152 \;=\; 6.08\%,$$

and the annual effective rate of interest is

$$(1.0152)^4 - 1 \;=\; 6.22\%.$$

The accumulated value of 1 in 2 years is, using (1.20),

$$a(2) = \left[1 - \frac{0.06}{4}\right]^{-8} = 1.13.$$

Note that this can also be calculated as

$$(1 + i)^2 = (1.0622)^2 = 1.13.$$

Example 1.12: The discount rate of a 6-month Treasury Bill is 8% per annum, what is the annual effective rate of interest? What is the accumulated value of 1 in 3 years?

Solution: The rate of interest charged for the 6-month period is

$$\frac{0.08 \times \dfrac{1}{2}}{1 - 0.08 \times \dfrac{1}{2}} = 4.17\%.$$

Therefore, the annualized equivalent nominal rate of interest compounded semiannually is

$$2 \times 0.0417 = 8.34\%,$$

and the annual effective rate of interest is

$$(1.0417)^2 - 1 = 8.51\%.$$

The accumulated value of 1 in 3 years is

$$a(3) = \left[1 - \frac{0.08}{2}\right]^{-6} = 1.28,$$

which can also be computed as

$$(1 + i)^3 = (1.0851)^3 = 1.28.$$

1.6   Force of Interest

Given any accumulation function $a(t)$, the effective rate of interest over the time interval $(t, t + \Delta t)$ can be computed as $i(t, t + \Delta t)$ using (1.15), which measures how fast the investment accumulates in value at time t. The rate computed by (1.15), however, is not annualized. But if we divide $i(t, t + \Delta t)$ by Δt, we obtain the rate of interest of the investment *per unit time* in the interval $(t, t + \Delta t)$ (if t is in years, the rate of interest is per annum). A particularly interesting question is the *instantaneous* rate, which is obtained when Δt is infinitesimally small. Thus, we consider $\frac{i(t, t + \Delta t)}{\Delta t}$ when Δt tends to zero, which is given by

$$
\begin{aligned}
\lim_{\Delta t \to 0} \frac{i(t, t + \Delta t)}{\Delta t} &= \lim_{\Delta t \to 0} \frac{1}{\Delta t} \left[\frac{a(t + \Delta t) - a(t)}{a(t)}\right] \\
&= \frac{1}{a(t)} \lim_{\Delta t \to 0} \left[\frac{a(t + \Delta t) - a(t)}{\Delta t}\right] \\
&= \frac{a'(t)}{a(t)}, &\text{(1.24)}
\end{aligned}
$$

where $a'(t)$ is the derivative of $a(t)$ with respect to t. Thus, we define

$$\delta(t) = \frac{a'(t)}{a(t)}, \tag{1.25}$$

which is called the **force of interest**. As (1.24) shows, the force of interest is the instantaneous rate of increase of the accumulated amount, $a'(t)$, as a percentage of the accumulated amount at time t, $a(t)$.

Given $a(t)$, the force of interest $\delta(t)$ can be computed using (1.25). Now we show that the computation can be reversed, i.e., given $\delta(t)$ we can compute $a(t)$. First, we note that (1.25) can be written as

$$\delta(t) = \frac{d \ln a(t)}{dt},$$

from which we have

$$\begin{aligned}
\int_0^t \delta(s)\,ds &= \int_0^t d \ln a(s) \\
&= \ln a(s)\big]_0^t \\
&= \ln a(t) - \ln a(0) \\
&= \ln a(t),
\end{aligned}$$

as $a(0) = 1$. Hence, we conclude

$$a(t) = \exp\left(\int_0^t \delta(s)\,ds\right). \tag{1.26}$$

Equation (1.26) provides the method to calculate the accumulation function given the force of interest. In the case when the force of interest is constant (not varying with t), we denote $\delta(t) \equiv \delta$, and the integral in (1.26) becomes δt. Thus, we have

$$a(t) = e^{\delta t}. \tag{1.27}$$

Comparing (1.27) with (1.9) we can see that if the force of interest is constant, it is equal to the continuously compounded rate of interest, i.e., $\bar{r} = \delta$.

We now derive the force of interest for the simple- and compound-interest methods. For the simple-interest method, we obtain, from (1.2),

$$a'(t) = r,$$

so that

$$\delta(t) = \frac{r}{1 + rt}, \qquad \text{for } t \geq 0. \tag{1.28}$$

Hence, $\delta(t)$ decreases as t increases. In other words, the instantaneous rate of interest as a percentage of the accumulated amount drops with time.

For the compound-interest method, we have, from (1.4) and Appendix A.6 (with i replacing r irrespective of the compounding frequency),

$$a'(t) = (1 + i)^t \ln(1 + i),$$

so that

$$\delta(t) = \frac{(1 + i)^t \ln(1 + i)}{(1 + i)^t} = \ln(1 + i). \tag{1.29}$$

Thus, $\delta(t)$ does not vary with time and we write $\delta(t) \equiv \delta$, from which equation (1.29) implies

$$e^\delta = 1 + i.$$

Comparing this with (1.12), we again conclude that the force of interest is the continuously compounded rate of interest.

Example 1.13:   A fund accumulates at a simple-interest rate of 5%. Another fund accumulates at a compound-interest rate of 4%, payable yearly. When will the force of interest be the same for the two funds? After this time, which fund will have a higher force of interest?

Solution: From (1.28), the force of interest of the simple-interest fund at time t is

$$\delta(t) = \frac{0.05}{1 + 0.05t}.$$

From (1.29), the force of interest of the compound-interest fund is $\ln(1.04)$ at any time. The two funds have the same force of interest when

$$\frac{0.05}{1 + 0.05t} = \ln(1.04),$$

i.e.,

$$t = \frac{0.05 - \ln(1.04)}{0.05 \ln(1.04)} = 5.4967,$$

after which the force of interest of the simple-interest fund remains lower than that of the compound-interest fund.

Example 1.14:   If a fund accumulates at force of interest $\delta(t) = 0.02t$, find the annual effective rate of interest over 2 years and 5 years.

Solution: From (1.26), we have

$$a(2) = \exp\left(\int_0^2 0.02s\, ds\right) = \exp\left(0.01s^2\big]_0^2\right) = e^{0.04}.$$

We solve the annual effective rate of interest i over the 2-year period from the equation (compare this with (1.13))

$$(1+i)^2 = e^{0.04}$$

to obtain

$$i = e^{0.02} - 1 = 2.02\%.$$

Similarly,

$$a(5) = \exp\left(0.01s^2\big]_0^5\right) = e^{0.25},$$

so that the annual effective rate of interest i over the 5-year period satisfies

$$(1+i)^5 = e^{0.25}$$

and we obtain

$$i = e^{0.05} - 1 = 5.13\%.$$

1.7 Present and Future Values

At the effective rate of interest i, a 1-unit investment today will accumulate to $(1+i)$ units at the end of the year. In this respect, the accumulated amount $(1+i)$ is also called the **future value** of 1 at the end of the year. Similarly, the future value of 1 at the end of year t is $(1+i)^t$. This is the amount of money you can get t years later if you invest 1 unit today at the effective rate i.

Sometimes it may be desirable to find the initial investment that will accumulate to a targeted amount after a certain period of time. For example, a $\frac{1}{1+i}$-unit payment invested today will accumulate to 1 unit at the end of the year. Thus, $\frac{1}{1+i}$ is called the **present value** of 1 to be paid at the end of year 1. Extending the time frame to t years, the present value of 1 due at the end of year t is $\frac{1}{(1+i)^t}$.

Example 1.15: Given $i = 6\%$, calculate the present value of 1 to be paid at (a) the end of year 1, (b) the end of year 5 and (c) 6.5 years.

Solution: (a) The present value of 1 to be paid at the end of year 1 is

$$\frac{1}{1+0.06} = 0.9434.$$

The answers to (b) and (c) are, respectively,

$$\frac{1}{(1+0.06)^5} = 0.7473$$

and

$$\frac{1}{(1+0.06)^{6.5}} = 0.6847.$$

Example 1.16: An insurance agent offers a policy that pays a lump sum of $50,000 five years later. If the effective rate of interest is 8%, how much would you pay for the plan?

Solution: The *fair* amount to pay for this policy is the present value of the lump sum, which is equal to

$$\frac{50,000}{(1.08)^5} = \$34,029.16.$$

Example 1.17: A person wants to accumulate $100,000 eight years from today to sponsor his son's education. If an investment plan offers him 8% compounded monthly, what amount must he invest today?

Solution: We first calculate the effective rate of interest, which is

$$\left[1 + \frac{0.08}{12}\right]^{12} - 1 = 8.30\%.$$

The amount required today is

$$\frac{100,000}{(1.083)^8} = \$52,841.16.$$

We now denote

$$v = \frac{1}{1+i}, \tag{1.30}$$

which is the **present value** of 1 due 1 year later. It is also called the **discount factor**, as multiplying a payment at the end of the year by v gives its present value. Combining (1.17) and (1.30), we obtain

$$d = iv, \tag{1.31}$$

so that the present value of i is d. Also,

$$v + d = \frac{1}{1+i} + \frac{i}{1+i} = 1, \tag{1.32}$$

which says that a unit payment at time 1 is the sum of its present value and discount. Since $a(1) = 1 + i$, (1.30) can also be written as

$$v = \frac{1}{a(1)},$$

which says that the present value of 1 due 1 year later is the reciprocal of the accumulation function evaluated at time $t = 1$. For a general time t, we denote $v(t)$ as the present value of 1 to be paid at time t. Then

$$v(t) = \frac{1}{(1+i)^t} = \frac{1}{a(t)}, \tag{1.33}$$

which is the discount factor for payments at time t.

The above calculations apply to the case of the compound-interest method with a constant effective rate of interest. For a general accumulation function $a(\cdot)$, the discount factor for payments at time t is

$$v(t) = \frac{1}{a(t)}.$$

Thus, when the simple-interest method is used, the present value of 1 due t years later at the nominal rate of interest r is

$$v(t) = \frac{1}{a(t)} = \frac{1}{1+rt}. \tag{1.34}$$

Example 1.18: Find the sum of the present values of two payments of $100 each to be paid at the end of year 4 and 9, if (a) interest is compounded semiannually at the nominal rate of 8% per year, and (b) the simple-interest method at 8% per year is used.

Solution: We first calculate the discount factors $v(4)$ and $v(9)$. For case (a), the effective rate of interest is

$$(1.04)^2 - 1 = 0.0816,$$

so that

$$v(4) = \frac{1}{(1.0816)^4} = 0.7307$$

and

$$v(9) = \frac{1}{(1.0816)^9} = 0.4936.$$

Hence, the present value of the two payments is

$$100(0.7307 + 0.4936) = \$122.43.$$

For case (b), we have

$$v(4) = \frac{1}{1 + 0.08 \times 4} = 0.7576$$

and

$$v(9) = \frac{1}{1 + 0.08 \times 9} = 0.5814,$$

so that the present value of the two payments is

$$100(0.7576 + 0.5814) = \$133.90.$$

Note that as the accumulation function for simple interest grows slower than that for compound interest, the present value of the simple-interest method is higher.

We now consider a payment of 1 at a future time τ. What is the future value of this payment at time $t > \tau$? The answer to this question depends on how a payment at a future time accumulates with interest. Let us assume that any future payment starts to accumulate interest following the same accumulation function as a payment made at time 0.[2] As the 1-unit payment at time τ earns interest over a period of $t - \tau$ until time t, its accumulated value at time t is $a(t - \tau)$.

However, if we consider a different scenario in which the 1-unit amount at time τ has been accumulated from time 0 and is not a new investment, what is the future value of this amount at time t? To answer this question, we first determine the invested amount at time 0, which is the present value of 1 due at time τ, i.e., $\frac{1}{a(\tau)}$. The future value of this investment at time t is then given by

$$\frac{1}{a(\tau)} \times a(t) = \frac{a(t)}{a(\tau)}.$$

---

[2]We adopt this assumption for the purpose of defining future values for future payments. It is not claimed that the current accumulation function applies to all future investments in practice.

We can see that the future values of the two investments, i.e., a 1-unit investment at time τ versus a 1-unit amount at time τ accumulated from time 0, are not necessarily the same. However, they are equal if

$$a(t - \tau) = \frac{a(t)}{a(\tau)} \tag{1.35}$$

for $t > \tau > 0$. Figure 1.1 illustrates the evaluation of the future values at time t of these two investments.

Note that compound-interest accumulation satisfies the condition (1.35). The principal at time τ accumulates interest at the rate of i per year, whether the principal is invested at time τ or is accumulated from the past. Specifically, we have

$$\frac{a(t)}{a(\tau)} = \frac{(1+i)^t}{(1+i)^\tau} = (1+i)^{t-\tau} = a(t - \tau).$$

In contrast, simple-interest accumulation does not satisfy condition (1.35). The future value at time t of a unit payment at time τ is $a(t - \tau) = 1 + r(t - \tau)$. However, we have

$$\frac{a(t)}{a(\tau)} = \frac{1 + rt}{1 + r\tau} = \frac{1 + r\tau + r(t - \tau)}{1 + r\tau} = 1 + \frac{r(t - \tau)}{1 + r\tau} < 1 + r(t - \tau) = a(t - \tau).$$

The discrepancy is due to the fact that only the principal of $\frac{1}{a(\tau)}$ invested at time 0 is paid interest in the period τ to t, although the principal has accumulated to 1 unit at time τ. On the other hand, if 1 unit of payment is invested at time τ, this is the amount that generates interest in the period τ to t.

Figure 1.1: Present and future values of unit payment at time τ

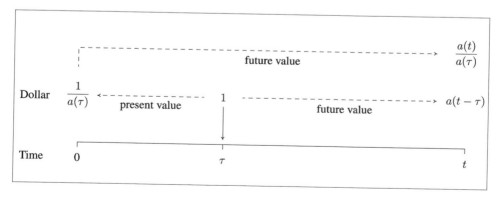

Example 1.19: Let $a(t) = 0.02t^2 + 1$. Calculate the future value of an investment at $t = 5$ consisting of a payment of 1 now and a payment of 2 at $t = 3$. You may assume that future payments earn the current accumulation function.

Solution: The future value at time 5 is

$$a(5) + 2 \times a(2) = [0.02(5)^2 + 1] + 2[0.02(2)^2 + 1] = 3.66.$$

Example 1.20: Let $\delta(t) = 0.01t$. Calculate the future value of an investment at $t = 5$ consisting of a payment of 1 now and a payment of 2 at $t = 2$. You may assume that future payments earn the current accumulation function.

Solution: We first derive the accumulation function from the force of interest, which is

$$a(t) = \exp\left(\int_0^t 0.01s\, ds\right) = \exp(0.005t^2).$$

Thus, $a(5) = \exp(0.125) = 1.1331$ and $a(3) = \exp(0.045) = 1.0460$, from which we obtain the future value of the investment as

$$a(5) + 2 \times a(3) = 1.1331 + 2(1.0460) = 3.2251.$$

1.8 Equation of Value

Consider a stream of cash flows occurring at different times. The present value of the cash flows is equal to the sum of the present values of each payment. To fix ideas, assume the payments are of values C_j occurring at time $j = 0, 1, \cdots, n$, and compound-interest accumulation is adopted. If the annual effective rate of interest is i with corresponding discount factor v, the present value P of the cash flows is given by

$$P = \sum_{j=0}^{n} C_j v^j \tag{1.36}$$

and the future value F of the cash flows at time n is

$$F = (1+i)^n P = (1+i)^n \left(\sum_{j=0}^{n} C_j v^j\right) = \sum_{j=0}^{n} C_j (1+i)^{n-j}. \tag{1.37}$$

Thus, equations (1.36) and (1.37) involve the quantities P, F, C_j, i and n.[3] We call these the **equations of value**. Given C_j, i and n, P and F can be calculated straightforwardly. Alternatively, if C_j and i are given, we can calculate the time n given the present value P or future value F. The examples below illustrate this point.

Example 1.21: At the annual effective rate of interest i, when will an initial principal be doubled?

Solution: This requires us to solve for n from the equation (note that $C_j = 0$ for $j > 0$, and we let $C_0 = 1$ and $F = 2$)

$$(1+i)^n = 2,$$

from which

$$n = \frac{\ln(2)}{\ln(1+i)}.$$

Thus, n is generally not an integer but can be solved exactly from the above equation.

To obtain an approximate solution for n, we note that $\ln(2) = 0.6931$ so that

$$n = \frac{0.6931}{i} \times \frac{i}{\ln(1+i)}.$$

We approximate the last fraction in the above equation by taking $i = 0.08$ to obtain

$$n \approx \frac{0.6931}{i} \times 1.0395 = \frac{0.72}{i}.$$

Thus, n can be calculated approximately by dividing 0.72 by the effective rate of interest. This is called the **rule of 72**. It provides a surprisingly accurate approximation to n for a wide range of values of i. For example, when $i = 2\%$, the approximation gives $n = 36$ while the exact value is 35. When $i = 14\%$, the approximate value is 5.14 while the exact value is 5.29.

Example 1.22: How long will it take for \$100 to accumulate to \$300 if interest is compounded quarterly at the nominal rate of 6% per year?

---

[3]Note that as we are assuming compound interest, (1.35) holds. Thus, we can compute the future value of future payments as the future value of their corresponding present values, as in equation (1.37).

Solution: Over one quarter, the interest rate is 1.5%. With $C_0 = \$100$, $C_j = 0$ for $j > 0$, and $F = \$300$, from (1.37) the equation of value is (n is in quarters)

$$300 = 100(1.015)^n,$$

so that

$$n = \frac{\ln(3)}{\ln(1.015)} = 73.79 \text{ quarters},$$

i.e., 18.45 years.

■

Another problem is the solution of the rate of interest that will give rise to a targeted present value or future value with given cash flows. The example below illustrates this point.

Example 1.23: A student takes out a tuition loan of \$15,000, and is required to pay back with a step-up payment \$7,000 in year 1 and \$8,500 in year 2. What is the effective rate of interest she is charged?

Solution: The equation of value is, from (1.36),

$$15,000 = 7,000v + 8,500v^2.$$

Solving for the quadratic equation (see Appendix A.3), we obtain, after dropping the negative root,

$$v = \frac{-7 + \sqrt{7^2 + 4 \times 8.5 \times 15}}{2 \times 8.5} = 0.979,$$

which implies

$$i = \frac{1}{0.979} - 1 = 2.14\%.$$

■

Note that the solution of the above problem can be obtained analytically by solving a quadratic equation, as there are only two payments. When there are more payments, the solution will require the use of numerical methods, the details of which can be found in Chapter 4.

Example 1.24: A savings fund requires the investor to pay an equal amount of installment each year for 3 years, with the first installment to be paid immediately. At the end of the 3 years, a lump sum will be paid back to the investor. If the effective interest rate is 5%, what is the amount of the installment such that the investor can receive a lump sum of $10,000?

Solution: Let k be the installment. From (1.37), the equation of value is

$$10{,}000 = k[(1.05)^3 + (1.05)^2 + 1.05] = 3.31k,$$

so that the installment is

$$k = \frac{10{,}000}{3.31} = \$3{,}021.03.$$

It can be observed that if the horizon of the savings fund is long, the computation of the above can be quite tedious. In the next chapter, we will see how the computation can be made easier for installments over a long horizon.

1.9 Summary

1. The amount function and accumulation function trace the accumulation of an investment over a period of time. The interest incurred in each period can be calculated from the amount function.

2. The simple-interest and compound-interest methods are two commonly used methods for calculating interest incurred. For the compound-interest method, the frequency of compounding is an important determinant of how interest accrues. To compare schemes with different compounding frequencies, the effective rate of interest should be used.

3. Discount instruments are popular in raising short-term loans. The effective rate of interest is always higher than the discount rate as the effective principal is less than the nominal principal or face value.

4. The force of interest is the instantaneous rate of interest as a percentage of the accumulated amount. It is a useful measure of how investment accumulates, especially when the rate of interest is time varying. If the force of interest is constant, it is equal to the continuously compounded rate of interest.

5. The present value of a stream of payments is equal to the sum of the present values of each payment. It aggregates the payments by properly weighting each of them by a discount factor that takes account of the differences in the time the payments are made.

6. The equation of value links the present value or the future value with the installments, the period of the payments and the interest rate. It can be used to solve for one variable given the others.

7. Table 1.3 summarizes the accumulated value and present value for various accumulation methods.

Exercises

1.1 An investor invests $20,000 into a fund for 4 years. The annual nominal interest rate remains at 8% in each year although it is convertible semiannually in the first year, quarterly in the second year, bi-monthly in the third year, and monthly in the fourth year. Find the accumulated value of the fund at the end of the fourth year.

1.2 For the compound-interest method over fraction of a compounding period, show that the second method described in Section 1.3 provides a larger accumulation amount over the first method.

1.3 If $A(4) = 1{,}200$ and $i(t) = 0.01t^2$, find $I(5)$ and $A(6)$.

1.4 It is given that $A(0) = 300, I(1) = 5, I(2) = 7, I(3) = 9$ and $I(4) = 14$. Find $A(3)$ and $i(4)$.

1.5 Find the accumulated value of $1,000 at the end of the fourth year

  (a) if the simple discount rate is 6% per annum,

  (b) if the simple interest rate is 6% per annum,

  (c) if the effective rate of interest is 6% per annum,

  (d) if the annual nominal interest rate is 6% payable quarterly,

  (e) if the annual nominal discount rate is 6% compounded monthly,

  (f) if the constant force of interest is 6% per annum.

1.6 Assume that $a(t) = \ln(0.5t^2 + e) + 0.05t^{0.3}$, find

  (a) $i(2)$ and $i(3)$,

  (b) the amount of interest earned in the third period if the principal is $1,200.

Table 1.3: Summary of accumulated value and present value formulas (all rates quoted per year)

Accumulation method	Freq of conversion per year	Rate of interest or discount	Future value of 1 at time t (in years): $a(t)$	Present value of 1 due at time t (in years): $1/a(t)$	Equations in book	Remarks
Compound interest	1	$r\,(=i)$	$(1+r)^t$	$(1+r)^{-t}$	(1.4)	also applies to non-integer $t>0$
Compound interest	m	$r^{(m)}$	$\left[1+\frac{r^{(m)}}{m}\right]^{mt}$	$\left[1+\frac{r^{(m)}}{m}\right]^{-mt}$	(1.6)	$m>1$ if compounding is more frequent than annually
Compound interest	∞	$\bar{r}$	$e^{\bar{r}t}$	$e^{-\bar{r}t}$	(1.9)	$\bar{r}$ is the constant force of interest δ
Compound discount	1	d	$(1-d)^{-t}$	$(1-d)^t$	(1.4), (1.7)	
Compound discount	m	$d^{(m)}$	$\left[1-\frac{d^{(m)}}{m}\right]^{-mt}$	$\left[1-\frac{d^{(m)}}{m}\right]^{mt}$	(1.19)	$m>1$ for loan period shorter than 1 year
Simple interest		r	$1+rt$	$(1+rt)^{-1}$	(1.2)	
Simple discount		d	$(1-dt)^{-1}$	$1-dt$	(1.23)	

1.7 It is given that $i(t) = 0.01 + 0.005t$.

(a) Find $a(t)$ for t being an integer.

(b) If the principal is \$100, find the total amount of interest earned in year 3, 4 and 5.

1.8 Which of the following is a valid accumulation function?

(a) $a(t) = t^2 + 2t + 2$,

(b) $a(t) = t^2 - 2t + 1$,

(c) $a(t) = t^2 + 2t + 1$.

1.9 If $d^{(4)} = 0.0985$, find

(a) i,

(b) $d^{(2)}$,

(c) $r^{(4)}$,

(d) δ,

(e) $a(t)$.

1.10 A security is sold at a discount of 7%, compounded semiannually. Find the effective rate of interest.

1.11 Prove that $i - d = id$ by using formulas (1.30) and (1.31). What does this relation tell you?

1.12 \$1,500 is deposited into a savings account that pays 3.5% interest with monthly compounding. What is the accumulated amount after four and a quarter years? What is the amount of interest earned over this period?

1.13 \$10,000 is deposited into a savings account that earns 3% per annum compounded quarterly.

(a) How much interest will be credited in the second month?

(b) How much interest will be credited in the second year?

1.14 Using the rule of 72, calculate the approximate number of years for an initial principal to double if the annual effective rate of interest is 4%. Compare your answer with the true value.

1.15 Find the present value of $500 to be paid at the end of 28 months.

(a) if the nominal interest rate is 6% convertible monthly,

(b) if the nominal discount rate is 6% compounded every 4 months,

(c) if the nominal interest rate is 4% compounded semiannually,

(d) if the nominal discount rate is 5% payable annually.

Apply the simple-interest method for the remaining fraction of the conversion period if necessary.

1.16 When does the rule of 72 hold exactly?

1.17 You wish to borrow $10,000. The following is the information you gathered from two lenders:

(a) Lender A charges 7% compounded quarterly,

(b) Lender B charges an annual effective rate of interest of 7.25%.

Which lender would you choose?

1.18 A Treasury Bill for $100 is purchased for $95 four months before due. Find the nominal rate of discount convertible three times a year earned by the purchaser.

1.19 You are given the following stream of cash flows:

t	C_t
0	950
1	800
2	150
3	400
4	120

Find the present value and the future value (after 5 years) of the cash flows evaluated at $i = 2\%$.

1.20 (a) Extend formula (1.36) to the case when the interest rate is not constant over time.

(b) It is given that

t	$v(t)$
1	0.98
2	0.95
3	0.92
4	0.90

Find the present value of the following stream of payments:

t	C_t (\$)
0	1,000
1	800
2	600
3	400
4	200

1.21 Let $v(t) = \dfrac{20}{20 + t}$.

(a) Find $i(1), i(2)$ and $i(3)$.

(b) How is the interest credited?

1.22 Beda wishes to accumulate \$3,000 in a fund at the end of 4 years. He makes deposits of \$$K$, \$$2K$, \$$3K$ at the beginning of year 1, 2 and 3, respectively. Find the value of K if the fund earns

(a) simple interest of 5% per year,

(b) compound interest of 5% per year.

1.23 Eddy deposits \$2,000 into a savings account. The bank credits interest at a rate of i convertible yearly for the first 4 years and a nominal rate of $4i$ convertible quarterly thereafter. If the accumulated value of the account is \$2,918.70 after 6 years, find the accumulated value of the account after 8.5 years.

1.24 Ada pays \$1,000 today and \$1,200 after 2 years to Andrew in exchange for a payment of \$2,198 one year from today.

(a) Set up an equation of value with i as unknown by equating the future values of the two cash-flow streams.

(b) Solve the equation of value obtained in (a).

(c) What can you observe?

1.25 $2,000 is put into an account which credits interest at 4% per annum and $1,500 is put into another account which credits interest at 6% per annum. How long does it take for the balances of the two accounts to be equal? Apply the compound-interest method for the remaining fraction of the conversion period.

1.26 $2,000 is put into an account which credits interest at 4% per annum and $1,500 is put into another account which credits interest at 6% per annum. How long does it take for the balances of the two accounts to be equal? Apply the simple-interest method for the remaining fraction of the conversion period. Compare your answer with that in Exercise 1.25.

1.27 Which of the following are valid graphs for the amount function $A(t)$?

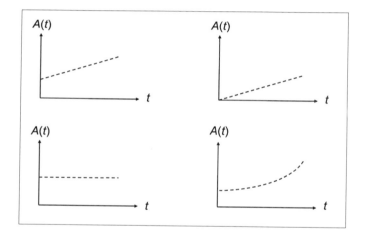

1.28 Irene invests $5,000 in an account that credits interest during the first two years at a nominal interest rate of $r^{(2)}$ convertible semiannually. During the third year, the account earns interest at a nominal discount rate of $d^{(4)}$ convertible quarterly. At the end of the third year, the fund has accumulated to $5,375.70. If $r^{(2)} = d^{(4)} = x$, find x.

1.29 Betty deposits $200 at the beginning of each year for 10 years into an account which credits simple interest at an annual interest rate of i payable every year. Find i if the accumulated value is $2,440 after 10 years.

1.30 You are given the following information:

t	$v(t)$
1	0.97
2	0.94
3	0.91
4	0.88
5	0.85

(a) You want to accumulate $10,000 five years from today. What amount should you invest today?

(b) You want to accumulate $10,000 five years from today by two install-ments of equal amount, to be paid at the beginning of the first and the third year. How much are the two installments? You may follow the assumption in Section 1.7 for the computation of the future value of future payments.

1.31 The present value of two payments, the first payment of $500 paid at the end of n years, and the second payment of $1,000 at the end of $2n$ years, is $1,158. If $i = 4\%$, find the value of n.

1.32 Albert takes out a loan of $30,000, and is required to pay back with a pay-ment of $20,000 at the end of the second year, and $11,000 at the end the fourth year. Interest is payable quarterly. What is the nominal rate of interest charged on the loan?

1.33 Let $a(t) = \dfrac{1}{1 - 0.01t}$ for $0 \le t < 100$.

(a) Draw the graph of $v(t)$ for $0 \le t < 100$.

(b) How is the interest credited?

1.34 Let $A(t) = t^2 + 2t + 4$. Find $\delta(5)$.

1.35 Which of the following are properties of the force of interest $\delta(t)$?

(a) It is non-negative.

(b) It is increasing with t.

(c) It is continuous.

1.36 Assume that $\delta(t) = \dfrac{1}{10(1 + t)^3}$ and $A(0) = 100$. Find the amount of interest earned in the fifth year.

1.37 Calculate the future value of an investment at $t = 5$ consisting of a payment of 1 at $t = 2$ and a payment of 3 at $t = 4$, if

    (a) $a(t) = 1 + 0.05t$,

    (b) $a(t) = (1.05)^t$,

    (c) $\delta(t) = 0.05t$.

1.38 In Fund P, money accumulates at a force of interest $\delta(t)$ whose graph is given below.

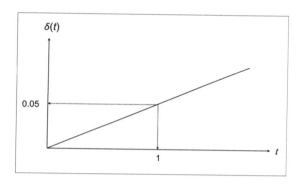

    (a) Find $a(5)$.

    (b) Fund Q accumulates at a constant force of interest δ_Q. If the value of the two funds are equal at $t = 0$ and $t = 5$, find δ_Q.

1.39 You are given the following stream of cash flows:

t	0.5	1	1.5	2	2.5	3
C_t	10	10	10	10	10	110

Find the present value of the cash flows given that the nominal rate of interest is 8% compounded half-yearly.

1.40 Certificates of deposit (CDs) are short- to medium-term investment instruments issued by banks which provides a fixed rate of interest for a period of time. CDs offer stability in interest earned but have penalty for early withdrawal.

A 1-year CD pays a nominal rate of interest of 8% compounded quarterly. You are offered two options of penalty for early withdrawal:

(a) loss of 3-month interest;

(b) a reduction in the nominal rate of interest to 6%.

If you wish to withdraw after 9 months, which option would you choose?

Advanced Problems

1.41   (a) For $c > 0$, let $f(x) = 1 + cx$ and $g(x) = (1+c)^x$, where $0 \le x \le 1$.

       (1) Show that $f(0) = g(0)$, and $f(1) = g(1)$.

       (2) By using the fact that $g(\cdot)$ is increasing in x, show that $f(x) \ge g(x)$ for $0 \le x \le 1$.

       (3) Letting $c = r$ in (a)(2), what conclusion can you draw?

    (b) Let $[x]$ be the integer part of x. For examples, $[4.2] = 4$, $[9.99] = 9$ and $[1] = 1$. By using the result in (a)(2), show that for $t \ge 0$,

$$\left(1 + \frac{r^{(m)}}{m}\right)^{mt - [mt]} \le 1 + r^{(m)} \left(\frac{mt - [mt]}{m}\right).$$

    (c) Prove that when the loan period is not an integer multiple of the compounding period, applying the simple-interest method for the remaining fraction of the conversion part always gives a larger accumulation function when compared with extending (1.6) to any $mt \ge 0$.

1.42 The following graphs plot the force of interest for Fund X and Fund Y for $0 \le t \le 10$.

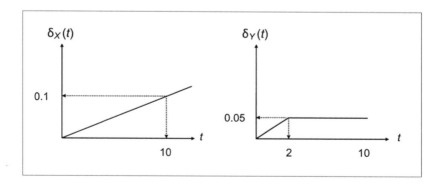

Find the points in time at which the values of the accumulation functions of the two funds are equal.

1.43 Assume that the force of interest is constant over time. Let the constant force of interest be δ and the equivalent effective rate of interest and discount be i and d, respectively.

    (a) Express δ in terms of i.

    (b) Express δ in terms of d.

    (c) By using the Taylor's expansion

$$\ln(1+x) = \sum_{k=1}^{\infty} \frac{(-1)^{k-1}x^k}{k} = x - \frac{x^2}{2} + \frac{x^3}{3} - \frac{x^4}{4} + \cdots,$$

and the expressions in (a) and (b), show that

$$\delta = \frac{1}{2}\left[\frac{i+d}{1} - \frac{i^2-d^2}{2} + \frac{i^3+d^3}{3} + \frac{i^4-d^4}{4} + \cdots\right].$$

The formula above shows that δ is very close to the average of i and d.

2

Annuities

An annuity is a series of payments made at equal intervals. There are many practical examples of financial transactions involving annuities, such as

- a car loan being repaid with equal monthly installments

- a retiree purchasing an annuity from an insurance company upon his retirement

- a life insurance policy being purchased with monthly premiums

- a bondholder receiving an annuity in the form of semiannual coupon payments

In this chapter we consider annuities of level or varying amounts, the payments of which are *certain*. Thus, we assume there is no default risk in the case of a bond or an annuity purchased from an insurance company. We shall discuss the calculation of the present and future values of these annuities. When there is uncertainty in the annuity payments, as in the case of the default of a car loan, the payments are contingent upon some random events. Such annuities will not be discussed in this book.

Learning Objectives

- *Annuity-immediate and annuity-due*
- *Present and future values of annuities*
- *Perpetuities and deferred annuities*
- *Other accumulation methods*
- *Payment periods and compounding periods*
- *Varying annuities*

2.1 Annuity-Immediate

Consider an annuity with payments of 1 unit each, made at the end of every year for n years. This kind of annuity is called an **annuity-immediate** (also called an **ordinary annuity** or an **annuity in arrears**). The **present value of an annuity** is the sum of the present values of each payment. The computation of the present value of an annuity can be explained in tabular form, as illustrated by the following example.

Example 2.1:   Calculate the present value of an annuity-immediate of amount $100 paid annually for 5 years at the rate of interest of 9% per annum.

Solution: Table 2.1 summarizes the present values of the payments as well as their total.

Table 2.1:   Present value of annuity

Year	Payment ($)	Present value ($)
1	100	$100\,(1.09)^{-1} = 91.74$
2	100	$100\,(1.09)^{-2} = 84.17$
3	100	$100\,(1.09)^{-3} = 77.22$
4	100	$100\,(1.09)^{-4} = 70.84$
5	100	$100\,(1.09)^{-5} = 64.99$
Total		388.97

Figure 2.1 illustrates the **time diagram** of an annuity-immediate of payments of 1 unit at the end of each period for n periods. As the payments occur at different times, their *time values* are different. We are interested in the value of the annuity at time 0, called the present value, and the accumulated value of the annuity at time n, called the future value.

Figure 2.1: Time diagram for an n-payment annuity-immediate

Suppose the rate of interest per period is i, and we assume the compound-interest method applies. Let $a_{\overline{n}|i}$ denote the present value of the annuity, which is sometimes denoted as $a_{\overline{n}|}$ when the rate of interest is understood. As the present value of the jth payment is v^j, where $v = \frac{1}{1+i}$ is the discount factor, the present value of the annuity is (see Appendix A.5 for the sum of a geometric progression)

$$
\begin{aligned}
a_{\overline{n}|} &= v + v^2 + v^3 + \cdots + v^n \\
&= v \times \left[\frac{1 - v^n}{1 - v} \right] \\
&= \frac{1 - v^n}{i} \\
&= \frac{1 - (1 + i)^{-n}}{i}.
\end{aligned}
\tag{2.1}
$$

The accumulated value of the annuity at time n is denoted by $s_{\overline{n}|i}$ or $s_{\overline{n}|}$. This is the future value of $a_{\overline{n}|}$ at time n. Thus, we have

$$
\begin{aligned}
s_{\overline{n}|} &= a_{\overline{n}|} \times (1 + i)^n \\
&= \frac{(1 + i)^n - 1}{i}.
\end{aligned}
\tag{2.2}
$$

$s_{\overline{n}|}$ will be referred to as the future value of the annuity. If the annuity is of level payments of P, the present and future values of the annuity are $Pa_{\overline{n}|}$ and $Ps_{\overline{n}|}$, respectively.

Example 2.2: Calculate the present value of an annuity-immediate of amount $100 paid annually for 5 years at the rate of interest of 9% per annum using formula (2.1). Also calculate its future value at the end of 5 years.

Solution: From (2.1), the present value of the annuity is

$$100\, a_{\overline{5}|} = 100 \times \left[\frac{1 - (1.09)^{-5}}{0.09} \right] = \$388.97,$$

which agrees with the solution of Example 2.1. The future value of the annuity is

$$(1.09)^5 \times (100\, a_{\overline{5}|}) = (1.09)^5 \times 388.97 = \$598.47.$$

Alternatively, the future value can be calculated as

$$100\, s_{\overline{5}|} = 100 \times \left[\frac{(1.09)^5 - 1}{0.09} \right] = \$598.47.$$

■

Example 2.3: Calculate the present value of an annuity-immediate of amount $100 payable quarterly for 10 years at the annual rate of interest of 8% convertible quarterly. Also calculate its future value at the end of 10 years.

Solution: Note that the rate of interest per payment period (quarter) is $\frac{8}{4}\% = 2\%$, and there are $4 \times 10 = 40$ payments. Thus, from (2.1) the present value of the annuity-immediate is

$$100\, a_{\overline{40}|0.02} = 100 \times \left[\frac{1 - (1.02)^{-40}}{0.02} \right] = \$2,735.55,$$

and the future value of the annuity-immediate is

$$2,735.55 \times (1.02)^{40} = \$6,040.20.$$

■

A common problem in financial management is to determine the installments required to pay back a loan. Note that we may use (2.1) to calculate the amount of level installments required. The example below illustrates this.

Example 2.4: A man borrows a loan of $20,000 to purchase a car at annual rate of interest of 6%. He will pay back the loan through monthly installments over 5 years, with the first installment to be made one month after the release of the loan. What is the monthly installment he needs to pay?

Solution: The rate of interest per payment period is $\frac{6}{12}\% = 0.5\%$. Let P be the monthly installment. As there are $5 \times 12 = 60$ payments, from (2.1) we have

$$
\begin{aligned}
20{,}000 &= P\, a_{\overline{60}|0.005} \\
&= P \times \left[\frac{1 - (1.005)^{-60}}{0.005} \right] \\
&= P \times 51.7256,
\end{aligned}
$$

so that

$$
P = \frac{20{,}000}{51.7256} = \$386.66.
$$

In the example above, we have assumed that the period of conversion of interest is equal to the payment period, i.e., both are monthly. We shall consider later the case when the two are not equal. Note that the quoted rate of interest of 6% in the above example is nominal and not the effective rate of interest.

The example below illustrates the calculation of the required installment for a targeted future value.

Example 2.5: A man wants to save \$100,000 to pay for his son's education in 10 years' time. An education fund requires the investors to deposit equal installments annually at the end of each year. If interest of 7.5% per annum is paid, how much does the man need to save each year in order to meet his target?

Solution: We first calculate $s_{\overline{10}|}$, which is equal to

$$
\frac{(1.075)^{10} - 1}{0.075} = 14.1471.
$$

Then the required amount of installment is

$$
P = \frac{100{,}000}{s_{\overline{10}|}} = \frac{100{,}000}{14.1471} = \$7{,}068.59.
$$

2.2 Annuity-Due

An **annuity-due** is an annuity for which the payments are made at the beginning of the payment periods. The time diagram in Figure 2.2 illustrates the payments of an annuity-due of 1 unit in each period for n periods.

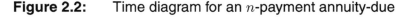

Figure 2.2: Time diagram for an n-payment annuity-due

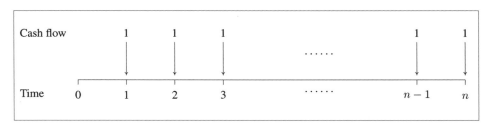

Note that the first payment is made at time 0, and the last payment is made at time $n - 1$. We denote the present value of the annuity-due at time 0 by $\ddot{a}_{\overline{n}|i}$ (or $\ddot{a}_{\overline{n}|}$ if the rate of interest i per payment period is understood), and the future value of the annuity at time n by $\ddot{s}_{\overline{n}|i}$ (or $\ddot{s}_{\overline{n}|}$ if the rate of interest i per payment period is understood).

The formula for $\ddot{a}_{\overline{n}|}$ can be derived as follows

$$
\begin{aligned}
\ddot{a}_{\overline{n}|} &= 1 + v + \cdots + v^{n-1} \\
&= \frac{1 - v^n}{1 - v} \\
&= \frac{1 - v^n}{d}.
\end{aligned}
\tag{2.3}
$$

Also, we have

$$
\begin{aligned}
\ddot{s}_{\overline{n}|} &= \ddot{a}_{\overline{n}|} \times (1 + i)^n \\
&= \frac{(1 + i)^n - 1}{d}.
\end{aligned}
\tag{2.4}
$$

As each payment in an annuity-due is paid one period ahead of the corresponding payment of an annuity-immediate, the present value of each payment in an annuity-due is $(1 + i)$ times the present value of the corresponding payment in an annuity-immediate. Thus, we conclude

$$
\ddot{a}_{\overline{n}|} = (1 + i)\, a_{\overline{n}|}
\tag{2.5}
$$

and, similarly,

$$
\ddot{s}_{\overline{n}|} = (1 + i)\, s_{\overline{n}|}.
\tag{2.6}
$$

Equation (2.5) can also be derived from (2.1) and (2.3). Likewise, (2.6) can be derived from (2.2) and (2.4).

As an annuity-due of n payments consists of a payment at time 0 and an annuity-immediate of $n - 1$ payments, the first payment of which is to be made at time 1, we have

$$\ddot{a}_{\overline{n}|} = 1 + a_{\overline{n-1}|}. \tag{2.7}$$

Similarly, if we consider an annuity-immediate with $n + 1$ payments at time 1, $2, \cdots, n+1$ as an annuity-due of n payments starting at time 1 plus a final payment at time $n + 1$, we can conclude

$$s_{\overline{n+1}|} = \ddot{s}_{\overline{n}|} + 1. \tag{2.8}$$

Equations (2.7) and (2.8) can also be proved algebraically using (2.1) through (2.4). Readers are invited to do this as an exercise.

Example 2.6: A company wants to provide a retirement plan for an employee who is aged 55 now. The plan will provide her with an annuity-immediate of $7,000 every year for 15 years upon her retirement at the age of 65. The company is funding this plan with an annuity-due of 10 years. If the rate of interest is 5%, what is the amount of installment the company should pay?

Solution: We first calculate the present value of the retirement annuity. This is equal to

$$7,000 \, a_{\overline{15}|} = 7,000 \times \left[\frac{1 - (1.05)^{-15}}{0.05} \right] = \$72,657.61.$$

This amount should be equal to the future value of the company's installments P, which is $P\ddot{s}_{\overline{10}|}$. Now from (2.4), we have

$$\ddot{s}_{\overline{10}|} = \frac{(1.05)^{10} - 1}{1 - (1.05)^{-1}} = 13.2068,$$

so that

$$P = \frac{72,657.61}{13.2068} = \$5,501.53.$$

2.3 Perpetuity, Deferred Annuity and Annuity Values at Other Times

A **perpetuity** is an annuity with no termination date, i.e., there is an infinite number of payments, with $n \to \infty$. An example that resembles a perpetuity is the dividends of a preferred stock. As a stock has no maturity date, if the dividend amounts are fixed, the payments are like a perpetuity. To calculate the present value of a perpetuity, we note that, as $v < 1$, $v^n \to 0$ when $n \to \infty$. Thus, from (2.1), we conclude that the present value of a perpetuity of payments of 1 unit when the first payment is made one period later, is

$$a_{\overline{\infty}|} = \frac{1}{i}. \tag{2.9}$$

For the case when the first payment is made immediately, we have, from (2.3),

$$\ddot{a}_{\overline{\infty}|} = \frac{1}{d}. \tag{2.10}$$

A **deferred annuity** is one for which the first payment starts some time in the future. Consider an annuity with n unit payments for which the first payment is due at time $m + 1$. This can be regarded as an n-period annuity-immediate to start at time m, and its present value is denoted by $_{m|}a_{\overline{n}|i}$ (or $_{m|}a_{\overline{n}|}$ for short). Thus, we have

$$
\begin{aligned}
_{m|}a_{\overline{n}|} &= v^m \, a_{\overline{n}|} \\
&= v^m \times \left[\frac{1 - v^n}{i} \right] \\
&= \frac{v^m - v^{m+n}}{i} \\
&= \frac{(1 - v^{m+n}) - (1 - v^m)}{i} \\
&= a_{\overline{m+n}|} - a_{\overline{m}|}. \tag{2.11}
\end{aligned}
$$

To understand the above equation, note that the deferred annuity can be regarded as a $(m+n)$-period annuity-immediate with the first m payments removed. It can be seen that the right-hand side of the last line of (2.11) is the present value of a $(m + n)$-period annuity-immediate minus the present value of a m-period annuity-immediate. Figure 2.3 illustrates (2.11).

From (2.11), we have the following results (note that the roles of m and n can be interchanged)

$$
\begin{aligned}
a_{\overline{m+n}|} &= a_{\overline{m}|} + v^m \, a_{\overline{n}|} \\
&= a_{\overline{n}|} + v^n \, a_{\overline{m}|}. \tag{2.12}
\end{aligned}
$$

Multiplying the above equations throughout by $1 + i$, we have

$$
\begin{aligned}
\ddot{a}_{\overline{m+n}|} &= \ddot{a}_{\overline{m}|} + v^m \, \ddot{a}_{\overline{n}|} \\
&= \ddot{a}_{\overline{n}|} + v^n \, \ddot{a}_{\overline{m}|}. \tag{2.13}
\end{aligned}
$$

Figure 2.3:   Illustration of equation (2.11)

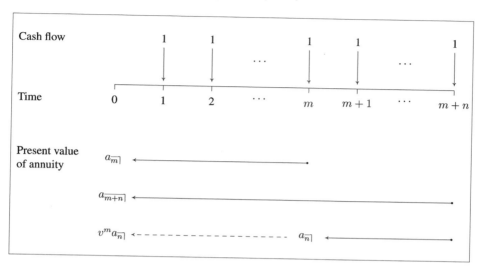

We also denote $v^m \ddot{a}_{\overline{n}|}$ as $_{m|}\ddot{a}_{\overline{n}|}$, which is the present value of a n-payment annuity of unit amounts due at time $m, m+1, \cdots, m+n-1$.

If we multiply the equations in (2.12) throughout by $(1+i)^{m+n}$, we obtain

$$
\begin{aligned}
s_{\overline{m+n}|} &= (1+i)^n s_{\overline{m}|} + s_{\overline{n}|} \\
&= (1+i)^m s_{\overline{n}|} + s_{\overline{m}|}.
\end{aligned}
\tag{2.14}
$$

Note that a $(m+n)$-period annuity-immediate can be regarded as the sum of a m-period annuity-immediate to start at time 0 and a n-period annuity-immediate to start at time m. The first line in (2.14) is the sum of the future values of the two annuity-immediates at time $m+n$. Finally, note that the roles of m and n can be interchanged so that the second line of (2.14) is an alternative way to write the future value of the $(m+n)$-period annuity-immediate. Figure 2.4 illustrates the first line of (2.14).

It is also straightforward to see that

$$
\begin{aligned}
\ddot{s}_{\overline{m+n}|} &= (1+i)^n \ddot{s}_{\overline{m}|} + \ddot{s}_{\overline{n}|} \\
&= (1+i)^m \ddot{s}_{\overline{n}|} + \ddot{s}_{\overline{m}|}.
\end{aligned}
\tag{2.15}
$$

We now return to (2.2) and write it as

$$
s_{\overline{m+n}|} = (1+i)^{m+n} a_{\overline{m+n}|},
$$

from which we multiply both sides of the equation by v^m to obtain

$$
v^m s_{\overline{m+n}|} = (1+i)^n a_{\overline{m+n}|},
\tag{2.16}
$$

Figure 2.4: Illustration of equation (2.14)

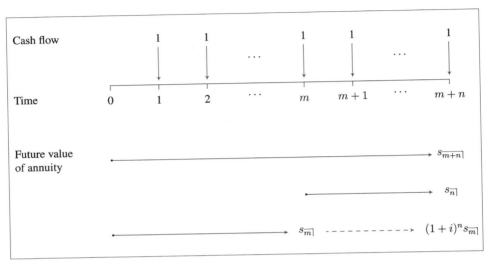

for arbitrary positive integers m and n. This equation expresses the value at time n of a $(m+n)$-period annuity-immediate starting at time 0 in two different ways. The left-hand side discounts the future value at time $m + n$ backwards by m periods, while the right-hand side brings the present value at time 0 forward by n periods. Figure 2.5 illustrates (2.16).

Figure 2.5: Illustration of equation (2.16)

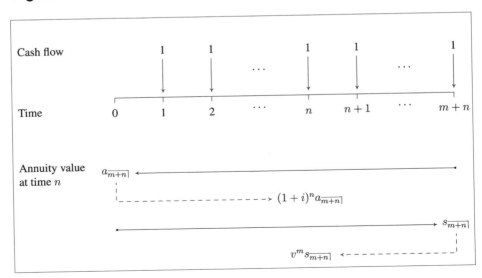

Also, it can be checked that the following result holds:

$$v^m \, \ddot{s}_{\overline{m+n}|} = (1+i)^n \, \ddot{a}_{\overline{m+n}|}.$$

2.4 Annuities under Other Accumulation Methods

We have so far discussed the calculations of the present and future values of annuities assuming compound interest. In this section we shall extend our discussion to other interest-accumulation methods. We shall consider a general accumulation function $a(\cdot)$ and *assume* that the function applies to any cash-flow transactions in the future. Thus, as stated in Section 1.7, any payment at time $t > 0$ starts to accumulate interest according to $a(\cdot)$ as a payment made at time 0.

Given the accumulation function $a(\cdot)$, the present value of a unit payment due at time t is $\frac{1}{a(t)}$. Thus, the present value of a n-period annuity-immediate of unit payments is

$$a_{\overline{n}|} = \sum_{t=1}^{n} \frac{1}{a(t)}. \tag{2.17}$$

Likewise, the future value at time n of a unit payment at time $t < n$ is $a(n - t)$. Thus, the future value of a n-period annuity-immediate of unit payments is

$$s_{\overline{n}|} = \sum_{t=1}^{n} a(n - t). \tag{2.18}$$

If (1.35) is satisfied so that $a(n - t) = \frac{a(n)}{a(t)}$ for $n > t > 0$, then

$$s_{\overline{n}|} = \sum_{t=1}^{n} \frac{a(n)}{a(t)} = a(n) \sum_{t=1}^{n} \frac{1}{a(t)} = a(n) \, a_{\overline{n}|}. \tag{2.19}$$

This result is satisfied for the compound-interest method, but not the simple-interest method or other accumulation schemes for which equation (1.35) does not hold.

Example 2.7: Suppose $\delta(t) = 0.02t$ for $0 \le t \le 5$, find $a_{\overline{5}|}$ and $s_{\overline{5}|}$.

Solution: We first calculate $a(t)$, which, from (1.26), is

$$a(t) = \exp\left(\int_0^t 0.02s \, ds\right)$$
$$= \exp(0.01t^2).$$

Hence, from (2.17),

$$a_{\overline{5}|} = \frac{1}{e^{0.01}} + \frac{1}{e^{0.04}} + \frac{1}{e^{0.09}} + \frac{1}{e^{0.16}} + \frac{1}{e^{0.25}} = 4.4957,$$

and, from (2.18),

$$s_{\overline{5}|} = 1 + e^{0.01} + e^{0.04} + e^{0.09} + e^{0.16} = 5.3185.$$

Note that $a(5) = e^{0.25} = 1.2840$, so that

$$a(5)\, a_{\overline{5}|} = 1.2840 \times 4.4957 = 5.7724 \neq s_{\overline{5}|}.$$

Note that in the above example, $a(n - t) = \exp[0.01(n - t)^2]$ and

$$\frac{a(n)}{a(t)} = \exp[0.01(n^2 - t^2)],$$

so that $a(n - t) \neq \frac{a(n)}{a(t)}$ and (2.19) does not hold.

Example 2.8: Calculate $a_{\overline{3}|}$ and $s_{\overline{3}|}$ if the nominal rate of interest is 5% per annum, assuming (a) compound interest, and (b) simple interest.

Solution: (a) Assuming compound interest, we have

$$a_{\overline{3}|} = \frac{1 - (1.05)^{-3}}{0.05} = 2.7232,$$

and

$$s_{\overline{3}|} = (1.05)^3 \times 2.7232 = 3.1525.$$

(b) For simple interest, the present value is

$$a_{\overline{3}|} = \sum_{t=1}^{3} \frac{1}{a(t)} = \sum_{t=1}^{3} \frac{1}{1 + rt} = \frac{1}{1.05} + \frac{1}{1.1} + \frac{1}{1.15} = 2.7310,$$

and the future value at time 3 is

$$s_{\overline{3}|} = \sum_{t=1}^{3} a(3 - t) = \sum_{t=1}^{3} (1 + r(3 - t)) = 1.10 + 1.05 + 1.0 = 3.15.$$

At the same nominal rate of interest, the compound-interest method generates higher interest than the simple-interest method. Therefore, the future value under the compound-interest method is higher, while its present value is lower. Also, note that for the simple-interest method, $a(3)\, a_{\overline{3}|} = 1.15 \times 2.7310 = 3.1407$, which is different from $s_{\overline{3}|} = 3.15$.

2.5 Payment Periods, Compounding Periods and Continuous Annuities

We have so far assumed that the payment period of an annuity coincides with the interest-conversion period. Now we consider the case where the payment period differs from the interest-conversion period. In general, the formulas derived in the previous sections can be applied with i being the effective rate of interest for the *payment period* (not the interest-conversion period). The examples below illustrate this point.

Example 2.9: Find the present value of an annuity-due of $200 per quarter for 2 years, if interest is compounded monthly at the nominal rate of 8%.

Solution: This is the situation where the payments are made less frequently than interest is converted. We first calculate the effective rate of interest per quarter, which is

$$\left[1 + \frac{0.08}{12}\right]^3 - 1 = 2.01\%.$$

As there are $n = 8$ payments, the required present value is

$$200\,\ddot{a}_{\overline{8}|0.0201} = 200 \times \left[\frac{1 - (1.0201)^{-8}}{1 - (1.0201)^{-1}}\right] = \$1{,}493.90.$$

Example 2.10: Find the present value of an annuity-immediate of $100 per quarter for 4 years, if interest is compounded semiannually at the nominal rate of 6%.

Solution: This is the situation where payments are made more frequently than interest is converted. We first calculate the effective rate of interest per quarter, which is

$$\left[1 + \frac{0.06}{2}\right]^{\frac{1}{2}} - 1 = 1.49\%.$$

Thus, the required present value is

$$100\,a_{\overline{16}|0.0149} = 100 \times \left[\frac{1 - (1.0149)^{-16}}{0.0149}\right] = \$1{,}414.27.$$

It is possible to derive algebraic formulas to compute the present and future values of annuities for which the period of installment is different from the period of compounding. We first consider the case where payments are made less frequently than interest conversion, which occurs at time 1, 2, $\cdots$, etc. Let i denote the effective rate of interest per interest-conversion period. Suppose an m-payment annuity-immediate consists of unit payments at time k, $2k$, $\cdots$, mk. We denote $n = mk$, which is the number of interest-conversion periods for the annuity. Figure 2.6 illustrates the cash flows for the case of $k = 2$.

Figure 2.6:   Payments less frequent than interest conversion ($k = 2$)

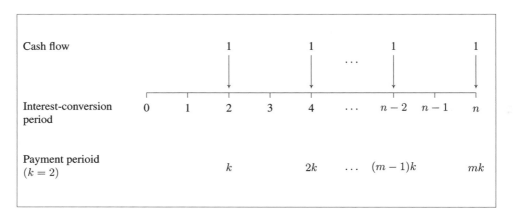

The present value of the above annuity-immediate is (we let $w = v^k$)

$$
\begin{aligned}
v^k + v^{2k} + \cdots + v^{mk} &= w + w^2 + \cdots + w^m \\
&= w \times \left[\frac{1 - w^m}{1 - w} \right] \\
&= v^k \times \left[\frac{1 - v^n}{1 - v^k} \right] \\
&= \frac{1 - v^n}{(1 + i)^k - 1} \\
&= \frac{a_{\overline{n}|}}{s_{\overline{k}|}},
\end{aligned}
\tag{2.20}
$$

and the future value of the annuity is

$$
(1 + i)^n \frac{a_{\overline{n}|}}{s_{\overline{k}|}} = \frac{s_{\overline{n}|}}{s_{\overline{k}|}}.
\tag{2.21}
$$

Note that (2.20) has a convenient interpretation. Consider an annuity-immediate with installments of $1/s_{\overline{k}|}$ each at time $1, \cdots, k$. The future value of these installments at time k is 1. Thus, the m-payment annuity-immediate of unit payments at time $k, 2k, \cdots, mk$ has the same present value as an mk-payment of annuity-immediate with installments of $1/s_{\overline{k}|}$ at time $1, 2, \cdots, n$, which is $a_{\overline{n}|}/s_{\overline{k}|}$.

We now consider the case where the payments are made more frequently than interest conversion. Let there be an mn-payment annuity-immediate due at time $\frac{1}{m}, \frac{2}{m}, \cdots, 1, 1 + \frac{1}{m}, \cdots, 2, \cdots, n$, and let i be the effective rate of interest per interest-conversion period. Thus, there are mn payments over n interest-conversion periods. Suppose each payment is of the amount $\frac{1}{m}$, so that there is a nominal amount of unit payment in each interest-conversion period. Figure 2.7 illustrates the cash flows for the case of $m = 4$.

We denote the present value of this annuity at time 0 by $a_{\overline{n}|i}^{(m)}$, which can be computed as follows (we let $w = v^{\frac{1}{m}}$)

$$
\begin{aligned}
a_{\overline{n}|i}^{(m)} &= \frac{1}{m}\left(v^{\frac{1}{m}} + v^{\frac{2}{m}} + \cdots + v + v^{1+\frac{1}{m}} + \cdots + v^n\right) \\
&= \frac{1}{m}(w + w^2 + \cdots + w^{mn}) \\
&= \frac{1}{m}\left[w \times \frac{1 - w^{mn}}{1 - w}\right] \\
&= \frac{1}{m}\left[v^{\frac{1}{m}} \times \frac{1 - v^n}{1 - v^{\frac{1}{m}}}\right] \\
&= \frac{1}{m}\left[\frac{1 - v^n}{(1+i)^{\frac{1}{m}} - 1}\right] \\
&= \frac{1 - v^n}{r^{(m)}},
\end{aligned}
\tag{2.22}
$$

where

$$
r^{(m)} = m\left[(1+i)^{\frac{1}{m}} - 1\right]
\tag{2.23}
$$

is the equivalent nominal rate of interest compounded m times per interest-conversion period (see (1.19)). The future value of the annuity-immediate is

$$
\begin{aligned}
s_{\overline{n}|i}^{(m)} &= (1+i)^n a_{\overline{n}|i}^{(m)} \\
&= \frac{(1+i)^n - 1}{r^{(m)}} \\
&= \frac{i}{r^{(m)}} s_{\overline{n}|}.
\end{aligned}
\tag{2.24}
$$

Figure 2.7: Payments more frequent than interest conversion ($m = 4$)

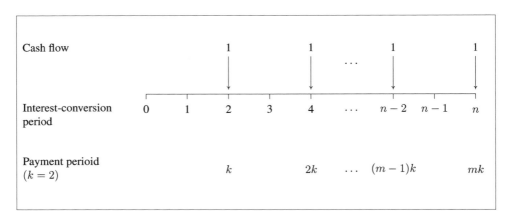

The above equation parallels (2.22), which can also be written as

$$a^{(m)}_{\overline{n}|i} = \frac{i}{r^{(m)}}\, a_{\overline{n}|}.$$

If the mn-payment annuity is due at time $0, \frac{1}{m}, \frac{2}{m}, \cdots, n - \frac{1}{m}$, we denote its present value at time 0 by $\ddot{a}^{(m)}_{\overline{n}|}$, which is given by

$$\ddot{a}^{(m)}_{\overline{n}|} = (1+i)^{\frac{1}{m}}\, a^{(m)}_{\overline{n}|} = (1+i)^{\frac{1}{m}} \times \left[\frac{1 - v^n}{r^{(m)}}\right]. \tag{2.25}$$

Thus, from (1.22) we conclude

$$\ddot{a}^{(m)}_{\overline{n}|} = \frac{1 - v^n}{d^{(m)}} = \frac{d}{d^{(m)}}\, \ddot{a}_{\overline{n}|}. \tag{2.26}$$

The future value of this annuity at time n is

$$\ddot{s}^{(m)}_{\overline{n}|} = (1+i)^n\, \ddot{a}^{(m)}_{\overline{n}|} = \frac{d}{d^{(m)}}\, \ddot{s}_{\overline{n}|}. \tag{2.27}$$

For deferred annuities, the following results apply

$$_{q|}a^{(m)}_{\overline{n}|} = v^q\, a^{(m)}_{\overline{n}|}, \tag{2.28}$$

and

$$_{q|}\ddot{a}^{(m)}_{\overline{n}|} = v^q\, \ddot{a}^{(m)}_{\overline{n}|}. \tag{2.29}$$

Example 2.11: Solve the problem in Example 2.9 using (2.20).

Solution: We first note that $i = \frac{0.08}{12} = 0.0067$. Now $k = 3$ and $n = 24$ so that from (2.20), the present value of the annuity-immediate is

$$200 \times \frac{a_{\overline{24}|0.0067}}{s_{\overline{3}|0.0067}} = 200 \times \left[\frac{1 - (1.0067)^{-24}}{(1.0067)^3 - 1} \right]$$
$$= \$1,464.27.$$

Finally, the present value of the annuity-due is

$$(1.0067)^3 \times 1,464.27 = \$1,493.90.$$

Example 2.12: Solve the problem in Example 2.10 using (2.22) and (2.23).

Solution: Note that $m = 2$ and $n = 8$. With $i = 0.03$, we have, from (2.23)

$$r^{(2)} = 2 \times [\sqrt{1.03} - 1] = 0.0298.$$

Therefore, from (2.22), we have

$$a_{\overline{8}|0.03}^{(2)} = \frac{1 - (1.03)^{-8}}{0.0298}$$
$$= 7.0720.$$

As the total payment in each interest-conversion period is $200, the required present value is

$$200 \times 7.0720 = \$1,414.27.$$

Now we consider (2.22) again. Suppose the annuities are paid *continuously* at the rate of 1 unit per interest-conversion period over n periods. Thus, $m \to \infty$ and we denote the present value of this continuous annuity by $\bar{a}_{\overline{n}|}$. As $\lim_{m \to \infty} r^{(m)} = \delta$, we have, from (2.22),

$$\bar{a}_{\overline{n}|} = \frac{1 - v^n}{\delta} = \frac{1 - v^n}{\ln(1 + i)} = \frac{i}{\delta} a_{\overline{n}|}. \tag{2.30}$$

For a continuous annuity there is no distinction between annuity-due and annuity-immediate. While theoretically it may be difficult to visualize annuities that are paid continuously, (2.30) may be a good approximation for annuities that are paid daily. Note that (2.30) does not depend on the frequency of interest conversion.

The present value of an n-period continuous annuity of unit payment per period with a deferred period of q is given by

$$_{q|}\bar{a}_{\overline{n}|} = v^q \, \bar{a}_{\overline{n}|} = \bar{a}_{\overline{q+n}|} - \bar{a}_{\overline{q}|}. \tag{2.31}$$

To compute the future value of a continuous annuity of unit payment per period over n periods, we use the following formula

$$\bar{s}_{\overline{n}|} = (1+i)^n \, \bar{a}_{\overline{n}|} = \frac{(1+i)^n - 1}{\ln(1+i)} = \frac{i}{\delta} \, s_{\overline{n}|}. \tag{2.32}$$

We now generalize the above results to the case of a general accumulation function $a(\cdot)$, which is not necessarily based on the compound-interest method. The present value of a continuous annuity of unit payment per period over n periods is

$$\bar{a}_{\overline{n}|} = \int_0^n v(t) \, dt = \int_0^n \exp\left(-\int_0^t \delta(s) \, ds\right) dt. \tag{2.33}$$

To compute the future value of the annuity at time n, we assume that, as in Section 1.7, a unit payment at time t accumulates to $a(n - t)$ at time n, for $n > t \geq 0$.[1] Thus, the future value of the annuity at time n is

$$\bar{s}_{\overline{n}|} = \int_0^n a(n-t) \, dt = \int_0^n \exp\left(\int_0^{n-t} \delta(s) \, ds\right) dt. \tag{2.34}$$

2.6 Varying Annuities

We have so far considered annuities with level payments. Certain financial instruments may provide cash flows that vary over time. For example, a bond may pay coupons with a step-up coupon rate, making lower coupon payments (or even deferred payments) initially with increased payments later. We illustrate how varying annuities may be evaluated. In particular, we consider annuities the payments of which vary according to an arithmetic progression. Thus, we consider an annuity-immediate and assume the initial payment is P, with subsequent payments $P + D$, $P + 2D, \cdots$, etc., so that the jth payment is $P + (j - 1)D$. Note that we allow D to be negative so that the annuity can be either stepping up or stepping down. However, for a n-payment annuity, $P + (n - 1)D$ must be positive so that negative cash flow is ruled out. Figure 2.8 presents the time diagram of this annuity.

---

[1] Note that this is not the only assumption we can adopt, nor is it the most reasonable. In Chapter 3 we shall see another possible assumption.

Figure 2.8:   Increasing annuity-immediate

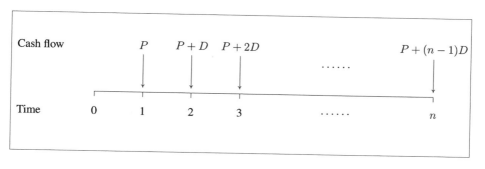

We can see that the annuity can be regarded as the sum of the following annuities: (a) an n-period annuity-immediate with constant amount P, and (b) $n-1$ deferred annuities, where the jth deferred annuity is a $(n-j)$-period annuity-immediate with level amount D to start at time j, for $j = 1, \cdots, n-1$. Thus, the present value of the varying annuity is

$$
\begin{aligned}
P a_{\overline{n}|} + D \left[\sum_{j=1}^{n-1} v^j a_{\overline{n-j}|} \right] &= P a_{\overline{n}|} + D \left[\sum_{j=1}^{n-1} v^j \frac{(1 - v^{n-j})}{i} \right] \\
&= P a_{\overline{n}|} + D \left[\frac{\left(\sum_{j=1}^{n-1} v^j \right) - (n-1)v^n}{i} \right] \\
&= P a_{\overline{n}|} + D \left[\frac{\left(\sum_{j=1}^{n} v^j \right) - nv^n}{i} \right] \\
&= P a_{\overline{n}|} + D \left[\frac{a_{\overline{n}|} - nv^n}{i} \right].
\end{aligned}
\tag{2.35}
$$

For an n-period *increasing* annuity with $P = D = 1$, we denote its present and future values by $(Ia)_{\overline{n}|}$ and $(Is)_{\overline{n}|}$, respectively. Readers are invited to show that

$$
(Ia)_{\overline{n}|} = \frac{\ddot{a}_{\overline{n}|} - nv^n}{i}
\tag{2.36}
$$

and

$$
(Is)_{\overline{n}|} = \frac{s_{\overline{n+1}|} - (n+1)}{i} = \frac{\ddot{s}_{\overline{n}|} - n}{i}.
\tag{2.37}
$$

For an increasing n-payment annuity-due with payments of $1, 2, \cdots, n$ at time $0, 1, \cdots, n-1$, the present value of the annuity is

$$
(I\ddot{a})_{\overline{n}|} = (1 + i)(Ia)_{\overline{n}|}.
\tag{2.38}
$$

This is the sum of an n-period level annuity-due of unit payments and a $(n-1)$-payment increasing annuity-immediate with starting and incremental payments of 1. Thus, we have

$$(I\ddot{a})_{\overline{n}|} = \ddot{a}_{\overline{n}|} + (Ia)_{\overline{n-1}|}. \tag{2.39}$$

For the case of a n-period *decreasing* annuity with $P = n$ and $D = -1$, we denote its present and future values by $(Da)_{\overline{n}|}$ and $(Ds)_{\overline{n}|}$, respectively. Figure 2.9 presents the time diagram of this annuity.

Figure 2.9: Decreasing annuity-immediate with $P = n$ and $D = -1$

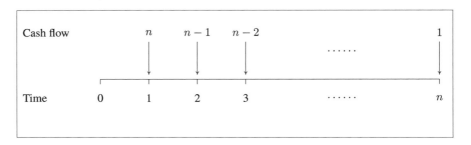

Readers are invited to show that

$$(Da)_{\overline{n}|} = \frac{n - a_{\overline{n}|}}{i} \tag{2.40}$$

and

$$(Ds)_{\overline{n}|} = \frac{n(1+i)^n - s_{\overline{n}|}}{i}. \tag{2.41}$$

We consider two types of increasing continuous annuities. First, we consider the case of a continuous n-period annuity with level payment (i.e., at a constant rate) of τ units from time $\tau - 1$ through time τ. We denote the present value of this annuity by $(I\bar{a})_{\overline{n}|}$, which is given by

$$(I\bar{a})_{\overline{n}|} = \sum_{\tau=1}^{n} \tau \int_{\tau-1}^{\tau} v^s \, ds = \sum_{\tau=1}^{n} \tau \int_{\tau-1}^{\tau} e^{-\delta s} \, ds. \tag{2.42}$$

The above equation can be simplified to (see Exercise 2.42)

$$(I\bar{a})_{\overline{n}|} = \frac{\ddot{a}_{\overline{n}|} - nv^n}{\delta}. \tag{2.43}$$

Second, we may consider a continuous n-period annuity for which the payment in the interval t to $t + \Delta t$ is $t\Delta t$, i.e., the instantaneous rate of payment at time t is t. We denote the present value of this annuity by $(\bar{I}\bar{a})_{\overline{n}|}$, which is given by (see Exercise 2.42)

$$(\bar{I}\bar{a})_{\overline{n}|} = \int_0^n tv^t \, dt = \int_0^n te^{-\delta t} \, dt = \frac{\bar{a}_{\overline{n}|} - nv^n}{\delta}. \tag{2.44}$$

We now consider an annuity-immediate with payments following a geometric progression. Let the first payment be 1, with subsequent payments being $1 + k$ times the previous one. Thus, the present value of an annuity with n payments is (for $k \neq i$)

$$
\begin{aligned}
v + v^2(1+k) + \cdots + v^n(1+k)^{n-1} &= v \sum_{t=0}^{n-1} [v(1+k)]^t \\
&= v \sum_{t=0}^{n-1} \left[\frac{1+k}{1+i}\right]^t \\
&= v \left[\frac{1 - \left(\dfrac{1+k}{1+i}\right)^n}{1 - \dfrac{1+k}{1+i}}\right] \\
&= \frac{1 - \left(\dfrac{1+k}{1+i}\right)^n}{i - k}. \tag{2.45}
\end{aligned}
$$

Note that in the above equation, if $k = i$ the present value of the annuity is nv, as can be concluded from the first line of (2.45).

Example 2.13: An annuity-immediate consists of a first payment of $100, with subsequent payments increased by 10% over the previous one until the 10th payment, after which subsequent payments decreases by 5% over the previous one. If the effective rate of interest is 10% per payment period, what is the present value of this annuity with 20 payments?

Solution: The present value of the first 10 payments is (note that $k = i$)

$$100 \times 10(1.1)^{-1} = \$909.09.$$

For the next 10 payments, $k = -0.05$ and their present value at time 10 is (note that the payment at time 11 is $100(1.10)^9(0.95)$)

$$100(1.10)^9(0.95) \times \frac{1 - \left(\dfrac{0.95}{1.1}\right)^{10}}{0.1 + 0.05} = 1{,}148.64.$$

Hence, the present value of the 20 payments is

$$909.09 + 1,148.64(1.10)^{-10} = \$1,351.94.$$

Example 2.14: An investor wishes to accumulate $1,000 at the end of year 5. He makes level deposits at the beginning of each year for 5 years. The deposits earn a 6% annual effective rate of interest, which is credited at the end of each year. The interests on the deposits earn 5% effective interest rate annually. How much does he have to deposit each year?

Solution: Let the level annual deposit be A. The interest received at the end of year 1 is $0.06A$, which increases by $0.06A$ annually to $5 \times 0.06A$ at the end of year 5. Thus, the interests from the deposits form a 5-payment increasing annuity with $P = D = 0.06A$, earning annual interest of 5%. Hence, we have the equation of value

$$1,000 = 5A + 0.06A(Is)_{\overline{5}|0.05}.$$

From (2.37) we obtain $(Is)_{\overline{5}|0.05} = 16.0383$, so that

$$A = \frac{1,000}{5 + 0.06 \times 16.0383} = \$167.7206.$$

2.7 Term of Annuity

Given the rate of interest, the term of the annuity and the sizes of the annuity payments, the formulas derived above enable us to calculate the present and future values of the annuity. The problem, however, may sometimes be reversed. For example, we may consider the following: (a) given an initial investment that generates level annuity payments at a given rate of interest, how long will the annuity payments last? (b) given an initial investment that generates a fixed number of level annuity payments, what is the rate of return for this investment? Obviously the first question requires us to solve for the value of n given other information, while the second requires the solution of i.

We now consider the case where the annuity period may not be an integer. This will throw light on the first question above. For example, we consider $a_{\overline{n+k}|}$, where

n is an integer and $0 < k < 1$. We note that

$$\begin{aligned}
a_{\overline{n+k}|} &= \frac{1 - v^{n+k}}{i} \\
&= \frac{(1 - v^n) + (v^n - v^{n+k})}{i} \\
&= a_{\overline{n}|} + v^{n+k}\left[\frac{(1+i)^k - 1}{i}\right] \\
&= a_{\overline{n}|} + v^{n+k} s_{\overline{k}|}.
\end{aligned} \tag{2.46}$$

Thus, $a_{\overline{n+k}|}$ is the sum of the present value of a n-period annuity-immediate with unit amount and the present value of an amount $s_{\overline{k}|}$ paid at time $n + k$. Note that $s_{\overline{k}|}$ should not be taken as the future value of an annuity-immediate as k is less than 1, the time of the first payment.

When the equation of value does not solve for an integer n, care must be taken to specify how the last payment is to be calculated. The example below illustrates this problem.

Example 2.15: A principal of \$5,000 generates income of \$500 at the end of every year at an effective rate of interest of 4.5% for as long as possible. Calculate the term of the annuity and discuss the possibilities of settling the last payment.

Solution: The equation of value

$$500\, a_{\overline{n}|0.045} = 5{,}000$$

implies $a_{\overline{n}|0.045} = 10$, which can be solved to obtain $n = 13.5820$. Thus, the investment may be paid off with 13 payments of \$500, plus an additional amount A at the end of year 13. Computing the future value at time 13, we have the equation of value

$$500\, s_{\overline{13}|0.045} + A = 5{,}000\,(1.045)^{13},$$

which implies $A = \$281.02$. We conclude that the last payment is $500 + 281.02 = \$781.02$. Alternatively, if A is not paid at time 13 the last payment B may be made at the end of year 14, which is given by

$$B = 281.02 \times 1.045 = \$293.67.$$

Finally, if we adopt the approach in (2.46), we let $n = 13$ and $k = 0.58$ so that the last payment C to be paid at time 13.58 years is given by

$$C = 500 s_{\overline{k}|} = 500 \times \left[\frac{(1.045)^{0.58} - 1}{0.045}\right] = \$288.32.$$

Note that $A < C < B$, which is as expected, as this follows the order of the occurrence of the payments. In principle, all three approaches are justified.

◼

Generally, the effective rate of interest cannot be solved analytically from the equation of value. Numerical methods must be used for this purpose.

Example 2.16: A principal of $5,000 generates income of $500 at the end of every year for 15 years. What is the effective rate of interest?

Solution: The equation of value is

$$a_{\overline{15}|i} = \frac{5,000}{500} = 10,$$

so that

$$a_{\overline{15}|i} = \frac{1 - (1+i)^{-15}}{i} = 10.$$

A simple grid search provides the following results

i	$a_{\overline{15}|i}$
0.054	10.10
0.055	10.04
0.056	9.97

A finer search provides the answer 5.556%.

◼

The solution of Example 2.16 requires the computation of the root of a nonlinear equation. This can be done numerically using the Excel Solver, which is illustrated in Exhibit 2.1. We enter a guessed value of 0.05 in Cell A1 in the Excel worksheet. The following expression is then entered in Cell A2: $(1 - (1 + A1)^{\hat{}}(-15))/A1$, which computes $a_{\overline{15}|i}$ with i set to the value at Cell A1. The Solver is then called up (from **Tools**, followed by **Solver**). In the **Solver Parameters** window we set the target cell to A2, and the target value to 10 by changing the value in Cell A1. The answer is found to be 0.05556.[2]

---

[2]Note that the exact procedure depends on the version of the Excel Solver.

Exhibit 2.1: Use of Excel Solver for Example 2.16

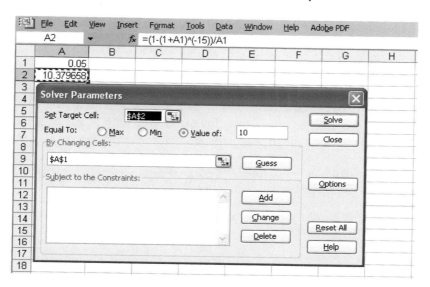

Alternatively, we can use the Excel function **RATE** to calculate the rate of interest that equates the present value of an annuity-immediate to a given value. Specifically, consider the equations

$$a_{\overline{n}|i} - A = 0 \qquad \text{and} \qquad \ddot{a}_{\overline{n}|i} - A = 0. \tag{2.47}$$

Given n and A, we wish to solve for i, which is the rate of interest per payment period of the annuity-immediate or annuity-due. The use of the Excel function **RATE** to compute i is described as follows:[3]

Excel function: RATE(np,1,pv,type,guess)

$np = n$,
$pv = -A$,
type = 0 (or omitted) for annuity-immediate, 1 for annuity-due
guess = starting value, set to 0.1 if omitted
Output = i, rate of interest per payment period of the annuity

---

To use **RATE** to solve for Example 2.16 we key in "**=RATE(15,1,-10)**".

---

[3]We use bold face fonts to denote Excel functions or the inputs of an Excel function that are mandatory. Input variables that are optional are denoted in normal fonts. For brevity we have adapted the specification of the functions for our usage. Readers should refer to the Excel Help Menu for the complete specification of the functions.

2.8 Summary

1. Annuities are series of payments at equal intervals. An annuity-immediate makes payments at the end of the payment periods, and an annuity-due makes payments at the beginning of the periods.

2. Algebraic formulas for the present and future values of annuity-immediate and annuity-due can be derived using geometric progression. These formulas facilitate the calculation of installments to pay off a loan, or installments required to accumulate to a targeted amount in the future.

3. Perpetuity has no maturity and makes payments indefinitely. Deferred annuity makes the first payment some time in the future.

4. Present- and future-value formulas can be derived for a general accumulation function.

5. When the payment period and the interest-conversion period are not the same, a simple approach is to compute the effective rate of interest for the payment period and do the computations using this rate. Algebraic approach can be used for both the cases of payments more frequent than interest conversion and less frequent than interest conversion.

6. Computations for continuous annuity can be used as approximations to frequent payments such as daily annuities.

7. Annuities involving simple step-up or step-down of payments in an arithmetic progression can be computed using basic annuity formulas.

8. The equation of value can be adopted to solve for n or i given other information. The calculation of i from the equation of value generally admits no analytic solution. Numerical methods such as grid search may be used.

Exercises

2.1 Let the effective rate of interest be 5%. Evaluate

    (a) $s_{\overline{10}|}$,

    (b) $\ddot{a}_{\overline{5}|}$,

    (c) $(Is)_{\overline{7}|}$,

    (d) $(Ia)_{\overline{7}|}$,

    (e) $a_{\overline{\infty}|}$.

2.2 Let $d^{(2)} = 2\%$. Evaluate each of the following and draw a time diagram for the cash flows involved.

(a) $a^{(2)}_{\overline{2}|}$,

(b) $\ddot{s}^{(4)}_{\overline{4}|}$,

(c) $\ddot{a}^{(\infty)}_{\overline{12}|}$.

2.3 Describe the meaning of $a_{\overline{20.3}|}$ evaluated at annual rate of interest 2%.

2.4 (a) Explain why $\ddot{a}_{\overline{n}|} \geq a_{\overline{n}|}$.

(b) Explain why $a^{(12)}_{\overline{n}|} \geq a_{\overline{n}|}$.

2.5 Let the effective rate of interest be 4%. Find the accumulated value of an annuity which pays $750

(a) annually for 8 years,

(b) biennially for 8 years,

(c) semiannually for 4 years,

assuming the payments are due at the end of every payment period.

2.6 A loan of $10,000 is repaid by 20 level installments at the end of every 6 months. The nominal rate of interest is 8%, convertible half yearly. Find the total amount of interest payment made over the 10-year period.

2.7 The present value of a series of payments of $5 at the end of every 3 years is $10. Find the effective rate of interest per year.

2.8 Find the present value of a 20-year annuity-due of $50 per year if the effective rate of interest is 6% for the first 12 years and 5% thereafter.

2.9 Assuming simple interest at 4%, evaluate

(a) $(Ia)_{\overline{3}|}$,

(b) $(Is)_{\overline{3}|}$.

Does the formula $a(3)(Ia)_{\overline{3}|} = (Is)_{\overline{3}|}$ hold?

2.10 Find the present value (evaluated at the beginning of year 2006) of the perpetuity which pays $1,000 at the beginning of every year starting from year 2006, but provides no payment at the beginning of every leap year. Express your answer in terms of the effective rate of interest i.

2.11 Novia deposits $1,000 into her bank account at the beginning of every year. The bank credits annual interest of 6%. At the end of every year, she takes out the interest earned from the bank account and puts it into an investment fund which earns 3% every half year. Find the interest earned in the fund during the first half of the ninth year.

2.12 The price of a watch is $25,000 and you finance it with a down payment and 18 installments of $1,000 payable at the end of every month. The nominal interest rate is 2.5% convertible monthly. Find the down payment.

2.13 The price of a LCD monitor is $1,649. Find the monthly payments commencing at time 0 and continuing for 1.5 years for the purchase if the interest charged is 2% convertible monthly.

2.14 Let $\delta(t) = 0.01(t + 1)$, $t \geq 0$. Find the current value at time 3 for $1 payable at time 1 and 5, $2 payable at time 2 and 4, and $3 payable at time 3. You may adopt the assumption in Section 1.7 for the future values of future payments.

2.15 Prove (2.7) and (2.8) algebraically.

2.16 A person plans to accumulate a sum of $50,000 at the end of 48 months by equal installments at the beginning of each month. If the effective rate of interest is 1% per month, what is the amount of the installment?

2.17 A sum of $20,000 is used to buy a deferred perpetuity-due that pays $2,100 every year for the first 5 years and $1,000 per year thereafter. If the annual effective rate is 6%, find the deferred period.

2.18 Find the present value of a 10-year annuity that pays $500 at the end of each month for the first 4 years and $2,000 at the end of each quarter for the last 6 years. The annual effective rate of interest is 7%.

2.19 A sum of $20,000 is used to buy a 4-year deferred perpetuity-immediate that pays M every quarter. If the annual effective rate of interest is 8%, find M.

2.20 Prove (2.36) and (2.37).

2.21 Prove (2.40) and (2.41).

2.22 Consider an annuity-due that pays 1 unit at the beginning of every k other interest-conversion periods, for a total of m payments. Derive the present value of this annuity. What is the future value of this annuity at time $n = mk$?

2.23 Express $\dfrac{s^{(52)}_{\overline{n}|}}{\ddot{s}^{(12)}_{\overline{n}|}}$ in terms of the nominal rates of interest and discount.

2.24 A couple want to save $100,000 to pay for their daughter's education. They put $2,000 into a fund at the beginning of every month. Interest is compounded monthly at a nominal rate of 7%. How long does it take for the fund to reach $100,000?

2.25 Denote the present value and future value (at time n) for 1 at time 0; 2 at time 1; $\cdots$, n at time $n - 1$, by $(I\ddot{a})_{\overline{n}|}$ and $(I\ddot{s})_{\overline{n}|}$, respectively. Show that

$$(I\ddot{a})_{\overline{n}|} = \frac{\ddot{a}_{\overline{n}|}}{d} - \frac{nv^{n-1}}{i}$$

and

$$(I\ddot{s})_{\overline{n}|} = \frac{\ddot{s}_{\overline{n}|} - n}{d}$$

with the help of formulas (2.36) and (2.37).

2.26 John deposits $500 into the bank at the end of every month. The bank credits monthly interest of 1.5%. Find the amount of interest earned in his account during the 13th month.

2.27 Consider lending $1 at the beginning of each year for n years. The borrower is required to repay interest at the end of every year. After n years, the principal is returned.

(a) Draw a time diagram and find the present value of all interests.

(b) How much principal is returned after n years?

(c) Formula (2.36) can be written as

$$\ddot{a}_{\overline{n}|} = i(Ia)_{\overline{n}|} + nv^n.$$

Explain verbally the meaning of the expression above.

(d) Using $(Ia)_{\overline{n}|} + (Da)_{\overline{n}|} = (n+1)a_{\overline{n}|}$ and (2.36), derive formula (2.40).

2.28 Payments of $500 per quarter are made over a 5-year period commencing at the end of the first month. Show that the present value of all payments 2 years prior to the first payment is

$$\$2,000(\ddot{a}^{(4)}_{\overline{7}|} - \ddot{a}^{(4)}_{\overline{2}|}),$$

where the annuity symbols are based on an effective rate of interest. What is the accumulated value of all payments 7 years after the first payment? Express your answers in a form similar to the expression above.

2.29 Find the accumulated value at the end of 12 years of a fund where $1,000 is deposited at the beginning of each year for the first 4 years, $2,000 is deposited at the beginning of each year for the subsequent 4 years, and $3,000 is deposited at the beginning of each year for the final 4 years. Express your answer in terms of a sum of accumulated values $\ddot{s}_{\overline{n}|}$.

2.30 Let $\delta(t) = (2+t)^{-1}, t \geq 0$.

    (a) Find $v(t)$.

    (b) Find $a_{\overline{3}|}$.

2.31 Deposits of $1,000 per year are placed into a fund continuously for 20 years at 4% force of interest. After 20 years, annual withdrawals commence and continue for 30 years at the same effective rate of interest, with the first payment to be made 1 year after the last deposit. Find the amount of each withdrawal.

2.32 Assuming simple rate of discount d, find an expression for $\ddot{a}_{\overline{n}|}$ for $n < 1/d$.

2.33 Describe the meaning of the following with the help of a time diagram:

    (a) $\dfrac{a_{\overline{18}|}}{a_{\overline{2}|}}$,

    (b) $\dfrac{1}{i\, s_{\overline{3}|}}$,

    (c) $\dfrac{s_{\overline{9}|}}{s_{\overline{3}|}}$.

2.34 Express, in terms of $a_{\overline{n}|}$ and $s_{\overline{n}|}$,

    (a) the present value at time 0 of $1 payable at time 4, 8, 12, 16, 20, $\cdots$, 60,

    (b) the accumulated value at time 25 of $1 payable at time 5, 8, 11, 14, 17 and 20.

2.35 Show that the current value at time 16 of $1 payable at time 3, 7, 11, $\cdots$, 31 is

$$\frac{s_{\overline{16}|} + a_{\overline{16}|}}{s_{\overline{3}|} + a_{\overline{1}|}}.$$

2.36 Find the present value of monthly payments of $2,400, $2,300, $\cdots$, $1,400, $1,300 commencing at time 0 at $d^{(12)} = 12\%$.

2.37 A paused rainbow is a cash-flow stream which pays $1 at time 1 and $2n$; $2 at time 2 and $2n - 1$; $\cdots$; $\$(n - 1)$ at time $n - 1$ and $n + 2$; and $\$n$ at time n and $n + 1$. Find the present value of the paused rainbow.

2.38 (a) Find the present value of a perpetuity of $1 at time 0, $2 at time 3, $3 at time 6, $4 at time 9, $\cdots$ at an effective rate of interest of 3%. [**Hint**: Use the result in Exercise 2.25.]

 (b) Hence, find the present value of a perpetuity which pays $1 at the end of the 3rd, 4th and 5th year, $2 at the end of the 6th, 7th and 8th year, $3 at the end of the 9th, 10th, 11th year and so on, at an effect rate of interest of 3%.

2.39 Express $(D\ddot{s})_{\overline{n}|}$ in terms of i and n under simple interest. [**Hint**: The symbol $(D\ddot{s})_{\overline{n}|}$ is defined similarly as in Exercise 2.25.]

2.40 Eric makes deposits into a retirement fund earning an annual effective rate of 7%. The first deposit of $1,000 is made on his 38th birthday and the last deposit is made on his 64th birthday. Every year his deposit increases by 3%. When he attains age 65, he will withdraw all the money in the retirement fund to purchase an annuity-immediate which provides him with monthly payment for 25 years. The nominal rate of interest on the annuity is convertible monthly at 6%. Find the amount of each monthly payment.

2.41 Albert purchased a house for $1,500,000 fifteen years ago. He put 30% down and financed the balance by a 20-year real estate mortgage at 6%, convertible monthly. Albert decides to pay the remaining loan balance in full by a single payment together with the installment just due. Find the prepayment penalty, which is one-third of the lender's interest loss.

2.42 Prove (2.43) and (2.44).

2.43 An investor wishes to accumulate $1,000 at the end of year 5. He makes level deposits at the end of each year. The deposits earn a 6% annual effective rate of interest, which is credited at the end of each year. The interests on the deposits earn 5% effective interest rate annually. How much does he have to deposit each year?

2.44 A principal of $20,500 generates income of $3,000 at the end of every 2 years at an effective rate of interest of 3% per annum for as long as possible. Calculate the term of the annuity and discuss the possibilities of settling the last payment.

2.45 You wish to accumulate $50,000 by semiannual deposits of $800 commencing at time 0 and for as long as necessary. The nominal rate of interest is 6% convertible monthly. Find how many regular deposits are necessary.

2.46 An investment of $1,000 is to be used to make payments of $15 at the end of the first year, $30 at the end of the second year, $45 at the end of the third year, etc., every year for as long as possible. A drop payment is paid 1 year after the last regular payment. Calculate the time and the amount of the drop payment at an annual rate of interest of 4%. [**Hint**: Use a trial-and-error approach, but start with a reasonable number of payments.]

2.47 Use the Excel **RATE** function to solve for the effective interest rate i of the following:

(a) $a_{\overline{18}|i} = 11$,

(b) $\ddot{a}_{\overline{18}|i} = 11$,

(c) $s_{\overline{18}|i} = 28$,

(d) $\ddot{s}_{\overline{18}|i} = 28$.

[**Hint**: Refer to the Excel Help Menu for the full specification of the **RATE** function.]

Advanced Problems

2.48 If $\bar{a}_{\overline{t}|} = \dfrac{t}{1+t}$ for $t \geq 0$, find $\delta(t)$. [**Hint**: Differentiate $\bar{a}_{\overline{t}|}$ with respect to t.]

2.49 Draw time diagrams and give interpretations to the following two formulas:

(a) $\sum_{t=1}^{n} s_{\overline{t}|} = (Is)_{\overline{n}|}$,

(b) $\sum_{t=1}^{n} a_{\overline{t}|} = (Da)_{\overline{n}|}$.

Hence, prove formulas (2.37) and (2.40).

2.50 Philip borrowed a loan of $12,000 for 29 years and financed it by 15 level payments payable at the end of every alternate year, with the first payment due at the end of the first year. The effective annual interest rate is 4%. Just before the fifth payment was due, Philip lost his job and the lender reduced the level payment by extending the loan for 6 more years.

(a) Find the amount of the original installments.

(b) Find the outstanding loan balance just before the fifth payment is due.

(c) Find the amount of extra interest that Philip has to pay because of the extension of the loan.

2.51 Ada, Betty and Chara receive an inheritance in the form of a series of level payments of \$4,000 at the end of every year. They decide to let Ada start receiving the payments first, followed by Betty and finally Chara such that they receive the same present value at an annual interest of 4%.

    (a) How many regular payments should Ada receive and how large is the final irregular payment?

    (b) Describe the payment pattern of Betty.

2.52 A rainbow is a cash flow stream which pays \$1 at time 1 and $2n - 1$, \$2 at time 2 and $2n - 2, \cdots$, \$$(n - 1)$ at time $n - 1$ and $n + 1$, and \$$n$ at time n for $n > 1$.

    (a) With the use of a time diagram, argue that the current value at time n of a rainbow is $s_{\overline{n}|}\ddot{a}_{\overline{n}|}$.

    (b) By using the formula $x + y \geq 2\sqrt{xy}$ for $x, y \geq 0$, show that $v^k + (1 + i)^k \geq 2$ for any positive integer k.

    (c) Hence or otherwise, show that $s_{\overline{n}|}\ddot{a}_{\overline{n}|} \geq n^2$. When does the equality hold? What is the significance of this result?

2.53 It is given that $s_{\overline{n}|} = x$ and $s_{\overline{2n}|} = y$. Express $s_{\overline{kn}|}$ in terms of x and y for k being a positive integer.

3 Spot Rates, Forward Rates and the Term Structure

The annuity formulas in Chapter 2 are derived based on the assumption that the rates of interest are constant through time and do not vary with the periods of the payments due. In practice, however, we would expect interest rates to change over time. Furthermore, the rates of interest may vary according to the time to maturity (the due date) of the payments. In this chapter we introduce the spot rate of interest and discuss the relationship between the rates of interest and the time to maturity, called the term structure of interest rates. We also define the notion of the forward rate of interest, and describe the relationship between the spot and forward rates of interest.

We discuss the relationship between the present and future values assuming future payments earn the forward rates of interest. We show the linkage between the accumulation function, and the spot and forward rates of interest. The definition of the accumulation function is extended so that it can be used to represent the term structure of the forward rate of interest.

An interest rate swap is an agreement between two parties to exchange cash flows based on interest rate movements in the future. It can be used to convert a floating rate loan to a fixed rate debt or vice versa. We discuss the determination of the swap rate and market value of the swap agreement prior to its termination.

This chapter lays the background for term structure modeling. The estimation of the yield curve and the theories for the determination of the term structure of interest rates will be discussed in Chapter 7.

- *Spot rate of interest*
- *Forward rate of interest*
- *Yield curve*
- *Term structure of interest rates*
- *Interest rate swap*
- *Swap rate*

3.1 Spot and Forward Rates of Interest

In Chapter 2 we discussed the computation of the present and future values of annuities under the compound-interest method. These results are derived assuming that the rate of interest is constant through time, irrespective of the investment horizon and the timing of the investment. We now relax this assumption and allow the rate of interest to vary with the time period of the investment. Specifically, we consider the case where investments over different horizons earn different rates of interest, although the principle of compounding still applies. To this effect, we consider two notions of interest rates, namely, the **spot rate of interest** and the **forward rate of interest**.

Consider an investment at time 0 earning interest over t periods. We assume that the period of investment is fixed at the time of investment, but the rate of interest earned per period varies according to the investment horizon. Thus, we define i_t^S as the spot rate of interest, which is the annualized effective rate of interest for the period from time 0 to t. Note that the subscript t in i_t^S highlights that the annual rate of interest varies with the investment horizon. Hence, a unit payment at time 0 accumulates to

$$a(t) = (1 + i_t^S)^t \tag{3.1}$$

at time t. This expression is also the future value at time t of a unit payment at time 0. Likewise, the present value of a unit payment due at time t is

$$\frac{1}{a(t)} = \frac{1}{(1 + i_t^S)^t}. \tag{3.2}$$

We now define i_t^F as the rate of interest applicable to the period $t-1$ to t, called the forward rate of interest. Unlike i_t^S, which applies to t periods (from time 0 to t), i_t^F applies to only one period (from time $t-1$ to t). Also, this rate is determined at time 0, although the payment is due at time $t-1$ (thus, the use of the term *forward*). By convention, we have $i_1^S \equiv i_1^F$. However, i_t^S and i_t^F are generally different for $t = 2, 3, \cdots$. Figure 3.1 illustrates the definitions of i_t^S and i_t^F.

Figure 3.1:   Spot and forward rates of interest

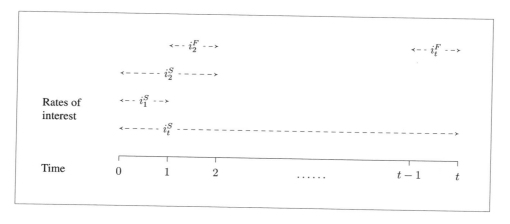

A plot of i_t^S against t is called the **yield curve**, and the mathematical relationship between i_t^S and t is called the **term structure of interest rates**. While we have defined two sets of interest rates, the spot and forward rates, they are not free to vary independently of each other. To illustrate this point, we consider the case of $t = 2$. If an investor invests a unit amount at time 0 over 2 periods, the investment will accumulate to $(1 + i_2^S)^2$ at time 2. Alternatively, she can invest a unit payment at time 0 over 1 period, and enter into a forward agreement to invest $1 + i_1^S$ unit at time 1 to earn the forward rate of i_2^F for 1 period. This rollover strategy will accumulate to $(1+i_1^S)(1+i_2^F)$ at time 2. We shall argue that the two strategies will accumulate to the same amount at time 2, so that

$$(1 + i_2^S)^2 = (1 + i_1^S)(1 + i_2^F). \tag{3.3}$$

The above equation holds if the capital market is *perfectly competitive*, so that no arbitrage opportunities exist. An assumption for a perfectly competitive capital market is that the lending and borrowing rates are the same.[1] Thus, if the left-hand

---

[1] This is an *idealized* condition to facilitate the proof. Equation (3.3) holds approximately when the capital market is nearly perfectly competitive.

side of equation (3.3) is less than the right-hand side, an arbitrageur will borrow 1 unit at time 0 over 2 years.[2] She will then lend 1 unit at time 0 over 1 year and at the same time lend $1 + i_1^S$ units, due at time 1 in the forward market (by entering into such an agreement at time 0) over 1 year. This strategy will guarantee a profit of $(1 + i_1^S)(1 + i_2^F) - (1 + i_2^S)^2 > 0$ without risk. On the other hand, if the left-hand side of (3.3) is larger than the right-hand side, she will lend 2 years in the spot market using capital borrowed for 1 year in the spot market with a forward agreement to roll over the loan for 1 year at time 1. Thus, such arbitrage activities will induce the two sides of equation (3.3) to be equal.

Equation (3.3) can be generalized to the following relationship concerning spot and forward rates of interest

$$(1 + i_t^S)^t = (1 + i_{t-1}^S)^{t-1}(1 + i_t^F), \tag{3.4}$$

for $t = 2, 3, \cdots$. Readers are invited to formulate arbitrage arguments for the proof of this equation. By repeatedly writing $(1 + i_{t-1}^S)$ in terms of $(1 + i_{t-2}^S)$ and $(1 + i_{t-1}^F)$, we can also conclude that

$$(1 + i_t^S)^t = (1 + i_1^F)(1 + i_2^F) \cdots (1 + i_t^F), \tag{3.5}$$

which is illustrated in Figure 3.2.

Given i_t^S, the forward rates of interest i_t^F satisfying equations (3.4) and (3.5) are called the *implicit* forward rates. Note that the *quoted* forward rates in the market may differ from the implicit forward rates in practice, as when the market is noncompetitive. Unless otherwise stated, however, we shall assume that equations (3.4) and (3.5) hold, so that it is the implicit forward rates we are referring to in our discussions.

Using equation (3.5) we can compute the spot rates given the forward rates. To compute the forward rates from the spot rates, we derive, from equation (3.4),

$$i_t^F = \frac{(1 + i_t^S)^t}{(1 + i_{t-1}^S)^{t-1}} - 1. \tag{3.6}$$

The following examples illustrate the applications of these results.

Example 3.1: Suppose the spot rates of interest for investment horizons of 1, 2, 3 and 4 years are, respectively, 4%, 4.5%, 4.5%, and 5%. Calculate the forward rates of interest for $t = 1, 2, 3$ and 4.

---

[2] An arbitrageur is an investor who exploits mispricings in the financial markets by making simultaneous offsetting trades aimed at creating riskless profits.

Solution: First, $i_1^F = i_1^S = 4\%$. The rest of the calculation, using (3.6), is as follows

$$i_2^F = \frac{(1+i_2^S)^2}{1+i_1^S} - 1 = \frac{(1.045)^2}{1.04} - 1 = 5.0024\%,$$

$$i_3^F = \frac{(1+i_3^S)^3}{(1+i_2^S)^2} - 1 = \frac{(1.045)^3}{(1.045)^2} - 1 = 4.5\%,$$

and

$$i_4^F = \frac{(1+i_4^S)^4}{(1+i_3^S)^3} - 1 = \frac{(1.05)^4}{(1.045)^3} - 1 = 6.5144\%.$$

Figure 3.2: Illustration of equation (3.5)

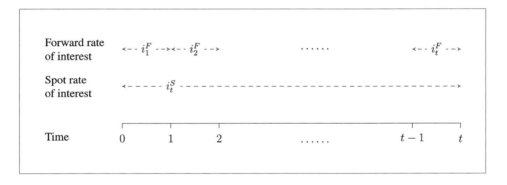

Example 3.2: Suppose the forward rates of interest for investments in year 1, 2, 3 and 4 are, respectively, 4%, 4.8%, 4.8% and 5.2%. Calculate the spot rates of interest for $t = 1, 2, 3$ and 4.

Solution: First, $i_1^S = i_1^F = 4\%$. From (3.5) the rest of the calculation is as follows

$$i_2^S = \left[(1+i_1^F)(1+i_2^F)\right]^{\frac{1}{2}} - 1 = \sqrt{1.04 \times 1.048} - 1 = 4.3992\%,$$

$$i_3^S = \left[(1+i_1^F)(1+i_2^F)(1+i_3^F)\right]^{\frac{1}{3}} - 1 = (1.04 \times 1.048 \times 1.048)^{\frac{1}{3}} - 1$$
$$= 4.5327\%,$$

$$i_4^S = \left[(1+i_1^F)(1+i_2^F)(1+i_3^F)(1+i_4^F)\right]^{\frac{1}{4}} - 1,$$
$$= (1.04 \times 1.048 \times 1.048 \times 1.052)^{\frac{1}{4}} - 1,$$
$$= 4.6991\%.$$

We have defined forward rates of interest that are applicable over a single period. We now define the multi-period forward rate $i^F_{t,\tau}$ as the annualized rate of interest applicable over τ periods from time t to $t+\tau$, for $t \geq 1$ and $\tau > 0$, with the rate being determined at time 0. Figure 3.3 illustrates the definition of $i^F_{t,\tau}$.

Figure 3.3: Illustration of equation (3.7)

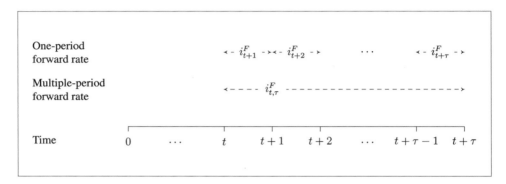

Using arbitrage arguments involving rollover strategies, we can see that the following no-arbitrage relationships hold.[3]

$$(1 + i^F_{t,\tau})^\tau = (1 + i^F_{t+1})(1 + i^F_{t+2}) \cdots (1 + i^F_{t+\tau}), \quad \text{for } t \geq 1, \tau > 0, \quad (3.7)$$

and

$$(1 + i^S_{t+\tau})^{t+\tau} = (1 + i^S_t)^t (1 + i^F_{t,\tau})^\tau, \quad \text{for } t \geq 1, \tau > 0. \quad (3.8)$$

Example 3.3: Based on the spot rates of interest in Example 3.1, calculate the multi-period forward rates of interest $i^F_{1,2}$ and $i^F_{1,3}$.

Solution: Using (3.7) we obtain

$$i^F_{1,2} = [(1 + i^F_2)(1 + i^F_3)]^{\frac{1}{2}} - 1 = (1.050024 \times 1.045)^{\frac{1}{2}} - 1 = 4.7509\%.$$

Similarly, we have

$$i^F_{1,3} = (1.050024 \times 1.045 \times 1.065144)^{\frac{1}{3}} - 1 = 5.3355\%.$$

We may also use (3.8) to compute the multi-period forward rates. Thus,

$$i^F_{1,2} = \left[\frac{(1 + i^S_3)^3}{1 + i^S_1} \right]^{\frac{1}{2}} - 1 = \left[\frac{(1.045)^3}{1.04} \right]^{\frac{1}{2}} - 1 = 4.7509\%,$$

---

[3]Note that i^F_t applies to the period $t - 1$ to t, whereas $i^F_{t,\tau}$ applies to the period t to $t + \tau$. It should be noted that $i^F_{t,1} = i^F_{t+1}$.

and similarly,

$$i_{1,3}^F = \left[\frac{(1+i_4^S)^4}{1+i_1^S}\right]^{\frac{1}{3}} - 1 = \left[\frac{(1.05)^4}{1.04}\right]^{\frac{1}{3}} - 1 = 5.3355\%.$$

3.2 The Term Structure of Interest Rates

Empirically the term structure can take various shapes, and its determination and dynamic evolution has been one of the most widely researched topics in finance. A sample of four yield curves of the US market are presented in Figure 3.4, and they illustrate some of the most commonly observed term structures in history.[4]

It can be seen that the spot-rate curve on 1998/06/30 is generally flat. The forward rate is also flat at the short end of the time to maturity and overlaps with the spot rate. Beyond maturity of 10 years, the spot rate increases gradually, and the forward rate starts to exceed the spot rate. This is an example of a nearly **flat term structure**. On 2000/03/31 we have a **downward sloping term structure**, where the long-term spot rate is lower than the short-term spot rate. In this case the forward rate drops below the spot rate, although it starts to climb up when the slope of the spot rate is getting flatter beyond maturity of 10 years. In contrast, we have an **upward sloping term structure** on 2001/08/31. Indeed, the spot rate increases quite sharply at the short end of the yield curve, although its slope is gradually flattening out as the time to maturity increases. Unlike the case of a downward sloping yield curve, the forward rate exceeds the spot rate when the yield curve is upward sloping. An upward sloping yield curve is also said to have a **normal term structure** as this is the most commonly observed term structure empirically. Finally, we have an inverted **humped yield curve** on 2007/12/31. The spot rate drops at the short end of the maturity before it starts to increase at around maturity of 3 years. The forward-rate curve crosses the spot-rate curve from below and varies quite a lot with the time to maturity.

Some questions may arise from a cursory examination of this sample of yield curves. For example: How are the yield curves obtained empirically? What determines the shape of the term structure? Why are upward sloping yield curves observed more often? Does the term structure have any useful information about the real economy? We shall answer some of these questions later in this book. In particular, we shall discuss some methods for the estimation of the term structure. In addition, we shall summarize some theories concerning the determination of the term structure.

---

[4]These yield curves are estimated by J. H. McCulloch and can be downloaded from http://www.econ.ohio-state.edu/jhm/ts/ts.html.

Figure 3.4:   Yield curves of the US market

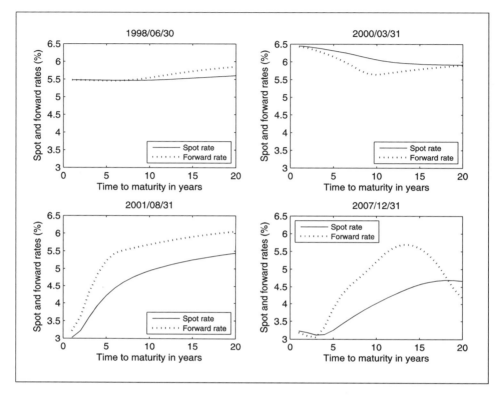

3.3   Present and Future Values Given the Term Structure

We now consider the present and future values of an annuity given the term structure. We shall continue to use the actuarial notations introduced in Chapter 2 for the present and future values of annuities, although their computation will depend on the whole term structure rather than a single effective rate of interest.

Using the present-value formula of a single payment given in (3.2), we compute the present value of a unit-payment annuity-immediate over n periods as

$$
a_{\overline{n}|} = \sum_{t=1}^{n} \frac{1}{a(t)}
$$

$$
= \sum_{t=1}^{n} \frac{1}{(1+i_t^S)^t}
$$

$$
= \frac{1}{(1+i_1^S)} + \frac{1}{(1+i_2^S)^2} + \cdots + \frac{1}{(1+i_n^S)^n}. \tag{3.9}
$$

From (3.5) we see that the future value at time t of a unit payment at time 0 can also be written as

$$a(t) = (1 + i_t^S)^t = \prod_{j=1}^{t}(1 + i_j^F) = (1 + i_1^F)(1 + i_2^F) \cdots (1 + i_t^F). \qquad (3.10)$$

Thus, the present value of a unit payment due at time t is

$$\frac{1}{a(t)} = \frac{1}{\prod_{j=1}^{t}(1 + i_j^F)}, \qquad (3.11)$$

and the present value of a n-period unit-payment annuity-immediate can also be written as

$$
\begin{aligned}
a_{\overline{n}|} &= \sum_{t=1}^{n} \frac{1}{a(t)} \\
&= \sum_{t=1}^{n} \frac{1}{\prod_{j=1}^{t}(1 + i_j^F)} \\
&= \frac{1}{(1 + i_1^F)} + \frac{1}{(1 + i_1^F)(1 + i_2^F)} + \cdots + \frac{1}{(1 + i_1^F) \cdots (1 + i_n^F)}. \quad (3.12)
\end{aligned}
$$

While the calculation of the present values remains straightforward when interest rates are varying deterministically, the computation of the future value at time n of a payment due at time t, where $0 < t < n$, requires additional assumptions. We now consider the assumption that a payment occurring in the future earns the forward rates of interest implicitly determined in (3.4) and (3.5). Therefore, the future value at time n of a unit payment due at time t is

$$(1 + i_{t,n-t}^F)^{n-t} = (1 + i_{t+1}^F) \cdots (1 + i_n^F). \qquad (3.13)$$

Hence, the future value at time n of a n-period annuity-immediate is

$$
\begin{aligned}
s_{\overline{n}|} &= \left[\sum_{t=1}^{n-1}(1 + i_{t,n-t}^F)^{n-t} \right] + 1 \\
&= \left[\sum_{t=1}^{n-1}\left(\prod_{j=t+1}^{n} (1 + i_j^F) \right) \right] + 1 \\
&= [(1 + i_2^F)(1 + i_3^F) \cdots (1 + i_n^F)] + [(1 + i_3^F)(1 + i_4^F) \cdots (1 + i_n^F)] + \cdots \\
&\quad \cdots + (1 + i_n^F) + 1. \qquad (3.14)
\end{aligned}
$$

Similarly, for a n-period unit-payment annuity-due, the future value at time n is

$$\ddot{s}_{\overline{n}|} = \sum_{t=0}^{n-1} \left(\prod_{j=t+1}^{n} (1 + i_j^F) \right)$$

$$= [(1 + i_1^F) \cdots (1 + i_n^F)] + [(1 + i_2^F) \cdots (1 + i_n^F)] + \cdots + (1 + i_n^F). \quad (3.15)$$

From (3.14) we can see that

$$s_{\overline{n}|} = \left[\prod_{t=1}^{n} (1 + i_t^F) \right] \times \left[\frac{1}{1 + i_1^F} + \frac{1}{(1 + i_1^F)(1 + i_2^F)} + \cdots + \frac{1}{(1 + i_1^F) \cdots (1 + i_n^F)} \right]. \quad (3.16)$$

Thus, from (3.10) and (3.12), we conclude

$$s_{\overline{n}|} = \left(\prod_{t=1}^{n} (1 + i_t^F) \right) a_{\overline{n}|} = a(n) a_{\overline{n}|}, \quad (3.17)$$

which shows that compound-interest accumulation with a given term structure satisfies (2.19) even when the rates of interest are not constant through time. Furthermore, we note that an alternative formula to calculate $s_{\overline{n}|}$ using the spot rates of interest is

$$s_{\overline{n}|} = (1 + i_n^S)^n a_{\overline{n}|}$$

$$= (1 + i_n^S)^n \left[\sum_{t=1}^{n} \frac{1}{(1 + i_t^S)^t} \right]. \quad (3.18)$$

Example 3.4: Suppose the spot rates of interest for investment horizons of 1, 2, 3 and 4 years are, respectively, 4%, 4.5%, 4.5%, and 5%. Calculate $a_{\overline{4}|}$, $s_{\overline{4}|}$, $a_{\overline{3}|}$ and $s_{\overline{3}|}$.

Solution: From (3.9) we have

$$a_{\overline{4}|} = \frac{1}{1.04} + \frac{1}{(1.045)^2} + \frac{1}{(1.045)^3} + \frac{1}{(1.05)^4} = 3.5763.$$

From (3.17) we obtain

$$s_{\overline{4}|} = (1.05)^4 \times 3.5763 = 4.3470.$$

Similarly,

$$a_{\overline{3}|} = \frac{1}{1.04} + \frac{1}{(1.045)^2} + \frac{1}{(1.045)^3} = 2.7536,$$

and

$$s_{\overline{3}|} = (1.045)^3 \times 2.7536 = 3.1423.$$

Example 3.5: Suppose the 1-period forward rates of interest for investments due at time 0, 1, 2 and 3 are, respectively, 4%, 4.8%, 4.8% and 5.2%. Calculate $a_{\overline{4}|}$ and $s_{\overline{4}|}$.

Solution: From (3.12) we have

$$
\begin{aligned}
a_{\overline{4}|} &= \frac{1}{1.04} + \frac{1}{1.04 \times 1.048} + \frac{1}{1.04 \times 1.048 \times 1.048} \\
&+ \frac{1}{1.04 \times 1.048 \times 1.048 \times 1.052} \\
&= 3.5867.
\end{aligned}
$$

As $a(4) = 1.04 \times 1.048 \times 1.048 \times 1.052 = 1.2016$, we have

$$
s_{\overline{4}|} = 1.2016 \times 3.5867 = 4.3099.
$$

Alternatively, from (3.14) we have

$$
\begin{aligned}
s_{\overline{4}|} &= 1 + 1.052 + 1.048 \times 1.052 + 1.048 \times 1.048 \times 1.052 \\
&= 4.3099.
\end{aligned}
$$

To further understand (3.17), we write (3.13) as (see (3.8))

$$
(1 + i_{t,n-t}^{F})^{n-t} = \frac{(1 + i_{n}^{S})^{n}}{(1 + i_{t}^{S})^{t}} = \frac{a(n)}{a(t)}. \tag{3.19}
$$

Thus, the future value of the annuity is, from (3.14) and (3.19),

$$
\begin{aligned}
s_{\overline{n}|} &= \left[\sum_{t=1}^{n-1} (1 + i_{t,n-t}^{F})^{n-t} \right] + 1 \\
&= \sum_{t=1}^{n} \frac{a(n)}{a(t)} \\
&= a(n) \sum_{t=1}^{n} \frac{1}{a(t)} \\
&= a(n) a_{\overline{n}|}. \tag{3.20}
\end{aligned}
$$

Similarly, for annuity-due we have

$$
\ddot{s}_{\overline{n}|} = a(n) \ddot{a}_{\overline{n}|}. \tag{3.21}
$$

Recall that in Chapter 2 we assume that the current accumulation function $a(t)$ (which defines the current term structure, i.e., all values of i_t^S, through (3.1)) applies to all future payments. Under this assumption, if condition (1.35) holds, equation (3.20) is valid. However, for a given general term structure, we note that

$$a(n - t) = (1 + i_{n-t}^S)^{n-t} \neq \frac{(1 + i_n^S)^n}{(1 + i_t^S)^t} = \frac{a(n)}{a(t)},$$

so that condition (1.35) does not hold. Thus, if future payments are assumed to earn spot rates of interest based on the current term structure, equation (3.20) does not hold in general.

Example 3.6: Suppose the spot rates of interest for investment horizons of 1 to 5 years are 4%, and for 6 to 10 years are 5%. Calculate the present value of an annuity-due of $100 over 10 years. Compute the future value of the annuity at the end of year 10, assuming (a) future payments earn forward rates of interest, and (b) future payments earn the spot rates of interest as at time 0.

Solution: We consider the 10-period annuity-due as the sum of an annuity-due for the first 6 years and a deferred annuity-due of 4 payments starting at time 6. The present value of the annuity-due for the first 6 years is

$$100 \times \ddot{a}_{\overline{6}|0.04} = 100 \times \left[\frac{1 - (1.04)^{-6}}{1 - (1.04)^{-1}} \right]$$

$$= \$545.18.$$

The present value at time 0 for the deferred annuity-due in the last 4 years is[5]

$$100 \times (\ddot{a}_{\overline{10}|0.05} - \ddot{a}_{\overline{6}|0.05}) = 100 \times \left[\frac{1 - (1.05)^{-10}}{1 - (1.05)^{-1}} - \frac{1 - (1.05)^{-6}}{1 - (1.05)^{-1}} \right]$$

$$= 100 \times (8.1078 - 5.3295)$$

$$= \$277.83.$$

Hence, the present value of the 10-period annuity-due is

$$545.18 + 277.83 = \$823.01.$$

We now consider the future value of the annuity at time 10. Under assumption (a) that future payments earn the forward rates of interest, the future value of the annuity at the end of year 10 is, by equation (3.20),

$$(1.05)^{10} \times 823.01 = \$1{,}340.60.$$

---

[5]Note that the effective rate of interest i for the 6-year annuity that is removed from the deferred annuity computation, $\ddot{a}_{\overline{6}|0.05}$, is 5%. The spot rate of interest of 4% for maturity of up to 5 years is not relevant.

Note that using (3.20) we do not need to compute the forward rates of interest to determine the future value of the annuity, as would be required if (3.16) is used.

Based on assumption (b), the payments at time $0, \cdots, 4$ earn interest at 5% per year (the investment horizons are 10 to 6 years), while the payments at time $5, \cdots, 9$ earn interest at 4% per year (the investment horizons are 5 to 1 years). Thus, the future value of the annuity is

$$100 \times (\ddot{s}_{\overline{10}|0.05} - \ddot{s}_{\overline{5}|0.05}) + 100 \times \ddot{s}_{\overline{5}|0.04} = \$1{,}303.78.$$

Thus, equation (3.20) does not hold under assumption (b).

We have seen two assumptions concerning how future payments may earn interests, namely, at the forward rate of interest and at the current spot rate of interest. When the timing and investment horizon of the payments are determined at time 0, and forward contracts are applicable, the forward-rate assumption would be appropriate. Otherwise, the choice of the assumption is ambiguous, and both assumptions may not apply. Indeed, in an environment in which interest rates are free to move, their future values are stochastic random variables. In Chapter 9 we shall discuss some approaches in modeling stochastic interest rates.

3.4 Accumulation Function and the Term Structure

Equation (3.1) relates the accumulation function to the spot rate of interest. This equation can be extended to any $t > 0$, which need not be an integer. Thus, the annualized spot rate of interest for time to maturity t, i_t^S, is given by

$$i_t^S = [a(t)]^{\frac{1}{t}} - 1. \tag{3.22}$$

We may also use an accumulation function to define the forward rates of interest. Let us consider the forward rate of interest for a payment due at time $t > 0$, and denote the accumulation function of this payment by $a_t(\cdot)$, where $a_t(0) = 1$. Now a unit payment at time 0 accumulates to $a(t + \tau)$ at time $t + \tau$, for $\tau > 0$. On the other hand, a strategy with an initial investment over t periods and a rollover at the forward rate for the next τ periods will accumulate to $a(t)a_t(\tau)$ at time $t + \tau$. By the no-arbitrage argument, we have

$$a(t)a_t(\tau) = a(t + \tau), \tag{3.23}$$

so that

$$a_t(\tau) = \frac{a(t + \tau)}{a(t)}. \tag{3.24}$$

If $\tau > 1$, the annualized (effective) forward rate of interest for the period t to $t + \tau$, $i_{t,\tau}^F$, satisfies

$$a_t(\tau) = (1 + i_{t,\tau}^F)^\tau,$$

so that

$$i_{t,\tau}^F = [a_t(\tau)]^{\frac{1}{\tau}} - 1. \tag{3.25}$$

If, however, $\tau < 1$, we define the forward rate of interest per unit time (year) for the fraction of a period t to $t + \tau$ as[6]

$$i_{t,\tau}^F = \frac{1}{\tau} \times \frac{a_t(\tau) - a_t(0)}{a_t(0)} = \frac{a_t(\tau) - 1}{\tau}. \tag{3.26}$$

The **instantaneous forward rate of interest** per unit time at time t is equal to $i_{t,\tau}^F$ for $\tau \to 0$, which is given by

$$\begin{aligned}
\lim_{\tau \to 0} i_{t,\tau}^F &= \lim_{\tau \to 0} \frac{a_t(\tau) - 1}{\tau} \\
&= \lim_{\tau \to 0} \frac{1}{\tau} \times \left[\frac{a(t + \tau)}{a(t)} - 1 \right] \\
&= \frac{1}{a(t)} \lim_{\tau \to 0} \left[\frac{a(t + \tau) - a(t)}{\tau} \right] \\
&= \frac{a'(t)}{a(t)} \\
&= \delta(t). \tag{3.27}
\end{aligned}$$

This shows that the instantaneous forward rate of interest per unit time is equal to the force of interest.

Example 3.7: Suppose $a(t) = 0.01t^2 + 0.1t + 1$. Compute the spot rates of interest for investments of 1, 2 and 2.5 years. Derive the accumulation function for payments due at time 2, assuming the payments earn the forward rates of interest. Calculate the forward rates of interest for a payment due at time 2 with time to maturity of 1, 2 and 2.5 years.

Solution: Using (3.22), we obtain $i_1^S = 11\%$, $i_2^S = 11.36\%$ and $i_{2.5}^S = 11.49\%$. Thus, we have an upward sloping spot-rate curve. To calculate the accumulation function of payments at time 2 we first compute $a(2)$ as

$$a(2) = 0.01(2)^2 + 0.1(2) + 1 = 1.24.$$

---

[6]Note the similarity of this definition versus the definition of the effective rate of interest per unit time over fraction of a period as stated in Footnote 1 of Chapter 1.

Thus, the accumulation function for payments at time 2 is

$$a_2(\tau) = \frac{a(2+\tau)}{a(2)} = \frac{0.01(2+\tau)^2 + 0.1(2+\tau) + 1}{1.24} = 0.00817\tau^2 + 0.1129\tau + 1.$$

Using the above equation, we obtain $a_2(1) = 1.1210$, $a_2(2) = 1.2581$ and $a_2(2.5) = 1.3327$, from which we conclude $i_{2,1}^F = 12.10\%$,

$$i_{2,2}^F = (1.2581)^{\frac{1}{2}} - 1 = 12.16\%$$

and

$$i_{2,2.5}^F = (1.3327)^{\frac{1}{2.5}} - 1 = 12.17\%.$$

Thus, the forward rates exceed the spot rates, which agrees with what might be expected of an upward sloping yield curve.

We can further establish the relationship between the force of interest and the forward accumulation function, and thus the forward rates of interest. From (3.24), we have

$$a_t(\tau) = \frac{a(t+\tau)}{a(t)} = \frac{\exp\left(\int_0^{t+\tau} \delta(s)\,ds\right)}{\exp\left(\int_0^t \delta(s)\,ds\right)} = \exp\left(\int_t^{t+\tau} \delta(s)\,ds\right), \qquad (3.28)$$

so that we can compute the forward accumulation function from the force of interest.

Example 3.8: Suppose $\delta(t) = 0.05t$. Derive the accumulation function for payments due at time 2, assuming the payments earn the forward rates of interest. Calculate the forward rates of interest for a payment due at time 2 for time to maturity of 1 and 2 years.

Solution: Using (3.28) we obtain

$$a_2(\tau) = \exp\left(\int_2^{2+\tau} 0.05s\,ds\right) = \exp\left(0.025(2+\tau)^2 - 0.025(2)^2\right)$$
$$= \exp(0.025\tau^2 + 0.1\tau).$$

Thus, we can check that $a_2(0) = 1$. Now, $a_2(1) = \exp(0.125) = 1.1331$, so that $i_{2,1}^F = 13.31\%$. Also, $a_2(2) = \exp(0.3) = 1.3499$, so that

$$i_{2,2}^F = (1.3499)^{\frac{1}{2}} - 1 = 16.18\%.$$

We now consider the evaluation of a stream of cash flows at arbitrary time points, assuming that future payments earn the forward rates of interest. Specifically, we consider payments of $C_1, C_2, \cdots, C_n$ at time $(0 \leq) t_1 < t_2 < \cdots < t_n$, respectively. Suppose we are interested in evaluating the value of this cash flow at any time $t \in (0, t_n)$. For the payment C_j at time $t_j \leq t$, its accumulated value at time t is $C_j a_{t_j}(t - t_j)$. On the other hand, if $t_j > t$, the discounted value of C_j at time t is $\frac{C_j}{a_t(t_j - t)}$. Thus, the value of the cash flows at time t is (see equation (3.24))

$$\sum_{t_j \leq t} C_j a_{t_j}(t - t_j) + \sum_{t_j > t} C_j \left[\frac{1}{a_t(t_j - t)} \right] = \sum_{t_j \leq t} C_j \left[\frac{a(t)}{a(t_j)} \right] + \sum_{t_j > t} C_j \left[\frac{a(t)}{a(t_j)} \right]$$

$$= \sum_{j=1}^{n} C_j \left[\frac{a(t)}{a(t_j)} \right]$$

$$= a(t) \sum_{j=1}^{n} C_j v(t_j)$$

$$= a(t) \times \text{present value of cash flows.}$$

$$(3.29)$$

An analogous result can be obtained if we consider a continuous cash flow. Thus, if $C(t)$ is the instantaneous rate of cash flow at time t for $0 \leq t \leq n$, so that the payment in the interval $(t, t + \Delta t)$ is $C(t)\Delta t$, the value of the cash flow at time $\tau \in (0, n)$ is

$$\int_0^{\tau} C(t) a_t(\tau - t) \, dt + \int_{\tau}^{n} \frac{C(t)}{a_{\tau}(t - \tau)} \, dt = \int_0^{\tau} \frac{C(t) a(\tau)}{a(t)} \, dt + \int_{\tau}^{n} \frac{C(t) a(\tau)}{a(t)} \, dt$$

$$= a(\tau) \int_0^{n} \frac{C(t)}{a(t)} \, dt$$

$$= a(\tau) \int_0^{n} C(t) v(t) \, dt. \qquad (3.30)$$

Example 3.9: Suppose $a(t) = 0.02t^2 + 0.05t + 1$. Calculate the value at time 3 of a 1-period deferred annuity-immediate of 4 payments of $2 each. You may assume that future payments earn the forward rates of interest.

Solution: We first compute the present value of the annuity. The payments of $2 are due at time 2, 3, 4 and 5. Thus, the present value of the cash flows is

$$2 \times \left[\frac{1}{a(2)} + \frac{1}{a(3)} + \frac{1}{a(4)} + \frac{1}{a(5)} \right].$$

Now, $a(2) = 0.02(2)^2 + 0.05(2) + 1 = 1.18$, and similarly we have $a(3) = 1.33$, $a(4) = 1.52$ and $a(5) = 1.75$. Thus, the present value of the cash flows is

$$2 \times \left[\frac{1}{1.18} + \frac{1}{1.33} + \frac{1}{1.52} + \frac{1}{1.75} \right] = 2 \times 2.82866 = \$5.6573,$$

and the value of the cash flows at time 3 is $a(3) \times 5.6573 = 1.33 \times 5.6573 = \$7.5242$.

Example 3.10: Suppose $\delta(t) = 0.02t$. An investor invests in a fund at the rate of $10t$ per period at time t, for $t > 0$. How much would she accumulate in the fund at time 2? You may assume that future payments earn forward rates of interest.

Solution: The amount she invests in the period $(t, t + \Delta t)$ is $10t\Delta t$, which would accumulate to $(10t\Delta t)a_t(2 - t)$ at time 2. Thus, the total amount accumulated at time 2 is

$$\int_0^2 10ta_t(2 - t)dt.$$

From (3.28), we have

$$a_t(2 - t) = \exp\left(\int_t^2 \delta(s)\, ds \right) = \exp\left(\int_t^2 0.02s\, ds \right).$$

Now, we have

$$\int_t^2 0.02s\, ds = 0.01s^2]_t^2 = 0.01(2)^2 - 0.01t^2,$$

so that

$$a_t(2 - t) = \exp(0.04 - 0.01t^2)$$

and

$$\begin{aligned}
\int_0^2 10ta_t(2 - t)dt &= 10 \int_0^2 te^{0.04 - 0.01t^2}\, dt \\
&= 10e^{0.04} \int_0^2 te^{-0.01t^2}\, dt \\
&= \frac{10e^{0.04}}{0.02} \left(-e^{-0.01t^2}]_0^2 \right) \\
&= \frac{10e^{0.04}(1 - e^{-0.04})}{0.02} \\
&= 20.4054.
\end{aligned}$$

Example 3.11: Suppose the principal is C and interest is earned at the force of interest $\delta(t)$, for $t > 0$. What is the present value of the interest earned over n periods?

Solution: As $\delta(t)$ is the instantaneous rate of interest per period at time t, the amount of interest earned in the period $(t, t + \Delta t)$ is $C\delta(t)\Delta t$, and the present value of this interest is $[C\delta(t)\Delta t]v(t)$. Thus, the present value of all the interest earned in the period $(0, n)$ is

$$\int_0^n C\delta(t)v(t)\, dt.$$

Now, we have

$$\begin{aligned}
\int_0^n \delta(t)v(t)\, dt &= \int_0^n \delta(t)\exp\left(-\int_0^t \delta(s)\, ds\right) dt \\
&= \left(-\exp\left(-\int_0^t \delta(s)\, ds\right)\right)\Big]_0^n \\
&= \exp\left(-\int_0^0 \delta(s)\, ds\right) - \exp\left(-\int_0^n \delta(s)\, ds\right) \\
&= 1 - v(n).
\end{aligned}$$

Hence, the present value of the interest earned is

$$C[1 - v(n)] = C - Cv(n),$$

which is the principal minus the present value of the principal redeemed at time n.

3.5 Interest Rate Swaps

An interest rate swap is an agreement between two parties to exchange cash flows based on interest rate movements in the future. A simple interest rate swap arrangement involves two companies. Company A agrees to pay cash flows to Company B equal to the amount of interest at a pre-fixed rate on a notional principal amount for a number of years. At the same time, Company B consents to pay interests to Company A at a floating rate on the same notional principal for the same period of time.

An interest rate swap is a formal contract between two **counterparties** (i.e., the two parties in the swap agreement). The following features of an interest rate swap are often agreed upon at the issue date.

Swap Term (or Swap Tenor): The contract period of the interest rate swap. It may be as short as a few months, or as long as 30 years.

Settlement Dates: The specified dates that two counterparties have to exchange interest payments.

Settlement Period: The time between settlement dates is called the settlement period. The settlement period specifies the frequency of interest payments. It can be annually, quarterly, monthly, or at any other interval determined by the parties.

Notional Amount: The notional principal amount is the predetermined dollar amount on which the exchanged interest payments are based. It should be noted that the amount is only used for the calculation of interest payments and the principal itself is never exchanged. This is why it is termed *notional*. In general the notional amount is a constant over the swap tenor. However, an **accreting swap** has the scheduled notional amount increasing over time, while an **amortizing swap** has the notional amount declining over time.

Swap Rate: The fixed interest rate specified in the interest rate swap contract.

Floating Interest Rate: This is the reference rate for calculating the floating interest payment at each settlement date. It must be specified in the interest rate swap contract. Commonly used floating reference interest rates in a swap agreement include: Treasury Bill Rate, Prime Rate, Federal Funds Rate in the US market, and the LIBOR (London Interbank Offer Rate) in the international markets. The floating rate can be specified with a spread to the reference rate, for example, 6-month LIBOR plus 20 basis points or 6-month Treasury Bill Rate minus 30 basis points.[7]

Interest rate swaps can be used to convert a floating rate loan to a fixed rate debt or vice versa. Suppose Company A has arranged to borrow US$10 million for five years. The amount of interest is payable at the end of each settlement year according to the 12-month US dollar LIBOR at the beginning of the settlement period. Company A, however, would like to transform this floating rate loan to a fixed one. On the other hand, Company B has arranged to borrow US$10 million at a fixed rate of 5% per annum for five years, but would prefer to convert this fixed rate loan to a floating rate loan. For this purpose, Company A and Company B may enter into a simple interest rate swap agreement, with Company A being the **fixed-rate payer** and Company B being the **floating-rate payer**. Figure 3.5 illustrates the arrangement of the swap.

---

[7]Note that one basis point is equal to 0.01%, or equivalently 100 basis points is equal to 1%. Some of the rates of interest in different markets will be described in Chapter 9.

Figure 3.5:   Illustration of cash flows of an interest rate swap

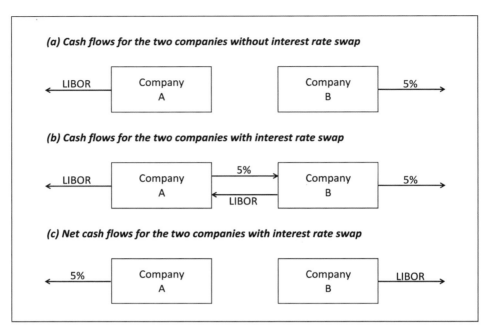

(a) Cash flows for the two companies without interest rate swap

LIBOR ← Company A   Company B → 5%

(b) Cash flows for the two companies with interest rate swap

LIBOR ← Company A   —5%→   Company B → 5%
                    ←LIBOR—

(c) Net cash flows for the two companies with interest rate swap

5% ← Company A   Company B → LIBOR

Suppose the 12-month US dollar LIBOR after one year is 4.75%. According to the swap agreement, Company B has to pay $10,000,000 × 4.75% = $475,000 to Company A at the end of the second year, while Company A needs to pay $10,000,000 × 5% = $500,000 to Company B at the same time. In order to avoid unnecessary transactions, most swap contracts require both parties to settle the netted amount only. In this example, the **interest rate swap net payment** in that settlement date is $25,000, payable from Company A to Company B.

The fixed interest rate in the interest rate swap contract is called the swap rate, which will be denoted by R_S. We now discuss a theoretical framework for deriving R_S such that the swap contract is equally attractive to both parties.[8]

Consider a n-year interest rate swap contract with notional amount m_t for year $t = 1, \cdots, n$. The settlement period is one year. At time 0, when the contract is initiated, the spot rates of interest i_t^S are known.[9] The floating interest rate is defined as the **realized** one-year spot rate i_t^* observed at the beginning of the tth future settlement period. It is obvious that $i_1^* = i_1^S$.

---

[8]It is assumed that the capital market is perfectly competitive (see Footnote 1 in this Chapter) and frictionless, where all costs and restraints associated with transactions are non-existent.

[9]These can be US Treasury spot rates, LIBOR spot rates or other types of spot rates specified in the swap agreement.

Figure 3.6: Cash flows of an interest rate swap with a market maker

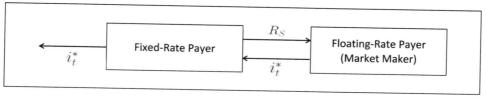

If the swap rate is R_S, at the end of year t, the fixed rate payer will receive $m_t(i_t^* - R_S)$ net interest rate swap payment from the counterparty. At the same time, the company has to repay a floating interest amount of $m_t i_t^*$ to its outside lender. Under this arrangement, the fixed rate payer has converted its floating rate debt to a fixed rate one using the swap with annual fixed rate payment $m_t R_S$. Suppose the counterparty (i.e., the floating rate payer) is a market maker who determines the swap rate R_S. Figure 3.6 illustrates the cash flows of these parties.

To understand the pricing of an interest rate swap (i.e., determination of R_S), we examine the cash flows of the market maker. At the end of year t, the market maker (floating-rate payer) pays the floating rate amount $m_t i_t^*$ and receives the fixed rate amount $m_t R_S$. It should be noted that i_t^* is unknown at time 0 when R_S is determined. The market maker can hedge this interest rate risk by entering into forward agreements with another financial institution and makes payments to it based on the forward rates of interest i_t^F. Table 3.1 summarizes the cash flows faced by the market maker.

Table 3.1: Cash flows of the market maker in Figure 3.6

Year	Net receipt on forward contract	Net receipt on swap contract	Overall
1	$m_1(i_1^* - i_1^F)$	$m_1(R_S - i_1^*)$	$m_1(R_S - i_1^F)$
2	$m_2(i_2^* - i_2^F)$	$m_2(R_S - i_2^*)$	$m_2(R_S - i_2^F)$
$\vdots$	$\vdots$	$\vdots$	$\vdots$
t	$m_t(i_t^* - i_t^F)$	$m_t(R_S - i_t^*)$	$m_t(R_S - i_t^F)$
$\vdots$	$\vdots$	$\vdots$	$\vdots$
n	$m_n(i_n^* - i_n^F)$	$m_n(R_S - i_n^*)$	$m_n(R_S - i_n^F)$

Note: At $t = 1$, $i_1^* = i_1^F$ and hence $m_1(i_1^* - i_1^F) = 0$.

Under the perfect and frictionless market assumption, the present value of the overall cash flows of the market maker should be zero.[10] Therefore, we have

$$m_1 \left[\frac{R_S - i_1^F}{(1 + i_1^S)} \right] + m_2 \left[\frac{R_S - i_2^F}{(1 + i_2^S)^2} \right] + \cdots + m_n \left[\frac{R_S - i_n^F}{(1 + i_n^S)^n} \right] = 0. \qquad (3.31)$$

Hence,

$$R_S = \frac{\displaystyle\sum_{t=1}^{n} m_t \, i_t^F (1 + i_t^S)^{-t}}{\displaystyle\sum_{t=1}^{n} m_t \, (1 + i_t^S)^{-t}}. \qquad (3.32)$$

For interest rate swaps with a constant notional principal amount for every year, equation (3.32) can be simplified to

$$R_S = \frac{\displaystyle\sum_{t=1}^{n} i_t^F (1 + i_t^S)^{-t}}{\displaystyle\sum_{t=1}^{n} (1 + i_t^S)^{-t}}. \qquad (3.33)$$

Example 3.12: A company enters into a 5-year interest rate swap contract with a level notional amount of $1 million. The settlement period is one year. The floating interest rate is defined as the realized one-year spot rate observed at the beginning of each settlement period. The spot rates of interest at the initiation of the swap for investment horizons of 1, 2, 3, 4 and 5 years are, respectively, 3.5%, 3.8%, 4.3%, 4.9% and 5.2%. Determine the swap rate.

Solution: The forward rates of interest i_t^F for $t = 1, 2, 3, 4$ and 5 can be calculated using equation (3.6). Table 3.2 shows the computation of the swap rate via equation (3.33). Hence,

$$R_S = \frac{0.223894}{4.377604} = 5.1145\%$$

---

[10]Note that if this value is positive, other market makers will bid down the swap rate to compete with this market maker. On the other hand, if this value is negative, the swap contract is not attractive.

Table 3.2: Computation results for Example 3.12

t	i_t^S	i_t^F	$i_t^F(1+i_t^S)^{-t}$	$(1+i_t^S)^{-t}$
1	0.035000	0.035000	0.033816	0.966184
2	0.038000	0.041009	0.038061	0.928122
3	0.043000	0.053072	0.046775	0.881347
4	0.049000	0.067208	0.055503	0.825844
5	0.052000	0.064086	0.049738	0.776106
Total			0.223894	4.377604

Example 3.13: Consider the swap contract in Example 3.12. Instead of a level notional amount of $1 million, the notional amounts m_t for $t = 1, 2, 3, 4$ and 5 are now assumed to be $1 million, $2 million, $\cdots$, and $5 million, respectively. Determine the swap rate of this accreting swap.

Solution: Table 3.3 shows the computation of the swap rate via equation (3.32). Hence,

$$R_S = \frac{0.720965}{12.650379} = 5.6992\%.$$

Table 3.3: Computation results for Example 3.13

t	i_t^S	i_t^F	m_t	$m_t i_t^F(1+i_t^S)^{-t}$	$m_t(1+i_t^S)^{-t}$
1	0.035000	0.035000	1	0.033816	0.966184
2	0.038000	0.041009	2	0.076122	1.856245
3	0.043000	0.053072	3	0.140326	2.644042
4	0.049000	0.067208	4	0.222013	3.303376
5	0.052000	0.064086	5	0.248688	3.880532
Total				0.720965	12.650379

A **deferred swap** is an interest rate swap for which the exchange of interest payments starts after a deferred period. The swap rate and the length of the deferred period are determined at time 0, the moment when the two parties enter into the contract. The cash flows of the market maker of a deferred swap with a deferred period t^* are analogous to those in Table 3.1, with the first t^* rows deleted. By modifying equation (3.32) the swap rate of the deferred swap can be obtained as follows

$$R_S = \frac{\displaystyle\sum_{t=t^*+1}^{n} m_t i_t^F (1 + i_t^S)^{-t}}{\displaystyle\sum_{t=t^*+1}^{n} m_t (1 + i_t^S)^{-t}}. \tag{3.34}$$

Example 3.14: Consider the accreting swap contract in Example 3.13. Suppose both parties agree to have a two-year deferred period. Determine the swap rate of this deferred swap.

Solution: Using the results in Table 3.3 and equation (3.34) with $t^* = 2$, we have

$$R_S = \frac{0.140326 + 0.222013 + 0.248688}{2.644042 + 3.303376 + 3.880532} = \frac{0.611026}{9.827950} = 6.2172\%. \tag{3.35}$$

A party who enters into an interest rate swap contract can close its outstanding position by selling the swap (i.e., transferring all the rights and obligations under the swap contract to another party) or terminating the swap (i.e., cancelling the swap contract with the counterparty) for a price at any time during the swap term. This price is called the **market value** of the swap. Under the perfect and frictionless market assumption, the market value of the swap is the present value of the remaining expected cash flows specified in the contract. The present value is computed using the prevailing spot rates of interest at the time of the swap termination. It should be noted that the market value may be positive or negative. A negative swap market value means that the outstanding swap is not competitive under the current yield curve condition and the seller would need to compensate the buyer (or the counterparty) to take over its position. The seller could be either the floating-rate payer or the fixed-rate payer of the swap. The market values of the swap with respect to both counterparties have the same absolute value but opposite signs.

Example 3.15: Consider the interest rate swap contract in Example 3.12. Suppose the market maker (i.e., the floating-rate payer) would like to sell the contract at the beginning of the fourth year to a third party and close its position. The prevailing spot rates of interest at that time for investment horizons of 1 and 2 years are, respectively, 4.5% and 4.7%. Determine the market value of the swap with respect to the seller. What is the market value of the swap with respective to the fixed-rate payer at that time?

Solution: For the interest rate swap contract in Example 3.12, at the beginning of the fourth year, there are two remaining expected cash flows before the end of the contract, namely, $m_4(R_S - i_1^F)$ and $m_5(R_S - i_2^F)$ payable at the end of the first and second year, respectively, after the market maker has closed his position. For the expected values of these two cash flows, i_1^F and i_2^F should be computed using the prevailing spot rates of interest at the time of the swap termination. We have $i_1^F = 4.5\%$ and $i_2^F = \frac{1.047^2}{1.045} - 1 = 4.9\%$. From the solutions of Example 3.12, we have $R_S = 5.1145\%$ and $m_4 = m_5 = \$1$ million. The numerical values of these two expected cash flows are $\$1,000,000 \times (5.1145\% - 4.5\%) = \$6,145$ and $\$1,000,000 \times (5.1145\% - 4.9\%) = \$2,145$. Hence, the market value of the swap for the market maker is

$$\frac{6,145}{1.045} + \frac{2,145}{(1.047)^2} = \$7,837.12.$$

The market value of the swap to the fixed-rate payer is –$7,837.12.

3.6 Summary

1. Investment outlays at time 0 earn the spot rates of interest, which may vary according to the time horizon of the investment. Investments that are committed at time 0 but due in the future earn the forward rates of interest, which may also vary with the time horizon of the investment.

2. A plot of the spot rates of interest is called the yield curve. The mathematical relationship between the spot rates of interest and time to maturity is called the term structure of interest rates.

3. Yield curves may take various shapes. They may be flat, upward sloping, download sloping or humped. Yield curves have important implications for future movements of interest rates and the real economy.

4. Spot and forward rates of interest are related through no-arbitrage conditions. Forward rates of interest that satisfy such conditions are called the implicit forward rates, which may differ from the forward rates quoted in the market in practice.

5. Present values of future payments can be computed straightforwardly given the term structure. To compute the future value of a future payment, we have to make additional assumptions, such as (a) future payments earn forward rates of interest, and (b) future payments earn current spot rates of interest. In practice, under a varying interest rate environment, both assumptions may not hold.

6. Spot and forward rates may be computed from accumulation functions. The accumulation function of the forward rates of interest can be derived from the current yield curve or the current accumulation function.

7. An interest rate swap is an agreement between two parties to exchange cash flows based on interest rate movements in the future. It can be used to convert a floating rate loan to a fixed rate debt or vice versa.

Exercises

3.1 Suppose the spot rates of interest for investment horizons of 1, 2 and 3 years are, respectively, 4.0%, 4.2% and 4.3%, and the 1-year forward rates of interest for payments due at time 1 and 2 are, respectively, 4.4% and 4.6%.

   (a) Do the above rates violate the no-arbitrage relationship concerning spot and forward rates of interest?

   (b) If so, describe an arbitrageur's strategy to make riskless profits.

3.2 Suppose the spot rates of interest for investment horizons of 1, 2, 3 and 4 years are, respectively, 3%, 3.5%, 3.5% and 3.75%.

   (a) Calculate the forward rates of interest i_1^F, i_2^F, i_3^F and i_4^F.

   (b) Calculate $a_{\overline{4}|}$ and $s_{\overline{3}|}$.

3.3 Suppose the forward rates of interest for investments in year 1, 2, 3 and 4 are, respectively, 6%, 6.2%, 6.5% and 7%.

   (a) Calculate the spot rates of interest i_1^S, i_2^S, i_3^S and i_4^S.

   (b) Calculate $a_{\overline{4}|}$ and $s_{\overline{4}|}$.

3.4 You are given the following information: $i_1^S = 2.1\%, i_2^F = 2.6\%, i_3^S = 3.1\%$ and $i_4^F = 3.6\%$.

   (a) Calculate the rates of interest i_1^F, i_2^S, i_3^F and i_4^S.

   (b) Calculate $\ddot{a}_{\overline{4}|}$ and $\ddot{s}_{\overline{4}|}$.

3.5 Suppose the spot rates of interest for investment horizons of 1, 2, 3 and 4 years are, respectively, 4%, 4.3%, i_3^S and 4.8%. You are given that $(Da)_{\overline{4}|}$ is 5% large than $(Ia)_{\overline{4}|}$.

    (a) Calculate the spot rate of interest i_3^S.

    (b) Calculate the values of $(Da)_{\overline{4}|}$ and $(Ia)_{\overline{4}|}$.

3.6 You are given the following information about various annuities available in the market. All the annuities pay $100 at the end of each year over the period of the investment. It is also given that the spot rate of interest for 1-year maturity is 3%.

Period of investment (in years)	Price (in $)
2	190.89
3	281.96
4	369.53

Calculate the forward rates of interest i_t^F for $t = 2, 3$ and 4. You want to accumulate $10,000 after four years by putting a single payment into a bank account. Based on the information above, calculate the deposit required.

3.7 Let $\delta(t) = 0.01t$, for $t \geq 0$. Find i_2^S and i_3^F.

3.8 The following table shows the spot rates of interest over a number of horizons:

Period of investment (in years)	Spot rate (in %)
1	6.00
2	7.00
3	7.75
4	8.25

    (a) Find the present value of payments of $100 at the end of each year for 4 years.

    (b) What is the effective rate of interest earned by this annuity-immediate if it were constant through the whole investment period? [**Hint:** Use the Excel function **Rate** to compute the rate of interest.]

3.9 Suppose that the spot rates of interest over a number of horizons (in quarters) with *continuous compounding* are as follows:

Period of investment (in quarters)	Spot rate (% per annum)
1	3.80
2	3.90
3	4.00
4	4.25
5	4.30
6	4.50

Calculate the forward rates of interest for the second, third, fourth, fifth, and sixth quarters.

3.10 Fill in the following table of forward rates of interest:

						$i_{t,\tau}^F$				
t	i_t^S	i_t^F	$\tau =$	1	2	3	4	5	6	7
1	4.00%									
2	4.20%								—	
3	4.40%								—	—
4	4.60%							—	—	—
5	4.70%						—	—	—	—
6	4.50%					—	—	—	—	—
7	4.30%				—	—	—	—	—	—
8	4.10%			—	—	—	—	—	—	—

3.11 Denote the spot rates of interest for investment horizons of 1 to n years by i_t^S for $t = 1, 2, \cdots, n$. Derive an expression (in terms of i_t^S) of the future value of the \$1-payment annuity-immediate at the end of year n, assuming future payments earn the spot rates of interest as at time 0.

3.12 Suppose the spot rates of interest for investment horizons of 1 to 5 years are 4%, and for 6 to 10 years are 5%.

(a) Compute the forward rates of interest i_t^F for $t = 1, 2, \cdots, 10$.

(b) Calculate the present value of an annuity-immediate of \$100 over 10 years.

(c) Compute the future value of the annuity-immediate at the end of year 10, assuming future payments earn the forward rates of interest, using equation (3.18).

(d) Repeat part (c) using equation (3.14). You should get the same answer as in part (c).

(e) Show that the future value of the annuity-immediate at the end of year 10, assuming future payments earn the spot rates of interest as at time 0, is

$$100 \times (s_{\overline{10}|0.05} - s_{\overline{6}|0.05}) + 100 \times s_{\overline{6}|0.04}.$$

(f) Solve the problem in (e) numerically using the formula in Exercise 3.11. Do you get the same answer as using the formula in (e)?

3.13 Consider the accumulation function $a(t) = 1 + 0.05t$.

(a) Compute the spot rates of interest for investments of 1, 2 and 2.5 years.

(b) Derive the accumulation function for payments due at time 2, assuming the payments earn the forward rates of interest.

(c) Calculate the forward rates of interest for a payment due at time 2 with time to maturity of 1, 2 and 2.5 years.

3.14 Suppose $\delta(t) = \dfrac{10 + t}{200}$.

(a) Derive the accumulation function for payments due at time 5, assuming the payments earn the forward rates of interest.

(b) Calculate the forward rates of interest for a payment due at time 5 with time to maturity of 1 and 2 years.

3.15 Under the compound-interest accumulation function, i.e.,

$$a(t) = (1 + i)^t,$$

show that

(a) $i_t^S = i$, for all $t > 0$.

(b) The accumulation function for payments due at time t, assuming the payments earn the forward rates of interest, is

$$a_t(\tau) = (1 + i)^\tau.$$

(c) $i_{t,\tau}^F = i$, for $t > 0$ and $\tau > 0$.

3.16 Suppose $v(t) = \dfrac{20}{20 + t}$. Assuming that future payments earn the forward rates of interest, calculate the value at time 2 of the following stream of payments:

t	C_t (\$)
0	1,000
1	800
2	600
3	400
4	200

3.17 Suppose $\delta(t) = 0.05$. An investor invests in a fund at the rate of kt per period at time t, for $t > 0$.

  (a) If k is constant, derive an expression (in terms of k) for the amount that she would accumulate in the fund at time 10? You may assume that future payments earn the forward rates of interest.

  (b) If $k = \frac{1}{t}$ find the accumulated amount at time 10.

  (c) Using equation (2.32), compute $\bar{s}_{\overline{n}|}$ with $n = 10$ and $\delta = 0.05$. Compare your answer with the one in part (b).

3.18 Company Z enters into a 5-year interest rate swap contract on 1 January 2015 as the fixed-rate payer party. The settlement period is one year. The settlement dates are 31 December of each year from 2015 to 2019. The spot rates of interest at the beginning of various years for investment horizons of $t = 1, 2, 3, 4$ and 5 years are given in the following table.

t	1 Jan 2015	1 Jan 2016	1 Jan 2017	1 Jan 2018	1 Jan 2019
1	0.71%	0.79%	0.42%	0.31%	0.35%
2	1.43%	1.24%	0.34%	0.38%	0.64%
3	2.05%	1.72%	0.47%	0.57%	1.05%
4	2.94%	2.59%	0.95%	1.08%	1.78%
5	3.55%	3.24%	1.47%	1.58%	2.31%

  (a) Assuming a level notional amount of \$1 million for the contract, determine the swap rate.

  (b) Suppose the contract is an accreting swap with notional amounts of \$1 million, \$3 million, \$5 million, \$7 million and \$9 million. Determine the swap rate.

  (c) Suppose the contract is an amortizing swap with notional amounts of \$5 million, \$4 million, \$3 million, \$2 million and \$1 million. Determine the swap rate.

(d) Calculate the interest rate swap net payment on 31 December 2016 for Company Z, assuming a level notional amount of $1 million for the contract.

(e) Immediately after the net payment is settled on 31 December 2016, calculate the market value of the interest rate swap with a level notional amount of $1 million, if Company Z would like to sell the contract to another party.

(f) Determine the swap rate on 1 January 2015 if it is a one-year deferred swap contract with a level notional amount of $1 million.

Advanced Problems

3.19   (a) Find an expression for the derivative

$$\frac{\partial\, i_t^F}{\partial\, i_t^S}$$

and hence show that it is larger than zero.

(b) Find an expression for the derivative

$$\frac{\partial\, i_t^F}{\partial\, i_{t-1}^S}$$

and hence show that it is less than zero.

(c) Show that $i_t^F > i_t^S$ when $i_t^S > i_{t-1}^S$.

3.20 Given that

$$i_t^S = \begin{cases} 0.04 + 0.002(t-1), & \text{for integral } t \le 5, \\ 0.05, & \text{for integral } t \ge 6. \end{cases}$$

(a) Find $a_{\overline{\infty}|}$.

(b) Find i_1^F, i_2^F, i_3^F, i_4^F, i_5^F and i_6^F.

(c) Show that $i_t^F = 0.05$ for integral $t \ge 7$.

3.21 Suppose $\delta(t) = 0.08 + 0.005t$. An investor invests in a fund at the rate of $100t$ per period at time t, for $t > 0$. How much would she accumulate in the fund at time 5? You may assume that future payments earn the forward rates of interest.

4

Rates of Return

The performance of investment projects, funds and portfolios of assets is typically measured by their rates of return. The most important measure of the return of a project or fund is the internal rate of return, also called the yield rate. In this chapter we define the internal rate of return and explain how it can be applied to various investment projects. We discuss measures of 1-period rate of return, including methods such as the dollar-weighted rate of return, time-weighted rate of return, as well as some approximation methods. Performance of funds over an extended period of time can be measured by the geometric mean rate of return and arithmetic mean rate of return. We also show how returns of a portfolio can be calculated from the returns of its component assets.

Short selling is a strategy through which investors can leverage. We consider the computation of the rate of return of a short-selling strategy. We also discuss methods of crediting interests in a fund, including the investment-year method and the portfolio method. Finally, we discuss methods of project appraisal, namely, the criteria of deciding whether or not to invest in a project.

- *Internal rate of return (yield rate)*
- *1-period rate of return of a fund: time-weighted rate of return and dollar-weighted (money-weighted) rate of return*
- *Rate of return over longer periods: geometric mean rate of return and arithmetic mean rate of return*
- *Portfolio return*
- *Return of a short-selling strategy*
- *Crediting interest: investment-year method and portfolio method*
- *Capital budgeting and project appraisal*

4.1   Internal Rate of Return

Consider a project with initial investment C_0 to generate a stream of future cash flows. For simplicity, we assume the cash flows occur at regular intervals, say, annually. The project lasts for n years and the future cash flows are denoted by $C_1, \cdots, C_n$. We adopt the convention that cash inflows to the project (investments) are positive and cash outflows from the project (withdrawals) are negative. We define the **internal rate of return (IRR)** (also called the **yield rate**) as the rate of interest such that the sum of the present values of the cash flows is equated to zero. Denoting the internal rate of return by y, we have

$$\sum_{j=0}^{n} \frac{C_j}{(1+y)^j} = 0, \tag{4.1}$$

where j is the time at which the cash flow C_j occurs. This equation can also be written as

$$C_0 = -\sum_{j=1}^{n} \frac{C_j}{(1+y)^j}. \tag{4.2}$$

The right-hand side of the above equation is the present value of future outflows (withdrawals) minus the present value of future inflows (investments). Thus, the net present value of all future withdrawals (injections are negative withdrawals) evaluated at the IRR is equal to the initial investment C_0.

Example 4.1: A project requires an initial cash outlay of $2,000 and is expected to generate $800 at the end of year 1 and $1,600 at the end of year 2, at which time the project will terminate. Calculate the IRR of the project.

Solution: If we denote $v = \frac{1}{1+y}$, we have, from (4.2)

$$2,000 = 800v + 1,600v^2,$$

or

$$5 = 2v + 4v^2.$$

Dropping the negative answer from the quadratic equation, we have

$$v = \frac{-2 + \sqrt{4 + 4 \times 4 \times 5}}{2 \times 4} = 0.8956.$$

Thus, $y = \frac{1}{v} - 1 = 11.66\%$. Note that $v < 0$ implies $y < -1$, i.e., the loss is larger than 100%, which will be precluded from consideration.

Equation (4.1) is formally the same as the equation of value (1.36), with the focus being on the solution of y given the cash flows C_j, $j = 0, \cdots, n$. Indeed, Example 4.1 is similar to Example 1.23, with the problem viewed as one on investment rather than loan. In many practical situations, the cash flows can be calculated or estimated, and the IRR provides a measure of the attractiveness of the project.

There is generally no analytic solution for y in (4.1) when $n > 2$, and numerical methods have to be used. The Excel function **IRR** enables us to compute the answer easily. Its usage is described as follows:

Excel function: IRR(values, guess)

values = an array of values containing the cash flows
guess = starting value, set to 0.1 if omitted
Output = IRR of cash flows

Example 4.2: An investor pays $5 million for a 5-year lease of a shopping mall. He will receive $1.2 million rental income at the end of each year. Calculate the IRR of his investment.

Solution: We use Excel to solve the problem. The cash flows are entered into cells A1 through A6, with A1 being 5, and A2 through A6 being -1.2. In cell

A7, we key in "=IRR(A1:A6, 0.1)". The first argument in the IRR function, namely, A1:A6, specifies the cells for the data of the cash flows. The second argument, namely, 0.1, provides the program with an initial value to do the numerical calculation (this input may be omitted). The answer returned is 6.4022%. Exhibit 4.1 shows the Excel worksheet for the computation of the IRR.

Exhibit 4.1:   IRR computation in Example 4.2

	File Edit View Insert Format Tools Data			
	A7 ▼ f_x =IRR(A1:A6,0.1)			
	A	B	C	D
1	5			
2	-1.2			
3	-1.2			
4	-1.2			
5	-1.2			
6	-1.2			
7	6.4022%			
8				

If the cash flows occur more frequently than once a year, such as monthly or quarterly, y computed from (4.1) is the IRR for the payment interval. Specifically, suppose cash flows occur m times a year, the nominal IRR in annualized term is $m \times y$, while the annual effective rate of return is $(1 + y)^m - 1$.

Example 4.3: A cash outlay of $100 generates incomes of $20 after 4 months and 8 months, and $80 after 2 years. Calculate the IRR of the investment.

Solution: If we treat one month as the interest conversion period, the equation of value can be written as

$$100 = \frac{20}{(1 + y_1)^4} + \frac{20}{(1 + y_1)^8} + \frac{80}{(1 + y_1)^{24}},$$

where y_1 is the IRR on monthly interval. The nominal rate of return on monthly compounding is $12y_1$. Alternatively, we can use the 4-month interest conversion interval, and the equation of value is

$$100 = \frac{20}{1 + y_4} + \frac{20}{(1 + y_4)^2} + \frac{80}{(1 + y_4)^6},$$

where y_4 is the IRR on 4-month interval. The nominal rate of return on 4-monthly compounding is $3y_4$. The effective annual rate of return is $y = (1 + y_1)^{12} - 1 = (1 + y_4)^3 - 1$.

The above equations of value have to be solved numerically for y_1 or y_4. Using Excel to solve for y_1, we enter 100 into Cell A1, -20 into Cells A5 and A9, and -80 into Cell A25. The rest of the cells in column A, from A2 up to A24 are filled with zeros. Using **IRR** with **A1:A25** as the cash stream, we obtain 1.0406% as the IRR per month, namely, y_1. The effective annualized rate of return is then $(1.010406)^{12} - 1 = 13.23\%$. The nominal annualized rate is $12 \times 0.0104 = 12.49\%$ for monthly compounding. On the other hand, solving for y_4 with Excel, we obtain the answer 4.2277%. Hence, the annualized effective rate is $(1.042277)^3 - 1 = 13.23\%$, which is equal to the effective rate computed using y_1.

When cash flows occur irregularly, we can define y as the annualized rate and express all time of occurrence of cash flows in years. Suppose there are $n + 1$ cash flows occurring at time $0, t_1, \cdots, t_n$, with cash amounts $C_0, C_1, \cdots, C_n$. Equation (4.2) is rewritten as

$$C_0 = -\sum_{j=1}^{n} \frac{C_j}{(1 + y)^{t_j}}. \tag{4.3}$$

Note that C_j occurs at time t_j and is discounted by $(1 + y)^{t_j}$. Equation (4.3) requires numerical methods for the solution of y, which can be computed using Excel Solver. Alternatively, we may also use the Excel function **XIRR** to solve for y. Unlike **IRR**, **XIRR** allows the cash flows to occur at *irregular* time intervals. The specification of **XIRR** is as follows:

Excel function: XIRR (values, dates, guess)

values = C_j, an array of values containing the cash flows in (4.3)
dates = t_j, an array of values containing the timing of the cash flows in (4.3)
guess = guess starting value, set to 0.1 if omitted
Output = IRR, value of annualized y satisfying (4.3)

To enter the values of the timing of the cash flows for **XIRR**, two methods may be used. First, we may use the **DATE** function in Excel, with input values of the calendar year, month and day of the time of cash flows. Second, we may enter the numerical values of the number of days from the first payment. Example 4.4

illustrates the solution of the IRR of an irregular cash flow using the Excel Solver and **XIRR**.

Example 4.4: A project requires an outlay of $2.35 million in return for $0.8 million after 9 months, $1 million after 15 months and $1 million after 2 years. What is the IRR of the project?

Solution: Returns of the project occur at time (in years) 0.75, 1.25 and 2. We solve for v numerically from the following equation using Excel Solver (see Exhibit 4.2)

$$235 = 80v^{0.75} + 100v^{1.25} + 100v^2$$

to obtain $v = 0.879$, so that

$$y = \frac{1}{0.879} - 1 = 13.78\%,$$

which is the effective annualized rate of return of the project.

Exhibit 4.2:   Solution of Example 4.4 using Solver

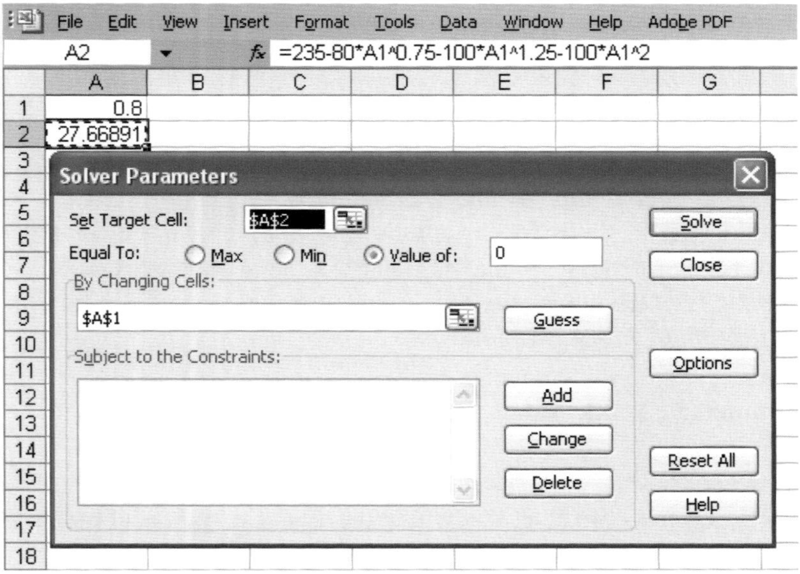

Alternatively, we may use the Excel function **XIRR** as shown in Exhibit 4.3. Note that the cash flows are entered in Cells A1 through A4. The timing of the cash flows in years is entered in Cells B1 through B4, and then converted to days in Cells C1 through C4. The **XIRR** function is entered in Cell A5, from which we obtain the solution of 13.78% per annum.

Exhibit 4.3:   Solution of Example 4.4 using `XIRR`

	File	Edit	View	Insert	Format	Tools	Data	Window
	A5		▼		f_x =XIRR(A1:A4,C1:C4)			
	A	B	C	D		E		
1	-235	0	0					
2	80	0.75	273.75					
3	100	1.25	456.25					
4	100	2	730					
5	0.137751							
6								

In the above examples, C_j, $j = 1, \cdots, n$, are all negative so that there are no subsequent outlays after the initial investment. Such projects are called **simple projects**. For simple projects, (4.1) has a unique solution with $y > -1$, so that IRR is well defined. However, some projects may require further cash outlays after time 0. In this circumstance, (4.1) generally has multiple roots, and IRR may not be well defined. The example below illustrates this situation.

Example 4.5: A project requires an initial outlay of $8 million, generates returns of $50 million 1 year later, and requires $50 million to terminate at the end of year 2. Solve for y in (4.1).

Solution: We are required to solve

$$8 = 50v - 50v^2,$$

which has $v = 0.8$ and 0.2 as solutions. This implies y has multiple solutions of 25% and 400%.

The use of IRR as a measure of the rate of return of a project is based on some implicit assumptions. First, as the same rate of interest y is used to discount all cash flows irrespective of the time of occurrence, the term structure is assumed to be flat and does not vary with the timing of the cash flows. Second, cash generated within the duration of the project is assumed to earn the same rate of return y. Third, both cash injections and withdrawals are discounted by the same rate of interest, i.e., borrowing rate is assumed to be equal to lending rate. However, despite the shortcomings of the IRR, it takes proper account of the time value of money in evaluating cash flows and has a firm theoretical underpinning.

4.2 One-Period Rate of Return

For the purpose of performance comparison and reporting, the rate of return of a fund is calculated on a regular basis, such as quarterly or annually. Theoretically, the methodology of the IRR may be used with the modification that the "project" terminates at the end of the reporting period. Thus, the last cash flow C_n in (4.1) is set equal to the negative of the end-of-period fund value (the project terminates by withdrawing the end-of-period balance). In practice, this method is rarely used, due to the complexity in solving for the IRR numerically, as well as the problem of multiple roots. As there are typically multiple fund injections and withdrawals within the reporting interval, the cash flows change signs and the problem of multiple root is prevalent.

We now discuss methods of calculating the return of a fund over a 1-period interval. The methodology adopted depends on the data available. We start with the situation where the exact amounts of fund withdrawals and injections are known, as well as the time of their occurrence. For illustration, we consider a 1-year period with initial fund amount B_0 (equal to C_0). Cash flow of amount C_j occurs at time t_j (in fraction of a year) for $j = 1, \cdots, n$, where $0 < t_1 < \cdots < t_n < 1$. As before, we adopt the convention that C_j is positive for cash injection and negative for cash withdrawal. Note that C_j are usually fund redemptions and new investments, and do not include investment incomes such as dividends and coupon payments.

Denoting the fund value before and after the transaction at time t_j by B_j^B and B_j^A, respectively, we have $B_j^A = B_j^B + C_j$ for $j = 1, \cdots, n$. The difference between B_j^B and B_{j-1}^A, i.e., the balance before the transaction at time t_j and after the transaction at time t_{j-1}, is due to investment incomes, as well as capital gains and losses. To complete the notations, let the fund balance at time 1 be B_1, and define $B_{n+1}^B = B_1$ and $B_0^A = B_0$ (this notation will allow us to express the gross return as (4.4) below). Figure 4.1 illustrates the time diagram of the fund balances and the cash flows.

We now introduce two methods to calculate the 1-year rate of return. These are the **time-weighted rate of return** (TWRR) and the **dollar-weighted rate of return** (DWRR).[1] To compute the TWRR we first calculate the return over each subinterval between the occurrences of transactions by comparing the fund balances just before the new transaction to the fund balance just after the last transaction. If we denote R_j as the rate of return over the subinterval t_{j-1} to t_j, we have

$$1 + R_j = \frac{B_j^B}{B_{j-1}^A}, \quad \text{for } j = 1, \cdots, n + 1. \tag{4.4}$$

---

[1]The dollar-weighted rate of return is also called the **money-weighted rate of return**.

Figure 4.1: Cash flows and fund values in period (0,1)

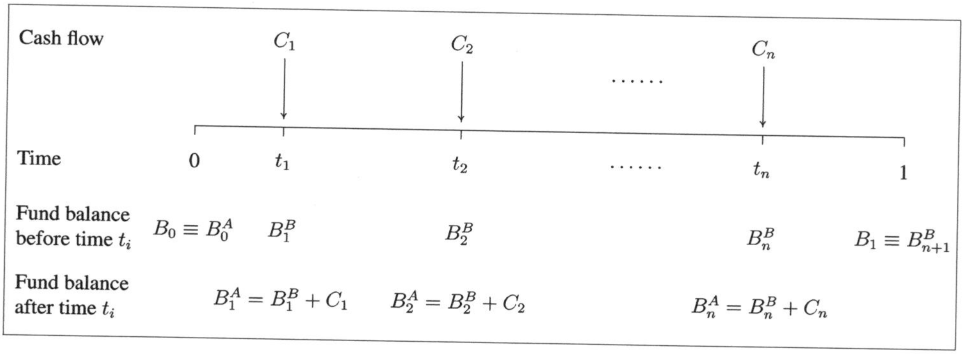

Then TWRR over the year, denoted by R_T, is

$$R_T = \left[\prod_{j=1}^{n+1}(1 + R_j)\right] - 1. \tag{4.5}$$

The TWRR requires data of the fund balance prior to each withdrawal or injection. In contrast, the DWRR does not require this information. It only uses the information of the amounts of the withdrawals and injections, as well as their time of occurrence. In principle, when cash of amount C_j is injected (withdrawn) at time t_j, there is a gain (loss) of capital of amount $C_j(1 - t_j)$ for the remaining period of the year. Thus, the *effective capital* of the fund over the 1-year period, denoted by B, is given by

$$B = B_0 + \sum_{j=1}^{n} C_j(1 - t_j).$$

Denoting $C = \sum_{j=1}^{n} C_j$ as the net injection of cash (withdrawal if negative) over the year and I as the interest income earned over the year, we have $B_1 = B_0 + I + C$, so that

$$I = B_1 - B_0 - C. \tag{4.6}$$

Hence the DWRR over the 1-year period, denoted by R_D, is

$$R_D = \frac{I}{B} = \frac{B_1 - B_0 - C}{B_0 + \sum_{j=1}^{n} C_j(1 - t_j)}. \tag{4.7}$$

Example 4.6: On January 1, a fund was valued at 100. On May 1, the fund increased in value to 112 and 30 of new principal was injected. On November 1, the fund value dropped to 125, and 42 was withdrawn. At the end of the year, the fund was worth 100. Calculate the DWRR and the TWRR.

Solution: Figure 4.2 illustrates the cash flows. As $C = 30 - 42 = -12$, there is a net withdrawal. From (4.6), the interest income earned over the year is

$$I = 100 - 100 - (-12) = 12.$$

Figure 4.2:   Illustration for Example 4.6

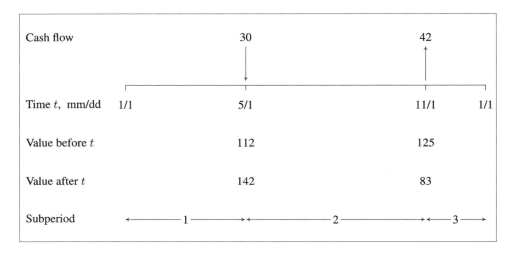

Hence, from (4.7), the DWRR is

$$R_D = \frac{12}{100 + \dfrac{2}{3} \times 30 - \dfrac{1}{6} \times 42} = 10.62\%.$$

The fund balance just after the injection on May 1 is $112 + 30 = 142$, and its value just after the withdrawal on November 1 is $125 - 42 = 83$. From (4.4), the fund-value relatives over the three subperiods are

$$1 + R_1 = \frac{112}{100} = 1.120,$$

$$1 + R_2 = \frac{125}{142} = 0.880,$$

$$1 + R_3 = \frac{100}{83} = 1.205.$$

Hence, from (4.5), the TWRR is

$$R_T = 1.120 \times 0.880 \times 1.205 - 1 = 18.76\%.$$

The above example shows that R_D and R_T may differ significantly. While the TWRR requires the fund values at the transaction dates, it compounds the returns of the fund over subperiods after purging the effects of the timing and amount of cash injections and withdrawals. As fund managers have no control over the timing of fund injection and withdrawal, the TWRR appropriately measures the *performance of the fund manager*. On the other hand, the DWRR is sensitive to the timing and amount of the cash flows. For example, if a fund manager receives a large cash injection at a time when the market is at a peak and on the way to a downturn, the DWRR will be adversely affected.

In Example 4.6, the fund manager is seen to perform well when the TWRR is used. He received cash injection in the second period, which happened to be a period of low return. This results in pulling down his performance if the DWRR is used. However, note that if the purpose is to measure the *performance of the fund*, the DWRR is appropriate. It allows superior market timing to impact the return of the fund.

For funds with frequent cash injections and withdrawals, the computation of the TWRR may not be feasible. The difficulty lies in the evaluation of the fund value B_j^B, which requires the fund to be constantly **marked to market**. If mark-to-market is not viable, DWRR may be adopted, which requires only the timing of the cash flows.

However, in some situations the exact timing of the cash flows may be difficult to identify. For example, consider an insurance portfolio for which the cash flows consist of receipts of premium payments, outlays for policy benefits, as well as interest incomes. While the total inflows and outflows can be calculated, full details of the timing may not be available. In this situation, we may approximate (4.7) by assuming the cash flows to be evenly distributed throughout the 1-year evaluation period. Hence, we replace $1 - t_j$ by its mean value of 0.5 so that $\sum_{j=1}^{n} C_j(1 - t_j) = 0.5C$, and (4.7) can be written as

$$
\begin{aligned}
R_D &\approx \frac{I}{B_0 + 0.5C} \\
&= \frac{I}{B_0 + 0.5(B_1 - B_0 - I))} \\
&= \frac{I}{0.5(B_1 + B_0 - I)}.
\end{aligned}
\tag{4.8}
$$

Example 4.7: For the data in Example 4.6, calculate the approximate value of the DWRR using (4.8).

Solution: With $B_0 = B_1 = 100$, and $I = 12$, the approximate R_D is

$$R_D = \frac{12}{0.5(100 + 100 - 12)} = 12.76\%.$$

Note that in the above example, the timing of the cash flows is not used in the calculation.

4.3   Rate of Return over Multiple Periods

We now consider the rate of return of a fund over an m-year period. We first consider the case where only annual data of returns are available. Suppose the annual rates of return of the fund have been computed as $R_1, \cdots, R_m$. Note that $-1 \le R_j < \infty$ for all j. The average return of the fund over the m-year period can be calculated as the mean of the sample values. We call this measure the **arithmetic mean rate of return**, denoted by R_A, which is given by

$$R_A = \frac{1}{m} \sum_{j=1}^{m} R_j. \tag{4.9}$$

An alternative is to use the geometric mean to calculate the average. We call this measure the **geometric mean rate of return**, denoted by R_G, which is given by

$$R_G = \left[\prod_{j=1}^{m} (1 + R_j) \right]^{\frac{1}{m}} - 1$$

$$= [(1 + R_1)(1 + R_2) \cdots (1 + R_m)]^{\frac{1}{m}} - 1. \tag{4.10}$$

Note that in the above formula, $(1 + R_G)$ is the geometric mean of $(1 + R_j)$ for $j = 1, \cdots, m$. As we have precluded R_j from being less than -1, $(1 + R_j) > 0$ and (4.10) is well defined.

Example 4.8: The annual rates of return of a bond fund over the last 5 years are (in %) as follows:

$$6.4 \quad 8.9 \quad 2.5 \quad -2.1 \quad 7.2$$

Calculate the arithmetic mean rate of return and the geometric mean rate of return of the fund.

Solution: The arithmetic mean rate of return is

$$R_A = \frac{6.4 + 8.9 + 2.5 - 2.1 + 7.2}{5}$$

$$= \frac{22.9}{5}$$

$$= 4.58\%,$$

and the geometric mean rate of return is

$$R_G = (1.064 \times 1.089 \times 1.025 \times 0.979 \times 1.072)^{\frac{1}{5}} - 1$$

$$= (1.246)^{\frac{1}{5}} - 1$$

$$= 4.50\%.$$

Example 4.9: The annual rates of return of a stock fund over the last 8 years (in %) are as follows:

$$15.2 \quad 18.7 \quad -6.9 \quad -8.2 \quad 23.2 \quad -3.9 \quad 16.9 \quad 1.8$$

Calculate the arithmetic mean rate of return and the geometric mean rate of return of the fund.

Solution: The arithmetic mean rate of return is

$$R_A = \frac{15.2 + 18.7 + \cdots + 1.8}{8} = 7.10\%$$

and the geometric mean rate of return is

$$R_G = (1.152 \times 1.187 \times \cdots \times 1.018)^{\frac{1}{8}} - 1 = 6.43\%.$$

Given any sample of data, the arithmetic mean is always larger than the geometric mean. This is verified in the two examples above. Generally, the two means will differ more when the variance of the returns is larger. As the variance of the returns in the stock fund is much higher than that in the bond fund, the discrepancy of the two return measures for the stock fund is larger than that for the bond fund.

Indeed, while the arithmetic mean of the bond fund exceeds the geometric mean by only 8 basis points (i.e., 0.08%), the arithmetic mean of the stock fund exceeds the geometric mean by 67 basis points.

As the arithmetic mean is always larger than the geometric mean, there is reason for fund managers to report their performance using the arithmetic mean. However, if the purpose is to measure the return of the fund over the *holding period* of m years, the geometric mean rate of return is the appropriate measure. It provides the annualized average rate of return over m years assuming a buy-and-hold portfolio. On the other hand, the arithmetic mean rate of return describes the average performance of the fund for a single year taken randomly from the sample period.

If there are more data about the history of the fund, alternative measures of the performance of the fund can be used. The methodology of the time-weighted rate of return in Section 4.2 can be extended to beyond 1 period (year). We first measure the returns over subperiods between cash injections and withdrawals. Suppose there are n subperiods, with returns denoted by $R_1, \cdots, R_n$, over a period of m years. Then we can measure the m-year return by compounding the returns over each subperiod to form the TWRR using the formula

$$
R_T = \left[\prod_{j=1}^{n} (1 + R_j) \right]^{\frac{1}{m}} - 1. \tag{4.11}
$$

We shall use the notation R_T for the TWRR of both 1- and multiple-year returns. Equation (4.11) is a generalization of (4.5) for $m \geq 1$, with a slight change of notation for the number of subperiods in the m-year period. The computation of the TWRR over m years is also similar to the calculation of the geometric mean rate of return R_G in equation (4.10). However, while the returns R_j in equation (4.10) are over equal intervals of 1 year, the subinterval for each return observation in equation (4.11) is determined by fund injections and withdrawals.

We can also compute the return over a m-year period using the IRR. To do this, we extend the notations for cash flows in Section 4.2 to the m-year period. Suppose cash flows of amount C_j occur at time t_j for $j = 1, \cdots, n$, where $0 < t_1 < \cdots < t_n < m$. Let the fund value at time 0 and time m be B_0 and B_1, respectively. We treat $-B_1$ as the last transaction, i.e., fund withdrawal of amount B_1. The rate of return of the fund is calculated as the IRR which equates the discounted values of $B_0, C_1, \cdots, C_n$, and $-B_1$ to zero. Unlike the TWRR defined in (4.11), this rate is sensitive to the amount of cash flows C_j. Hence, it is referred to as the DWRR over the m-year period. Like the DWRR for the 1-year return given in (4.7), we shall denote it as R_D, which solves the following equation

$$B_0 + \sum_{j=1}^{n} \frac{C_j}{(1 + R_D)^{t_j}} - \frac{B_1}{(1 + R_D)^m} = 0. \qquad (4.12)$$

As a measure of return over a m-year interval, the methodology used in (4.12) takes account of the time value of money. The cost for using the IRR approach is that situations of multiple roots must be avoided. For the evaluation of a close-ended stock fund or bond fund where the cash flows are usually outflows of dividends or coupon payments, the DWRR method can be applied.

The example below concerns the returns of a bond fund. When a bond makes the periodic coupon payments, the bond value drops and the coupons are cash amounts to be withdrawn from the fund. Further description of bonds will be found in Chapter 6.

Example 4.10: A bond fund has an initial value of $20 million. The fund records coupon payments in 6-month periods. Coupons received from January 1 through June 30 are regarded as paid on April 1. Likewise, coupons received from July 1 through December 31 are regarded as paid on October 1. For the 2-year period 2016 and 2017, the fund values and coupon payments were recorded in Table 4.1.

Table 4.1: Cash flows of the fund

Time mm/dd/yy	Coupon received ($ millions)	Fund value before date ($ millions)
01/01/16		20.0
04/01/16	0.80	22.0
10/01/16	1.02	22.8
04/01/17	0.97	21.9
10/01/17	0.85	23.5
12/31/17		25.0

Calculate the TWRR and the DWRR of the fund.

Solution: As the coupon payments are withdrawals from the fund (the portfolio of bonds), the fund drops in value after the coupon payments. For example, the bond value drops to $22.0 - 0.80 = \$21.2$ million on April 1, 2016 after the coupon payments. Thus, the TWRR is calculated as

$$R_T = \left[\frac{22}{20} \times \frac{22.80}{22.0 - 0.8} \times \frac{21.90}{22.80 - 1.02} \times \frac{23.50}{21.90 - 0.97} \times \frac{25.0}{23.50 - 0.85} \right]^{0.5} - 1$$

$$= 21.42\%.$$

To calculate the DWRR we solve R_D from the following equation

$$20 = \frac{0.8}{(1+R_D)^{0.25}} + \frac{1.02}{(1+R_D)^{0.75}} + \frac{0.97}{(1+R_D)^{1.25}} + \frac{0.85}{(1+R_D)^{1.75}} + \frac{25}{(1+R_D)^2}$$

$$= 0.8v + 1.02v^3 + 0.97v^5 + 0.85v^7 + 25v^8,$$

where $v = (1+R_D)^{-0.25}$. We let $(1+y)^{-1} = v$ and use Excel to obtain $y = 4.949\%$, so that the annual effective rate of return is $R_D = (1.04949)^4 - 1 = 21.31\%$. Exhibit 4.4 provides an Excel worksheet for the computation of y using the **IRR** function.[2]

Exhibit 4.4:   DWRR computation in Example 4.10

	File	Edit	View	Insert	Format	Tools	Data
	A10		▼		f_x =IRR(A1:A9,0.05)		

	A	B	C	D
1	20			
2	-0.8			
3	0			
4	-1.02			
5	0			
6	-0.97			
7	0			
8	-0.85			
9	-25			
10	4.9487%			
11				

As discussed before, the DWRR method assumes the rate of return to be the same throughout the period of evaluation. Thus, all cash flows are discounted at the same rate R_D. In contrast, the TWRR method does not make this assumption and computes the return over the period of evaluation by compounding the returns over the subintervals. Hence, the TWRR is a more appropriate measure if the returns are volatile over the evaluation period. However, data for the fund value at each time point of transaction must be available if the TWRR method is to be used.

---

[2] Alternatively, the **XIRR** function may also be used to solve this problem.

4.4 Portfolio Return

We now consider the return of a portfolio of assets. Suppose a portfolio consists of N assets denoted by $A_1, \cdots, A_N$. Let the value of asset A_j in the portfolio at time 0 be A_{0j}, for $j = 1, \cdots, N$. We allow A_{0j} to be negative for some j, so that asset A_j is sold short in the portfolio.[3] The portfolio value at time 0 is $B_0 = \sum_{j=1}^{N} A_{0j}$. Let the asset values at time 1 be A_{1j}, so that the portfolio value is $B_1 = \sum_{j=1}^{N} A_{1j}$. Denote R_P as the return of the portfolio in the period from time 0 to time 1. Thus,

$$R_P = \frac{B_1 - B_0}{B_0} = \frac{B_1}{B_0} - 1.$$

We define

$$w_j = \frac{A_{0j}}{B_0},$$

which is the proportion of the value of asset A_j in the initial portfolio, so that

$$\sum_{j=1}^{N} w_j = 1,$$

and $w_j < 0$ if asset j is short sold in the portfolio. We also denote

$$R_j = \frac{A_{1j} - A_{0j}}{A_{0j}} = \frac{A_{1j}}{A_{0j}} - 1,$$

which is the rate of return of asset j. Thus,

$$
\begin{aligned}
1 + R_P &= \frac{B_1}{B_0} \\
&= \frac{1}{B_0} \sum_{j=1}^{N} A_{1j} \\
&= \sum_{j=1}^{N} \frac{A_{0j}}{B_0} \times \frac{A_{1j}}{A_{0j}} \\
&= \sum_{j=1}^{N} w_j (1 + R_j),
\end{aligned}
$$

which implies

$$R_P = \sum_{j=1}^{N} w_j R_j, \tag{4.13}$$

---

[3]The mechanism of short selling will be discussed in the next section.

so that the return of the portfolio is the weighted average of the returns of the individual assets.

Note that (4.13) is an identity, and applies to realized returns as well as returns as random variables. If we take the expectations of (4.13), we obtain (see Appendix A.11)

$$E(R_P) = \sum_{j=1}^{N} w_j E(R_j), \tag{4.14}$$

so that the expected return of the portfolio is equal to the weighted average of the expected returns of the component assets. The variance of the portfolio return is given by

$$\text{Var}(R_P) = \sum_{j=1}^{N} w_j^2 \text{Var}(R_j) + \underbrace{\sum_{h=1}^{N} \sum_{j=1}^{N} w_h w_j \text{Cov}(R_h, R_j)}_{h \neq j}. \tag{4.15}$$

For example, consider a portfolio consisting of two funds, a stock fund and a bond fund, with returns denoted by R_S and R_B, respectively. Likewise, we use w_S and w_B to denote their weights in the portfolio. Then, we have

$$E(R_P) = w_S E(R_S) + w_B E(R_B), \tag{4.16}$$

and

$$\text{Var}(R_P) = w_S^2 \text{Var}(R_S) + w_B^2 \text{Var}(R_B) + 2 w_S w_B \text{Cov}(R_S, R_B), \tag{4.17}$$

where $w_S + w_B = 1$.

Example 4.11: A stock fund has an expected return of 0.15 and variance of 0.0625. A bond fund has an expected return of 0.05 and variance of 0.0016. The correlation coefficient between the two funds is -0.2.

(a) What is the expected return and variance of the portfolio with 80% in the stock fund and 20% in the bond fund?

(b) What is the expected return and variance of the portfolio with 20% in the stock fund and 80% in the bond fund?

(c) How would you weight the two funds in your portfolio so that your portfolio has the lowest possible variance?

Solution: For (a), we use (4.16) and (4.17), with $w_S = 0.8$, $w_B = 0.2$ and

$$\text{Cov}(R_S, R_B) = (-0.2)\sqrt{(0.0016)(0.0625)} = -0.002$$

to obtain

$$E(R_P) = (0.8)(0.15) + (0.2)(0.05) = 13\%$$
$$\text{Var}(R_P) = (0.8)^2(0.0625) + (0.2)^2(0.0016) + 2(0.8)(0.2)(-0.002)$$
$$= 0.03942.$$

Thus, the portfolio has a standard deviation of $\sqrt{0.03942} = 19.86\%$. For (b), we do similar calculations, with $w_S = 0.2$ and $w_B = 0.8$, to obtain $E(R_P) = 7\%$, $\text{Var}(R_P) = 0.002884$ and a standard deviation of $\sqrt{0.002884} = 5.37\%$.

Hence, we observe that the portfolio with a higher weightage in stock has a higher expected return but also a higher standard deviation, i.e., higher risk.

For (c) we rewrite (4.17) as

$$\text{Var}(R_P) = w_S^2\text{Var}(R_S) + (1 - w_S)^2\text{Var}(R_B) + 2w_S(1 - w_S)\text{Cov}(R_S, R_B).$$

To minimize the variance, we differentiate $\text{Var}(R_P)$ with respect to w_S to obtain

$$2w_S\text{Var}(R_S) - 2(1 - w_S)\text{Var}(R_B) + 2(1 - 2w_S)\text{Cov}(R_S, R_B).$$

Equating the above to zero, we solve for w_S to obtain

$$w_S = \frac{\text{Var}(R_B) - \text{Cov}(R_S, R_B)}{\text{Var}(R_B) + \text{Var}(R_S) - 2\text{Cov}(R_S, R_B)}$$
$$= 5.29\%.$$

The expected return of this portfolio is 5.53%, its variance is 0.001410, and its standard deviation is 3.75%, which is lower than the standard deviation of the bond fund of 4%. Hence, this portfolio *dominates* the bond fund, in the sense that it has a higher expected return and a lower standard deviation.

Note that the fact that the above portfolio indeed minimizes the variance can be verified by examining the second-order condition.

4.5 Short Sales

A **short sale** is the sale of a security that the seller does not own. It can be executed through a **margin account** with a brokerage firm. The seller *borrows* the security from the brokerage firm to deliver to the buyer. The sale is based on the belief that the security price will go down in the future so that the seller will be able to buy back the security at a lower price, thus keeping the difference in price as profit.

   In many markets, short selling is only allowed when the last recorded price change is positive. This is to prevent excessive speculation against the security. Proceeds from the short sale are kept in the margin account, and cannot be invested to earn income. In addition, the seller is required to place cash or securities into the margin account. This is to ensure that the brokerage firm can cover any losses incurred when the short sold security's price goes up. The **initial percentage margin** m is the percentage of the proceeds of the short sold security that the seller must place into the margin account. Thus, if P_0 is the price of the security when it is sold short, the initial deposit D is $P_0 m$. The seller will earn interest from the deposit. At any point in time, there is a **maintenance margin** m^*, which is the minimum percentage of the seller's equity in relation to the current value of the security sold short. Thus, if the current security price is P_1, the equity E is $P_0 + D - P_1$ and $\frac{E}{P_1}$ must be larger than m^*. If $\frac{E}{P_1}$ falls below m^*, the seller will get a **margin call** from the broker instructing him to top up his margin account.

Example 4.12: A person sold 1,000 shares of a stock short at \$20. If the initial margin is 50%, how much should he deposit in his margin account? If the maintenance margin is 30%, how high can the price go up before there is a margin call?

Solution: The initial deposit is

$$1,000 \times 20 \times 0.5 = \$10,000.$$

At price P_1, the percent of equity is

$$\frac{10,000 + 1,000(20 - P_1)}{1,000 P_1},$$

which must be more than 0.3. Thus, the maximum P_1 is

$$\frac{30}{1.3} = \$23.08.$$

To calculate the rate of return of a short-sale strategy we note that the capital is the deposit D in the margin account. The return includes the interest earned in the deposit. The seller, however, pays the dividend to the buyer if there is any dividend payout. The net rate of return will thus take account of the interest earned and the dividend paid.

Example 4.13: A person sells a stock short at $30. The stock pays a dividend of $1 at the end of the year, after which the man covers his short position by buying the stock back at $27. The initial margin is 50% and interest rate is 4%. What is his rate of return over the year?

Solution: The capital investment per share is $15. The gross return after one year is $(30 - 27) - 1 + 15 \times 0.04 = \$2.6$. Hence, the return over the 1-year period is

$$\frac{2.6}{15} = 17.33\%.$$

Note that in the above calculation we have assumed that there was no margin call throughout the year.

4.6 Crediting Interest: Investment-Year Method and Portfolio Method

A fund pools the investments of individual investors. The investors may invest new money into the fund at any time. While the fund invests the aggregate of the investments, there is an issue of how to credit interest to the individual investors' accounts. A simple method is to credit the average return of the fund to all investors. This is called the **portfolio method**. The portfolio method, however, may not be equitable when the individual investments are made at different times. For example, at a time when returns to securities are going up, new investments are likely to achieve higher returns compared to old investments. In this case, crediting the average return will not be attractive to new investments. On the other hand, when security returns are declining, the portfolio method may be crediting higher returns to new investors at the expense of the old ones.

Alternatively, the fund may pay interests to the accounts according to their year of investment. This method is called the **investment-year method.** Under this method, new investments are credited the investment-year rates of interest over a period of time, after which the investors are credited the portfolio rate of interest. A two-dimensional table is set up to specify the rates of interest depending on the year of investment. Table 4.2 gives an example. For simplicity of exposition, we assume that investments are made at the beginning of the calendar year and interests are credited at the end of the year.

Table 4.2:   An example of investment-year rates and portfolio rates

Calendar year	Investment-year rates (%)			Portfolio rates (%)
of investment (Y)	i_1^Y	i_2^Y	i_3^Y	i^{Y+3}
2012	5.6	5.6	5.7	5.9
2013	5.6	5.7	5.8	6.2
2014	5.8	5.9	6.0	6.3
2015	6.2	6.3	6.6	
2016	6.7	6.4		
2017	7.1			

In Table 4.2, investments are credited the investment-year rates in the first 3 years. The calendar year of the investment is denoted by Y, the rate of interest credited for the tth year of the investment made in calendar year Y is i_t^Y for $t = 1, 2, 3$, and i^Y is the portfolio rate credited for calendar year Y. Thus, using these notations, $i_t^Y = i^{Y+t-1}$ for $t > 3$. For example, in Table 4.2, an investment made in 2012 earns 5.6%, 5.6% and 5.7% in 2012, 2013 and 2014, respectively, which are the investment-year rates. Subsequent to that, the investment earns 5.9%, 6.2% and 6.3% in 2015, 2016 and 2017, respectively, which are the portfolio rates.

Example 4.14:   A fund credits interest according to Table 4.2. Find the total interest credited in the period 2015 through 2017 for (a) an investment in 2010, (b) an investment in 2014, (c) an investment in 2015, (d) an investment in 2015, withdrawn every year and reinvested in the fund as new money. All investments, including reinvestments, are made on January 1.

Solution: The last column of the table gives the portfolio rate of interest in 2015 through 2017. For (a), the investment made in 2010 earns the portfolio rate of interest in 2015 through 2017. Thus, the total return over the 3-year period is

$$1.059 \times 1.062 \times 1.063 - 1 = 19.55\%.$$

For (b), the investment made in 2014 earns the investment-year rates in 2015 and 2016 of 5.9% and 6.0%, respectively, and the portfolio rate in 2017 of 6.3%. The total return is

$$1.059 \times 1.06 \times 1.063 - 1 = 19.33\%.$$

For (c), the investment made in 2015 earns the investment-year rates in 2015 through 2017 to give the total return

$$1.062 \times 1.063 \times 1.066 - 1 = 20.34\%.$$

Finally, for (d) if an investment made in 2015 is withdrawn every year and reinvested at the new money rate, the total return is

$$1.062 \times 1.067 \times 1.071 - 1 = 21.36\%.$$

4.7 Capital Budgeting and Project Appraisal

Capital budgeting and project appraisal refer to the managerial decision of investing in a project. We shall introduce some methods of making such decisions, and discuss some fallacies underlying the application of these methods.

One approach is called the **IRR rule**, which requires the manager to calculate the IRR of the project. The IRR is then compared against the **required rate of return** of the project, which is the minimum rate of return of an investment needed to make it acceptable. We denote the required rate of return by R_R. The IRR rule accepts the project if IRR $\geq R_R$. However, R_R is often a difficult quantity to identify. It depends on factors such as the market rate of interest, the horizon of the investment and the risk of the project. In what follows, we shall assume R_R to be given and focus on the application of the budgeting rules.

An alternative approach is the **net present value (NPV) rule**. To illustrate the application of the NPV rule, we consider a project with annual cash flows and adopt the notations in Section 4.1. Discounting the future cash flows by R_R, we rewrite (4.2) and define the NPV of the project as

$$\text{NPV} = -\sum_{j=1}^{n} \frac{C_j}{(1 + R_R)^j} - C_0. \tag{4.18}$$

Recall that cash outflows (withdrawals) are negative and inflows (investments) are positive. Hence, a positive NPV implies that the sum of the present values of cash outflows created by the project exceeds the sum of the present values of all investments. This forms the basis of the NPV rule, which states that managers should invest in projects with positive NPV.

As we have seen in Section 4.1, the IRR may not be unique. For the case of a simple project with a unique IRR, the NPV decreases as R_R increases. Thus, the IRR is greater than R_R if and only if the NPV evaluated at R_R is positive. In this case, the IRR rule and the NPV rule give identical conclusion. However, when there are multiple IRRs, the decision is ambiguous. First, it is not clear which IRR should be used to compare against R_R. Second, the modification of the IRR rule to accept the project if the minimum of the IRRs is larger than R_R turns out to be invalid. The following example illustrates this point.

Example 4.15: Consider a 2-year project with an initial investment of $1,000. A cash amount of $2,230 will be generated after 1 year, and the project will be terminated with fund injection of $1,242 at the end of year 2. What conclusion can be drawn regarding the acceptance of this project?

Solution: The cash-flow diagram is given in Figure 4.3.
To calculate the IRR we solve for the equation

$$1,000 - 2,230v + 1,242v^2 = 0,$$

where $v = \frac{1}{1+y}$ and y is the IRR. Note that we have adopted the convention of cash inflow being positive and outflow being negative. Solving for the above equation we obtain $y = 8\%$ or 15%. For R_R lying between the two roots of y, the IRR rule cannot be applied. However, if R_R is below the minimum of the two solutions of y, say 6%, can we conclude the project be accepted?

Figure 4.3:   Time diagram of the project in Example 4.15

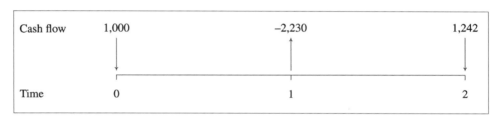

Evaluating the NPV at $R_R = 6\%$, we obtain

$$\text{NPV} = -1,000 + \frac{2,230}{1.06} - \frac{1,242}{(1.06)^2}$$

$$= -\$1.60.$$

Thus, the project has a negative NPV and should be rejected. Figure 4.4 plots the NPV of the project as a function of the interest rate. It shows that the NPV is positive for $0.08 < R_R < 0.15$, which is the region of R_R for which the project should be accepted. Outside this region, the project has a negative NPV and should be rejected.

Figure 4.4:   NPV versus R_R for project in Example 4.15

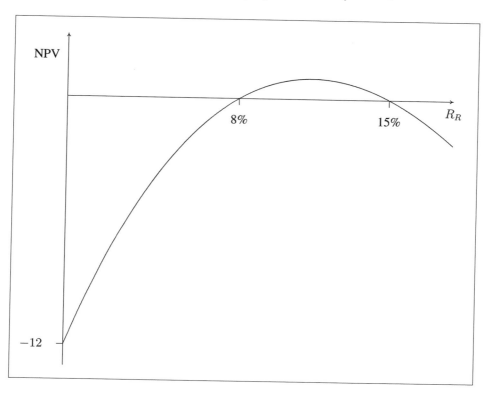

The above example shows that the NPV rule avoids the pitfalls of the IRR rule. A potential pitfall of the NPV rule, however, is to conclude that if the NPV of a project is positive for a discount rate R, the project is acceptable at any required rate of return $R_R < R$. Example 4.15 has demonstrated a counter-example.

Example 4.16: You are given two projects to invest. Project A requires an investment of \$1,000 at time 0. You will then receive \$100 yearly in arrears for 18 years. Project B requires a capital of \$1,200, and you will be paid \$70 yearly in arrears for 15 years, with the return of the capital at the end of the period. Discuss the choice of the two projects.

Solution: The NPV of Project A is

$$\text{NPV}_A = 100a_{\overline{18}|i} - 1,000.$$

Setting the above to zero, we solve for the IRR of Project A to obtain $\text{IRR}_A =$

7.8176%. Similarly, the NPV of Project B is

$$\mathrm{NPV_B} = 70a_{\overline{15}|i} + \frac{1,200}{(1+y)^{15}} - 1,200,$$

from which we obtain the IRR of Project B as $\mathrm{IRR_B} = 5.8333\%$. The IRR of both projects are unique. Thus, if the required rate of return is less than 5.8333%, both project are acceptable. Suppose the rate of interest is 4%, we have $\mathrm{NPV_A} = \$265.9297 > \mathrm{NPV_B} = \$244.6045$. Thus, if only one project is to be taken, Project A is preferred. However, suppose the rate of interest is 2%, then $\mathrm{NPV_A} = \$499.2031 < \mathrm{NPV_B} = \$591.0661$, in which case Project B is preferred. We can further show that the NPV of the two projects are both equal to \$311.5285 if the rate of interest is 3.5683%, in which case both projects are acceptable and the investor would be indifferent.

The NPV rule can be applied with varying interest rates that reflects a term structure which is not flat. We can modify (4.18) to calculate the NPV, where the cash flow at time j is discounted by the rate of interest R_j. Thus, equation (4.18) becomes

$$\mathrm{NPV} = -\sum_{j=1}^{n} \frac{C_j}{(1+R_j)^j} - C_0. \tag{4.19}$$

However, if the IRR method is adopted, the term structure must be assumed to be flat.

We have so far postulated that the rate of interest is the same whether cash flows are injection or withdrawal. If capital is raised for investment they will incur a cost based on the borrowing rate. On the other hand, when a project generates cash incomes they can only be invested to earn the lending rate. The NPV calculation in (4.18) and (4.19) does not recognize the difference in lending and borrowing.

We now consider capital budgeting decision when the lending and borrowing rates are different. We denote the lending and borrowing rates by R_L and R_B, respectively, with the condition $R_B \geq R_L$. Suppose the initial fund in the project is $B_0 = C_0 > 0$. Thus, the project requires an initial investment, which is raised by a loan. We trace the balance in the fund through time. If the balance is positive at time t, the project is in debt and the investment incurs interest at the rate R_B. The balance at time $t+1$ is $B_{t+1} = B_t(1 + R_B) + C_{t+1}$. On the other hand, if the balance at time t is negative, the project has generated positive net cash, which earns interest at the rate R_L. The balance at time $t+1$ is $B_{t+1} = B_t(1+R_L) + C_{t+1}$. Combining these two possibilities, we have

$$B_{t+1} = \begin{cases} B_t(1 + R_B) + C_{t+1}, & \text{if } B_t \geq 0, \\ B_t(1 + R_L) + C_{t+1}, & \text{if } B_t < 0. \end{cases} \tag{4.20}$$

When the project terminates at time n, the fund balance is B_n after the cash flow C_n. As a positive fund balance implies the project is in debt and a negative fund balance implies the fund has generated positive net cash flow (withdrawal), the project should be rejected if $B_n \geq 0$ and accepted if $B_n < 0$.

Example 4.17: Consider a 2-year project with an initial investment of $1,000. A cash amount of $2,200 will be generated after 1 year, and the project will be terminated with fund injection of $1,180 at the end of year 2. If $R_B = 15\%$ and $R_L = 14\%$, is the project profitable? What is your conclusion if $R_L = 12\%$?

Solution: When $R_B = 15\%$ and $R_L = 14\%$,

$$B_1 = 1{,}000 \times 1.15 - 2{,}200 = -\$1{,}050$$

and

$$B_2 = -1{,}050 \times 1.14 + 1{,}180 = -\$17.$$

Hence, the project has net cash and is profitable, implying that it should be accepted. When $R_B = 15\%$ and $R_L = 12\%$, B_1 remains unchanged, while B_2 becomes

$$B_2 = -1{,}050 \times 1.12 + 1{,}180 = \$4,$$

so that the project incurs net debt at the end and should be rejected. Keeping $R_B = 15\%$ unchanged, the fund is in net debt if R_L is less than

$$\frac{1{,}180}{1{,}050} - 1 = 12.3\%,$$

in which case it should be rejected.

While (4.18) computes the NPV of the project upon its completion, it can be modified to compute the NPV of the project at a time prior to its completion. Thus, for $t \leq n$, we define the NPV of the project up to time t as

$$\text{NPV}(t) = -\sum_{j=1}^{t} \frac{C_j}{(1 + R_R)^j} - C_0. \tag{4.21}$$

If $\text{NPV}(t)$ changes sign only once in the duration of the project, we can calculate the value of t at which $\text{NPV}(t)$ first becomes positive. This value of t is called the **discounted payback period** (DPP). Formally, DPP is defined as

$$\text{DPP} = \min \{t : \text{NPV}(t) > 0\}. \tag{4.22}$$

Thus, the smaller the DPP, the earlier the project recovers its investment. Hence, a capital budgeting criterion is to choose the project with the lowest DPP. The example below illustrates this criterion.

Example 4.18: Consider the two projects in Example 4.16. Discuss the choice of the two projects based on the DPP criterion.

Solution: For Project B, as the most substantial cash flow generated is at the end of the project duration, the DPP of the project is 15 years. For Project A, Table 4.3 summarizes the results for several required rates of interest R_R.

Table 4.3: NPV of Project A

R_R	t	NPV(t)	DPP
0.03	12	–4.5996	13
	13	63.4955	
0.04	13	–1.4352	14
	14	56.3123	
0.05	14	–10.1359	15
	15	37.9658	
0.06	15	–28.7751	16
	16	10.5895	

For required rates of interest of 3%, 4%, 5% and 6%, the DPP of Project A are, respectively, 13, 14, 15 and 16 years. When the required rate of interest is 6%, Project B has a negative NPV and the DPP is not defined. When the required interest rate is 5%, Project B has the same DPP as Project A, namely, 15 years. For other required rates of interest considered, the DPP of Project A is shorter.

■

If R_R in (4.21) is set equal to zero, the resulting value of t at which NPV(t) first becomes positive is called the **payback period**. Although a project appraisal method may be based on the minimum payback period, this method lacks theoretical rigor as the time value of money is not taken into account.

4.8 Summary

1. The internal rate of return is the discount rate that equates the present value of cash outflows to the present value of cash inflows for a project. It is a

measure of the rate of return of the project and takes account of the time value of money.

2. The internal rate of return usually cannot be calculated analytically, and its computation requires numerical methods. Although simple projects have unique internal rate of return, more complicated projects may have multiple solutions of internal rate of return.

3. The 1-period rate of return of a fund can be computed using the time-weighted rate of return or the dollar-weighted rate of return. The time-weighted rate of return requires data for the cash flows as well as the value of the fund at the time of cash flows. The dollar-weighted rate of return does not require the fund value to be marked to market.

4. Multiple-period return of a fund can be measured using the geometric mean rate of return or the arithmetic mean rate of return. The geometric mean rate of return measures the fund's performance over the period based on the buy-and-hold assumption. The arithmetic mean rate of return measures the average return of the fund in a random year over the period.

5. The time-weighted and dollar-weighted methods can be used to measure the return of a fund over an extended period, if the data about of the cash flows over the period are available.

6. The rate of return of a portfolio is equal to the weighted average of the rates of return of its component assets. Portfolio diversification may lead to reduction in standard deviation over individual assets in the portfolio.

7. Short sale is the sale of a security that the seller does not own. Short selling involves the creation of a margin account, and the return of the short-sale strategy should be based on the margin deposits.

8. Investment-year method and portfolio method are two methods of crediting interests to investors of a fund. The purpose is to have a more equitable method of crediting interests with respect to the different timings of the investments.

9. The net present value rule accepts projects with positive net present value discounted at the required rate of return. This method can be extended to allow the required rate of return to vary with the horizons of the cash flows. The IRR and DPP methods are two alternative methods of project appraisal.

Exercises

4.1 A project requires an initial cash outlay of $100 and an investment of $150 at the end of year 1, and is expected to generate $300 at the end of year 2, at which time the project will terminate. Calculate the internal rate of return of the project.

4.2 A project requires an initial cash outlay of $1,000 and a final investment of $600 at the end of year 2, and is expected to generate $1,750 at the end of the first year. Calculate the internal rate of return of the project.

4.3 Calculate the net present value of the cash flows in Exercise 4.1 by using:

   (a) a constant interest rate of 6%,

   (b) $i_1^S = 4\%$ and $i_2^S = 5.5\%$.

4.4 Calculate the net present value of the cash flows in Exercise 4.2 by using:

   (a) a constant interest rate of 6%,

   (b) $i_1^F = 4\%$ and $i_2^F = 5.5\%$.

4.5 You are given the following cash flows for an investment project. Calculate the yield rate of the project, assuming that all cash flows occur at year end.

Year	Contribution	Investment income	Withdrawal
0	10,000	1,550	0
1	1,000	500	0
2	1,000	500	3,000
3	0	200	7,000
4	0	200	7,000

4.6 Paul pays $5 million for a 7-year lease of a building and rented it out. He will receive $1 million rental income at the end of the first and the second year, and will receive $1.3 million at the end of the remaining years.

   (a) Calculate the internal rate of return of his investment.

   (b) Stock X is expected to generate a return of 14.5% per annum over the next 7 years. Which investment should Paul choose? Explain why.

4.7 Which of the following cannot be the yield rate of a stock? Explain why.

    (a) -110%.

    (b) -10%.

    (c) 10%.

    (d) 110%.

4.8 A deposit of $1,000 is made into an investment fund at time 0. After 3 months, $300 is injected into the fund. After 8 months, $200 is withdrawn from the fund. No other deposits or withdrawals are made. The fund balance after 1 year is $1,000.

    (a) Find the internal rate of return.

    (b) Find the effective capital of the fund over the 1-year period.

    (c) Compute the DWRR of the fund.

4.9 Deposits of $2,000 are made into an investment fund at time 0 and 1. The fund balance is $2,200 at time 1 before the new investment and $3,500 at time 2. Compute the TWRR of the fund over the whole period.

4.10 On January 1, a fund was valued at 100. On April 1, the fund increased in value to 140 and 40 of new principal was injected. On October 16, the fund value dropped to 125, and 10 was withdrawn. At the end of the year, the fund was worth 135. Calculate the DWRR and the TWRR.

4.11 The annual rate of return of a unit trust over the last 5 years are (in %) as follows:
$$12.50 \quad -10.25 \quad 24.11 \quad 11.00 \quad -8.33$$

Calculate the arithmetic mean rate of return and the geometric mean rate of return of the unit trust.

4.12 Cindy invested in a small stock whose price was $5.60. The following table shows the prices of the stock at the end of the first year, second year, and so on.

Year	Price ($)
1	7.71
2	7.07
3	14.41
4	21.71
5	14.71

Calculate the arithmetic mean rate of return and the geometric mean rate of return of the stock.

4.13 The annual rate of return of a bond fund over the last 8 years are (in %) as follows:

$$-0.53 \quad 15.29 \quad 32.68 \quad 23.96 \quad -2.65 \quad 8.40 \quad 19.49 \quad 7.13$$

Calculate the arithmetic mean rate of return and the geometric mean rate of return of the fund.

4.14 A fund has a value of $10,000 at the beginning of the year. A deposit of $300 was made at the end of every 4 months. A withdrawal of $200 was made at the end of 9 months. At the end of the year, the fund balance after the final deposit is $11,000. Find the DWRR earned by the fund. Also calculate the approximate DWRR using equation (4.8).

4.15 A portfolio made up of two coupon bonds has an initial value of $20,000. The fund records coupon payments in 6-month periods. For the 2-year period 2016 and 2017, the following fund values and coupon payments were recorded:

Time mm/dd/yy	Coupon payment received	Fund value before date
01/01/16		20,000
07/01/16	550	21,250
01/01/17	1,000	18,500
07/01/17	550	19,750
12/31/17		20,500

Calculate the TWRR and the DWRR of the fund.

4.16 A project requires investments of $1,000 and $1,176 at the end of the first year and the third year, respectively, and generates income of $2,170 at the end of 2 years. Find the internal rate of return of the project.

4.17 A project requires an initial cash outlay of $1,000 and a final investment of $800 at the end of year 2, and is expected to generate $1,750 at the end of the first year. Calculate the internal rate of return of the project.

4.18 A cash outlay of $600 generates incomes of $300 after 3 months and 9 months, and $50 after 1 year. Calculate the yield rate of the investment.

4.19 A 7-year project requires an initial cash injection of $10,000. Expenses of $500 are incurred at the end of every year. The project starts to generate income of $3,000 after 3 years, and the income increases at a rate of 10% every year.

(a) Calculate the yield rate of the project.

(b) Repeat (a), assuming that at the end of each year, the company has to pay 5% tax on investment income after expenses. (If the net income in the year is negative, no tax is paid.) Compare your answer with that obtained in (a).

4.20 On June 1, 2016, an investment account is worth $200. On November 1, 2016, the value has increased to $225 and X is deposited into the account. On April 1, 2017, the balance becomes $270, and $90 is withdrawn. On June 1, 2017, the account balance is $168. The TWRR of the account is 5%. Find the DWRR of the account.

4.21 On January 1, an account is worth $70,000. After k months, the balance increases by 20%, and $4,000 is withdrawn. $k+2$ months prior to the end of the year, the balance becomes $88,000 and $2,000 is deposited. After 1 year, the account is worth $80,000. The DWRR of the account is 17.69%.

(a) Find k.

(b) Calculate the TWRR of the account.

4.22 Consider the following table for the cash flows of an investment account:

Time mm/dd/yy	Contribution	Fund value before contribution
01/01/2017		1,000
04/01/2017	−300	500
08/01/2017	+2,000	250
12/31/2017		2,750

(a) Calculate the TWRR and the DWRR of the fund.

(b) Comment on the results.

4.23 The following shows the returns and standard deviations of three stock indices: US, Germany and Japan:

	Expected return	Standard deviation
US	16%	21%
Germany	20%	25%
Japan	17%	27%

The correlation matrix of the three stock indices is as follows:

	US	Germany	Japan
US	100%		
Germany	37%	100%	
Japan	26%	33%	100%

You construct a portfolio of the three markets with 15% weight in US, 40% weight in Germany and 45% weight in Japan. Calculate the expected return and standard deviation of the return of the portfolio.

4.24 The value of Ms Sweetheart Company is sensitive to the price of cocoa. If the cocoa crop fails due to bad weather, the price of cocoa rises and the company suffers losses. The following shows the three scenarios of the company:

	Bearish market	Bullish market	Crop failure
Rate of return	13%	20%	−15%
Probability	40%	50%	10%

Kenny has a portfolio of risk-free bonds and Ms Sweetheart stock. The risk-free interest rate is 5% per annum. The expected return of Kenny's portfolio is 9%. Calculate the standard deviation of the return of Kenny's portfolio.

4.25 The values of Ms Sweetheart Company and Mr Sugar Company are sensitive to the price of cocoa. If the cocoa crop fails due to bad weather, Ms Sweetheart suffers from huge losses while Mr Sugar generates more profit. The following shows the three scenarios of Mr Sugar (refer to Exercise 4.24 for Ms Sweetheart):

	Bearish market	Bullish market	Crop failure
Rate of return	8%	13%	20%
Probability	40%	50%	10%

(a) Calculate the correlation between the returns of Ms Sweetheart and Mr Sugar.

(b) Kitty wants to construct a portfolio with the lowest possible variance using the two stocks. Find the weight of Ms Sweetheart in the portfolio and compute the expected return of this minimum-variance portfolio.

4.26 A stock fund has an expected return of 0.16 and variance of 0.0784. A bond fund has an expected return of 0.08 and variance of 0.0196. The correlation between the two funds is -0.3.

(a) What is the expected return and standard deviation of the portfolio with 80% in the stock fund and 20% in the bond fund?

(b) What is the expected return and standard deviation of the portfolio with 20% in the stock fund and 80% in the bond fund?

4.27 Let r_A and r_B be the returns of two assets A and B, with standard deviation σ_A and σ_B, respectively. Let $\rho < 0$ be the correlation between r_A and r_B. A portfolio is constructed using the two assets.

(a) Show that the weight of asset A in the minimum-variance portfolio is

$$w_A = \frac{\sigma_B^2 - \rho\sigma_A\sigma_B}{\sigma_A^2 + \sigma_B^2 - 2\rho\sigma_A\sigma_B}.$$

(b) Show that if the two assets are perfectly negatively correlated,

$$w_A = \frac{\sigma_B}{\sigma_A + \sigma_B}.$$

4.28 Most exchanges allow short sale only when the last change in the stock price is positive (that is, an "uptick"). Suggest a reason for this.

4.29 You sell short 300 shares of a stock for $80 per share and give your broker 55% margin deposit, which earns no interest. Your broker requires a maintenance margin of 30%.

(a) How far can the price of the stock go up before you receive a margin call?

(b) What will be your rate of return or loss if the price of the stock increases by 5%?

4.30 Mary sells short 200 shares of Conron and gives the broker the minimum amount of $6,700 to establish the margin account. The initial margin requirement is 50% and the margin deposit earns no interest.

(a) Find the price of the stock when Mary sells short.

(b) After 3 months, Mary covers the short position, resulting in a return of -10%. The interest credited to the margin account in the 3-month period is $50. Find the price of the stock when Mary covers the short position.

4.31 You sold short 100 shares in Outel at $33 per share. After 4 months, the stock paid $3 of dividend. After 2 more months you covered the short position by purchasing the stock at a price of $26. If the initial margin requirement is 50%, the margin deposit earns $30 interest in the half-year period, and each share incurs a transaction cost of $1 when you sold short the stock, find the rate of return over the half-year period.

4.32 Suppose you sell short 100 shares of a stock for $50 per share and give your broker 50% margin. The margin deposit earns no interest. When the stock price decreases by 12%, you close the short position. Calculate the rate of return if the stock pays a dividend of (a) $0.5 per share, (b) $1 per share, and (c) $2 per share before you close the short position. What is the effect of the dividend on the rate of return?

4.33 A fund credits interest according to the following table:

Calendar year of investment (Y)	Investment-year rates (%)				Portfolio rates (%)
	i_1^Y	i_2^Y	i_3^Y	i_4^Y	i^{Y+4}
2009	5.6	5.6	5.7	5.9	5.9
2010	5.6	5.6	5.7	5.9	5.8
2011	5.6	5.7	5.8	6.2	5.9
2012	5.8	5.9	6.0	6.3	X
2013	6.2	6.3	6.6	6.5	
2014	6.7	6.4	6.8		
2015	7.1	7.3			
2016	Z				

Assume all investments are made at the beginning of the year, and let

$M1$ = the total interest credited in the period 2013 through 2016 for an investment in 2009,

$M2$ = the total interest credited in the period 2013 through 2016 for an investment in 2013,

$M3$ = the total interest credited in the period 2013 through 2016 for an investment in 2013, if the balance is withdrawn at the end of every year and re-invested in the fund as new money in the following year.

Given that $M1 = M2 = M3$, find the two missing rates, X and Z, in the above table.

4.34 Find the investment-year rates and the portfolio rate credited in calendar year 2016 in Table 4.2.

4.35 An investment of $500 is made at the beginning of 2013 in the fund crediting interest according to Table 4.2. Find the total interest credited in calender years 2015 through 2017 inclusive.

4.36 You invest in the fund crediting interest according to Table 4.2 at the beginning of 2012 for two years and then withdraw and reinvest the money at the beginning of 2014 for two more years. Find the equivalent level effective interest rate for your 4-year holding period.

4.37 Find $\ddot{s}_{\overline{3}|}$ using Table 4.2, assuming that the first payment is made in the beginning of 2013 and that there is no withdrawal from the fund.

4.38 Consider the investment fund in Table 4.2. An investment of $1,000 at the beginning of 2011 has an accumulated value of $1,220 at the beginning of 2015. At the end of 2017, the money is withdrawn. Find the equivalent level effective rate of interest over the investment horizon.

4.39 Consider a fund which earns interest according to Table 4.2 and assume that the force of interest over each year is constant. You invest $1,000 in the beginning of 2014 and withdraw the investment after two and a half years. Find the amount of interest credited.

4.40 The cash flows for the first 3 years of an investment are as follows:

Year	Cash flow ($)
0	500
1	−600
2	1,000
3	−1,200

Let the borrowing rate be 12% and the lending rate be 10%. Calculate the balance after 3 years.

4.41 The cash flows of a 5-year investment are as follows:

Year	Cash flow ($)
0	1,500
1	500
2	−2,500
3	700
4	−1,000
5	450

Let the borrowing rate be 10% and the lending rate be 8%. Calculate the balance after 5 years. Will you accept the investment if it terminates in 5 years?

4.42 Consider a 4-year project with an initial investment of $10,000. A cash amount of $23,100 will be generated after 2 years, and the project will be terminated with fund injection of $13,300 at the end of year 4.

(a) Draw a graph of the NPV versus the required rate of return for the project.

(b) If you have a required rate of return of 8% per annum, will you be interested in the project based on the NPV rule? Will the IRR rule work in this problem?

4.43 Consider a 2-year project requiring a cash injection of $200 immediately and $230 after 1 year for an income of $500 at the end of year 2.

(a) Draw a graph of the NPV versus the required rate of return for the project.

(b) Will you be interested in this project based on the NPV rule at 8%? Will the IRR rule work in this problem?

4.44 Consider a 3-year project with an initial investment of $10,000. Cash amounts of $11,500 and $12,100 will be generated after 1 year and 2 years, respectively, and the project will be terminated with fund injection of $13,915 at the end of year 3. What conclusion can be drawn regarding the acceptance of this project?

4.45 You are given the following information obtained from the balance sheet of a company selling automobile insurance:

Type of cash flow	Amount of cash flow ($)
Balance at the beginning	10,000,000
Premium income	2,000,000
Investment income	744,000
Total benefit paid out	862,540
Operating expenses	20,000
Investment expenses	35,000
Tax	100,000

The total amount of interest earned can be approximated by the investment income net of investment expenses. Calculate the rate of interest earned during the year using a suitable method. Explain why your method makes sense.

4.46 The forward borrowing and lending rates are shown in the table below:

Year	Borrowing	Lending
i_1^F	7.0%	5.00%
i_2^F	7.5%	5.25%
i_3^F	8.2%	5.50%

The cash flows for the first 3 years of an investment are as follows:

Year	Cash flow ($)
0	500
1	−600
2	100
3	−120

Calculate the balance of the fund after 3 years. Is the project profitable?

4.47 A used scanner can be purchased for $150 cash or for $65 down payment and $50 at the end of each of the next two half-years. If you have a nominal interest preference rate of 7% convertible semiannually, will you pay cash now or pay by installments?

4.48 Consider the investment project given in the following table:

Year	Cash flow ($)
0	919.15
0.5	−42.00
1.0	−42.00
1.5	−42.00
2.0	−1,092.00

At what required rate of return (expressed as a nominal rate convertible semi-annually) will you accept the project? Will the NPV rule and the IRR rule give you the same result?

4.49 Beda borrows a $10,000 loan from Wendy for 5 years at an effective rate of interest of 8% per year. Wendy offers two options for Beda to repay the loan.

1: Interest payments due at year end are paid at year end, and the principal is repaid after 5 years.

2: The loan is repaid by five level payments over the 5 years. Wendy can only reinvest the repayments of Beda at 7% per annum.

(a) Calculate the yield rate of Wendy under Option 1.

(b) Calculate the yield rate of Wendy under Option 2. Explain why the answer obtained is smaller than that in (a).

4.50 Judy is considering whether she should buy a junk bond. The price of the bond is $4,429 and the cash flows of the bond are shown in the table below.

Time (year)	Cash flow ($)
0.5	500
1.0	500
1.5	5,500

(a) Calculate the annualized internal rate of return of the junk bond.

(b) Judy calculated the net present value of the junk bond using the annualized 3-month Treasury Bill rate, which is 4% per annum. Calculate the NPV of this investment based on Judy's assumption.

(c) Give two reasons why the price of the junk bond is so low when compared with that in (b).

Advanced Problem

4.51 When you are bearish on a stock you may try to make profit by short selling. When you are bullish on a stock you may borrow extra money from a broker to buy more stocks in order to earn a higher return. This is called "buy on margin." However, just like short selling, in buy-on-margin you have to maintain a margin level in your margin account, which is defined as

$$\frac{\text{Equity in your account}}{\text{Value of security you own}}.$$

In the definition above, the value of the security you own is the value of the stock you purchase as your own investment plus the extra stock you own by borrowing money from the broker. The equity in your account is the value of the security you own minus the amount of money you borrow from the broker. If the margin level falls below a margin maintenance requirement, you will receive a broker's call.

(a) Andrew is bullish on Orange Corporation whose current market price is $40 per share, and he has $9,200 to invest. To leverage his position Andrew borrows $4,000 from the broker at an interest rate of 5% per year. After 1 year, the price of Orange Corporation pays $2 dividend and the ex-dividend price has increased by 7%. Find the rate of return.

(b) How far can the price of the stock fall before Andrew receives a margin call, supposing that the margin maintenance requirement is 40%? You may ignore the interest incurred in the margin account.

5

Loans and
Costs of Borrowing

Loans are usually paid back by periodic installments. Upon payment of the installments, the balance of the loan reduces. We introduce two methods of calculating the balance of the loan, namely, the prospective method and the retrospective method. The two methods are mathematically equivalent.

The quantum of each installment can be determined by the amortization method or the sinking fund method. In the amortization method, each installment is used to offset the interest incurred over the period and to reduce the principal. For the sinking fund method, installments are made up of a portion used to offset the interest and another portion used to accumulate an amount to repay the principal. We extend our analysis to installments that are of unequal amounts, as well as to the case where interest rates are varying.

Lending and borrowing serve an important function in varying a person's consumption pattern and timing. The quoted rate of interest, however, may not adequately reflect the true cost in borrowing. To compare different loan schemes on the same basis we propose to use the equivalent nominal rate of interest, which is appropriate for comparing loans with the same frequency of repayment installments.

Learning Objectives

- *Calculation of loan balance: prospective method and retrospective method*
- *Amortization schedule*
- *Sinking fund*
- *Varying installments and varying interest rates*
- *Quoted rate of interest and equivalent nominal rate of interest in monthly rest*
- *Flat rate loan and flat rate discount loan*
- *Annual percentage rate, annual percentage yield, effective rate of interest, and comparison rate of interest*

5.1   Loan Balance: Prospective and Retrospective Methods

We consider a loan with a fixed term of maturity, which is to be redeemed by a series of repayments. If the repayments prior to maturity are only to offset the interests, followed by a final payment to redeem the principal upon maturity, the loan is called an **interest-only loan**. On the other hand, if the repayments include both payment of interest and partial redemption of the principal, the loan is called a **repayment loan**.

If a repayment includes a component to partially redeem the principal, the balance of the loan is reduced. We consider two approaches to compute the balance of the loan: the **prospective method** and the **retrospective method**. The prospective method is forward looking. It calculates the loan balance as the present value of all future payments. The retrospective method is backward looking. It calculates the loan balance as the accumulated value of the loan at the time of evaluation minus the accumulated value of all installments paid up to the time of evaluation.

Let the loan amount be L, and the rate of interest per payment period be i. If the loan is to be paid back in n installments of an annuity-immediate, the installment amount A is given by

$$A = \frac{L}{a_{\overline{n}|i}}. \tag{5.1}$$

We also denote $L = B_0$, which is the loan balance at time 0. Immediately after the mth payment has been made $(m < n)$, the loan is redeemable by a $n - m$ annuity-immediate. We denote the loan balance after the mth installment by B_m, which can be computed using the prospective method as follows:

$$
\begin{aligned}
B_m &= A\, a_{\overline{n-m}|i} \\
&= \frac{L\, a_{\overline{n-m}|i}}{a_{\overline{n}|i}}.
\end{aligned}
\tag{5.2}
$$

To use the retrospective method to compute the balance, we first calculate the accumulated loan amount at time m, which is $L(1+i)^m$. The accumulated value of the installments is $As_{\overline{m}|i}$. Thus, the loan balance can also be written as

$$
L(1+i)^m - As_{\overline{m}|i}.
\tag{5.3}
$$

To show that the two methods are equivalent, we simplify (5.3). Thus, we have

$$
\begin{aligned}
Aa_{\overline{n}|i}(1+i)^m - As_{\overline{m}|i} &= A\left[\frac{1-v^n}{i}(1+i)^m - \frac{(1+i)^m - 1}{i}\right] \\
&= A\left[\frac{1-v^{n-m}}{i}\right] \\
&= A\, a_{\overline{n-m}|i},
\end{aligned}
$$

which is equal to (5.2).

Example 5.1: A housing loan of \$400,000 was to be repaid over 20 years by monthly installments of an annuity-immediate at the nominal rate of 5% per year. After the 24th payment was made, the bank increased the interest rate to 5.5%. If the lender was required to repay the loan within the same period, how much would be the increase in the monthly installment. If the installment remained unchanged, how much longer would it take to pay back the loan?

Solution: We first demonstrate the use of the prospective and retrospective methods for the calculation of the loan balance after the 24th payment. From (5.1), the amount of the monthly installment is

$$
\begin{aligned}
A &= \frac{400{,}000}{a_{\overline{240}|\frac{0.05}{12}}} \\
&= \frac{400{,}000}{151.525} \\
&= \$2{,}639.82.
\end{aligned}
$$

By the prospective method, after the 24th payment the loan would be redeemed with a 216-payment annuity-immediate so that the balance is

$$
\begin{aligned}
A\, a_{\overline{216}|\frac{0.05}{12}} &= 2{,}639.82 \times 142.241 \\
&= \$375{,}490.
\end{aligned}
$$

By the retrospective method, the balance is

$$400,000 \left(1 + \frac{0.05}{12}\right)^{24} - 2,639\, s_{\overline{24}|\frac{0.05}{12}} = 441,976.53 - 2,639.82 \times 25.186$$

$$= \$375,490.$$

Hence, the two methods give the same answer. After the increase in the rate of interest, if the loan is to be repaid within the same period, the revised monthly installment is

$$\frac{375,490}{a_{\overline{216}|\frac{0.055}{12}}} = \frac{375,490}{136.927}$$

$$= \$2,742.26,$$

so that the increase in installment is $102.44. Let m be the remaining number of installments if the amount of installment remained unchanged. Thus,

$$a_{\overline{m}|\frac{0.055}{12}} = a_{\overline{216}|\frac{0.05}{12}} = 142.241,$$

from which we solve for $m = 230.88 \approx 231$. Thus, it takes 15 months more to pay back the loan.

Example 5.2: A housing loan is to be repaid with a 15-year monthly annuity-immediate of $2,000 at a nominal rate of 6% per year. After 20 payments, the borrower requests for the installments to be stopped for 12 months. Calculate the revised installment when the borrower starts to pay back again, so that the loan period remains unchanged. What is the difference in the interest paid due to the temporary stoppage of installments?

Solution: The loan is to be repaid over $15 \times 12 = 180$ payments. After 20 payments, the loan still has 160 installments to be paid. Using the prospective method, the balance of the loan after 20 payments is

$$2,000 \times a_{\overline{160}|0.005} = \$219,910.$$

Note that if we calculate the loan balance using the retrospective method, we need to compute the original loan amount. The full calculation using the retrospective method is

$$2,000\, a_{\overline{180}|0.005} (1.005)^{20} - 2,000\, s_{\overline{20}|0.005} = 2,000\,(130.934 - 20.979)$$

$$= \$219,910.$$

Due to the delay in payments, the loan balance 12 months after the 20th payment is

$$219,910\,(1.005)^{12} = \$233,473,$$

which has to be repaid with a 148-payment annuity-immediate. Hence, the revised installment is

$$\frac{233,473}{a_{\overline{148}|0.005}} = \frac{233,473}{104.401}$$
$$= \$2,236.31.$$

The difference in the interest paid is

$$2,236.31 \times 148 - 2,000 \times 160 = \$10,973.$$

Working out the balance of a loan is often the first step in deciding whether to re-finance the loan if a more attractive interest rate is available. The example below illustrates this application.

Example 5.3: A man borrows a housing loan of $500,000 from Bank A to be repaid by monthly installments over 20 years at nominal rate of interest of 4% per year. After 24 installments Bank B offers the man a loan at rate of interest of 3.5% to be repaid over the same period. However, if the man wants to re-finance the loan he has to pay Bank A a penalty equal to 1.5% of the outstanding balance. If there are no other re-financing costs, should the man re-finance the loan?

Solution: The monthly installment paid to Bank A is

$$\frac{500,000}{a_{\overline{240}|\frac{0.04}{12}}} = \frac{500,000}{165.02}$$
$$= \$3,029.94.$$

The outstanding balance after paying the 24th installment is

$$3,029.94\, a_{\overline{216}|\frac{0.04}{12}} = 3,029.94 \times 153.80$$
$$= \$466,004.$$

If the man re-finances with Bank B, he needs to borrow

$$466,004 \times 1.015 = \$472,994,$$

so that the monthly installment is

$$\frac{472{,}994}{a_{\overline{216}|\frac{0.035}{12}}} = \frac{472{,}994}{160.09}$$

$$= \$2{,}954.56.$$

As this is less than the installments of $3,029.94 he pays to Bank A, he should re-finance.

5.2 Amortization

If a loan is repaid by the amortization method, each installment is first used to offset the interest incurred since the last payment. The remaining part of the installment is then used to reduce the principal. Consider a loan to be repaid by a n-payment unit annuity-immediate. The principal is $a_{\overline{n}|i}$ and the interest incurred in the first payment period is $i\, a_{\overline{n}|i} = 1 - v^n$. Thus, out of the unit payment, $1 - v^n$ goes to paying the interest and the principal is reduced by the amount v^n. The principal is then reduced to

$$\begin{aligned}
a_{\overline{n}|i} - v^n &= \frac{1 - v^n}{i} - v^n \\
&= \frac{1 - v^n(1+i)}{i} \\
&= \frac{1 - v^{n-1}}{i} \\
&= a_{\overline{n-1}|i}.
\end{aligned}$$

This result is consistent with the computation of the loan balance using the prospective method, and can be obtained as a special case of (2.11). Making use of this result we can construct an **amortization schedule** that separates each installment into the interest and principal components. Table 5.1 presents an amortization schedule constructed based on this principle.

Example 5.4: Construct an amortization schedule of a loan of $5,000 to be repaid over 6 years with a 6-payment annuity-immediate at effective rate of interest of 6% per year.

Solution: The annual payment is

$$\frac{5{,}000}{a_{\overline{6}|0.06}} = \frac{5{,}000}{4.9173}$$

$$= \$1{,}016.81.$$

Using Table 5.1 with installments of 1,016.81 in place of 1, we obtain the amortization schedule in Table 5.2.

Table 5.1: Amortization of a loan of $a_{\overline{n}|i}$ by a n-payment unit annuity-immediate at effective interest rate of i per period

Time	Installment	Interest payment	Principal payment	Outstanding balance
0				$a_{\overline{n}|}$
1	1	$i\,a_{\overline{n}|} = 1 - v^n$	v^n	$a_{\overline{n}|} - v^n = a_{\overline{n-1}|}$
$\cdot$	$\cdot$	$\cdot$	$\cdot$	$\cdot$
$\cdot$	$\cdot$	$\cdot$	$\cdot$	$\cdot$
t	1	$i\,a_{\overline{n-t+1}|}$ $= 1 - v^{n-t+1}$	v^{n-t+1}	$a_{\overline{n-t+1}|} - v^{n-t+1}$ $= a_{\overline{n-t}|}$
$\cdot$	$\cdot$	$\cdot$	$\cdot$	$\cdot$
$\cdot$	$\cdot$	$\cdot$	$\cdot$	$\cdot$
n	1	$i\,a_{\overline{1}|} = 1 - v$	v	$a_{\overline{1}|} - v = 0$
Total	n	$n - a_{\overline{n}|}$	$a_{\overline{n}|}$	

Table 5.2: Amortization of a loan of $5,000 by a 6-payment annuity-immediate at effective interest rate of 6% per year

Year	Installment	Interest payment	Principal payment	Outstanding balance
0				5,000.00
1	1,016.81	300.00[a]	716.81[b]	4,283.19[c]
2	1,016.81	256.99[d]	759.82	3,523.37
3	1,016.81	211.40	805.41	2,717.96
4	1,016.81	163.08	853.73	1,864.23
5	1,016.81	111.85	904.96	959.26
6	1,016.81	57.55	959.26	0.00
Total	6,100.86	1,100.86	5,000.00	

The details of the computation in Table 5.2 are given as follows:

[a] Interest incurred in the first period: $5,000 \times 0.06 = \$300$.

[b] Principal reduction with the first installment: $1,016.81 - 300 = \$716.81$.

[c] Outstanding balance at the end of the first year: $5,000 - 716.81 = \$4,283.19$.

[d] Interest incurred in the second period: $4,283.19 \times 0.06 = \$256.99$.

The rest of the computations follow similarly.

5.3　Sinking Fund

A loan may also be served by payments of interest on a periodic basis, with a lump sum equal to the original principal paid at the end of the loan period. The borrower deposits an amount periodically into a **sinking fund** so as to accumulate to the principal. Consider a loan of amount $a_{\overline{n}|i}$. Using the amortization method, the borrower makes periodic payments of unit amount over n periods. By the sinking fund method, the borrower pays an amount $i\,a_{\overline{n}|i} = 1 - v^n$ each period to serve the interest. In addition, he deposits installments into a sinking fund. Suppose the sinking fund accumulates interest at the rate of interest i. To accumulate to $a_{\overline{n}|i}$ at time n, each sinking fund installment is $a_{\overline{n}|i}/s_{\overline{n}|i} = v^n$. Thus, the total amount the borrower has to pay each period is

$$(1 - v^n) + v^n = 1,$$

which is the same as the amount paid in amortization. Table 5.3 presents the sinking fund schedule based on a loan of $a_{\overline{n}|i}$.

Note that the interest paid in Table 5.3 remains constant at $1 - v^n$, while the interest paid in Table 5.1 using the amortization method decreases with the time period t. This apparent discrepancy is due to the interest earned in the sinking fund. At time t, the interest earned in the sinking fund over the payment period is $iv^n s_{\overline{t-1}|} = v^n[(1+i)^{t-1} - 1] = v^{n-t+1} - v^n$. We subtract this amount from the interest served to obtain the net interest paid as

$$1 - v^n - (v^{n-t+1} - v^n) = 1 - v^{n-t+1},$$

which is the same as the value in Table 5.1.

Table 5.3:　Sinking fund schedule of a loan of $a_{\overline{n}|i}$ by an n-payment unit annuity-immediate at effective interest rate of i per period

Time	Installment	Interest payment	Sinking fund deposit	Sinking fund balance
1	1	$i\,a_{\overline{n}|} = 1 - v^n$	v^n	$v^n s_{\overline{1}|} = v^n$
2	1	$i\,a_{\overline{n}|} = 1 - v^n$	v^n	$v^n s_{\overline{2}|}$
.	.	.	.	.
.	.	.	.	.
t	1	$i\,a_{\overline{n}|} = 1 - v^n$	v^n	$v^n s_{\overline{t}|}$
.	.	.	.	.
.	.	.	.	.
n	1	$i\,a_{\overline{n}|} = 1 - v^n$	v^n	$v^n s_{\overline{n}|} = a_{\overline{n}|}$
Total	n	$n - nv^n$	nv^n	

Example 5.5: Construct a sinking fund schedule for the loan in Example 5.4.

Solution: The interest payment is $5,000 \times 0.06 = \$300$, and the sinking fund deposit is

$$\frac{5,000}{s_{\overline{6}|0.06}} = \$716.81.$$

Hence, the total annual installment is $300 + 716.81 = \$1,016.81$. The sinking fund schedule is presented in Table 5.4.

Table 5.4: Sinking fund schedule of a loan of $5,000 by a 6-payment annuity-immediate at effective interest rate of 6% per year

Year	Installment	Interest payment	Sinking fund deposit	Sinking fund interest	Sinking fund balance
1	1,016.81	300.00	716.81	0.00	716.81
2	1,016.81	300.00	716.81	43.01	1,476.63
3	1,016.81	300.00	716.81	88.60	2,282.04
4	1,016.81	300.00	716.81	136.92	3,135.77
5	1,016.81	300.00	716.81	188.15	4,040.73
6	1,016.81	300.00	716.81	242.44	5,000.00
Total	6,100.86	1,800.00	4,300.86	699.14	

At the end of year 2, the sinking fund generates interest of $716.81 \times 0.06 = \$43.01$. Throughout the 6 years the sinking fund accumulates interest of $699.14, which is the difference between the interest paid under the sinking fund method and the interest paid using amortization, namely, $1,800 - 1,100.86$.

When the rates of interest charged to the loan and earned by the sinking fund are the same, the dollar amounts of payment computed using the amortization and sinking fund methods are equal. The choice between the two methods may then depend on the tax implications with respect to the interest costs of a loan and the interest earned on deposits.

We now consider the case where the sinking fund earns a rate of interest different from that charged to the loan. Specifically, suppose the sinking fund earns interest at the rate of j per payment period. For a loan of amount $a_{\overline{n}|i}$, to accumulate to the principal in the sinking fund over n periods the periodic installment is

$$\frac{a_{\overline{n}|i}}{s_{\overline{n}|j}}.$$

Hence, the total installment is

$$i\,a_{\overline{n}|i} + \frac{a_{\overline{n}|i}}{s_{\overline{n}|j}} = a_{\overline{n}|i}\left(i + \frac{1}{s_{\overline{n}|j}}\right). \tag{5.4}$$

When $i = j$, the sinking fund method and the amortization method are the same, so that the monthly payment in (5.4) is equal to 1. Hence, we have

$$i + \frac{1}{s_{\overline{n}|i}} = \frac{1}{a_{\overline{n}|i}}. \tag{5.5}$$

Note that in (5.5), the right-hand side is the n-payment annuity-immediate to pay back a loan of 1 by amortization, and the left-hand side states that the annuity consists of payment of i for the interest and $1/s_{\overline{n}|i}$ for the sinking fund.

From (5.4) we can see that a loan of unit amount can be redeemed over n periods by a sinking fund that charges rate of interest i to the loan and credits rate of interest j to the sinking fund by periodic payment of amount

$$i + \frac{1}{s_{\overline{n}|j}}.$$

If this amount is used to redeem a loan of unit amount by the amortization method at the rate of interest i^*, then we have

$$\frac{1}{a_{\overline{n}|i^*}} = i + \frac{1}{s_{\overline{n}|j}}. \tag{5.6}$$

We interpret i^* as the interest rate for the amortization method that is equivalent to the sinking fund method charging interest rate i to the loan and crediting interest rate j to the sinking fund. If $i > j$, it can be shown that $i^* > i$ (see Exercise 5.6). Thus, if the interest charged to the loan is higher than the interest credited to the sinking fund, the equivalent interest rate of the loan redeemed by amortization is higher. The example below illustrates this result.

Example 5.6: A 5-year loan of $500 is to be repaid by a 5-payment annuity-immediate using the sinking fund method. The loan charges 6% interest and the sinking fund credits 4% interest. What is the annual installment? If this installment is used to pay back a loan of the same amount by amortization, what is the rate of interest?

Solution: The installment is

$$500 \times 0.06 + \frac{500}{s_{\overline{5}|0.04}} = \$122.31.$$

We solve for i^* in the equation

$$122.31 a_{\overline{5}|i^*} = 500$$

to obtain $i^* \approx 7.11\%$.

Example 5.7: A loan is to be repaid by an 8-payment annual annuity-immediate of \$200 at interest of 5% for both the loan charge and the sinking fund credit. What is the interest component of the 4th payment in the amortization schedule? What is the interest credited to the sinking fund at the end of year 5?

Solution: In the amortization schedule, the loan balance after the third payment is

$$200 a_{\overline{5}|0.05} = \$865.90.$$

Hence, in amortization the interest in the 4th payment is

$$865.90 \times 0.05 = \$43.30.$$

For the sinking fund method, we first calculate the loan amount, which is

$$200 a_{\overline{8}|0.05} = \$1,292.64.$$

Thus, the sinking fund payment is

$$\frac{1,292.64}{s_{\overline{8}|0.05}} = \$135.37.$$

In the beginning of year 5, the sinking fund balance is

$$135.37 s_{\overline{4}|0.05} = \$583.46,$$

so that the interest credited to the sinking fund at the end of year 5 is

$$583.46 \times 0.05 = \$29.17.$$

We now consider a fund in which the interest on the sinking fund deposits earns a **reinvestment rate of interest** different from the sinking fund deposits. Specifically, we assume the installments paid to the sinking fund generate interest at the rate j, while the interest received is reinvested at the rate of interest j'. To calculate the accumulated amount, we first consider the case of a unit payment to the sinking fund at time 0. Interest of amount j is paid at time $1, 2, \cdots, n$. These interest payments earn interest at the rate j'. The time diagram of the fund is given in Figure 5.1.

Figure 5.1:   Single payment earning interest at the rate j for n periods

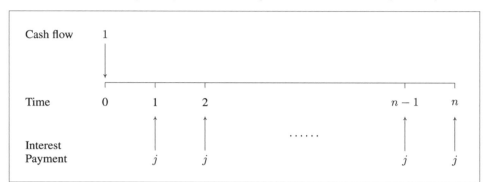

The accumulated amount at time n is made up of the unit-payment at time 0 and the n-payment annuity-immediate of amount j which earns interest at rate j'. Thus, the accumulated value is $1 + js_{\overline{n}|j'}$. If $j = j'$, this expression reduces to $(1 + j)^n$.

If an n-payment annuity-immediate of unit amount is paid to the sinking fund, the interest generated is an increasing annuity of amount $j, 2j, \cdots, (n-1)j$ paid at time 2, 3, $\cdots$, n, which earns interest at the rate j'. The accumulated value of this annuity is (see (2.37) for the formula of the increasing annuity)

$$n + j(Is)_{\overline{n-1}|j'} = n + j\left(\frac{s_{\overline{n}|j'} - n}{j'}\right). \tag{5.7}$$

Figure 5.2 illustrates the time diagram of the payments and the interests.

Figure 5.2:   A unit-payment annuity generating interests at rate j

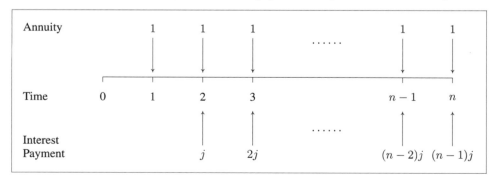

Example 5.8: A loan of $1,000 at effective rate of interest of 6% per year is to be redeemed over 5 years by a sinking fund that credits interest at 5.5% with reinvestment rate of interest of 5%. Calculate the annual installments of the annuity-immediate required to redeem the loan. What is the equivalent rate of interest using the amortization method?

Solution: The interest payment per year is $1,000 \times 0.06 = \$60$. Let X be the annuity payments to the sinking fund, which, after 5 years accumulate to

$$X\left[5 + 0.055(Is)_{\overline{4}|0.05}\right] = X\left[5 + 0.055\left(\frac{s_{\overline{5}|0.05} - 5}{0.05}\right)\right]$$
$$= 5.5782X.$$

Setting this to 1,000, we obtain $X = 179.27$. Hence, the annual installment is $60 + 179.27 = \$239.27$. If this payment redeems the load by amortization, the rate of interest i^* solves the equation

$$239.27 a_{\overline{5}|i^*} = 1,000,$$

from which we obtain $i^* \approx 6.29\%$.

5.4 Varying Installments and Varying Interest Rates

Installments to repay a loan need not be level. Suppose a loan over n periods at rate of interest i is to be paid back by a varying n-payment annuity-immediate of amounts $A_1, \cdots, A_n$ at times $1, \cdots, n$, respectively. The loan amount L is given by

$$L = \sum_{t=1}^{n} A_t v^t. \tag{5.8}$$

To determine the amount of interest and principal repayment in the kth payment, we first work out the balance of the loan B_{k-1} after the $(k-1)$th payment, which is, by the prospective method, given by

$$B_{k-1} = \sum_{t=k}^{n} A_t v^{t-k+1}.$$

Thus, the interest in the kth payment is iB_{k-1} and the principal is reduced by the amount $A_k - iB_{k-1}$.

Example 5.9: A 20-year loan is to be repaid by installments of $100 at the end of year 1, $200 at the end of year 2, and so on, increasing by $100 each year, up to $600 at the end of the 6th year. From then onwards, a level installment of $600 will be paid. The rate of interest charged is 6%. Calculate the loan amount. What is the interest and the principal reduction in the 3rd and the 12th payments?

Solution: The time diagram of the repayments is shown in Figure 5.3. The loan amount L is

$$100(Ia)_{\overline{6}|} + 600v^6 a_{\overline{14}|} = 100 \times \left[\frac{5.2124 - 6(1.06)^{-6}}{0.06} \right] + 3{,}931.56$$

$$= \$5{,}569.22.$$

To calculate the balance after the second installment, we use the retrospective method to obtain

$$B_2 = 5{,}569.22(1.06)^2 - 100(1.06) - 200 = \$5{,}951.57.$$

Note that the loan amount has actually increased, as the initial payments are not sufficient to cover the interest. This is the case of a *negative amortization*. The interest in the third payment is

$$0.06 \times 5{,}951.57 = \$357.09.$$

The third installment of $300 is not sufficient to pay for the interest, and there is an increase of loan balance by $57.09 to $6,008.66.

To split the 12th installment into interest and principal, we first calculate the loan balance after the 11th payment using the prospective method, which is

$$B_{11} = 600a_{\overline{9}|}$$
$$= \$4{,}081.02.$$

Thus, the interest in the 12th payment is $4{,}081.02 \times 0.06 = \$244.86$, so that the principal reduction is $600 - 244.86 = \$355.14$.

$\blacksquare$

Figure 5.3: Illustration of payments in Example 5.9

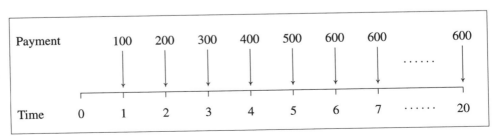

For the sinking fund method in which the loan charges rate of interest i and the sinking fund credits interest at the rate j, the interest in each installment is iL. If the sinking fund contribution at time t is S_t for $t = 1, \cdots, n$, then

$$\sum_{t=1}^{n} S_t (1+j)^{n-t} = L, \tag{5.9}$$

and the tth installment is

$$A_t = S_t + iL.$$

Example 5.10: Suppose a 20-year loan of $1,000 at rate of interest 6% is to be redeemed by the sinking fund method with an annuity-immediate crediting sinking fund deposits at 5.5%. If the sinking fund deposit increases by 5% in each payment, what is the amount of the 6th installment of this loan? What is the total amount of installments to repay this loan?

Solution: Let S be the first sinking fund deposit made at time 1. The tth sinking fund deposit is $S(1.05)^{t-1}$ for $t = 1, \cdots, 20$. As the deposits accumulate to $1,000 in 20 years, we have

$$\begin{aligned}
1,000 &= \sum_{t=1}^{20} S(1.05)^{t-1}(1.055)^{20-t} \\
&= \frac{S(1.055)^{20}}{1.05} \sum_{t=1}^{20} \left(\frac{1.05}{1.055}\right)^t \\
&= 2.7788S \sum_{t=1}^{20} (0.9953)^t \\
&= 52.91S,
\end{aligned}$$

from which we solve for $S = \$18.90$. Thus, the 6th installment is

$$1,000 \times 0.06 + 18.90(1.05)^5 = \$84.12.$$

The total amount paid is

$$1,000 \times 0.06 \times 20 + 18.90 \sum_{t=0}^{19} (1.05)^t = \$1,824.95.$$

For comparison, the total payments using the amortization method is

$$20 \times \frac{1,000}{a_{\overline{20}|0.06}} = \$1,743.69.$$

Equation (5.9) can be generalized to the case where the rate of interest varies with the time of the payment. For loans with floating rates of interest, the loan balance has to be updated with each payment to facilitate the calculation of the installments whenever interest rate changes. The example below illustrates a floating-rate loan.

Example 5.11: A man borrows a housing loan of $300,000 from a bank for 20 years, to be paid back by monthly installments. In the first year the bank charges an interest rate of 2.5%, followed by the second year of 3%. From then onwards, the interest rate will be 5%. All rates quoted are nominal per year. The bank calculates installments *as if* the loan is to be repaid over the remaining term at the ongoing rate. Thus, the first year installment assumes rate of interest of 2.5% for 20 years.

(a) Calculate the installments in the first, second and third year.
(b) What are the interests paid in the first and second year?

Solution: (a) The first-year payment is

$$\frac{300,000}{a_{\overline{240}|\frac{0.025}{12}}} = \frac{300,000}{188.71}$$

$$= \$1,589.71.$$

Using the prospective method, the loan balance after 12 payments is

$$1,589.71 a_{\overline{228}|\frac{0.025}{12}} = \$288,290$$

so that the revised installment is

$$\frac{288,290}{a_{\overline{228}|\frac{0.03}{12}}} = \frac{288,290}{173.63}$$

$$= \$1,660.38.$$

Repeating the same calculation, the balance after 24 payments is $1,660.38\, a_{\overline{216}|\frac{0.03}{12}} = \$276,858$. The revised installment is

$$\frac{276,858}{a_{\overline{216}|\frac{0.05}{12}}} = \$1,946.41.$$

For (b), the total amount of payments in the first year is $12 \times 1,589.71 = \$19,076.52$, and the reduction in principal is $300,000 - 288,290 = \$11,710$. Thus, the interest served is $19,076 - 11,710 = \$7,366$. Likewise, the interest served in the second year is $12 \times 1,660.38 - (288,290 - 276,858) = \$8,492.56$.

5.5 Comparison of Borrowing Costs

The cost of a loan depends on the **quoted rate of interest** and the way the interest is calculated. For example, the balance of a loan may be computed on a **periodic rest basis**, where the period is specified in the loan agreement. This means that interest is charged on the outstanding balance at the beginning of the period for the whole period, although installments may be made prior to the end of the period. To illustrate, we consider an annual-rest versus a monthly-rest loan. An annual-rest loan charges interest for the whole year, even though installments may be made monthly throughout the year. Thus, an annual-rest loan with monthly installments charges a higher effective rate of interest compared to a monthly-rest loan with monthly installments.

Example 5.12: A man is borrowing a housing loan of $500,000 from a bank. The quoted rate of interest is 6.5% per annum. Calculate the monthly installments in arrears if the loan is based on (a) annual rest, and (b) monthly rest. Compare the results for a 15-year loan and a 20-year loan.

Solution: For the annual-rest loan, we first calculate the annual payment, which, for the 15-year loan, is

$$\frac{500,000}{a_{\overline{15}|0.065}} = \frac{500,000}{9.4027}$$
$$= \$53,176.22.$$

The monthly installment is

$$\frac{53,176.22}{12} = \$4,431.35.$$

For the monthly-rest loan, the monthly installment is

$$\frac{500,000}{a_{\overline{180}|\frac{0.065}{12}}} = \frac{500,000}{114.796}$$
$$= \$4,355.55.$$

For the 20-year loan, the monthly installments for the annual-rest and monthly-rest loans are, respectively, $3,781.52 and $3,727.87.

When the quoted rates of interest are the same for the annual-rest and monthly-rest loans, the monthly-rest loan has a lower installment for the same term of the loan. When the quoted rates are different, however, the answer may depend on the term of the loan. The following example illustrates this point.

Example 5.13: A bank offers two options of housing loans. Option A is annual-rest at a quoted rate of 6.25% per annum. Option B is monthly-rest at 6.5% per annum. Both options require repayment by monthly installments in arrears. If a 10-year loan is required, which option should be preferred? What is your answer for a 20-year loan?

Solution: We consider an arbitrary loan amount of $500,000. For a 10-year loan, the monthly installments of the annual-rest and monthly-rest loans are, respectively, $5,728.40 and $5,677.40. Thus, the monthly-rest loan is preferred.

For a 20-year loan, the installments for the annual-rest and monthly-rest loans are, respectively, $3,706.75 and 3,727.85. Thus, the annual-rest loan is preferred.

When loans are paid back by installments of the same payment interval, they can be compared by converting the quoted rates to an equivalent nominal rate with compounding frequency equal to the payment frequency. For the examples above we can convert the quoted rate of interest for the loan on annual rest to an **equivalent nominal rate (ENR) of interest based on monthly rest**. Consider a principal of amount L. For a n-year annual-rest loan at quoted rate r to be repaid by monthly installments, the installment amount is

$$\frac{L}{12a_{\overline{n}|r}}. \tag{5.10}$$

We denote the annualized ENR on monthly rest by r^*, so that the monthly installment

$$\frac{L}{a_{\overline{12n}|\frac{r^*}{12}}} \tag{5.11}$$

is equal to (5.10). This implies

$$12a_{\overline{n}|r} = a_{\overline{12n}|\frac{r^*}{12}}, \tag{5.12}$$

from which we can solve for r^* numerically.

Example 5.14: For the loans in Example 5.13, calculate the ENR of the annual-rest loan for a 10-year and 20-year loan.

Solution: For the 10-year loan, the ENR is 6.70%. This can be checked by verifying the equation

$$12a_{\overline{10}|0.0625} = a_{\overline{120}|\frac{0.067}{12}}.$$

Similarly, we can verify that the ENR of the 20-year annual-rest loan is 6.43%. Thus, the ENR of the 10-year annual-rest loan is higher than the quoted rate of the monthly-rest loan, which shows that the monthly-rest loan is preferred. On the other hand, the ENR of the 20-year annual-rest loan is lower than the quoted rate of the monthly-rest loan, which means that the annual-rest loan should be preferred. This is consistent with the answer in Example 5.13.

It should be noted that the ENR r^* defined in (5.12) is actually $r^{(12)}$ defined in Chapter 1. If the installment is made m times a year, we can modify (5.11) to define the ENR accordingly, and we shall denote it simply by $r^{(m)}$. We conclude this section by stating that the ENR is a *nominal* rate; it is not an *effective* rate as defined in Chapter 1.

5.6   Flat Rate Loan and Flat Rate Discount Loan

Some short-term loans are charged on a flat rate basis. This means that interest is charged on the original principal for the whole term of the loan, even though the loan is progressively repaid by periodic installments. For a n-year loan of amount L charged on a quoted flat rate of interest of r per annum, the monthly installment A is computed by

$$A = \frac{L(1 + rn)}{12n}. \tag{5.13}$$

If the installments are paid in arrears, the loan is called a **flat rate loan**. To compute the ENR of this loan, we solve for $r^{(12)}$ from the equation

$$A a_{\overline{12n}|\,\frac{r^{(12)}}{12}} = L,$$

or, equivalently,

$$a_{\overline{12n}|\,\frac{r^{(12)}}{12}} = \frac{12n}{1 + rn}. \tag{5.14}$$

Example 5.15: A bank charges a car loan at 3% per annum flat. If the loan period is 5 years, and the repayments are by monthly installments in arrears, what is the ENR? What is the effective rate of interest?

Solution: Using (5.14), we solve for $r^{(12)}$ in

$$a_{\overline{60}|\,\frac{r^{(12)}}{12}} = \frac{12 \times 5}{1 + 0.03 \times 5} = 52.1739$$

to obtain $r^{(12)} = 5.64\%$. The effective rate of interest is

$$\left(1 + \frac{0.0564}{12}\right)^{12} - 1 = 5.79\%.$$

If a loan is to be repaid by monthly installments in *advance*, i.e., by an annuity-due, to solve for the ENR, we modify (5.14) to

$$\ddot{a}_{\overline{12n}|\frac{r^{(12)}}{12}} = \frac{12n}{1 + rn}. \tag{5.15}$$

A loan with such repayments is called a **flat rate discount loan**.

Example 5.16: Solve the problem in Example 5.15, assuming now the monthly installments are to be paid in advance.

Solution: We solve for $\frac{r^{(12)}}{12}$ from

$$\ddot{a}_{\overline{60}|\frac{r^{(12)}}{12}} = 52.1739,$$

to obtain $\frac{r^{(12)}}{12} = 0.004876$. Thus the ENR is $r^{(12)} = 5.84\%$ and the effective rate of interest is $(1.004876)^{12} - 1 = 6.00\%$. Hence we can see that the effective cost of the payments-in-advance loan is about 21 basis points higher than that of the payments-in-arrears loan, although the quoted rates of interest are the same.

■

Note that the *timing* of the installments of a payments-in-arrears loan and a payments-in-advance loan is different. Thus, it is not appropriate to compare the loans by the amounts of monthly installments. A more appropriate comparison is to use the ENR. The example below illustrates this point.

Example 5.17: A car buyer is offered two options of car loan. Option A charges interest at 4% flat with monthly installments paid in arrears. Option B charges 3.75% flat with monthly installments paid in advance. A loan of $50,000 is required, and the man is considering whether to borrow for 2 years or 5 years. Which option should he prefer?

Solution: For a 2-year loan, Option A requires installments of

$$\frac{50,000(1 + 2 \times 0.04)}{2 \times 12} = \$2,250.00,$$

while Option B requires

$$\frac{50,000(1 + 2 \times 0.0375)}{2 \times 12} = \$2,239.58.$$

Similarly, the installments for the 5-year loans of Option A and Option B are, respectively, $1,000.00 and $989.58. As Option B has a lower quoted rate of interest, its monthly repayment is always lower than that of Option A for the same loan period.

We solve the ENR of the loans using (5.14) and (5.15). The ENR of Option A for the 2- and 5-year loans are, respectively, 7.5% and 7.42%. Similarly, the ENR of Option B for the 2- and 5-year loans are, respectively, 7.68% and 7.23%. Thus, based on the ENR, Option A is preferred if a 2-year loan is required, while Option B is preferred if a 5-year loan is required. In contrast, if we compare the loans by the monthly installments, we will erroneously conclude that Option B is preferred due to its lower monthly payment.

When the payment frequencies of different loans are not the same, the ENR is not a valid measure to compare the loans' actual costs. The appropriate measure is the effective rate of interest computed from the ENR. Below is an example.

Example 5.18: A bank offers a loan of $100,000 for 2 years under three different options. Option A charges 6.75% per annum on monthly rest, with repayment installments made monthly. Option B charges 5.50% per annum on annual rest, with repayment installments made quarterly. Option C charges interest flat at 3.5% in year 1 and flat at 4.00% in year 2. The principal is repaid by equal monthly installments, and the interest in each year is repaid by equal monthly installments in that year. If all payments are made in arrears, which option is preferred?

Solution: Option A is straightforward. The effective rate of interest is

$$\left[1 + \frac{0.0675}{12}\right]^{12} - 1 = 6.96\%.$$

For Option B, the quarterly installment is

$$\frac{100,000}{4a_{\overline{2}|0.055}} = \$13,540.59,$$

and we solve for r^* from the equation

$$13,540.59\, a_{\overline{8}|r^*} = 100,000$$

to obtain $r^* = 0.01812$. Hence, the ENR in quarterly rest is $4 \times 0.01812 = 7.25\%$. The effective rate of interest for Option B is

$$(1.01812)^4 - 1 = 7.45\%.$$

For Option C, the monthly installment for the principal is

$$\frac{100,000}{24} = \$4,166.67.$$

Therefore, the total monthly installment for the first year is

$$4{,}166.67 + \frac{100{,}000 \times 0.035}{12} = \$4{,}458.34$$

while that for the second year is

$$4{,}166.67 + \frac{100{,}000 \times 0.040}{12} = \$4{,}500.00.$$

We solve for r^* from the equation

$$4{,}458.34 \, a_{\overline{12}|r^*} + 4{,}500.00 \, a_{\overline{12}|r^*}(1 + r^*)^{-12} = 100{,}000$$

to obtain $r^* = 0.005856$, so that the ENR in monthly rest is $12 \times 0.005856 = 7.03\%$. The effective rate of interest of Option C is

$$(1.005856)^{12} - 1 = 7.26\%.$$

Hence, Option A has the lowest effective rate of interest, and Option B has the highest effective rate of interest.

5.7 Borrowing Costs and Reference Rates

Apart from the differences in the ways interest is calculated, loans may vary in the manner they charge other related fees. These may include administrative fees, application fees, monthly fees and so on. To the effect that such fees may form a significant portion of the costs in serving the loan, a loan that apparently charges a lower rate of interest in nominal terms prior to such costs may turn out to be more costly when such costs are properly accounted for. To help consumers choose a loan in a well informed manner, regulators impose some guidelines that lenders have to follow. Generally speaking, these regulations require the lenders to present their loan offers in a *representative* or *reference rate of interest* that takes proper account of any possible hidden costs and differences in computing the installments. The terminology used by various regulatory bodies, however, does not always agree with each other, or with the terms defined in the academic literature. These representative rates or reference rates may be called by different names in different countries. Furthermore, fine details are usually not available as to how the rates should be computed. An accurate summary of the methodology used in different countries is a difficult task.

Notwithstanding the caveat, Table 5.5 summarizes the main reference rates in several countries. The term **Annual Percentage Rate (APR)** is commonly used in Canada, Hong Kong, UK and US. The equivalence of the APR in the academic literature is $r^{(m)}$, and in particular, for $m = 12$. Australia uses the term **Comparison Rate**, which takes account of most fee costs. In Singapore, the term used is the **Effective Interest Rate** (EIR), which is actually the Equivalent Nominal Rate defined in Section 5.5.

To illustrate the hidden costs that are applicable to consumer loans, the example below considers a short-term car loan. The loan is charged on a flat rate basis at the quoted rate of r per annum, with monthly repayment installments in advance. The loan balance in early exit is determined by the so-called **Rule of 78.** For a n-year loan of amount L with k installments made, the Rule of 78 determines the balance B after the kth payment as

$$B = \text{Principal} + \text{Interest} - \text{Installments Paid} - \text{Interest Rebate},$$

where Interest is the total interest charged over the whole term of the loan, and the Interest Rebate, denoted by R, is

$$R = \frac{(12n - k)(12n - k + 1)Lrn}{12n(12n + 1)}. \tag{5.16}$$

Hence, B is given by

$$B = L(1 + rn) - Ak - R, \tag{5.17}$$

where A is the monthly installment given in (5.13).

Example 5.19: A 6-year car loan charges flat rate at 2.5% per annum, to be repaid by a monthly annuity-due. Calculate the ENR in monthly rest of the loan. If the borrower decides to redeem early after 12, 24, 36, 48 and 60 payments, calculate the ENR in monthly rest charged over these periods.

Solution: The ENR in monthly rest is the value of r^* that satisfies the equation (see (5.15)):

$$\ddot{a}_{\overline{72}|\frac{r^*}{12}} = \frac{72}{1 + 6 \times 0.025} = 62.6087,$$

from which we obtain $r^* = 4.853\%$. If the loan is redeemed after k payments, the ENR in monthly rest is r^* that solves

$$L = \left[\sum_{t=0}^{k-1} \frac{A}{\left(1 + \dfrac{r^*}{12}\right)^t} \right] + \frac{B}{\left(1 + \dfrac{r^*}{12}\right)^{k-1}},$$

where A and B are given in (5.13) and (5.17), respectively. Solving the above equation for various values of k we obtain the following results:

k	12	24	36	48	60
r^* (%)	5.369	5.085	4.972	4.906	4.867

If the loan is redeemed at maturity, the annual effective rate of interest is $(1 + \frac{0.04853}{12})^{12} - 1 = 4.9624\%$. However, if the loan is redeemed after 1 year, the effective rate of interest is $(1 + \frac{0.05369}{12})^{12} - 1 = 5.5503\%$. In the case the loan involves a further penalty for early redemption, the difference in the borrowing costs may be even higher.

5.8 Summary

1. The balance of a loan can be computed using the prospective or retrospective methods. The prospective method computes the present value of the future installments required to pay back the loan. The retrospective method computes the accumulated value of the installments that have been paid, and subtracts this figure from the original loan amount with accumulated interest.

2. The amortization method of redeeming a loan computes the interest incurred since the last installment. The current installment is used to offset the interest with the remaining part applied to reduce the principal.

3. The sinking fund method of redeeming a loan involves two part payments. There is a portion that serves the interest calculated on the original principal. Another portion is deposited into a sinking fund that accumulates with interest to redeem the principal. The interest credited to the sinking fund may differ from the interest charged to the loan. If the interest credited to the sinking fund is the same as the interest charged on the principal, the total installments in the two methods are the same.

4. If the interest credited to the sinking fund is less than the interest charged on the loan, then the total amount of payments in the sinking fund method is higher than the total amount of payments in the amortization method.

5. To compare the costs of different loans, we may use the repayment installments or the rates of interest. When loans are repaid by installments of the same frequency and timing, they can be compared by the required repayment installments. When the frequencies or timing of the repayments are different, it is appropriate to compare the loans by their rates of interest.

Table 5.5: Summary of reference rates in selected countries

Country	Name of reference rate	Equivalent to	Remarks
Australia	Comparison Rate	APR, taking into account all interest and most fees and charges	Fees and charges include government fees, charges and duties. Early exit fees or early termination costs are not included in the Comparison Rate calculation. The Comparison Rate is higher than the APR.
Canada	Actual Interest Rate (AIR) Annual Percentage Rate (APR)	$APR = r^{(m)}$	AIR is the annual interest rate used to calculate the monthly payments. APR includes both the interest and any additional costs or prepaid finance charges, mortgage insurance, closing fees.
Hong Kong	Annual Percentage Rate (APR)	$APR = r^{(m)}$	APR should include interest on loans as well as any other fees and charges to reflect the total cost of credit. However, institutions are not obliged to quote the APR. Nonetheless, they should show all fees and charges related to the product in a clear and prominent manner.
Singapore	Effective Interest Rate (EIR)	$EIR = r^{(m)}$	Fees and early exit charges are not taken into account.
UK	Annual Percentage Rate (APR)	$APR = r^{(m)}$	Takes account of other charges such as arrangement fees.
US	Annual Percentage Rate (APR) Annual Percentage Yield (APY)	$APR = r^{(m)}$ $APY = i$	Takes account of application fee, closing fee and title fee, etc.

6. As the quoted rates of interest may not reflect the true cost of the loan, we propose to compare the costs of loans using the equivalent nominal rate. The equivalent nominal rate may be further compounded to obtain the effective annual rate of interest, which is sometimes called the Annual Percentage Yield.

7. We have illustrated the use of the equivalent nominal rate using the flat rate loans as examples. The actual costs of a loan should also take account of scenarios of early exit and any other fees or administration costs.

Exercises

5.1 Though the prospective method and the retrospective method yield the same outstanding loan balance, one method may be more efficient than the other depending on the information given. Discuss which method is more efficient in the following three scenarios.

(a) You are given the size of the loan and the time it started, the interest rate, and the level annual payment only.

(b) You are given the stream of varying annual repayments, the interest rate, and the term of the loan only.

(c) You are given the outstanding balance 2 years ago, the interest rate, and the installments in the previous 2 years only.

5.2 A loan is being repaid with 20 payments of $1,000 at the end of each quarter. Given that the nominal rate of interest is 8% per year compounded quarterly, find the outstanding balance of the loan immediately after 10 payments have been made

(a) by the prospective method,

(b) by the retrospective method.

5.3 A loan is to be repaid with quarterly installments over 3 years at 8% per annum convertible quarterly. Given that the outstanding loan balance after 2 years, B_2, is $1,440.23, find $B_{1.5}$.

5.4 A loan is to be repaid with $1,000, $2,000, and $3,000 at the end of the first, second, and third year. Interest is at the rate of 5% compounded semiannually. Find the outstanding balance immediately after the second payment is paid

(a) by the prospective method,

(b) by the retrospective method.

5.5 A loan of amount $3,000 is to be repaid with bi-monthly payments of $269.36 for 2 years.

    (a) Find the nominal rate of interest and the outstanding loan balance immediately after the 6th payment is made.

    (b) Explain why the answer in (a) is larger than one half of the initial loan balance.

5.6 A loan of amount $5,000 is to be repaid with P, $0.95P$, 0.95^2P and 0.95^3P at the end of the first 4 years. The annual rate of interest is 7%.

    (a) Find P.

    (b) Find the outstanding loan balance after 2 years.

5.7 A debt of $10,000 is to be repaid with quarterly installments of $4,000, $3,000, $2,000, $1,000 plus a final payment which pays off the loan after 5 quarters. Interest rate is 12% compounded quarterly. Find the outstanding loan balance after the second payment.

5.8 A loan is to be repaid with annual installments $P_t = n - t + 1$ for $t = 1, 2, \cdots, n$. Show that the prospective method and the retrospective method give the same outstanding balance.

5.9 Construct an amortization schedule for the loan in Exercise 5.6.

5.10 The following shows an amortization schedule for a loan which calls for level semi-annual payments over 2 years. Fill in the missing values in the amortization schedule and calculate the effective rate of interest.

Year	Installment	Interest paid	Principal repaid	Outstanding balance
0				
0.5				9,088.51
1			2,969.71	
1.5		122.38		
2	3,151.49			0

5.11 In the amortization schedule in Table 5.1, show that for $t = 1, 2, \cdots, n - 1$ and $i > 0$,

$$B_t > \frac{1}{2}(B_{t-1} + B_{t+1}).$$

Hence, describe the shape of the plot of B_t versus t.

5.12 The following shows an amortization schedule for a debt to be repaid with level annual payments over 3 years. Fill in the missing values in the amortization schedule.

Year	Installment	Interest paid	Principal repaid	Outstanding balance
0				
1				6,145.12
2				3,147.50
3				0

5.13 Consider a loan which is being repaid with level installments at the end of each year for 10 years. The interest rate is 9% per annum. It is given that the outstanding loan balance immediately after the 5th installment is made, B_5, is $30,304.29. Find the interest portion in the 3rd payment.

5.14 Johnny takes out a loan at 5% effective. He makes payments at the end of each year for 10 years. The first payment is $500, and each of the subsequent payment increases by $20 per year. Find the principal portion of the 6th payment.

5.15 A loan of $20,000 is to be amortized in 10 level annual payments. The interest rate for the first 3 years is 4% while the interest rate for the subsequent 7 years is 6%. Calculate the loan balance B_6 by

(a) the prospective method,

(b) the retrospective method.

Hence find the interest portion in the 7th annual payment.

5.16 Brian borrows $15,000 from Mary and agrees to repay with 12 installments payable half-yearly. The effective interest rate is 6.09% per annum. When the 6th payment is due, Brian repays the outstanding loan balance by a lump sum.

(a) Calculate the lump sum payment of Brian.

(b) Calculate the loss of interest income of Mary.

5.17 Irene borrowed a loan of $1,000,000 at an interest rate of 5% amortized over 30 years by annual payments. The first 15 payments were made on time but the next 3 were defaulted. A new agreement was then made to pay the remaining obligation in 12 equal annual payments at 6%, the first payment being made 1 year after the 3rd defaulted payment. Calculate the amount of the principal repaid in the 6th rescheduled payment.

5.18 Warren purchased a $100,000 house 5 years ago. The mortgage was to be repaid with monthly payments in arrears over 15 years. The nominal rate of interest is 8% compounded monthly. In order to shorten the term of the mortgage by 5 years so as to reduce interest, Warren negotiates with the lender so that the remaining outstanding loan balance is to be repaid in 5 years by larger monthly level payments. How much interest can Warren save?

5.19 Tim borrowed $10,000 at effective rate of 10% for 16 years and the loan was scheduled to be repaid with level annual installment payments at the end of each year until maturity. During the 6th year, the market interest rate dropped and Tim negotiated with the lender so that the interest rate charged in subsequent years after the 6th payment would be 8% and the term of the loan would be unchanged. Calculate

(a) the level annual installment payments after the 6th payment,

(b) the interest loss to the lender as a result of the negotiation.

5.20 Lily borrowed a loan to study in a university. Now that she has graduated, she needs to repay the loan with quarterly installments for 6 years. The first payment (due after 3 months) and the second payment (due after 6 months) are both $400, and the payment increases by $30 every half-year, until it reaches $610 and becomes level. The nominal interest rate is 8% compounded quarterly. Find the amount of principal repaid in the 9th payment.

5.21 Sally deposited $200 into a fund which earns 5% per year. The interest can only be reinvested at 4% per annum.

(a) Find the accumulated value of the investment after 5 years.

(b) Find the effective annual rate of interest of the investment.

5.22 Philip invests $500 at the beginning of each month into an account earning an effective rate of 6% for 2 years. The interest earned from the account can only be reinvested at an effective rate of 5%.

(a) Find the accumulated value of the investment after 3 years.

(b) Compare your answer with the case when all interests are reinvested at 6% effective.

5.23 A loan of amount L is to be repaid with level installments P at the end of each year for as long as necessary, plus a smaller final payment. The interest rate charged by the lender is i per year. Assume that $P > iL$ so that there is no negative amortization. Construct an amortization schedule by following the steps below.

    (a) Calculate the outstanding loan balance. [**Hint:** Prospective method does not work.]

    (b) Calculate the interest paid in each period.

    (c) Calculate the principal repaid in each period.

    (d) Determine n, the number of payments needed, and the size of the final irregular payment. How is this final payment split into interest and principal repaid?

Show that the principal repaid (except the one corresponding to the final installment) is an increasing geometric sequence. This observation is useful in the construction of the amortization schedule. Note that if the installments are level, then the principal repaid forms a geometric sequence in view of Table 5.1.

5.24 Construct an amortization schedule for the loan in Exercise 5.7.

5.25 A loan of $10,000 is to be repaid with level installments of $1,800 per month for as long as necessary, plus a smaller final payment. The nominal rate of interest convertible monthly is 12%. Construct an amortization schedule for the loan.

5.26 A loan is being repaid with level installments except for the final smaller adjustment payment. Complete the following amortization schedule:

Year	Installment	Interest paid	Principal repaid	Outstanding balance
0				
1			970.00	
2				
3			1,131.41	
4			351.00	0

5.27 A loan is being repaid with level installments except for the final smaller adjustment payment. Complete the following amortization schedule:

Year	Installment	Interest paid	Principal repaid	Outstanding balance
0				
1			1,550	
2		138		1,838
3				
4				0

5.28 A loan is being repaid with level installments except for the final smaller adjustment payment. Complete the following amortization schedule:

Year	Installment	Interest paid	Principal repaid	Outstanding balance
0				
1		200.00		
2		150.00		
3		97.50		
4				0

5.29 A loan is to be repaid with $1,000, $2,000, and $3,000 at the end of the 1st, 2nd and 3rd year. Interest is payable semiannually at a nominal rate of 5%. Construct an amortization schedule for the loan. Interests payable in the middle of the year are debited into the loan balance.

5.30 A loan is originally scheduled to be repaid with 9 annual level payments of $500 at rate i. When the 6th payment is due, the borrower only pays the interest due. At the end of the 7th year, the borrower cannot even pay the interest then due, but finally pays off the loan by level installments of P at the end of the 8th, 9th, 10th and 11th year. Assuming that the lender does not charge a higher interest to penalize the borrower for delaying the payment, by how much is P greater than $500?

5.31 A loan of $1,000 is to be repaid with annual payments of $50, $100, $1,000 and P at the end of the 1st, 2nd, 3rd and 4th year. The interest rate is 10% per annum. Construct an amortization schedule for the loan and determine P.

5.32 Richard purchases a car for $30,000, paying down $7,000, and $800 at the end of each month until the debt is redeemed. If the interest rate charged on the loan is 6% convertible monthly, how long will it take to redeem the loan? What is the size of the final irregular payment?

5.33 A $200,000 real estate mortgage is to be repaid with monthly payments at 12% interest convertible monthly over 30 years. Calculate

   (a) the principal portion in the 100th monthly payment,

   (b) the total principal repaid in the 100th to 200th monthly payments,

   (c) the sum of the present value of the interest payments made in the 100th to 200th monthly payments.

   Comment on the results in (b) and (c).

5.34 Stephen takes out a 15-year loan at 6% effective, to be repaid with annual repayments at the end of each year. Each loan repayment is 10% more than the previous year's repayment. Let P be the first payment.

   (a) Show that for $t = 0, 1, \cdots, 15$,

   $$B_t = 25P \left[\frac{(1.1)^{15}}{(1.06)^{15-t}} - 1.1^t \right].$$

   (b) Show that negative amortization takes place only in the first 2 years.

   (c) It is given that the principal portion of the 9th repayment is $1,132.29. Find the interest portion of the 5th repayment.

5.35 Betty borrows $1,000 from Ada for 2 years at a nominal rate of 12% compounded quarterly. What is the difference in interest earned by Ada if Betty repays with semiannual level installments instead of quarterly level installments?

5.36 June takes out a 20-year loan at an effective rate i to be repaid with annual payments. The payments are 7 at the end of year 1 to 6, 13 at the end of year 7 to 13, and 9 at the end of year 14 to 20. If the interest portion of the 7th payment is twice as much as that of the 14th payment, find i.

5.37 A man borrows a housing loan of $500,000 from Bank A to be repaid by monthly installments over 20 years at nominal rate of interest of 5% per year. After 5 years Bank B offers the man a loan at rate of interest of 4.5% to be repaid over the same period. However, if the man wants to re-finance the loan he has to pay Bank A a penalty equal to j of the outstanding balance. If there are no other re-financing costs, what is the value of j such that the man is indifferent to the two options?

5.38 Payments of $1,000 are invested into an account at the end of each year for 8 years, earning 8% effective per annum. Interests can only be reinvested at 6% for the first 6 years and 7% thereafter. Find the accumulated value of the investment after 10 years.

5.39 A borrower takes out a loan of $5,000 for 2.25 years. Construct a sinking fund schedule if the lender receives 9% effective on the loan per year, with interest payments payable at the end of each quarter, and if the borrower accumulates a sinking fund with semiannual deposits earning 8% compounded quarterly.

5.40 Gordon borrows $5,000 at an effective rate of interest of 8% per annum. He agrees to pay interest payment at the end of each year for n years, and repays the capital after n years by making sinking fund deposits at the end of each year for n years. The first sinking fund payment is $800, the subsequent $n-1$ payments increase by 5% each, while the payment at the end of n years is an irregular payment (less than the regular payment) such that the capital can be repaid. The sinking fund earns interest at 7.5% per annum.

   (a) Find the final irregular sinking fund deposit.

   (b) Find the growth rate of the sinking fund deposit if the loan is to be paid at the end of n years and the growth rate is always regular (i.e., there is no final smaller irregular payment).

5.41 Raymond took out a loan and agreed to make interest payments every 2 months at a nominal annual rate of 12%. Raymond will repay the principal after $2n$ months by making bi-monthly deposits into a sinking fund which credits interest at a nominal rate of 9%. It is known that 40% of the 32nd interest payment paid to the lender is offset by the interest earned on the sinking fund.

   (a) Find n.

   (b) When will the interest earned on the sinking fund start to offset more than one half of the interest payment to the lender?

5.42 A loan of amount L with effective rate i is to be repaid with interest payments at the end of every year for n years. The borrower agrees to make level deposits of amount X into a sinking fund earning an effective rate of j $(< i)$ at the end of each year for n years to repay the loan. After $n - 1$ years, the interest rate of the sinking fund increases to i. Let X' be the adjusted final sinking fund deposit into the sinking fund such that the accumulated value of the sinking fund after n years is just enough to redeem the loan. Show that

$$X - X' = L \left(\frac{i - j}{1 + j} \right) \left(\frac{a_{\overline{n-1}|j}}{a_{\overline{n}|j}} \right).$$

5.43 Nikita takes out a 5-year loan at 8% and pays interest of $120 to the lender at the end of every year. She also makes deposits into a sinking fund at the end of each year for 5 years, earning an effective rate of j per annum to repay the loan. The following is the sinking fund schedule of Nikita.

Year	Sinking fund deposit	Sinking fund interest	Sinking fund balance
1			260.836
2			
3			
4			
5			

(a) Find j. Then fill in the missing values in the schedule and find the net amount of interest paid to the lender.

(b) If the sinking fund is actually invested by the lender, what is the overall yield rate of the lender?

5.44 The following is a sinking fund schedule for the accumulation of $2,000 in 6 years by annual level deposits. Fill in the missing values in the schedule.

Year	Sinking fund deposit	Sinking fund interest	Sinking fund balance
1			
2			
3			885.069
4			
5			
6			

5.45 Luke repays a debt at 6% effective with payments of $400 at the end of each of the first 5 years, which then decreases by $20 each year until it becomes $200 at the end of 15 years. Find the amount of the loan if the sinking fund used to accumulate the capital earns a rate of only 5% effective.

5.46 Construct a sinking fund schedule for a loan of $2,500 to be repaid over 5 years at 7%. It is assumed that the sinking fund earns 7% per year.

5.47 Construct a sinking fund schedule for a loan of $2,500 to be repaid over 5 years at 7%. It is assumed that the sinking fund earns 6% per year. Compare your results with that in Exercise 5.46.

5.48 Construct a sinking fund schedule for a loan of $2,500 to be repaid over 5 years at 7%. It is assumed that the sinking fund earns 6% per year, while the interest in the sinking fund can only be reinvested at 5% effective. Compare the results with those in Exercise 5.46 and Exercise 5.47.

5.49 Gary took out a loan of $2,300 at an annual effective rate of 6%. Level interest payments are made at the end of every year for 8 years, and the principal is repaid at the end of 8 years by the accumulation of a sinking fund earning 5% effective. Find the difference between the interest payment earned by the sinking fund and the interest payment on the loan.

5.50 Paul borrows $53,000 and repays the principal by making 10 payments at the end of each year into a sinking fund earning an effective rate of 7.5% per annum. The interest earned on the sinking fund in the kth year is $2,035.40. Find k.

5.51 Jennifer took out a $6,000 loan from a bank and agreed to make interest payments every 6 months at a nominal rate of 6% compounded semiannually. At the end of 3 years she would repay the principal. In the meantime, Jennifer made deposits into a sinking fund earning an annual effective rate of 4.04%.

 (a) Find the total payment made by Jennifer every 6 months.

 (b) Find the sinking fund balance after 2 years.

 (c) Find the net interest served to the loan in the 5th payment to the lender.

5.52 A loan of $3,000 at effective rate of interest of 4% per year is to be redeemed over 10 years by a sinking fund that credits interest at 3.5%. When the 5th payment is due, the borrower can only pay the interest payment to the lender but is not able to make the sinking fund deposit. In order to repay the loan on time, the borrower pays an extra K dollars in the 6th to 10th sinking fund deposits. Find K.

5.53 Eddy borrowed $10,000 from a bank for 15 years at an annual effective rate of 6%. He paid interest annually and also made annual level deposits in a sinking fund which would repay the debt at the end of 15 years. The sinking fund earns 5% in the first 8 years and then 6% in subsequent years.

(a) What is the annual payment for Eddy?

(b) Find the net amount of the loan after 9 years.

5.54 A man is borrowing a housing loan of $180,000 from a bank for 10 years. The quoted rate of interest is 8% per annum. Calculate the monthly install-ments in arrears if the loan is based on (a) annual rest, and (b) monthly rest.

5.55 You borrow a loan of $100,000 to be repaid with quarterly installments in 15 years. The quoted rate of interest is 9% per annum based on annual rest. Find the quarterly installments in arrears.

5.56 For a loan of $200,000 for 14 years to be repaid by monthly installments in arrears, the quoted rate of interest is 8.7% per annum. Find the annualized equivalent rate of interest on monthly rest if the loan is based on annual rest.

5.57 A loan of $10,000 is to be repaid in 10 years according to one of the following arrangements:

(a) monthly payments in arrears with an APR of 8%,

(b) monthly payments in arrears with an APR of 9%, with a cash back of $650 at the beginning (i.e., the loan amount is reduced by $650),

(c) monthly payments in arrears with a quoted interest rate of 7% on annual rest.

Calculate the monthly payments for the three arrangements. Which arrange-ment is more favorable to the borrower?

5.58 Calculate the annual effective rate for the three arrangements in Exercise 5.57.

5.59 A loan of $12,000 is to be repaid in 2 years according to one of the following arrangements:

(a) repayment at the end of each month with APR of 12%,

(b) repayment of $1,650 at the beginning of each quarter.

Calculate the annual effective rate of interest for the two arrangements. Which arrangement is more favorable to the borrower?

5.60 A 5-year automobile loan of amount $50,000 charges interest at a quoted flat rate of interest of 6% per annum. The monthly installments are to be paid in advance. Find the ENR and the effective rate of interest of the loan.

5.61 You have a credit card loan of 18% flat for 1 year, to be repaid by monthly installments in arrears. The bank offers you an alternative option of 30% per annum on monthly rest, installments payable in advance. Would you accept the alternative?

5.62 Give a reason why the flat rate is smaller than the effective rate of interest of the flat-rate loan.

5.63 You are offered 3 options of a $50,000 car loan over 2.5 years.

    (a) 5% flat with level monthly installments in arrears,

    (b) 4.6% flat with level quarterly installments in advance,

    (c) 8% APR in the first year, which increases to 9% afterwards, with level quarterly installments in arrears.

    Which option would you choose?

5.64 You are given the following two options to repay a 1-year loan of $10,000:

    (a) $1,400 monthly installments in arrears,

    (b) $4,200 quarterly installments in arrears.

    Without numerical calculations, state which option is more attractive. Explain why.

5.65 You are given the following three options to repay a 1-year loan of $10,000:

    (a) a flat rate of 4%, quarterly installments payable in arrears,

    (b) a flat rate of 4%, monthly installments payable in advance,

    (c) a flat rate of 4%, monthly installments payable in arrears.

    Without numerical calculations, state which option is more attractive and which option is the most costly. Explain why.

Advanced Problems

5.66 Nicola borrows a $24,000 loan from Steve. She agrees to pay interest on the loan at the end of each year for 8 years, and will repay the capital by the accumulation of a sinking fund. The sinking fund deposits are such that the net amount of the loan decreases linearly, resulting in a level repayment of principal at the end of each year. The interest rate on the loan is 5% over the first 4 years and 4.5% over the next 4 years. The sinking fund earns a fixed 4% interest rate per annum.

    (a) Find the total amount of the 5th installment paid by Nicola.

    (b) Compare this with the case when Nicola repays the loan with 8 equal annual installments.

5.67 James repays a debt of L at an effective rate of $i < 0.5$ by varying payments. For the first 10 payments, the size of the payments equals three times the interest. For the next nine payments, the size of the payments is twice the interest. The final payment at the end of 20 years pays the loan in full. Derive an expression for the final payment in terms of L and i.

5.68 Andrew borrows a loan of amount $a_{\overline{n+5}|}$ $(n > 10)$, originally scheduled to be repaid by level annual payments of 1 for $n+5$ years. At the end of the 5th, 7th, 9th and 11th year, Andrew pays an additional amount of v^n, v^{n-3}, v^{n-6} and v^{n-9} apart from the originally scheduled unit payment.

    (a) After how many years will the loan be paid off completely?

    (b) Show that the amount of interest saved due to the additional payments is

$$4 - v^{n-9}\left(\frac{a_{\overline{12}|}}{a_{\overline{3}|}}\right).$$

5.69 For i^* defined in (5.6), show that $a_{\overline{n}|i^*} = \dfrac{a_{\overline{n}|j}}{[1 + (i-j)a_{\overline{n}|j}]}$.

    (a) Give an alternative formula for $a_{\overline{n}|i^*}$ in terms of the accumulated value of annuities evaluated at rate j.

    (b) Hence, show that

$$\frac{s_{\overline{n}|j}}{a_{\overline{n}|i^*}} = 1 + is_{\overline{n}|j}.$$

    Give a verbal interpretation of the relation above and find the return of the lender if he can only reinvest at rate j in the n-year period.

    (c) Show that the return of the lender in (b) above is in between i and j if it is assumed that $i > j$.

5.70 This question explains formula (5.17). In the amortization schedule discussed in this chapter, each installment is split into interest payment and principal repaid, and the amount of interest payment is determined by the outstanding balance in the previous payment period. In the Rule of 78, an approximation using linearly declining interest payment is used to split each installment. We denote $m = 12n$, which is the number of installments, and let $S_m = 1 + 2 + \cdots + (m - 1) + m$. Thus, m is the term of the loan in months. In the Rule of 78, the borrower is *assumed* to pay $\frac{m}{S_m}$ of the total interest in the 1st month, $\frac{m-1}{S_m}$ of the total interest in the 2nd month, $\cdots$, $\frac{1}{S_m}$ of the total interest in the last month. Thus, the interest payment is linearly decreasing, and the amount of interest paid in the kth installment, denoted by I_k, is

$$I_k = \text{Total amount of interest paid} \times \frac{m+1-k}{S_m} = Lnr \times \frac{m+1-k}{S_m}.$$

(a) Show that

$$\sum_{k=1}^{m} I_k = Lnr.$$

(b) Show that if you decide to pay off the loan at the kth payment, the interest rebate, which is defined as the unpaid interest saved, is

$$R = \frac{(12n - k)(12n - k + 1)Lrn}{12n(12n + 1)}.$$

Note that if we apply the above rule to a 1-year loan, $m = 12$ and $S_{12} = 78$. That is why this method is called the "Rule of 78".

6   Bonds and Bond Pricing

A bond is a contract/certificate of debt for which the issuer promises to pay the holder a sequence of interest payments over a specified period of time, and to repay the principal at a specified terminal date. There are various types of bonds with different features: coupon-paying bonds, zero-coupon bonds, inflation-indexed bonds, callable bonds, etc. Different risks are involved in investing in different types of bonds.

In a bond transaction the investor determines the price in order to achieve a fair rate of return to compensate for the risks. We introduce three formulas for pricing a bond, namely, the basic formula, the premium/discount formula, and the Makeham formula. Bonds are loans from bondholders to issuers. Analogous to the concept of loan amortization, methods of constructing bond amortization schedules are discussed. When bonds are traded between two coupon-payment dates we need to extend the pricing formulas to include the accrued interest. We distinguish between the quoted price and the purchase price of a bond, with the difference being the accrued interest.

We will also discuss the pricing of a callable bond, which is a complex problem due to the uncertainty about the call event. Finally, while much of this chapter assumes a flat term structure for the purpose of pricing a bond, we show how to extend the pricing formula to the case of a known but nonflat term structure.

Learning Objectives

- *Types, features and risks of bond investments*
- *Formulas for pricing a bond*
- *Construction of bond amortization schedules*
- *Pricing a bond between two coupon-payment dates*
- *Callable bonds and their pricing*
- *Price of a bond under a nonflat term structure*

6.1 Basic Concepts

A **bond** is a contract/certificate of debt for which the issuer promises to pay the holder a sequence of interest payments over a specified period of time, and to repay the principal at a specified terminal date (called the **maturity** or **redemption date**).

Many entities issue bonds. National governments, provincial (or state) governments, governmental agencies and large corporations are common bond issuers. Governments issue bonds to fund public programs, infrastructure projects or even general government expenditures. Corporations issue bonds for expansion, acquisitions, investments in projects or other uses.

There are many risks involved in investing in bonds. We summarize below some of these risks.

Interest-rate risk: Most bonds are **coupon-paying bonds**. Bond investors receive interest payments periodically before the redemption date. The term "coupon-paying" is used because bonds once came with a book of coupons, which the holder had to clip and present to the issuer for interest payment. Typically, coupon payments are constant during the life of the bond. They depend on the **coupon rate**, which is usually fixed at the issue of the bond. After the investor purchases the bond, if the prevailing interest rate rises, the price of the bond will fall as the bond is less attractive to the investors. In general, the price of a bond changes in the opposite direction to the change in interest rate. This is called interest-rate risk.

Default risk: Default risk is the risk that the bond issuer is unable to make interest and/or redemption payments. Most investors consider bonds issued by national governments of modern industrialized countries to be default free. On the other hand, bonds issued by corporations, provincial governments and other institutions may not be default free. Based on the bond issuer's financial strength, bond rating agencies provide a rating (a measure of the quality and safety) of the bond. The evaluation by a rating service provider indicates the likelihood that the bond issuer will be able to meet scheduled interest and principal repayments. Bonds with strong credit standing are called **investment-grade bonds**, while bonds with weak credit standing are called **junk bonds** (a riskier class).

Reinvestment risk: For coupon-paying bonds, investors receive interest payments periodically before the redemption date. The reinvestment of these interest payments (sometimes referred to as interest-on-interest) depends on the prevailing interest-rate level at the time of reinvestment. Volatility in the reinvestment rate of return due to changes in market interest rates is called reinvestment risk. **Zero-coupon bonds** do not have reinvestment risk, as they do not have periodic coupon payments. Investors purchase a zero-coupon bond at a discount to its redemption value and receive a single redemption payment at a specified time in the future.

Call risk: The issuer of a **callable bond** has the right to redeem the bond prior to its maturity date at a preset **call price** under certain conditions, which are specified at the bond issue date and are known to the investors. The issuer will typically consider calling a bond if it is paying a higher coupon rate than the prevailing market interest rate. The **call risk** has three impacts on a bond investor: (a) the cash-flow pattern becomes uncertain, (b) the investor becomes exposed to reinvestment risk because she may receive redemption payments before maturity, and (c) the capital appreciation potential of the bond will be reduced, because bond issuers typically call the bond when its market price is higher than the call price. Callable bonds often carry a **call protection** provision. It specifies a period of time during which the bond cannot be called.

Inflation risk: Inflation risk arises because of the uncertainty in the real value (i.e., purchasing power) of the cash flows from a bond due to inflation. **Inflation-indexed bonds** are popular among investors who do not wish to bear the inflation risk. An indexed bond has a fixed coupon rate (just like a conventional bond), while its principal value may be adjusted upward or downward periodically based on a defined inflation index (usually the adjustment dates are set at the coupon-payment dates). In this manner, the interest income is also adjusted for inflation. However, the principal value of the bond may be reduced during the indexed bond's term if there is deflation.

In addition to the aforementioned, there may be other risks in investing in bonds. For examples, **market risk** is the risk that the bond market as a whole declines. **Event risk** arises when some events occur and they have negative impacts on a specific class of bonds. **Liquidity risk** is the risk that investors may have difficulty finding a buyer when they want to sell and may be forced to sell at a significant discount to the bond's fair value.

6.2   Bond Evaluation

A bond is a formal contract between the issuer and the investor. The following features of a bond are agreed upon at the issue date.

Face Value: Face value, denoted by F, also known as **par** or **principal** value, is the amount printed on the bond. This value is the base for the calculation of the amount of periodic interest payments.

Redemption Value: A bond's redemption value or **maturity value**, denoted by C, is the amount that the issuer promises to pay on the redemption date. In most cases the redemption value is the same as the face value.

Time to Maturity: Time to Maturity refers to the length of time before the redemption value is repaid to the investor. It may be as short as a few months, or as long as 30 years (or even longer).

Coupon Rate: The coupon rate, denoted by r, is the rate at which the bond pays interest on its face value at regular time intervals until the redemption date. For bonds issued in the European bond markets, coupon payments are often made once a year. However, in the North American bond markets, the usual practice is for the issuer to pay the coupon in two semiannual installments per year.

In this chapter we only consider the financial mathematics of default-free bonds. In other words, we assume that the issuer will pay all interest and principal repayments as scheduled, and defaults on such obligations will not occur. Before purchasing a bond the prospective investors need to consider several factors in relation to the bond features. These include: (a) the number of coupon payment periods, n, from the **date of purchase** (or the **settlement date**) to the maturity date, (b) the purchase price, P, and (c) the rate of return, i, of the investment (called the **yield rate**). The yield rate reflects the current market conditions and is determined by the market forces, giving investors a fair compensation in bearing the risks of investing in the bond. We assume that r and i are measured per coupon-payment period. Thus, for semiannual coupon bonds, r and i are the rate of interest per half-year.

The price of a bond is the sum of the present values of all coupon payments plus the present value of the redemption value due at maturity. We assume that a coupon has just been paid, and we are interested in pricing the bond after this payment. Figure 6.1 illustrates the cash-flow pattern of a typical coupon bond.

Figure 6.1: Cash-flow pattern of a coupon-paying bond with n coupons

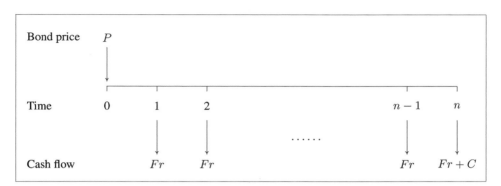

We shall assume that the term structure is flat, so that cash flows at all times are discounted at the same yield rate i. Thus, the *fair price* P of the bond is given by the following **basic price formula**

$$P = (Fr)a_{\overline{n}|} + Cv^n, \tag{6.1}$$

where the interest and annuity functions are calculated at the yield rate i.

Example 6.1: The following shows the results of a government bond auction:

Type of Bond	*Government bond*
Issue Date	*February 15, 2010*
Maturity Date	*February 15, 2040*
Coupon Rate	*4.500% payable semiannually*
Yield Rate	*4.530% convertible semiannually*

Assume that the redemption value of the bond is the same as the face value, which is $100. Find the price of the bond.

Solution: This is a 30-year bond and we can use the basic price formula (6.1) with

$$
\begin{aligned}
F &= 100, \\
C &= 100, \\
r &= \frac{0.045}{2} = 0.0225, \\
i &= \frac{0.0453}{2} = 0.02265, \\
n &= 60,
\end{aligned}
$$

to calculate the price of the bond, which is

$$
\begin{aligned}
P &= (Fr)a_{\overline{n}|} + Cv^n \\
&= 2.25a_{\overline{60}|0.02265} + 100(1.02265)^{-60} \\
&= \$99.51.
\end{aligned}
$$

Example 6.2: The following shows the information of a government bond traded in the secondary market:

Type of Bond	*Government bond*
Issue Date	*June 15, 2005*
Date of Purchase	*June 15, 2009*
Maturity Date	*June 15, 2020*
Coupon Rate	*4.2% payable semiannually*
Yield Rate	*4.0% convertible semiannually*

Assume that the redemption value of the bond is the same as the face value, which is $100. Find the purchase price of the bond immediately after its 8th coupon payment on June 15, 2009.

Solution: This is a 15-year bond at issue but there are only 22 remaining coupon-payment periods after its 8th coupon payment on June 15, 2009. We use the basic price formula (6.1) with

$$
\begin{aligned}
F &= 100, \\
C &= 100, \\
r &= \frac{0.042}{2} = 0.021, \\
i &= \frac{0.040}{2} = 0.020, \\
n &= 22,
\end{aligned}
$$

to obtain

$$
\begin{aligned}
P &= (Fr)a_{\overline{n}|} + Cv^n \\
&= 2.1a_{\overline{22}|0.02} + 100(1.02)^{-22} \\
&= \$101.77.
\end{aligned}
$$

Example 6.3: Find the price of a 18-month zero-coupon bond with redemption value of $100. The bond is bought to yield 4.24% convertible semiannually.

Solution: It should be noted that the basic price formula (6.1) can be used for zero-coupon bonds with $r = 0$. We obtain, with $i = 2.12\%$ and $n = 3$

$$
\begin{aligned}
P &= Cv^n \\
&= 100(1.0212)^{-3} \\
&= \$93.90.
\end{aligned}
$$

Example 6.4: Show that

$$
P = K + \frac{g}{i}(C - K),
$$

where $K = Cv^n$ is the present value of the redemption payment and $g = \frac{Fr}{C}$ is the **modified coupon rate**.

Solution: We start with (6.1) to obtain

$$
\begin{aligned}
P &= (Fr)a_{\overline{n}|} + Cv^n \\
&= (Fr)\left(\frac{1 - v^n}{i}\right) + K \\
&= Cg\left(\frac{1 - v^n}{i}\right) + K \\
&= \frac{g}{i}(C - Cv^n) + K \\
&= \frac{g}{i}(C - K) + K.
\end{aligned} \tag{6.2}
$$

This formula is called the **Makeham formula**.

6.3 Bond Amortization Schedule

We further develop the basic bond price formula as follows:

$$
\begin{aligned}
P &= (Fr)a_{\overline{n}|} + Cv^n \\
&= (Fr)a_{\overline{n}|} + C(1 - ia_{\overline{n}|}) \\
&= C + (Fr - Ci)a_{\overline{n}|}.
\end{aligned} \tag{6.3}
$$

The above equation is often called the **premium/discount formula** because

$$P - C = (Fr - Ci)a_{\overline{n}|} \tag{6.4}$$

represents the bond **premium** (when it is positive) or the bond **discount** (when it is negative). In other words, if the selling price of a bond is larger than its redemption value, the bond is said to be traded at a premium of value $P - C = (Fr - Ci)a_{\overline{n}|}$. On the other hand, if the selling price of a bond is less than its redemption value, the bond is said to be traded at a discount of amount $C - P = (Ci - Fr)a_{\overline{n}|}$. In most cases the redemption value is the same as the face value (i.e., $C = F$), so that the bond is traded at

Premium:	$P - F = F(r - i)a_{\overline{n}|}$,	if $r > i$,
Par:	$P - F = 0$,	if $r = i$,
Discount:	$F - P = F(i - r)a_{\overline{n}|}$,	if $i > r$.

Premium/discount arises in a bond trading transaction when the prevailing required yield rate i is different from the fixed coupon rate r, and the investor adjusts the price to reflect such differences.

In the bond premium situation the bondholder pays more than the face value. The premium represents an amount that the investor will not receive at maturity. This paid-in-advance premium (which is an asset for the bondholder) will be refunded (amortized) periodically from the coupon payments over the life of the bond. There are two commonly used methods to amortize the bond premium, namely, the **straight-line method** and the **effective interest method**. We shall only consider the effective interest method, which is analogous to the loan amortization schedule in Chapter 5.

As an illustrative example, we consider a $1,000 face value (same as the redemption value) 3-year bond with semiannual coupons at the rate of 5% per annum. The current required rate of return i for the bond is 4% convertible semiannually. The price of the bond is

$$\begin{aligned} P &= (1{,}000 \times 0.025)a_{\overline{6}|0.02} + 1{,}000(1.02)^{-6} \\ &= \$1{,}028.01, \end{aligned}$$

and the premium is $28.01. In each half-year period a $25 coupon payment is received. This amount is larger than the interest earned at the yield rate based on the book value, which is $1,028.01 \times 0.02 = \$20.56$ for the first half-year. The remaining part of the coupon payment is then used to reduce the unamortized premium. We can construct a bond premium amortization schedule based on this principle. The result is shown in Table 6.1.

Table 6.1: A bond premium amortization schedule

Half-year	Coupon payment	Effective interest earned	Amortized amount of premium	Book value
0				$1{,}028.01^a$
1	25.00^b	20.56^c	4.44^d	$1{,}023.57^e$
2	25.00	20.47	4.53	1,019.04
3	25.00	20.38	4.62	1,014.42
4	25.00	20.29	4.71	1,009.71
5	25.00	20.19	4.81	1,004.90
6	25.00	20.10	4.90	1,000.00
Total	150.00	121.99	28.01	

The details of the computation are as follows:

[a] The purchase price is the beginning balance of the book value.

[b] The coupon payment is $1{,}000 \times \frac{0.05}{2} = \$25.00$.

[c] Effective interest earned in the first half-year is $1{,}028.01 \times \frac{0.04}{2} = \$20.56$.

[d] Amortized amount of premium in the first half-year is $25.00 - 20.56 = \$4.44$.

[e] The book value after amortization is $1{,}028.01 - 4.44 = \$1{,}023.57$.

The rest of the computations follow similarly.

The bond amortization schedule is useful to bondholders for accounting and taxation purposes. In some countries the bond interest income is taxable. In the above example, however, the $25 coupon payment received each period should not be fully taxable. The actual (taxable) amount of interest earned in each period is computed in the schedule (the third column in Table 6.1). Furthermore, the book values, which should be entered into the bondholder's balance sheet at the end of each period, can also be obtained from the amortization table.

In the bond discount situation the bondholder purchases the bond for less than the face value. The discount represents an amount that must be paid by the issuer to the investor at the time of maturity. The discount (a form of pre-paid interest) will be amortized periodically from the coupon payments over the life of the bond.

We re-visit the illustrative example. For the $1,000 face value 3-year bond with semiannual coupons at the rate of 5% per annum, we now assume that the required rate of return is 6% convertible semiannually. The purchase price of this bond is $972.91, and the discount is $27.09. We construct a bond discount amortization schedule in Table 6.2. The computational steps follow closely those of Table 6.1.

Table 6.2:   A bond discount amortization schedule

Half-year	Coupon payment	Effective interest earned	Amortized amount of discount	Book value
0				972.91
1	25.00	29.19	−4.19	977.10
2	25.00	29.31	−4.31	981.41
3	25.00	29.44	−4.44	985.86
4	25.00	29.58	−4.58	990.43
5	25.00	29.71	−4.71	995.15
6	25.00	29.85	−4.85	1,000.00
Total	150.00	177.09	−27.09	

In general, the redemption value may not be the same as the face value (i.e., $C \neq F$). From equation (6.4), we obtain

$$\text{Premium:} \quad P - C = C(g - i)a_{\overline{n}|}, \qquad \text{if } g > i,$$
$$\text{Discount:} \quad C - P = C(i - g)a_{\overline{n}|}, \qquad \text{if } i > g,$$

where $g = \frac{Fr}{C}$ is the modified coupon rate as defined in Example 6.4. It should be noted that g is the coupon interest per unit amount of the redemption value, while r is the coupon interest per unit amount of the face value. A general bond amortization schedule for a n-period bond, with redemption value C, modified coupon rate g and yield rate i is given in Table 6.3.

Table 6.3:   Formulas for a general bond amortization schedule

Half-year	Coupon payment	Effective interest earned	Amortized amount	Book value
0				$P = C + C(g - i)a_{\overline{n}|}$
1	Cg	$i[C + C(g - i)a_{\overline{n}|}]$	$C(g - i)v^n$	$C + C(g - i)a_{\overline{n-1}|}$
2	Cg	$i[C + C(g - i)a_{\overline{n-1}|}]$	$C(g - i)v^{n-1}$	$C + C(g - i)a_{\overline{n-2}|}$
$\vdots$	$\vdots$	$\vdots$	$\vdots$	$\vdots$
t	Cg	$i[C + C(g - i)a_{\overline{n-t+1}|}]$	$C(g - i)v^{n-t+1}$	$C + C(g - i)a_{\overline{n-t}|}$
$\vdots$	$\vdots$	$\vdots$	$\vdots$	$\vdots$
n	Cg	$i[C + C(g - i)a_{\overline{1}|}]$	$C(g - i)v$	$C + C(g - i)a_{\overline{0}|} = C$
Total	nCg	$nCg - C(g - i)a_{\overline{n}|}$	$C(g - i)a_{\overline{n}|}$	

Note that the amortized amount $C(g - i)v^{n-t+1}$ at time t is positive for a premium bond ($g > i$) and negative for a discount bond ($i > g$). The book value at time t is equal to the book value at time $t - 1$ *minus* the amortized amount. Thus, the book value decreases through time for a premium bond and increases through time for a discount bond, and its value finally becomes the redemption value at maturity.

Example 6.5: Find the price of a $1,000 face value 15-year bond with redemption value of $1,080 and coupon rate of 4.32% payable semiannually. The bond is bought to yield 5.00% convertible semiannually. Show the first 5 entries, as well as entries of the 20th and 30th half-year periods, of its bond amortization schedule.

Solution: Using the bond price formula (6.3), we have

$$
\begin{aligned}
P &= C + (Fr - Ci)a_{\overline{n}|} \\
&= 1{,}080 + (21.6 - 27.0)a_{\overline{30}|0.025} \\
&= \$966.98.
\end{aligned}
$$

Entries of the amortization schedule, using formulas in Table 6.3, can be computed as in Table 6.4.

Table 6.4: Amortization schedule for Example 6.5

Half-year	Coupon payment	Effective interest earned	Amortized amount	Book value
0				966.98
1	21.60	24.17	−2.57	969.55
2	21.60	24.24	−2.64	972.19
3	21.60	24.30	−2.70	974.89
4	21.60	24.37	−2.77	977.67
⋮	⋮	⋮	⋮	⋮
20	21.60[a]	25.72[b]	−4.12[c]	1,032.74[d]
⋮	⋮	⋮	⋮	⋮
30	21.60	26.87	−5.27	1,080.00

The details of the computation are as follows:

[a] The modified coupon rate is $g = \frac{Fr}{C} = 2\%$ per half-year period. Coupon payment is $Cg = 1{,}080(0.02) = \$21.60$, and it is the same as $Fr = 1{,}000(0.0216) = \$21.60$, where r is $\frac{0.0432}{2} = 2.16\%$ per half-year period.

[b] Effective interest earned in the 20th half-year is $0.025[1{,}080 + 1{,}080(0.02 - 0.025)a_{\overline{11}|0.025}] = \$25.72$.

^{c} Amortized amount in the 20th half-year is $1{,}080(0.02 - 0.025)(1.025)^{-11} =$ $-\$4.12$. A negative amortized amount represents a discount situation. Alternatively, this is equal to $21.60 - 25.72$.

^{d} The ending balance (after the 20th coupon payment) of the book value is $1{,}080 + 1{,}080(0.02 - 0.025)a_{\overline{10}|0.025} = \$1{,}032.74$.

The rest of the computations follow similarly.

6.4   Valuation between Coupon-Payment Dates

The pricing formulas discussed so far are applicable to a bond at its issue date or at a date immediately after a coupon payment. However, bond transactions may occur any time before maturity. We now consider the pricing of a bond traded between coupon-payment dates.

In practice the price of a bond is stated as a percentage (e.g., 90.125, or 90.125%) of its face value, which is called the **quoted price** (or the **clean price**). When a bond is purchased between the coupon-payment dates, interest is earned by the seller of the bond from the last coupon-payment date, which is referred to as the **accrued interest**. In addition to the quoted price, the purchaser of the bond has to pay the accrued interest to the seller since the seller will not be entitled to any amount of the next coupon payment. The accrued interest is added to the quoted price to determine the **purchase price** (also called the **dirty price** or **invoice price**), i.e.,

$$\text{Purchase price} = \text{quoted price} + \text{accrued interest.} \qquad (6.5)$$

In a bond transaction the purchaser seeks a fair yield rate to compensate the risks of investing in the bond. The yield is often determined by the market forces and other economic factors. Thus, the yield earned by the purchaser is likely to be different from the seller's original yield.

Let us denote k as the time immediately after the kth coupon payment. We consider a bond traded in between two coupon-payment dates k and $k + 1$, at time $k + t$, where t measures the length of time since k as a fraction of the time between k and $k + 1$. While there are different market practices in defining t, we adopt the **actual/actual day count** convention and define t as

$$t = \frac{\text{Number of days since time } k}{\text{Number of days between } k \text{ and } k + 1}, \qquad (6.6)$$

so that $0 < t < 1$.

Figure 6.2: Value of a bond between coupon dates

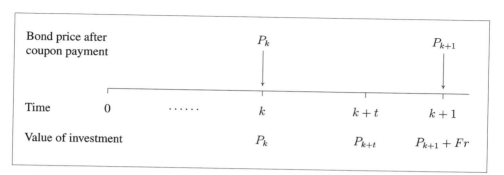

We denote the bond price at time k and $k + 1$ by P_k and P_{k+1}, respectively. These prices are the bond values after the coupon payments. For an investor who purchased the bond after the coupon payment at time k and held it till time $k + 1$, the value of her investment in the period is illustrated in Figure 6.2. If the yield rate remains unchanged from time k to $k + 1$, we have the following relationship

$$P_{k+t} = P_k(1 + i)^t = (P_{k+1} + Fr)(1 + i)^{-(1-t)}.$$ (6.7)

As shown in (6.5), there are two components in the purchase price P_{k+t}, namely the quoted price and the accrued interest. The accrued interest is the income earned, and the quoted price is the book value of the bond. For accounting purposes, these two items should be entered differently in the bondholder's financial statements. Therefore, it is important to decompose P_{k+t} into the two components. In common practice, the simple-interest method is used to calculate the accrued interest at time $k + t$, denoted by I_{k+t}. Using the simple-interest formula, we have

$$I_{k+t} = t(Fr).$$ (6.8)

The book value (quoted price) at time t, denoted by B_{k+t}, is then given by

$$B_{k+t} = P_{k+t} - I_{k+t}.$$ (6.9)

Example 6.6: Assume that the coupon dates for the government bond in Example 6.2 are June 15 and December 15 of each year. On August 18, 2009, an investor purchased the bond to yield 3.8% convertible semiannually. Find the purchase price, accrued interest and the quoted price of the bond at the date of purchase, based on a face value of 100.

Solution: We have $i = \frac{0.038}{2} = 1.9\%$, so that the values of P_k and P_{k+1} are

$$\begin{aligned}
P_k &= 2.1a_{\overline{22}|0.019} + 100(1.019)^{-22} = 103.5690, \\
P_{k+1} &= 2.1a_{\overline{21}|0.019} + 100(1.019)^{-21} = 103.4368.
\end{aligned}$$

The number of days between June 15, 2009 and August 18, 2009 is 64 and the number of days between the two coupon dates in 2009 is 183. Therefore $t = \frac{64}{183}$. Hence,

$$P_{k+t} = P_k(1+i)^t = 103.5690(1.019)^{\frac{64}{183}} = 104.2529,$$

or equivalently,

$$P_{k+t} = v^{1-t}(P_{k+1} + Fr) = (1.019)^{-\frac{119}{183}}(103.4368 + 2.1) = 104.2529.$$

The accrued interest is

$$I_{k+t} = t(Fr) = 0.7344,$$

and the quoted price (book value) is

$$B_{k+t} = P_{k+t} - I_{k+t} = 104.2529 - 0.7344 = 103.5185.$$

Figure 6.3 plots the values of P_{k+t}, I_{k+t} and B_{k+t} in Example 6.6. When $k = 8$, $P_k = 103.5690$, and P_{k+t} rises from P_k to $P_{k+1} + Fr = 105.5368$ just before the coupon payment at $k = 9$. Then, P_{k+1} drops by the amount $Fr = 2.1$ after the coupon payment. This cycle is repeated in each coupon period. On the other hand, the book value moves downward steadily (the bond was bought at a premium), approaching the redemption value at maturity. It should be noted that P_{k+t} in (6.7) is a non-linear function of t. However, the curvature of P_{k+t} is usually very small (due to fractional values of t and low rates of interest), leading to a function which is almost linear over time. Figure 6.3 depicts the schematic relationship between B, P and I.

The Excel function **PRICE** can be used to compute the quoted price of a bond between coupon-payment dates. Its specification is as follows:

Excel function: PRICE (smt,mty,crt,yld,rdv,frq,basis)

smt = settlement date
mty = maturity date
crt = coupon rate of interest per annum
yld = annual yield rate
rdv = redemption value per 100 face value
frq = number of coupon payments per year
basis = day count, 30/360 if omitted (or set to 0) and actual/actual if set to 1
Output = quoted price of bond at settlement date per 100 face value

---

The default for the input "basis" is the 30/360 convention. Under this convention, every month has 30 days and every year has 360 days. If selected, this convention is used to compute the number of days between two coupon-payment dates, as well as the number of days between the last coupon-payment date and the settlement date. Exhibit 6.1 illustrates the use of the function **PRICE** to compute the quoted bond price in Example 6.6.

Figure 6.3:   Bond price between coupon-payment dates

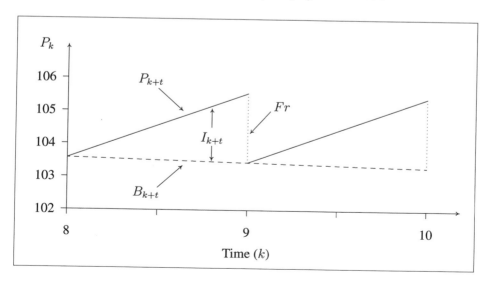

Exhibit 6.1:   Excel solution of Example 6.6

	File	Edit	View	Insert	Format	Tools	Data	Window	Help
	A5		▼	*fx*	=Price(A1,A2,A3,A4,100,2,1)				
	A		B	C	D	E			
1	8/18/2009								
2	6/15/2020								
3	0.042								
4	0.038								
5	103.51852								
6									

6.5 Callable Bonds

Callable bonds are bonds that can be redeemed by the issuer prior to the bonds' maturity date. Investors whose bonds are called are paid a specified **call price**, which was fixed at the issue date of the bond. The call price may be the bond's face value or higher. The difference between the call price and the face value is called the **call premium**. If a bond is called between coupon dates, the issuer must pay the investor accrued interest in addition to the call price.

Only the issuer (not the bondholders) has the right to call the bond before maturity. An issuer may choose to call a bond when the current interest rate drops below the coupon rate of the bond. In this circumstance, the issuer will save money by paying off the bond and issuing another bond at a lower interest rate. As a result, investors of callable bonds often require a higher yield to compensate for the call risk as compared to non-callable bonds.

In order to attract investors, some callable bonds offer a **call protection period**. The issuer is not allowed to call the bond before the ending date of the protection period. The **first call date** is the date after which the bond is fully callable.

The call option gives the right (not the obligation) to the issuer to redeem the bond at any time after the first call date. Theoretically, there is an optimal call date for the issuer to maximize the call benefit. However, in addition to the call benefit, there are many other factors (such as transaction costs, possible negative impact on the company's reputation and competition, etc.) affecting the decision of the issuer to make a call. Therefore, it is difficult to predict when the issuer will call.

The uncertainty of the possible call date is the main difficulty in pricing a callable bond. Here we consider a defensive pricing approach for the investor. Under this approach, an investor assumes that the issuer will call the bond at a date which will maximize the call benefit.

Assuming the yield rate remains unchanged, if a callable bond is traded at a discount and the call price is fixed at the bond's redemption value, the optimal call date for the issuer is at maturity. This can be easily seen by checking the bond amortization schedule. For example, in Table 6.2 the issuer makes $25 coupon payment per period, which is less than the effective interest to the investor. Thus, the issuer should keep this advantage as long as possible, even if the bond is callable.

On the other hand, if a callable bond is traded at a premium and the call price is fixed at the bond's redemption value, the optimal call date for the issuer is the first call date. In Table 6.1, the issuer makes $25 coupon payment per period, which is more than the effective interest to the investor. If this bond is callable, the issuer should cut short this disadvantage as soon as possible.

In general, when the call price is not a fixed constant but varies in a pre-fixed relation with the possible call dates, it is not easy to determine the issuer's optimal call date. In this situation, we can apply the alternative (but equivalent) interpretation of the defensive pricing approach. Under this strategy, the investor will pay the lowest price among the prices calculated by assuming all possible call dates.

Example 6.7: Assume that the bond in Table 6.1 is callable and the first call date is the date immediately after the 4th coupon payment. Find the price of the bond for the yield to be at least 4% compounded semiannually.

Solution: Assuming the first call date is the maturity date of the bond, the price of the bond is

$$25a_{\overline{4}|0.02} + 1{,}000(1.02)^{-4} = \$1{,}019.04.$$

We further compute the prices of the bond assuming all other possible call dates, namely, after the 5th and 6th coupon payments, with respectively prices

$$25a_{\overline{5}|0.02} + 1{,}000(1.02)^{-5} = \$1{,}023.57$$

and

$$25a_{\overline{6}|0.02} + 1{,}000(1.02)^{-6} = \$1{,}028.01.$$

Thus, the price of the bond is the lowest among all possible values, i.e., $1,019.04.

Example 6.8: Consider a $1,000 face value 15-year bond with coupon rate of 4.0% convertible semiannually. The bond is callable and the first call date is the date immediately after the 15th coupon payment. Assume that the issuer will only call the bond at a date immediately after the nth coupon ($15 \le n \le 30$) and the call price (i.e., redemption value) is

$$C = \begin{cases} 1{,}000, & \text{if } 15 \le n \le 20, \\ 1{,}000 + 10(n - 20), & \text{if } 20 < n \le 30. \end{cases}$$

Find the price of the bond if the investor wants to achieve a yield of at least 5% compounded semiannually.

Solution: First, we compute the prices of the bond assuming all possible call dates, with $r = 0.02$, $i = 0.025$, $F = 1,000$ and the value of C following the given call price formula. The results are given in Table 6.5.

Table 6.5: Results for Example 6.8

n	Redemption value C	Price
15	1,000	938.09
16	1,000	934.72
17	1,000	931.44
18	1,000	928.23
19	1,000	925.11
20	**1,000**	**922.05**
21	1,010	925.03
22	1,020	927.79
23	1,030	930.34
24	1,040	932.69
25	1,050	934.85
26	1,060	936.82
27	1,070	938.62
28	1,080	940.25
29	1,090	941.71
30	1,100	943.02

Thus, the minimum price is $922.05, which assumes the bond will be called after the 20th coupon payment. This is the price of the callable bond a defensive investor is willing to pay if she wants to obtain a yield of at least 5% compounded semiannually.

6.6 Bond Pricing under a General Term Structure

The basic price formula in equation (6.1) assumes a flat term structure such that the yield rate for all cash flows (coupons and redemption payment) is the same. In the case when the term structure is not flat the pricing formula has to be modified. Following the principle that the fair price of the bond is the present value of the cash flows, we can compute the price of the bond as the sum of the present values of the coupon and redemption payments.

We consider a bond with n coupon payments of amounts $C_1, \cdots, C_n$, and re-demption at time n (in number of coupon-payment periods) with redemption value C. Let i_j^S be the spot rate of interest for cash flows due in j years and r be the rate of interest per coupon payment. To compute the price of the bond, we sum the present values of the coupons and the redemption value. For the case of an annual level-coupon bond, the price P is given by

$$
\begin{aligned}
P &= \sum_{j=1}^{n} \frac{C_j}{(1+i_j^S)^j} + \frac{C}{(1+i_n^S)^n} \\
&= Fr \sum_{j=1}^{n} \frac{1}{(1+i_j^S)^j} + \frac{C}{(1+i_n^S)^n}.
\end{aligned}
\tag{6.10}
$$

For a semiannual level-coupon bond, the pricing formula is

$$
P = Fr \sum_{j=1}^{n} \frac{1}{\left(1+\dfrac{i_j^S}{2}\right)^j} + \frac{C}{\left(1+\dfrac{i_n^S}{2}\right)^n}.
\tag{6.11}
$$

Example 6.9: Consider a \$100 par bond with coupon rate of 4.0% per annum paid semiannually. The spot rates of interest in the market are given by

j (years)	0.5	1.0	1.5	2.0	2.5	3.0	3.5	4.0	4.5	5.0
i_j^S (%)	3.0	3.0	3.5	3.5	4.0	4.0	4.5	4.5	5.0	5.0

Find the price of the bond if it matures in (a) 3 years, and (b) 5 years.

Solution: For (a), the price of the bond is

$$
\begin{aligned}
P &= 2\left[\frac{1}{1.015} + \frac{1}{1.015^2} + \frac{1}{1.0175^3} + \frac{1}{1.0175^4} + \frac{1}{1.025^5} + \frac{1}{1.025^6}\right] + \frac{100}{1.025^6} \\
&= \$100.0608.
\end{aligned}
$$

Similarly, for (b), the price of the bond is

$$
\begin{aligned}
P &= 2\left[\frac{1}{1.015} + \frac{1}{1.015^2} + \cdots + \frac{1}{1.0225^8} + \frac{1}{1.025^9} + \frac{1}{1.025^{10}}\right] + \frac{100}{1.025^{10}} \\
&= \$95.9328.
\end{aligned}
$$

Note that we have a premium bond for the case of (a), with the price higher than the redemption value. This is due to the fact that the spot rates of interest are less than the coupon rate of interest for cash flows of maturity less than 3 years. On the other hand, for the case of (b) we have a discount bond, with the price lower than the redemption value. As the spot rates of interest for cash flows of maturity of more than 3 years are higher than the coupon rate, the present value contributions of the cash flows beyond 3 years are lower, causing the price of the bond to drop.

Hence, when the term structure is not flat the premium/discount relationship of a bond with respect to its redemption value may vary with the time to maturity even for bonds with the same coupon rate of interest.

6.7 Summary

1. There are many risks involved in investing in a bond, such as interest-rate risk, default risk, reinvestment risk, call risk, inflation risk, market risk, event risk and liquidity risk.

2. A typical coupon bond has definite (in terms of both timing and amount) cash-flow payments. The price of a bond can be calculated by discounting all the future cash flows by a specified interest rate, called the yield rate, which is determined by the prevailing market conditions.

3. Premium/discount arises in a bond transaction when the yield rate is different from the coupon rate. In a bond amortization schedule, each coupon payment is used to offset the effective interest incurred in the period, with the balance (positive or negative) used to offset the unamortized premium or discount.

4. In addition to the quoted price, the purchaser of the bond has to pay the accrued interest to the seller, since the seller will not be entitled to the next coupon payment. The problem of accrued interest arises when the bond is traded between two coupon-payment dates. The accrued interest is added to the quoted price to determine the purchase price.

5. A callable bond gives the issuer the right to redeem the bond after the first call date. As a result, investors of callable bonds require a higher return to compensate for the call risk as compared to non-callable bonds. In a defensive strategy, an investor would pay the lowest price among the prices of the callable bond calculated by assuming all possible call dates.

6. When the term structure is not flat, the basic bond price formula does not hold. The principle of pricing the bond as the present value of the coupon and redemption payments still applies, and the present values are evaluated based on the market term structure.

Exercises

6.1 Bond is classified as a fixed-income security, which is a large class of investment vehicles including mortgage loan and certificate of deposit (CD). Explain why it is so.

6.2 Find the price of a 6-year $100 par value bond bearing 8% annual coupon, redeemable at $103 with a yield of $2\%, 3\%, \cdots, 10\%$ and 11%. Give a rough sketch of the bond price versus the yield rate. What can you observe?

6.3 State two factors that a rating agency would use to determine the rating of a bond.

6.4 Which one of the following statements is true?

(a) A zero-coupon bond has no default risk.

(b) A zero-coupon bond has no market risk.

(c) A zero-coupon bond has no liquidity risk.

(d) A zero-coupon bond has no reinvestment risk.

(e) A zero-coupon bond has no inflation risk.

6.5 Which of the following statement(s) is/are true?

(a) Junk bonds have higher yield than government bonds.

(b) Junk bonds are too risky for individual investors.

(c) Junk bonds are issued by companies with deteriorating credit rating.

6.6 Construct a bond amortization schedule for a $100 par value 2-year bond with 7% coupons paid semiannually, redeemable at par and bought to yield 4% per annum.

6.7 The following shows the information of a government bond traded in the secondary market.

Type of Bond	Government bond
Issue Date	May 16, 2006
Maturity Date	May 16, 2016
Face Value	$100
Redemption Value	$108
Coupon Rate	5% payable semiannually
Yield Rate	8% convertible semiannually

Construct the bond amortization schedule for year 5 and year 6 (i.e., for the 9th coupon through the 12th coupon).

6.8 Consider the bond in Exercise 6.7 and assume the coupon dates are May 16 and November 16 each year. On September 20, 2010, an investor purchased the bond to yield 7% convertible semiannually. Find the purchase price, the accrued interest and the quoted price of the bond at the date of purchase.

6.9 Find the coupon rate of a 5-year $100 par semiannual coupon bond redeemable at par, yielding 5.7% convertible semiannually, if its price is the same as that of a zero-coupon bond with face value $100 maturing in 5 years and yielding 3.5% compounded annually.

6.10 Two $1,000 par value bonds both with 6% coupon rate payable annually are selling at $1,000. Bond A matures in 3 years while bond B matures in 10 years. Find the price of the two bonds if the market interest rate goes up or down by 1 percentage point. Which bond is more sensitive to the change in the prevailing interest rate?

6.11 You own a $1,000 face value 10-year bond with semiannual coupons that will mature in 6 years. Immediately after receiving the 8th coupon of $46, you sell the bond and purchase another newly issued $1,000 face value 10-year bond with semiannual coupons of $47.5 each. Given that the prevailing market interest rate is $r^{(2)} = 9\%$ and the bond you originally owned is redeemable at 104%, find the redemption value of the new bond that you purchase.

6.12 Fill in the missing values of the following bond amortization schedule for a $100 par value 2-year bond with semiannual coupons:

Half-year	Coupon payment	Effective interest earned	Amortized amount of premium	Book value
0				
1				
2				94.26
3			−1.05	95.31
4		3.34	−1.09	96.40

6.13 Samurai bonds are yen-denominated bonds issued in Japan by non-Japanese companies. State two possible reasons for non-Japanese companies to issue Samurai bonds.

6.14 Fill in the missing values of the following excerpt of a bond amortization schedule for a $100 par value 10-year bond with semiannual coupons and redeemable at par:

Half-year	Coupon payment	Effective interest earned	Amortized amount of premium	Book value
8				
9				
10		2.62	0.38	104.38
11				

6.15 The following shows the information of an investment-grade bond when it was issued in 2002.

Type of Bond	*Corporate bond*
Issue Date	*Oct 28, 2002*
Maturity Date	*Oct 28, 2012*
Face Value	*$1,000*
Coupon Rate	*6.8% payable semiannually*
Yield Rate	*7.4% convertible semiannually*

The bond is redeemable at par and coupons are payable on October 28 and April 28 every year. An investor purchased the bond on October 28, 2007 immediately after the coupon was paid at a purchase price of $967.5 under the prevailing interest rate, and sold the bond on March 30, 2008. Assuming that the market interest rate is constant in the holding period, calculate the bond's dirty price.

6.16 A $100 par value bond has semiannual coupons of 5% per annum and is callable at the end of the 7th through the 10th year at par. Find the most defensive price of the bond if

   (a) the yield rate is 6% compounded semiannually,

   (b) the yield rate is 4.5% compounded semiannually.

6.17 A $1,000 par value 10-year bond with annual coupons is redeemable at $1,055, and has a purchase price of $986 at a yield rate of 4% per annum. The coupons are non-level and increase at a rate of 3% per year. Find the amount amortized or discounted for the 5th coupon.

6.18 Two $1,000 bonds, redeemable on the same date at par to yield 4.5% have annual coupon rate of r and $2r$. If the total purchase price of the two bonds is $2,153.52 and the difference of the bond prices is $307.04, find r.

6.19 A $100 par value 5% bond with annual coupons has a call protection period of 5 years. The bond is callable at $109 at the end of year 6, 7 and 8; at $104 at the end of year 9, 10 and 11; and at $100 at the end of year 12.

   (a) If the yield rate is 6%, what is the optimal call date for the issuer?

   (b) If the yield rate is 3%, what is the optimal call date for the issuer?

6.20 In Section 6.4, the calculation of accrued interest is by assuming simple interest while the calculation of the dirty price is based on compound interest. While this approach is widely used and conforms to generally accepted accounting principles (GAAP), it is not consistent with compound interest theory. Consider a bond redeemable at par and that the yield rate is the same as the coupon rate. Find an expression for the book value B_{k+t} for $0 < t < 1$, with k being an integer between 0 to n. Comment on your results.

6.21 A $100 par value 8-year annual-coupon bond is redeemable at 105%. The coupon rate is 3% in the first 4 years and increases to 5% afterwards. Construct the amortization schedule for the bond in the 4th, 5th and 6th year, given that the price of the bond is $96.3. [**Hint**: Set up a bond amortization schedule and then use Excel Solver.]

6.22 A $100 par value bond maturing in n years with 5% annual coupons is sold at $103.3. Another bond with an annual coupon rate of 3% but otherwise the same is sold at $90.1. Both bonds are redeemable at par. Find the write-up/write-down of the book value for the second bond during the 5th year.

6.23 Show that

$$\frac{dP}{di} = -\frac{C}{1+i}\left[\frac{n}{(1+i)^n} + g(Ia)_{\overline{n}|}\right]$$

and that

$$\frac{d^2P}{di^2} > 0.$$

6.24 A \$1,000 par value 16-year bond with m coupons per annum has a price of \$910.63. If the total write-up value in the book value of the bond in the first 8 years is \$54 and the yield rate of the bond is 5.0945% effective per annum, find the redemption value of the bond.

6.25 One method of calculating the write-up or write-down of the book value of a bond is the straight-line method. This method is used for taxation purposes in the US for bonds purchased at premium and issued before the Tax Reform Act 1986. Under the straight-line method, the book value decreases from the purchase price to the redemption value linearly over the life of the bond. For the bond considered in Table 6.1, construct the bond amortization schedule using the straight-line method. Is this method consistent with the theory of compound interest or simple interest?

6.26 A \$100 par value 20-year callable bond paying 5.5% coupons annually has a call protection period of 10 years. The bond is redeemable

(a) at the end of the 11th to the 15th year, at 104%,
(b) at the end of the 16th to the 20th year, at par.

Find the price of the bond if the yield rate of the bond is not less than 5.3%.

6.27 For a \$1,000 par value 10-year bond with annual coupons, you are given the following information:

Time (in year)	Coupon payment	Effective interest earned	Amortized amount of premium	Book value
⋮		⋮		
5		54.099		
6		54.945		
7		55.842		
⋮		⋮		

Find the sum of the premiums or discounts in the last 2 years of the term of the bond.

6.28 For a $100 par value 5-year bond with 8% coupons paid semiannually and bought to yield 10% compounded semiannually, calculate the amount of premium or discount 2 years and 10 months after the date of purchase. Assume that each month has exactly 30 days.

6.29 Consider a $100 face value bond with coupon rate of 4.0% paid semiannually. The spot rates of interest in the market are given by

j (years)	0.5	1.0	1.5	2.0	2.5	3.0	3.5	4.0	4.5	5.0
i_j^S (%)	5.0	5.0	4.5	4.5	4.0	4.0	3.5	3.5	3.0	3.0

Find the price of the bond if it matures in (a) 3 years, and (b) 5 years. Compare your results with those in Example 6.9.

6.30 Johnny sold short a 10-year par value 8% semiannual coupon bond yielding 7% compounded semiannually at issue. The broker's initial margin requirement was 50% of the value of the short position. As predicted by Johnny, the prevailing market interest rate increased to 9% shortly after he sold short the bond. After 7 months, Johnny covered the short position by buying back the bond from the market.

  (a) Calculate the bond price when Johnny sold short the bond, and when he purchased the bond from the market.

  (b) Assuming that the margin deposit earned no interest, calculate the rate of return resulting from the short sale.

Advanced Problems

6.31 This question discusses the relation between bond and sinking fund.

  (a) Show that
$$(Fr - Pi)s_{\overline{n}|i} = P - C.$$

  (b) Interpret the result in (a). [**Hint**: First try the case when the bond is sold at a premium.]

6.32 A $2,000 par value bond with annual coupons of 5% is to be redeemed by $100 installments of principal at the end of the 10th through 29th years at $103. What is the price of the bond if it is bought to yield 7% annually? [**Hint**: Use the Makeham formula (6.2).]

7

Bond Yields and the Term Structure

We discuss the use of yield to maturity in measuring bond returns, which properly takes account of the time value of money and reflects the cash-flow pattern. When this method is applied to a callable bond assuming a known call date, the result is the yield to call. In addition, the par yield is often used as a summary of the spot-rate curve. To measure the return of a bond *ex post*, we can use the realized compound yield, which is also called the holding-period yield. Applying the realized compound yield over specific investment horizons with different interest-rate scenarios will provide useful information for bond management.

While the yield curve is very important in evaluating financial assets, it is not directly observable. It has to be estimated using bond prices observed in the market. We discuss the use of the bootstrap method and the least squares method for the estimation of the spot rates of interest with discrete compounding (usually semiannually). An alternative method is to estimate the instantaneous forward rate of interest under the continuous compounding assumption. This method can be applied to bonds with irregularly spaced coupon payments and maturity dates. Using the estimated forward-rate function, we can compute the spot-rate curve.

We discuss models of the determination of the term structure, including the expectations hypotheses, liquidity premium hypothesis, market segmentation hypothesis and preferred habitat hypothesis.

- *Yield to maturity, yield to call and par yield*
- *Realized compound yield and horizon analysis*
- *Estimation of the yield curve: bootstrap method and least squares method*
- *Estimation of the instantaneous forward rate and the term*
- *Models of the determination of the term structure*

7.1   Some Simple Measures of Bond Yield

Bond dealers often quote the potential return of a bond. A simple quote is the **current yield**, which is the annual dollar amount of coupon payment(s) divided by the quoted (clean) price of the bond. In other words, it is the annual coupon rate of interest divided by the quoted price of the bond per unit face value. For example, if a bond has a face value of $1,000 and pays a $22 coupon every 6 months with a current quoted price in the secondary market of $980, then the bond's current yield is $\frac{44}{980} = 4.49\%$.

The current yield does not adequately reflect the potential gain of the bond. First, it does not take account of the time value of money. Second, it does not take into consideration the capital gain or loss when the bond is held until maturity when the redemption payment is made. For example, if the bond is bought at a discount, there is a capital gain when the bond is redeemed. On the other hand, if the bond is bought at a premium, there is a capital loss when the bond is redeemed. Third, the computation of the current yield is based on the quoted price, while the actual investment is the purchase (dirty) price.

Another simple measure of bond yield is the **nominal yield**, which is the annual amount of coupon payment(s) divided by the face value, or simply the coupon rate of interest per annum. Like the current yield, the nominal yield is not a good measure of the potential return of the bond. These measures are used due to their simplicity in computation rather than sound theoretical justification.

7.2 Yield to Maturity

Given the yield rate applicable under the prevailing market conditions, we can compute the bond price using one of the pricing formulas in Chapter 6. The computed price reflects the fair value of the bond based on the prevailing rate of interest. This is especially important if an investor has to price a new issue of bonds. The pricing formula can be extended to the case of a general term structure with given spot rates i_t^S, forward rates i_t^F or accumulation function $a(t)$. The bond price is then computed using (6.10) (for an annual coupon bond) or (6.11) (for a semiannual coupon bond).

In practice, however, the yield rate or the term structure are not *observable*, while the transaction price of the bond can be observed from the market.[1] Given the transaction price, we can solve for the rate of interest that equates the discounted future cash flows (coupon payments and redemption value) to the transaction price. This rate of interest is called the **yield to maturity** (or the **yield to redemption**), which is the return on the bond investment if the investor holds the bond until it matures, assuming all the entitled payments are realized.

It can be seen that the yield to maturity is indeed the internal rate of return of the bond investment. Specifically, for a n-year annual coupon bond with transaction price P, the yield to maturity, denote by i_Y, is the solution of the following equation:

$$P = Fr \sum_{j=1}^{n} \frac{1}{(1+i_Y)^j} + \frac{C}{(1+i_Y)^n}. \qquad (7.1)$$

In the case of a n-year semiannual coupon bond, we solve i_Y from the equation (the coupon rate r is now per half-year)

$$P = Fr \sum_{j=1}^{2n} \frac{1}{\left[1 + \dfrac{i_Y}{2}\right]^j} + \frac{C}{\left[1 + \dfrac{i_Y}{2}\right]^{2n}}. \qquad (7.2)$$

Thus, for an annual coupon bond i_Y is an annual effective rate, while for a semiannual coupon bond i_Y is a nominal rate (per annum) convertible semiannually. Note that equations (6.10) and (6.11) are applicable from the *pricing* perspective, while equations (7.1) and (7.2) evaluate the *return* of the bond investment when an investor purchases it at the price P and holds it until it matures.

To calculate the solutions of equations (7.1) and (7.2) numerical methods are required. The Excel Solver may be used for the computation.

---

[1] We shall discuss the *estimation* of the term structure in Sections 7.5 and 7.6.

Figure 7.1:   Cash-flow diagram of the bond in Example 7.1

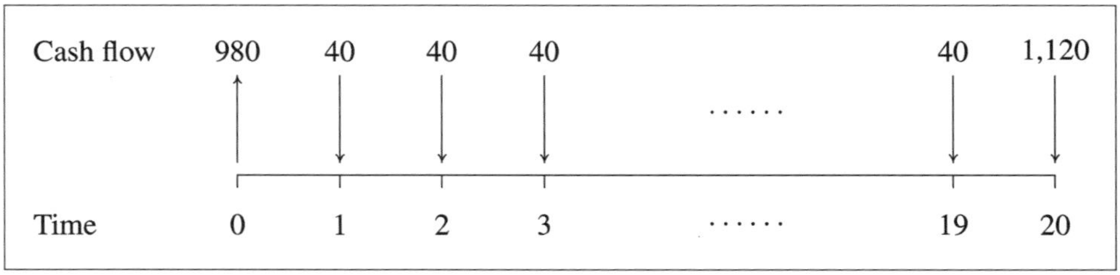

Example 7.1: A $1,000 par value 10-year bond with redemption value of $1,080 and coupon rate of 8% payable semiannually is purchased by an investor at the price of $980. Find the yield to maturity of the bond.

Solution: The cash flows of the bond in this example are plotted in Figure 7.1. We solve for i from the following equation:

$$980 = 40a_{\overline{20}|i} + 1,080(1 + i)^{-20}$$

to obtain $i = 4.41\%$, so that the yield to maturity i_Y is 8.82% per annum convertible semiannually.

Example 7.2: The following shows the information of a bond traded in the secondary market:

Type of Bond	*Non-callable government bond*
Issue Date	*March 10, 2002*
Maturity Date	*March 10, 2012*
Face Value	*$100*
Redemption Value	*$100*
Coupon Rate	*4% payable semiannually*

Assume that the coupon dates of the bond are March 10 and September 10 of each year. Investor A bought the bond on the issue date at a price of $105.25. On January 5, 2010 Investor B purchased the bond from A at the purchase (dirty) price of $104.75. Find (a) the yield to maturity of Investor A's purchase on March 10, 2002, (b) the realized yield for Investor A on the sale of the bond, and (c) the yield to maturity of Investor B's purchase on January 5, 2010.

Solution: (a) We need to solve for i in the basic price formula

$$P = (Fr)a_{\overline{n}|i} + Cv^n,$$

which, on the issue date, is

$$105.25 = 2a_{\overline{20}|i} + 100(1+i)^{-20}.$$

The numerical solution of i is 1.69% (per half-year). Thus, the yield to maturity is 3.38% per annum convertible semiannually.

(b) Investor A received the 15th coupon payment on September 10, 2009 and there are 117 days between September 10, 2009 and the sale date of January 5, 2010. The number of days between the two coupon payments, namely, September 10, 2009 and March 10, 2010 is 181. Thus, we need to compute i in the following equation:

$$105.25 = 2a_{\overline{15}|i} + 104.75(1+i)^{-15\frac{117}{181}},$$

the solution of which is 1.805% (per half-year). Thus, the realized yield is 3.61% per annum convertible semiannually.

(c) Investor B will receive the next 5 coupon payments starting on March 10, 2010. There are 64 days between the purchase date and the next coupon date. Investor B's return i per half-year is the solution of the following equation:

$$
\begin{aligned}
104.75 &= \left[2\ddot{a}_{\overline{5}|i} + 100(1+i)^{-4}\right](1+i)^{-\frac{64}{181}} \\
&= \left[2a_{\overline{5}|i} + 100(1+i)^{-5}\right](1+i)^{\frac{117}{181}},
\end{aligned}
$$

which is 1.18%. Thus, the yield to maturity is 2.36% per annum convertible semi-annually.

If a bond is callable prior to its maturity, a commonly quoted measure is the **yield to call**, which is computed in the same way as the yield to maturity, with the following modifications: (a) the redemption value in equations (7.1) and (7.2) is replaced by the call price, and (b) the maturity date is replaced by the call date. An investor will be able to compute a schedule of the yield to call as a function of the call date (which also determines the call price), and assess her investment over the range of possible yields.

Example 7.3: An investor purchased the callable bond in Example 6.8 at the price of $950. Find the minimum implied rate of return this investor is expected to obtain.

Solution: We solve the internal rate of return i of the bond at all possible call dates with $P = 950$, $r = 0.02$ and $F = 1,000$. Also, the value of C follows the given call price formula in Example 6.8. The results are summarized in Table 7.1.

Table 7.1: Results of Example 7.3

n	C	$i\ (\%)$
15	1,000	2.401
16	1,000	2.379
17	1,000	2.360
18	1,000	2.344
19	1,000	2.329
20	**1,000**	**2.315**
21	1,010	2.342
22	1,020	2.364
23	1,030	2.384
24	1,040	2.402
25	1,050	2.417
26	1,060	2.430
27	1,070	2.441
28	1,080	2.451
29	1,090	2.460
30	1,100	2.467

Thus, the minimum yield is 2.315% per half-year or 4.63% per annum convertible semiannually. This occurs when the bond is called after the 20th coupon payment.

Although the Excel Solver can be used to calculate the solution of equations (7.1) and (7.2), the computation can be more easily done using the Excel function **YIELD**, the specification of which is given as follows:

Excel function: YIELD(smt,mty,crt,prc,rdv,frq,basis)

smt = settlement date
mty = maturity date
crt = coupon rate of interest per annum
prc = quoted (clean) price of the bond per 100 face value
rdv = redemption value per 100 face value
frq = number of coupon payments per year
basis = day count, 30/360 if omitted and actual/actual if set to 1
Output = yield to maturity of the bond

Exhibit 7.1: Use of Excel function `YIELD`

	File Edit View Insert Format Tools Data Window Help Adc				
	N26		*fx*		
	A	B	C	D	E
1	3/10/2002				
2	1/5/2010				
3	3/10/2012				
4	3.38%	= YIELD(A1,A3,0.04,105.25,100,2,1)			
5	2.36%	= YIELD(A2,A3,0.04,103.4572,100,2,1)			
6					

Exhibit 7.1 illustrates the use of the function `YIELD` to solve Example 7.2. We first enter the dates March 10, 2002, January 5, 2010 and March 10, 2012 into Cells A1 through A3, respectively. In Cell A4, the `YIELD` function is entered, with settlement date A1, maturity date A3 and price of bond 105.25. The output is the yield to maturity of Investor A's purchase on March 10, 2002, i.e., 3.38%, which is the answer to Part (a). Part (b), however, cannot be solved by the `YIELD` function, as the bond was not sold on a coupon-payment date.[2] For Part (c), note that the input price of the bond required in the `YIELD` function is the quoted price. Thus, to use the `YIELD` function, we must first compute the quoted price of the bond on January 5, 2010, which is

$$104.75 - 2 \times \frac{117}{181} = \$103.4572.$$

The answer to Part (c) is shown in Cell A5 to be 2.36%.

7.3 Par Yield

Given the prevailing spot-rate curve and that bonds are priced according to the existing term structure, the yield to maturity i_Y is solved from the following equation (for an annual coupon bond):[3]

$$Fr \sum_{j=1}^{n} \frac{1}{(1+i_Y)^j} + \frac{C}{(1+i_Y)^n} = Fr \sum_{j=1}^{n} \frac{1}{\left(1+i_j^S\right)^j} + \frac{C}{(1+i_n^S)^n}, \qquad (7.3)$$

---

[2]The function `YIELD` assumes that the last payment consists of both coupon and redemption. It can be used to compute the internal rate of return of the bond (i.e., the return over the holding period of the bond, which will be discussed in Section 7.4) if the transaction occurs on a coupon-payment date. In this case, the "redemption value" is the quoted (clean) price of the bond.

[3]Note that the right-hand side of equation (7.3) is the price of the bond based on the prevailing term structure.

which is obtained from equations (6.10) and (7.1). Hence, i_Y is a nonlinear function *averaging* the spot rates i_j^S, $j = 1, \cdots, n$. As an averaging measure of the spot rates, however, i_Y has some disadvantages. First, no analytic solution of i_Y exists and it has to be computed using numerical methods. Second, i_Y varies with the coupon rate of interest, even for bonds with the same maturity. To overcome these difficulties, the **par yield** may be used, which is defined as the coupon rate of interest such that the bond is traded at par based on the prevailing term structure. Thus, denoting the par yield by i_P and setting $F = C = 100$, we have

$$100 = 100\, i_P \sum_{j=1}^{n} \frac{1}{\left(1 + i_j^S\right)^j} + \frac{100}{(1 + i_n^S)^n}, \tag{7.4}$$

from which we obtain

$$i_P = \frac{1 - \left(1 + i_n^S\right)^{-n}}{\sum_{j=1}^{n} \left(1 + i_j^S\right)^{-j}}. \tag{7.5}$$

More generally, if the bond makes level coupon payments at times $t_1, \cdots, t_n$, and the term structure is defined by the accumulation function $a(\cdot)$, the par yield is given by

$$
\begin{aligned}
i_P &= \frac{1 - [a(t_n)]^{-1}}{\sum_{j=1}^{n} [a(t_j)]^{-1}} \\
&= \frac{1 - v(t_n)}{\sum_{j=1}^{n} v(t_j)}.
\end{aligned}
\tag{7.6}
$$

The par yield can be computed easily without using numerical methods. Table 7.2 illustrates the par yields computed from two different spot-rate curves: an upward sloping curve and a downward sloping curve. In Case 1, the spot-rate curve is upward sloping, and we observe that the par yield increases with the time to maturity. Hence, we have an upward sloping par-yield curve as well, although the par yield is below the spot rate of the same maturity. In Case 2, we have a downward sloping spot-rate curve, which is accompanied by a downward sloping par-yield curve. The par-yield curve, however, is above the spot-rate curve and its slope is less steep.

Table 7.2: Par yields of two term structures

	Case 1		Case 2	
n	i_n^S	i_P	i_n^S	i_P
1	3.50	3.50	6.00	6.00
2	3.80	3.79	5.70	5.71
3	4.10	4.08	5.40	5.42
4	4.40	4.37	5.10	5.14
5	4.70	4.64	4.80	4.86
6	5.00	4.91	4.50	4.58
7	5.30	5.18	4.20	4.30
8	5.60	5.43	3.90	4.02
9	5.90	5.67	3.60	3.74
10	6.20	5.91	3.30	3.46
11	6.50	6.13	3.00	3.18
12	6.80	6.34	2.70	2.89

It should be noted that the par yield is more a summary measure of the existing term structure than a measure of the potential return of a bond. On the other hand, the yield to maturity is an *ex ante* measure of the return of a bond. It assumes that the bond is held to maturity and that all coupon payments are re-invested at the same yield. If the bond is sold before it matures, or if the **interest-on-interest** is different from the prevailing yield rate, the *ex post* return of the bond will be different. We now consider the evaluation of the return of a bond taking account of the possibility of varying interest rates prior to redemption as well as sale of the bond before maturity.

7.4 Holding-Period Yield

Bonds are actively traded in the secondary markets. For various reasons, investors often sell their bonds before maturity. The **holding-period yield**, also called the **realized compound yield** or the **total return**, is often computed on an *ex post* basis to evaluate the average return of the investment over the holding period of the bond (not necessarily until it matures or is called; for instance, see Example 7.2 (b)). This methodology, however, can also be applied to assess the possible return of the bond over a targeted horizon under different interest-rate scenarios. This application, called **horizon analysis**, is a useful tool for active bond management.

We shall denote the holding-period yield of a bond by i_H. To fix ideas, we first discuss the simple case of a **one-period holding yield**. Suppose a bond is purchased at time $t-1$ for P_{t-1}. At time t the bondholder receives a coupon of Fr and then sells the bond for P_t. The holding yield over the period $t-1$ to t, denoted by i_H, is then given by

$$i_H = \frac{(P_t + Fr) - P_{t-1}}{P_{t-1}}. \tag{7.7}$$

Example 7.4: A \$1,000 face value 3-year bond with semiannual coupons at 5% per annum is traded at a yield of 4% per annum convertible semiannually. If interest rate remains unchanged in the next 3 years, find the holding-period yield at the third half-year period.

Solution: Using the basic price formula, the prices of the bond after the second and third coupon payments are, respectively, $P_2 = 1,019.04$ and $P_3 = 1,014.42$. Therefore, the holding-period yield for the third half-year period is

$$i_H = \frac{(1,014.42 + 25.00) - 1,019.04}{1,019.04} = 2\%.$$

The above example illustrates that when the yield rate is unchanged after the purchase of the bond until it is sold prior to maturity, the holding-period yield in that period is equal to the yield to maturity. However, when the prevailing yield rate fluctuates, so will the bond's holding-period yield. An increase in the bond's required current yield reduces its price, which translates to a lower holding-period yield than the initial yield to maturity. On the other hand, a decline in the current yield will result in a higher holding-period yield than the initial yield to maturity.

The computation of the one-period holding yield can be extended to multiple periods. In order to calculate the n-period holding yield over n coupon-payment periods, we need to know the interest earned by the coupons when they are paid. Let P_0 be the beginning price of the bond, P_n be the ending price of the bond and V be the accumulated value of the coupons at time n. The n-period holding yield i_H is then the solution of the equation

$$P_0(1 + i_H)^n = P_n + V, \tag{7.8}$$

so that the annualized n-period holding yield is

$$i_H = \left[\frac{P_n + V}{P_0}\right]^{\frac{1}{n}} - 1. \tag{7.9}$$

Example 7.5: Consider a $1,000 face value 5-year non-callable bond with annual coupons of 5%. An investor bought the bond at its issue date at a price of $980. After receiving the third coupon payment, the investor immediately sold the bond for $1,050. The investor deposited all coupon income in a savings account earning an effective rate of 2% per annum. Find the annualized holding-period yield i_H of the investor.

Solution: We have $P_0 = \$980$ and $P_3 = \$1,050$. The accumulated interest-on-interest of the coupons, V, is

$$V = (1,000 \times 0.05)s_{\overline{3}|0.02} = 50 \times 3.0604 = \$153.02.$$

Thus, the annualized 3-period holding yield i_H is the solution of

$$980(1 + i_H)^3 = 1,050 + 153.02 = 1,203.02,$$

which implies

$$i_H = \left[\frac{1,203.02}{980}\right]^{\frac{1}{3}} - 1 = 7.0736\%.$$

In the above examples, the holding period yields are computed as *ex post* returns of the bonds over the holding periods, for which the interest-rate variations are known. This calculation can be used in a horizon analysis in which the interest-rate movements are assumed scenarios. The analyst examines the returns of different bond investment strategies under different scenarios and chooses the best strategy under the scenario that is deemed to be most likely. The following example illustrates this application.

Example 7.6: Consider two bonds, A and B. Bond A is a 10-year 2% annual-coupon bond, and Bond B is a 3-year 4% annual-coupon bond. The current spot-rate curve is flat at 3%, and is expected to remain flat for the next 3 years. A fund manager assumes two scenarios of interest-rate movements. In Scenario 1, the spot rate increases by 0.25 percentage point each year for 3 years. In Scenario 2, the spot rate drops to 2% next year and remains unchanged for 2 years. If the manager has an investment horizon of 3 years, what is her recommended strategy under each scenario? You may assume that all coupons and their interests are reinvested to earn the prevailing one-year spot rate.

Solution: We first compute the current bond prices. For Bond A, the current price is

$$2a_{\overline{10}|0.03} + 100(1.03)^{-10} = 91.4698,$$

and for Bond B, its current price is

$$4a_{\overline{3}|0.03} + 100(1.03)^{-3} = 102.8286.$$

Under Scenario 1, the price of Bond A after 3 years is

$$2a_{\overline{7}|0.0375} + 100(1.0375)^{-7} = 89.3987,$$

and the accumulated value of the coupons is

$$2 \times (1.0325 \times 1.035 + 1.035 + 1) = 6.2073.$$

Thus, the holding-period yield of Bond A over the 3 years is

$$\left[\frac{89.3987 + 6.2073}{91.4698}\right]^{\frac{1}{3}} - 1 = 1.4851\%.$$

Under Scenario 2, Bond A is traded at par in year 3 with the accumulated value of the coupons being

$$2 \times (1.02 \times 1.02 + 1.02 + 1) = 6.1208.$$

Thus, the holding-period yield is

$$\left[\frac{100 + 6.1208}{91.4698}\right]^{\frac{1}{3}} - 1 = 5.0770\%.$$

On the other hand, Bond B matures in 3 years so that its holding-period yield under Scenario 1 is

$$\left[\frac{100 + 4 \times (1.0325 \times 1.035 + 1.035 + 1)}{102.8286}\right]^{\frac{1}{3}} - 1 = 3.0156\%,$$

while under Scenario 2 its holding-period yield is

$$\left[\frac{100 + 4 \times (1.02 \times 1.02 + 1.02 + 1)}{102.8286}\right]^{\frac{1}{3}} - 1 = 2.9627\%.$$

Thus, Bond B is the preferred investment under Scenario 1, while Bond A is preferred under Scenario 2.

7.5 Discretely Compounded Yield Curve

We have so far used the prevailing term structure to price a bond or compute the net present value of a project, assuming the spot-rate curve is given. In practice, spot rates of interest are not directly observable in the market, although they can be estimated from the observed bond prices. In this section we discuss the estimation of the spot rates of interest, which are assumed to be compounded over discrete time intervals. Specifically, we consider the estimation of the spot rates of interest convertible semiannually using a series of semiannual coupon bonds.

The simplest way to estimate the spot-rate curve is by the **bootstrap method**. This method requires the bond-price data to follow a certain format. In particular, we assume that the coupon-payment dates of the bonds are synchronized and spaced out the same interval apart. The following example illustrates the use of the bootstrap method.

Example 7.7: Table 7.3 summarizes a series of semiannual coupon bonds with different time to maturity, coupon rate of interest r (in percent per annum) and price per 100 face value. Using the given bond data, estimate the spot rate of interest i_t^S over t years, for $t = 0.5, 1, \cdots, 6$.

Table 7.3: Bond price data

Maturity (yrs)	Coupon rate r (%)	Price per 100 face value
0.5	0.0	98.41
1.0	4.0	100.79
1.5	3.8	100.95
2.0	4.5	102.66
2.5	2.5	98.53
3.0	5.0	105.30
3.5	3.6	101.38
4.0	3.2	99.83
4.5	4.0	102.83
5.0	3.0	98.17
5.5	3.5	100.11
6.0	3.6	100.24

Solution: We first compute the spot rate of interest for payments due in half-year, which can be obtained from the first bond. Equating the bond price to the present value of the redemption value (there is no coupon), we have

$$98.41 = \frac{100}{1 + \frac{i_{0.5}^S}{2}},$$

which implies

$$i_{0.5}^S = 2 \times \left[\frac{100}{98.41} - 1\right] = 2 \times 0.016157 = 3.231\%.$$

For the second bond, there are two cash flows. As a coupon is paid at time 0.5 year and the spot rate of interest of which has been computed, we obtain the following equation of value for the bond:

$$100.79 = \frac{2}{1.016157} + \frac{102}{\left[1 + \frac{i_1^S}{2}\right]^2},$$

from which we obtain $i_1^S = 3.191\%$. Similarly, for the third bond the equation of value involves $i_{0.5}^S$, i_1^S and $i_{1.5}^S$, of which only $i_{1.5}^S$ is unknown and can be solved from the equation. Thus, for the bond with k semiannual coupons, price P_k and coupon rate r_k per half-year, the equation of value is

$$P_k = 100\, r_k \sum_{j=1}^{k} \frac{1}{\left[1 + \frac{i_j^S}{2}\right]^j} + \frac{100}{\left[1 + \frac{i_k^S}{2}\right]^k}.$$

These equations can be used to solve sequentially for the spot rates. Figure 7.2 plots the spot-rate curve for maturity of up to 6 years for the data given in Table 7.3.

Although the bootstrap method is simple to use, there are some data requirements that seriously limit its applicability. First, the data set of bonds must have synchronized coupon-payment dates. Second, there should not be any gap in the series of bonds in the time to maturity. We now consider the **least squares method**, which is less demanding in the data requirement.

Figure 7.2: Estimated spot-rate curve of Example 7.7

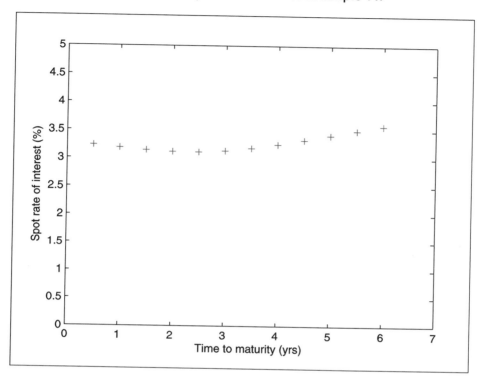

Let us assume we have a set of m bonds for which the coupon-payment dates are synchronized. We denote the prices of these bonds per 100 face value by P_j, their coupon rate by r_j per half-year and their time to maturity by n_j half-years, for $j = 1, \cdots, m$. We denote

$$v_h = \frac{1}{\left[1 + \dfrac{i^S_{\frac{h}{2}}}{2}\right]^h}, \tag{7.10}$$

which is the discount factor for payments due in h half-years. Thus, the equation of value for the jth bond is

$$P_j = 100\, r_j \sum_{h=1}^{n_j} v_h + 100 v_{n_j}.$$

If the last payment (redemption plus coupon) of the bonds occur in M periods (i.e., M is the maximum of all n_j for $j = 1, \cdots, m$), the pricing equations of the bonds can be written as

$$P_j = C_{j1}v_1 + C_{j2}v_2 + \cdots + C_{jM}v_M, \qquad j = 1, \cdots, m, \qquad (7.11)$$

in which C_{jh} are known cash-flow amounts and v_h are the unknown discount factors.[4] Thus, in equation (7.11) we have a **multiple linear regression model** with M unknown coefficients $v_1, \cdots, v_M$ and m observations (P_j is the **dependent variable** and $C_{j1}, \cdots, C_{jM}$ are the **independent variables**, for $j = 1, \cdots, m$). We can solve for the values of v_h using the least squares method, and subsequently obtain the values of $i^S_{\frac{h}{2}}$ from equation (7.10).

7.6 Continuously Compounded Yield Curve

We now introduce the estimation of the term structure assuming that interest is credited based on continuous compounding. Let us denote the current time by 0, and use i^S_t to denote the continuously compounded spot rate of interest for payments due at time t. As shown in equation (3.27), if we consider the limiting value of the forward rate of interest $i^F_{t,\tau}$ for τ approaching zero, we obtain the instantaneous forward rate, which is equal to the force of interest, i.e.,

$$\lim_{\tau \to 0} i^F_{t,\tau} = \delta(t).$$

An important method to construct the yield curve based on the instantaneous forward rate is due to Fama and Bliss (1987).[5] Note that if we denote the current price of a zero-coupon bond with unit face value maturing at time t by $P(t)$, we have

$$P(t) = v(t) = \frac{1}{a(t)} = \exp\left[-t\, i^S_t\right]. \qquad (7.12)$$

Thus, if we had a continuously observable sequence of zero-coupon bond prices $P(t)$ maturing at time $t > 0$, the problem of recovering the spot rates of interest is straightforward using equation (7.12). In practice, however, this sequence is not available. The Fama-Bliss method focuses on the estimation of the instantaneous forward rates, from which the spot-rate curve can be computed.

In equation (1.26), we have established that

$$a(t) = \exp\left[\int_0^t \delta(u)\, du\right]. \qquad (7.13)$$

---

[4] C_{jh} is the hth payment (coupon and/or redemption) of the jth bond. Note that these values are zero if h is larger than the maturity of the bond.

[5] See E. Fama and R. Bliss, "The information in long-maturity forward rates", *American Economic Review* 77, 1987, 680 – 692.

From (7.12) and (7.13), we conclude that

$$\exp\left[t\, i_t^S\right] = a(t) = \exp\left[\int_0^t \delta(u)\, du\right],$$

so that

$$i_t^S = \frac{1}{t} \int_0^t \delta(u)\, du, \tag{7.14}$$

which says that the continuously compounded spot rate of interest i_t^S is an *equally-weighted average* of the force of interest $\delta(t)$. Thus, if we have a sequence of estimates of the instantaneous forward rates, we can compute the spot-rate curve using (7.14).

To apply the Fama-Bliss method, we assume that we have a sequence of bonds with possibly irregularly spaced maturity dates. We assume that the force of interest between two successive maturity dates is constant. Making use of the equations of value for the bonds sequentially in increasing order of the maturity, we are able to compute the force of interest over the period of the sample data. The spot rates of interest can then be calculated using equation (7.14). Although this yield curve may not be smooth, it can be fine tuned using some spline smoothing methods. Example 7.8 illustrates the use of the Fama-Bliss method to estimate the force of interest and the spot-rate curve.

Example 7.8: You are given the bond data in Table 7.4. The jth bond matures at time t_j with current price P_j per unit face value, which equals the redemption value, for $j = 1, \cdots, 4$ and $0 < t_1 < t_2 < t_3 < t_4$. Bonds 1 and 2 have no coupons, while Bond 3 has two coupons, at time t_{31}^* with $t_1 < t_{31}^* < t_2$ and at maturity t_3. Bond 4 has three coupons, with coupon dates t_{41}^*, t_{42}^* and t_4, where $t_2 < t_{41}^* < t_3$ and $t_3 < t_{42}^* < t_4$.

Table 7.4: Bond data for Example 7.8

Bond	Coupon per unit face value	Coupon dates	Maturity	Bond price per unit face value
1	0	–	t_1	P_1
2	0	–	t_2	P_2
3	C_3	$t_{31}^*,\ t_1 < t_{31}^* < t_2$	t_3	P_3
	C_3	t_3		
4	C_4	$t_{41}^*,\ t_2 < t_{41}^* < t_3$	t_4	P_4
	C_4	$t_{42}^*,\ t_3 < t_{42}^* < t_4$		
	C_4	t_4		

It is assumed that the force of interest $\delta(t)$ follows a step function taking constant values between successive maturities, i.e., $\delta(t) = \delta_i$ for $t_{i-1} \leq t < t_i$, $i = 1, \cdots, 4$ with $t_0 = 0$. Estimate $\delta(t)$ and compute the spot-rate curve for maturity up to time t_4.

Solution: As Bond 1 is a zero-coupon bond, its equation of value is

$$P_1 = \exp\left[-t_1\, i_{t_1}^S\right] = \exp\left[-\int_0^{t_1} \delta(u)\, du\right] = \exp\left[-\delta_1 t_1\right],$$

so that

$$\delta_1 = -\frac{1}{t_1} \ln P_1,$$

which applies to the interval $(0, t_1)$. Now we turn to Bond 2 (which is again a zero-coupon bond) and write down its equation of value as

$$P_2 = \exp\left[-\int_0^{t_2} \delta(u)\, du\right] = \exp\left[-\delta_1 t_1 - \delta_2(t_2 - t_1)\right].$$

Solving the above equation for δ_2, we obtain

$$
\begin{aligned}
\delta_2 &= -\frac{1}{t_2 - t_1}\left[\ln P_2 + \delta_1 t_1\right] \\
&= -\frac{1}{t_2 - t_1} \ln\left[\frac{P_2}{P_1}\right].
\end{aligned}
$$

For Bond 3, there is a coupon payment of amount C_3 at time t_{31}^*, with $t_1 < t_{31}^* < t_2$. Thus, the equation of value for Bond 3 is

$$
\begin{aligned}
P_3 &= (1 + C_3)\exp\left[-\int_0^{t_3} \delta(u)\, du\right] + C_3\exp\left[-\int_0^{t_{31}^*} \delta(u)\, du\right] \\
&= (1 + C_3)\exp\left[-\delta_1 t_1 - \delta_2(t_2 - t_1) - \delta_3(t_3 - t_2)\right] \\
&\quad + C_3\exp\left[-\delta_1 t_1 - \delta_2(t_{31}^* - t_1)\right],
\end{aligned}
$$

from which we obtain

$$
\begin{aligned}
\delta_3 &= -\frac{1}{t_3 - t_2} \ln\left[\frac{P_3 - C_3\exp\left[-\delta_1 t_1 - \delta_2(t_{31}^* - t_1)\right]}{(1 + C_3)P_2}\right] \\
&= -\frac{1}{t_3 - t_2} \ln\left[\frac{P_3 - P_1 C_3\exp\left[-\delta_2(t_{31}^* - t_1)\right]}{(1 + C_3)P_2}\right].
\end{aligned}
$$

Going through a similar argument, we can write down the equation of value for Bond 4 as

$$P_4 = (1 + C_4)P_3^* \exp\left[-\delta_4(t_4 - t_3)\right] + P_2 C_4 \exp\left[-\delta_3(t_{41}^* - t_2)\right]$$
$$+ P_3^* C_4 \exp\left[-\delta_4(t_{42}^* - t_3)\right],$$

where[6]

$$P_3^* = \exp\left[-\delta_1 t_1 - \delta_2(t_2 - t_1) - \delta_3(t_3 - t_2)\right],$$

so that

$$(1 + C_4) \exp\left[-\delta_4(t_4 - t_3)\right] + C_4 \exp\left[-\delta_4(t_{42}^* - t_3)\right]$$
$$= \frac{P_4 - P_2 C_4 \exp\left[-\delta_3(t_{41}^* - t_2)\right]}{P_3^*}.$$

Thus, the right-hand side of the above equation can be computed, while the left-hand side contains the unknown quantity δ_4. The equation can be solved numerically for the force of interest δ_4 in the period (t_3, t_4). Finally, using (7.14), we obtain the continuously compounded spot interest rate as

$$i_t^S = \begin{cases} \delta_1, & \text{for } 0 < t < t_1, \\[2mm] \dfrac{\delta_1 t_1 + \delta_2(t - t_1)}{t}, & \text{for } t_1 \leq t < t_2, \\[2mm] \dfrac{\delta_1 t_1 + \delta_2(t_2 - t_1) + \delta_3(t - t_2)}{t}, & \text{for } t_2 \leq t < t_3, \\[2mm] \dfrac{\delta_1 t_1 + \delta_2(t_2 - t_1) + \delta_3(t_3 - t_2) + \delta_4(t - t_3)}{t}, & \text{for } t_3 \leq t < t_4. \end{cases}$$

The above example shows that the instantaneous forward rate of interest can be computed successively using the bond data, although numerical methods may be required in some circumstances. Using the estimated step function of instantaneous forward rates, the spot-rate curve can be computed by equation (7.14).[7]

---

[6]Note that P_3^* is the price of a unit par value zero-coupon bond maturing at time t_3.

[7]Empirically it may occur that the forward rates of interest over some intervals are found to be negative. Such *anomaly* is an indication of the existence of arbitrage opportunities in the market and may be due to the poor quality of the data. Thus, some *data cleaning* may be required prior to applying the Fama-Bliss method.

7.7   Term Structure Models

We have shown some samples of the yield curves of the US market in Chapter 3. Empirically the yield curve can take various shapes. Figure 7.3 presents the term structure of the UK market monthly from January 2002 through December 2015. Likewise, Figure 7.4 summarizes the term structure of the US market for the same period. It can be seen that the term structures took quite different shapes during this period. For the US market the yield curve was mostly upward sloping from 2002 through 2004. It showed inverted humps in parts of 2005 and 2006, while in 2007 and 2008 it was generally quite flat, even showing slightly downward slopes at long maturities. The US Federal Reserve has held short-term interest rates around 0.25% after the global financial crisis. The US yield curve has been mostly upward sloping after 2008. In comparison, the UK market showed more frequent occurrences of downward sloping yield curves. However, similar to the US market, it also experienced several years of rather steep normal yield curves in the early parts of the 2000s. It will be interesting to examine the factors determining the shapes of the yield curve, how the yield curve evolves over time, and whether the shape of the yield curve has any implications for the real economy such as the business cycle.

Figure 7.3:   Historical UK spot-rate curves
(Source: Bank of England, www.bankofengland.co.uk)

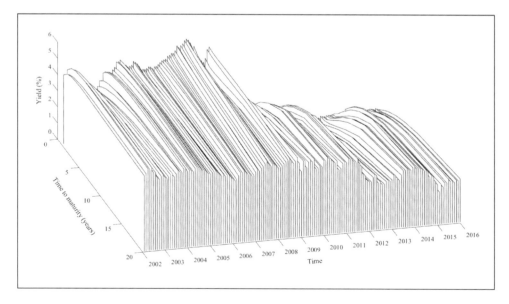

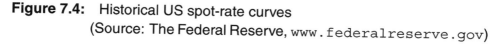

Figure 7.4: Historical US spot-rate curves
(Source: The Federal Reserve, www.federalreserve.gov)

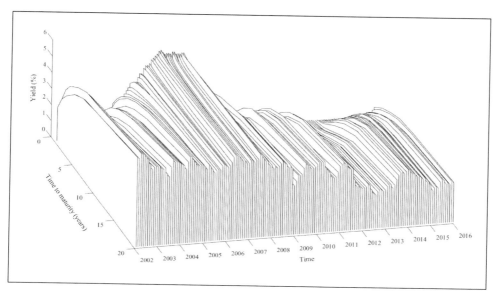

There are several approaches to defining the term-structure models. We shall examine the theories of the term structure in terms of the 1-period holding-period yield introduced in Section 7.4. For simplicity of exposition, we assume investments in zero-coupon bonds and relate different measures of returns to the bond prices. To this effect, we first define some notations prior to discussing the term-structure models.

We denote $i_H^{(n)}$ as the 1-period holding-period (from time 0 to 1) yield of a bond maturing at time n. The current time is 0 and the price of a bond at time t with remaining n periods to mature is denoted by $P_t(n)$. We introduce the new notation $_ti_\tau^S$ to denote the spot rate of interest at time t for payments due τ periods from t (i.e., due at time $t + \tau$). Thus, for $t > 0$, $_ti_\tau^S$ is a *random variable* at time 0.[8] Suppose an investor purchased a n-period bond at time 0 and held it for 1 period, the bond price at time 1 is $P_1(n-1)$, so that the 1-period holding-period yield from time 0 to 1 is

$$i_H^{(n)} = \frac{P_1(n-1) - P_0(n)}{P_0(n)}. \qquad (7.15)$$

---

[8]It is important to distinguish between $_ti_\tau^S$ and i_t^F. The former is an unknown quantity at time 0 as it can only be observed at time $t > 0$. It is the spot rate applicable to period t to $t + \tau$. On the other hand, i_t^F is a known quantity at time 0, determined by the no-arbitrage condition and satisfies equations (3.4) and (3.5).

Note that $P_1(n-1)$ is a random variable at time 0, and so is $i_H^{(n)}$. Furthermore, $P_t(\tau)(1 + {}_t i_\tau^S)^\tau = 1$, so that ${}_t i_\tau^S$ is given by

$$
{}_t i_\tau^S = \left[\frac{1}{P_t(\tau)} \right]^\tau - 1. \tag{7.16}
$$

If we assume that all market participants are **risk neutral** (they neither avoid nor love risks) and that they have no preference for the maturities of the investments, then their only criterion for the selection of an investment is its *expected return*. This assumption leads to the **pure expectations hypothesis**, which states that the *expected* 1-period holding-period yields for bonds of all maturities are equal, and thus equal to the 1-period spot rate of interest (which is the 1-period holding-period yield of a bond maturing at time 1). Thus, if we denote $E[i_H^{(n)}]$ as the expected value of $i_H^{(n)}$ at time 0, the pure expectations hypothesis states that

$$
E[i_H^{(n)}] = i_1^S, \qquad \text{for } n = 1, \cdots . \tag{7.17}
$$

However, while the 1-period holding-period yield for a 1-year zero-coupon bond is known at time 0 (i.e., i_1^S), it is unknown for bonds with longer maturities. Thus, bonds with longer maturities involve uncertainty and may have higher risks. Investors may demand higher expected return for bonds with maturities longer than a year, which is due to the **risk premium**. If the risk premium is constant for bonds of all maturities, we have the **expectations** (or **constant premium**) **hypothesis**, which states that

$$
E[i_H^{(n)}] = i_1^S + \varrho, \qquad \text{for } n = 2, \cdots , \tag{7.18}
$$

where ϱ is a positive constant independent of n. However, if investors prefer short-maturity to long-maturity assets due to their better liquidity, then the expected return for bonds with longer maturities must be higher to compensate the investors. This leads to the **liquidity premium hypothesis**, which states that

$$
E[i_H^{(n)}] = i_1^S + \varrho^{(n)}, \qquad \text{for } n = 2, \cdots , \tag{7.19}
$$

where the risk premium for a n-period bond $\varrho^{(n)}$ increases with n, so that $\varrho^{(2)} \leq \varrho^{(3)} \leq \cdots$.

Some theorists, however, argue that investors do not necessarily prefer short-maturity assets to long-maturity assets. Some institutions may prefer short-term assets (e.g., banks), while others may prefer long-term assets (e.g., insurance companies and pension funds). Thus, the risk premiums of bonds with different maturities $\varrho^{(n)}$ may not be a monotonic function of n, but may depend on other covariates

$w^{(n)}$, which are functions of the maturity n. This is called the **market segmenta-tion hypothesis**, for which we have

$$\mathrm{E}[i_H^{(n)}] = i_1^S + \varrho(w^{(n)}), \qquad \text{for } n = 2, \cdots, \tag{7.20}$$

so that the risk premium $\varrho(\cdot)$ is a function of the specific asset market. Finally, the **preferred habitat hypothesis** states that institutions do not have a rigid targeted maturity class of assets to invest, but will be influenced by the returns expected of assets with different maturities. Thus, bonds with similar maturities will be close substitutes of each other. Under this hypothesis, equation (7.20) is applicable and the risk premium $\varrho(\cdot)$ will be a slowly moving function of the maturity n.

We now examine the implications of the prevailing term structure for the future movements of interest rates under the aforementioned term-structure models. Let us consider the 1-period holding-period yield of a 2-period bond, $i_H^{(2)}$, which is given by (see equation (7.15))

$$i_H^{(2)} = \frac{P_1(1) - P_0(2)}{P_0(2)} = \frac{P_1(1)}{P_0(2)} - 1. \tag{7.21}$$

If we consider the spot rate of interest over the 2-period horizon, i_2^S, we have

$$\left(1 + i_2^S\right)^2 = \frac{1}{P_0(2)} = \frac{P_1(1)}{P_0(2)} \times \frac{1}{P_1(1)} = \left(1 + i_H^{(2)}\right)\left(1 + {}_1 i_1^S\right). \tag{7.22}$$

Note that i_2^S on the left-hand side is known at time 0, while $i_H^{(2)}$ and ${}_1 i_1^S$ on the right-hand side are unknown (random variables) at time 0. Using equation (3.3) (i.e., no-arbitrage condition) to rewrite $\left(1 + i_2^S\right)^2$, we have

$$\left(1 + i_H^{(2)}\right)\left(1 + {}_1 i_1^S\right) = \left(1 + i_1^S\right)\left(1 + i_2^F\right). \tag{7.23}$$

To the first-order approximation the above equation can be written as

$$i_H^{(2)} + {}_1 i_1^S = i_1^S + i_2^F. \tag{7.24}$$

Note that the left-hand side of the above equation involves two random variables, while the right-hand side involves two known quantities at time 0. Now we take expectations on both sides of the equation. If we adopt the pure expectations hypothesis, we have $\mathrm{E}[i_H^{(2)}] = i_1^S$, so that equation (7.24) implies

$$\mathrm{E}[{}_1 i_1^S] = i_2^F, \tag{7.25}$$

which says that the expected value of the *future* 1-period spot rate is equal to the prevailing 1-period forward rate for that period. This statement is called the **un-biased expectations hypothesis**, which is itself implied by the pure expectations hypothesis. Note that under the pure expectations hypothesis equation (7.25) can be generalized to

$$E[_t i_\tau^S] = i_{t,\tau}^F, \qquad \text{for } 0 < t, \tau, \tag{7.26}$$

so that the prevailing forward rates have important implications for the expected future values of the spot rates at any time t over any horizon τ.

We have seen that if the term structure is upward sloping, the forward rate of interest is higher than the spot rate of interest. Thus, under the pure expectations hypothesis, an upward sloping yield curve implies that the future spot rate is *expected* to be higher than the current spot rate.[9]

On the other hand, if long-term bonds command a risk premium, an upward sloping yield curve may not imply that the spot rate is expected to rise. For example, assuming the constant-premium model and taking expectations of equation (7.24), we have

$$E[_1 i_1^S] = i_1^S + i_2^F - E[i_H^{(2)}] = i_1^S + i_2^F - (i_1^S + \varrho) = i_2^F - \varrho.$$

Now as an upward sloping yield curve implies $i_2^F > i_1^S$, we conclude $E[_1 i_1^S] > i_1^S - \varrho$. However, this does not imply $E[_1 i_1^S] > i_1^S$. Thus, after taking account of the risk premium, the expected future spot rate may be lower than the current spot rate even if the term structure is upward sloping.

7.8 Summary

1. A bond's yield to maturity is the internal rate of return an investor would achieve if she purchases the bond at its current market price and holds it until maturity, assuming all coupon and principal payments are received as scheduled. There are other bond yield measures such as current yield, nominal yield and yield to call.

2. The par yield is the coupon rate of interest of a bond such that the bond price is at par based on the prevailing term structure. The par yield may be regarded as a summary measure of the existing term structure.

3. The holding-period yield is the average rate of return of a bond over the holding (multiple) period. It takes account of the actual interest-on-interest earned on an *ex post* basis, and is also called the realized compound yield or total return. On an *ex ante* basis, the holding-period yield may be computed under different assumed scenarios and is a useful tool in active bond management.

---

[9]For example, since $(1 + i_2^S)^2 = (1 + i_1^S)(1 + i_2^F)$, $i_2^S > i_1^S$ (upward sloping term structure) implies $E(_1 i_1^S) = i_2^F > i_2^S > i_1^S$.

4. The term structure may be estimated using bond price data in the market. The bootstrap method and the least squares method can be used to estimate the periodic compounding spot-rate curve. There are, however, data limitations which restrict the use of these methods.

5. Assuming continuous compounding, the instantaneous forward rate can be estimated using bond price data. The step function of instantaneous forward rates can be calculated from a sequence of bonds with possibly irregularly spaced maturities. This method is quite versatile and has fewer data limitations. Upon estimating the instantaneous forward rates, the spot-rate curve can be calculated by averaging the instantaneous forward rates.

6. There are several theories that explain the determination of the term structure. The most widely used theory is probably the pure expectations hypothesis, which implies that the forward rate is an unbiased estimate of the future spot rate. The expectations hypothesis, liquidity premium hypothesis, market segmentation hypothesis and preferred habitat hypothesis are other competing theories.

Exercises

7.1 A $1,000 par value 10-year bond with redemption value of $1,080 and coupon rate of 8% payable semiannually is purchased by an investor at price P.

(a) Find the yield to maturity of the bond if $P = \$1,000$.

(b) Find the yield to maturity of the bond if $P = \$1,080$.

(c) Determine P if the yield to maturity of the bond is 8% per annum convertible semiannually.

7.2 The following shows the information of an investment-grade bond.

Type of Bond	Corporate bond
Issue Date	March 2, 2015
Maturity Date	March 2, 2021
Face Value	$1,000
Redemption Value	$1,035
Coupon Rate	9% payable semiannually

If the 1-year forward rates are 7% for the first 3 years and 10% for the last 3 years, find the price of the bond at issue. What is the yield to maturity of the bond?

7.3 Louis bought a $100 par value 5-year bond with 10% semiannual coupons at a purchase price of $94. After receiving the 5th coupon, Louis sold the bond to Raymond. Find the yield to maturity for Raymond, if the realized yield for Louis is 12% compounded semiannually.

7.4 You are given the following incomplete bond amortization schedule for a $1,000 par value 10-year bond with semiannual coupons, purchased at $864.9. The bond is *not* redeemable at par.

Half-year	Coupon payment	Effective interest earned	Amortized amount of premium	Book value
11			-10.068	
12				
13			-10.827	

(a) Find the yield to maturity of the bond.

(b) Find the redemption value of the bond.

[**Hint**: Study the column "amount amortized" in Table 6.3 carefully.]

7.5 The following shows the information of a bond:

Type of Bond	*Non-callable municipal bond*
Issue Date	*June 20, 2011*
Maturity Date	*June 20, 2021*
Face Value	*$100*
Redemption Value	*$100*
Coupon Rate	*8% payable semiannually*

Assume that the coupon dates of the bond are June 20 and December 20 of each year. Isaac bought the bond on the issue date at a price of $89. Slightly over 4 years on August 5, 2015 Simon purchased the bond from Isaac at a purchase (dirty) price of $93.70. Find

(a) the yield to maturity of the bond upon issue,

(b) the realized yield (internal rate of return) to Isaac on the sale of the bond,

(c) the yield to maturity of Simon's purchase on August 5, 2015.

7.6 For a particular bond market, zero-coupon bonds with face value $100, redeemable at par, are priced as follows:

- bonds redeemable in exactly 1 year are priced at $98,
- bonds redeemable in exactly 2 years are priced at $93,
- bonds redeemable in exactly 3 years are priced at $89,
- bonds redeemable in exactly 4 years are priced at $85.50.

Find the yield to maturity of a bond redeemable at 103% of the face value in 4 years with annual coupons of 5%.

7.7 You are given that the risk-free force of interest $\delta(t)$ at time t is given by

$$\delta(t) = \begin{cases} 0.03, & \text{for } 0 < t \le 5, \\ 0.03 + 0.005(t - 5), & \text{for } t > 5. \end{cases}$$

(a) Find $a(t)$.

(b) A $100 par value 7-year bond has 8% semiannual coupons and is redeemable at 107%. Find the price of the bond.

(c) Find the yield to maturity of the bond in (b).

7.8 If the callable bond in Exercise 6.19 has a market price of $105, find the minimum implied required rate of return the investor is expected to obtain.

7.9 Given the term structure i_n^S, for $n = 1, 2, \cdots, 12$, in the following table, compute the corresponding forward rates and par yields.

n	i_n^S	i_n^F	i_P
1	3.50%		
2	3.80%		
3	4.10%		
4	4.40%		
5	4.70%		
6	5.00%		
7	4.50%		
8	4.30%		
9	4.10%		
10	3.90%		
11	3.80%		
12	3.50%		

7.10   (a) Rewrite equation (7.5) for a n-year semiannual coupon bond.

     (b) Given the term structure i_n^S, for $n = 0.5, 1, 1.5, \cdots, 6$, in the following table, compute the corresponding forward rates and par yields.

n	i_n^S	i_n^F	i_P
0.5	4.12%		
1	4.38%		
1.5	4.50%		
2	4.60%		
2.5	4.80%		
3	4.50%		
3.5	4.30%		
4	4.35%		
4.5	4.44%		
5	4.60%		
5.5	4.80%		
6	4.84%		

7.11 A term structure is defined by the following accumulation function:

$$a(t) = \begin{cases} e^{0.03t}, & \text{for } 0 < t \le 5, \\ e^{0.06+0.0025(1+t)^2}, & \text{for } t > 5. \end{cases}$$

If a 10-year bond makes level coupon payments at year 2, 4, 6, 8 and 10. Find the par yield of this bond.

7.12 Suppose the yields to maturity of 6-month, 12-month, 18-month and 24-month zero-coupon bonds are, respectively, 10%, 8%, 7% and 6% per annum convertible semiannually.

     (a) What is the 2-year par yield?

     (b) Find the price of a 2-year semiannual coupon bond with coupon rate of interest of 3.0407% per annum and face value 100.

     (c) Comment on the result in (b).

7.13 For the bond in Exercise 6.7, determine the following:

    (a) the nominal yield,

    (b) i_H for the 13th half-year period, assuming the rate of interest remains unchanged,

    (c) i_H for the 6th year, assuming the investor can reinvest the coupons at 13% per annum compounded semiannually.

7.14 A $100 par value non-callable bond has 4% semiannual coupons and is redeemable at $103 after 20 years. The bond is currently selling at $105.

    (a) Find the yield to maturity of the bond convertible yearly.

    (b) If coupons can be reinvested at 4.5% compounded semiannually, find the 20-year holding-period yield convertible yearly. Compare this with the answer obtained in (a).

7.15 A $100 par value bond has 7.5% annual coupons and is callable at the end of the 8th through the 12th years at par. The price of the bond at issue was determined by assuming that the yield to maturity is 7%. Mary purchased the bond and held it until it was called after 10 years.

    (a) Calculate the yield to maturity of Mary's investment in the 10-year period.

    (b) Calculate the 10-year holding-period yield of Mary if coupons can be reinvested at only 6%.

7.16 Consider two bonds, A and B. Bond A is a 5-year 2% annual-coupon bond, and Bond B is a 3-year 4% annual-coupon bond. In addition to the current spot-rate curve, a fund manager assumes 2 scenarios of spot-rate curve movements in the next 3 years. Scenario UP assumes an instantaneous 0.1% parallel shift upwards in the spot-rate curve in Year 0 and the shift continues annually for the next three years. Scenario DOWN assumes an instantaneous 0.1% parallel shift downwards in the spot-rate curve in Year 0 and the shift continues annually for the next three years. The spot-rate curves, under various scenarios, are summarised in the following table.

		t:	1	2	3	4	5
					i_t^S		
	Year 3		5.40%	5.50%	5.60%	5.70%	5.80%
Scenario	Year 2		5.30%	5.40%	5.50%	5.60%	5.70%
UP	Year 1		5.20%	5.30%	5.40%	5.50%	5.60%
	Year 0		5.10%	5.20%	5.30%	5.40%	5.50%
Current spot rate	Year 0		5.00%	5.10%	5.20%	5.30%	5.40%
	Year 0		4.90%	5.00%	5.10%	5.20%	5.30%
Scenario	Year 1		4.80%	4.90%	5.00%	5.10%	5.20%
DOWN	Year 2		4.70%	4.80%	4.90%	5.00%	5.10%
	Year 3		4.60%	4.70%	4.80%	4.90%	5.00%

If the manager has an investment horizon of 3 years and we assume that all coupons are invested at the prevailing one-year spot rate, what is her recommended strategy under each scenario?

7.17 The following table gives the prices of zero-coupon and semiannual coupon bonds:

Maturity (years)	Coupon rate r (% per annum)	Price per 100 face value
0.5	0.0	98
1.0	0.0	95
1.5	4.0	96
2.0	6.0	97

Calculate the spot rates for maturities of 0.5, 1, 1.5 and 2 years using the bootstrap method.

7.18 The following table gives the prices of some zero-coupon and annual-coupon bonds:

Maturity (years)	Coupon rate r (% per annum)	Price per 100 face value
1	0.0	98
2	0.0	95
3	4.0	96
4	6.0	97

Calculate the spot rates for maturities of 1, 2, 3 and 4 years using the bootstrap method.

7.19 The following table gives the prices of some zero-coupon and semiannual coupon bonds:

Maturity (years)	Coupon rate r (% per annum)	Price per 100 face value
0.25	0.000	99.46
0.50	0.000	98.82
1.00	2.250	99.66
1.50	2.250	99.23
2.00	2.500	99.15
2.50	2.875	99.47
3.00	3.000	99.47
3.50	3.125	99.64
4.00	3.500	100.54
4.50	3.375	99.60
5.00	3.500	99.68

Calculate the spot rates for maturities of $0.25, 0.5, 1.0, 1.5, \cdots$ and 5 years using the bootstrap method.

7.20 The following table gives the yield to maturity of some zero-coupon and semiannual coupon bonds:

Maturity (years)	Coupon rate r (% per annum)	Yield to maturity (% per annum)
0.50	0.000	2.38
1.00	2.250	2.61
1.50	2.250	2.85
2.00	2.500	3.11
2.50	2.875	3.23
3.00	3.000	3.38
3.50	3.125	3.46
4.00	3.500	3.50
4.50	3.375	3.68
5.00	3.500	3.80

Calculate the spot rates for maturities of $0.25, 0.5, 1.0, 1.5, \cdots$ and 5 years using the bootstrap method.

Advanced Problems

7.21 A 5-year 6% semiannual coupon bond with face value $100 currently sells for $98. A 5-year 2% semiannual coupon bond with face value $100 currently sells for $90. What is the current 5-year spot rate?

7.22 The following table gives the prices of some zero-coupon and semiannual coupon bonds:

Maturity (years)	Coupon rate r (% per annum)	Price per 100 face value
0.5	0.000	98.00
1.5	2.250	96.07
1.5	2.200	96.00
1.5	2.000	95.72
2.0	2.500	93.60
2.5	2.875	92.10
3.0	3.000	90.00

Calculate the spot rates for maturities of $0.5, 1.0, 1.5, \cdots$ and 3 years using the least squares method.

7.23 The cash prices of 3-month and 9-month zero-coupon bonds with face value 100 are 98.0 and 94.0, respectively. A 1-year semiannual coupon bond that pays coupons of $4 every 6 months from now currently sells for $99.50. A 34-month bond that pays annual coupons of $10 starting 10 months from now sells for $103.27. Calculate the force of interest in the periods (in years): $(0, \frac{3}{12}), [\frac{3}{12}, \frac{9}{12}), [\frac{9}{12}, 1)$ and $[1, 2\frac{10}{12})$. Hence, calculate the spot rates for maturities of $0.25, 0.5, 1.0$ and 1.5 years.

7.24 Let P_t^* be the current price of a zero-coupon bond (per 100 face value) with time to maturity t years. The spot rate of interest for investment horizon t can be obtained by solving the equation $P_t^* = 100(1 + i_t^S)^{-t}$. Given observed prices P_t^* at time 0 of zero-coupon bonds with time to maturity t for $t = 1, 2, \ldots, n$, show that the swap rate of an interest rate swap contract with a level notional amount as derived in equation (3.33) can be rewritten as

$$R_S = \frac{100 - P_n^*}{\sum_{t=1}^{n} P_t^*}.$$

8   Bond Management

The rate of interest affects the prices of bonds differently, depending on the coupon rate of interest and the time to maturity of the bond. We introduce the Macaulay duration and the modified duration as measures of the price sensitivity of a bond with respect to the rate of interest. Duration can also be used to compute the approximate change in the bond price when interest rate changes. If better approximation is desired, convexity may be used to enhance the accuracy.

Asset-liability management is an important task for many financial institutions. Given a stream of liability obligations to meet, managers are required to manage their assets to fund the liabilities. Most importantly, the assets should not be adversely affected by interest-rate changes to the extent that the liabilities are not sufficiently funded. We discuss bond asset-liability management strategies such as target-date immunization, cash-flow matching, dedication strategy and net-worth immunization. We also discuss passive bond management strategy such as indexation.

Duration measures can be extended to the case when the term structure is not flat, resulting in the Fisher-Weil duration. Immunization strategy under a nonflat term structure can be constructed based on the Fisher-Weil duration.

Learning Objectives

- *Macaulay duration and modified duration*
- *Duration and interest-rate sensitivity*
- *Convexity*
- *Some rules for duration calculation*
- *Asset-liability matching and immunization*
- *Target-date immunization and duration matching*
- *Effective duration and Fisher-Weil duration*

8.1   Macaulay Duration and Modified Duration

When an investor invests an amount P_0 at time 0 and receives an amount P_n at time n, the horizon of her investment is n periods. Now suppose an investor purchases a n-year semiannual coupon bond for P_0 at time 0 and holds it until maturity. She receives cash payments at time 0.5, 1, 1.5, $\cdots$, n years from now. It is not immediately obvious what the horizon of her investment is. As the amounts of the payments she receives are different at different times, one way to summarize the horizon is to consider the *weighted average* of the time of the cash flows. However, taking into account the fact that the payments are received at different times, we should use the present values of the cash flows (not their nominal values) to compute the weights.

Consider an investment that generates cash flows of amount C_t at time $t = 1, \cdots, n$, measured in payment periods. Suppose the rate of interest is i per payment period and the initial investment is P (for simplicity of notation we have dropped the suffix 0). We denote the present value of C_t due at time t by $\text{PV}(C_t)$, which is given by

$$\text{PV}(C_t) = \frac{C_t}{(1+i)^t}. \tag{8.1}$$

As the value of the investment is equal to the sum of the present values of the future cash flows it generates, we have

$$P = \sum_{t=1}^{n} \text{PV}(C_t). \tag{8.2}$$

Using $PV(C_t)$ as the factor of proportion, we define the weighted average of the time of the cash flows, denoted by D, as

$$D = \sum_{t=1}^{n} t \left[\frac{PV(C_t)}{P} \right]$$

$$= \sum_{t=1}^{n} t w_t, \tag{8.3}$$

where

$$w_t = \frac{PV(C_t)}{P}. \tag{8.4}$$

Note that $w_t \geq 0$ for all t and $\sum_{t=1}^{n} w_t = 1$, so that w_t are properly defined weights and D is the weighted average of $t = 1, \cdots, n$. We call D the **Macaulay duration**, which measures the *average period* of the investment. The value computed from (8.3) gives the Macaulay duration in terms of the number of payment periods. If there are k payments per year and we desire to express the duration in years, we replace t in (8.3) by $\frac{t}{k}$. Thus, if the payments are made twice a year, D is the weighted average of $0.5, 1, \cdots, \frac{n-1}{2}, \frac{n}{2}$ years, and the resulting value of D is then the Macaulay duration in years.

Figure 8.1 illustrates the cash flows of a coupon bond and the calculation of the Macaulay duration of the bond.

Figure 8.1: Present values of the cash flows of a coupon bond

Example 8.1: Calculate the Macaulay duration of a 4-year annual coupon bond with 6% coupon and a yield to maturity of 5.5%.

Solution: The present values of the cash flows can be calculated using (8.1) with $i = 5.5\%$. The computation of the Macaulay duration is presented in Table 8.1.

Table 8.1: Computation for Example 8.1

t (years)	C_t	PV(C_t)	w_t	tw_t
1	6	5.6872	0.0559	0.0559
2	6	5.3907	0.0530	0.1060
3	6	5.1097	0.0502	0.1506
4	106	85.5650	0.8409	3.3636
Total		101.7526	1.0000	3.6761

The price of the bond P is equal to the sum of the third column, namely 101.7526. Note that the entries in the fourth column are all positive and sum up to 1. The Macaulay duration is the sum of the last column, which is 3.6761 years. Thus, the Macaulay duration of the bond is less than its time to maturity of 4 years.

Example 8.2: Calculate the Macaulay duration of a 2-year semiannual coupon bond with 4% coupon per annum and a yield to maturity of 4.8% compounded semiannually.

Solution: The cash flows of the bond occur at time 1, 2, 3 and 4 half-years. The present values of the cash flows can be calculated using (8.1) with $i = 2.4\%$ per payment period (i.e., half-year). The computation of the Macaulay duration is presented in Table 8.2.

Table 8.2: Computation for Example 8.2

t (half-years)	C_t	PV(C_t)	w_t	tw_t
1	2	1.953	0.0198	0.0198
2	2	1.907	0.0194	0.0388
3	2	1.863	0.0189	0.0568
4	102	92.768	0.9419	3.7676
Total		98.491	1.0000	3.8830

The price of the bond is equal to the sum of the third column, namely 98.491. The Macaulay duration is the sum of the last column, namely 3.8830 half-years, which again is less than the time to maturity of the bond of 4 half-years. The Macaulay duration of the bond can also be stated as $\frac{3.8830}{2} = 1.9415$ years.

We introduce the Macaulay duration in (8.3) assuming the cash flows occur at regular intervals. The formula can be easily extended to the case when the cash flows occur at irregular *intervals*. In such case, i will be the rate of interest per base period, e.g., per year, and the discount factor $(1 + i)^t$ will be applied to any (possibly non-integral) value of t (years). The Macaulay duration computed will then be expressed in terms of the number of base periods (years).

Consider a bond with face value (also the redemption value) F, coupon rate r per payment, and time to maturity of n payment periods. The rate of interest i applicable to (8.3) is the yield to maturity per coupon-payment period. Now C_t is equal to Fr for $t = 1, \cdots, n - 1$ and $C_n = Fr + F$. Thus, from (8.3) we have

$$D = \frac{1}{P} \left[\sum_{t=1}^{n} \frac{tFr}{(1 + i)^t} + \frac{nF}{(1 + i)^n} \right]$$

$$= \frac{1}{P} \left[Fr \sum_{t=1}^{n} PV(t) + Fnv^n \right]. \tag{8.5}$$

From (6.1) we have $P = (Fr)a_{\overline{n}|} + Fv^n$. Hence, the Macaulay duration of the bond is (in terms of the number of payment periods)

$$D = \frac{Fr \sum_{t=1}^{n} PV(t) + Fnv^n}{(Fr)a_{\overline{n}|} + Fv^n}$$

$$= \frac{r(Ia)_{\overline{n}|} + n v^n}{r\, a_{\overline{n}|} + v^n}. \tag{8.6}$$

Example 8.3: Calculate the Macaulay duration of the bonds in Examples 8.1 and 8.2 using equation (8.6).

Solution: For Example 8.1, $r = 6\%$, $i = 5.5\%$ and $n = 4$. Thus, $a_{\overline{4}|} = 3.5052$ and we use (2.36) to obtain $(Ia)_{\overline{4}|} = 8.5285$. Now using (8.6) we have

$$D = \frac{0.06 \times 8.5294 + 4(1.055)^{-4}}{0.06 \times 3.5052 + (1.055)^{-4}} = 3.6761 \text{ years,}$$

which is the answer in Example 8.1. For Example 8.2, we have $r = 2\%$, $i = 2.4\%$ and $n = 4$. Thus, $a_{\overline{4}|} = 3.7711$ and $(Ia)_{\overline{4}|} = 9.3159$. Hence, we have

$$D = \frac{0.02 \times 9.3159 + 4(1.024)^{-4}}{0.02 \times 3.7711 + (1.024)^{-4}} = 3.8830 \text{ half-years.}$$

While the Macaulay duration was originally proposed to measure the average horizon of an investment, it turns out that it can be used to measure the price sensitivity of the investment with respect to interest-rate changes. To measure this sensitivity we consider the derivative $\frac{dP}{di}$. As the price of the investment P drops when interest rate i increases, $\frac{dP}{di} < 0$. We consider (the negative of) the percentage change in the price of the investment per unit change in the rate of interest, i.e., $-\frac{dP}{di}\frac{1}{P}$. Using (8.1) and (8.2), this quantity is given by

$$
\begin{aligned}
-\frac{1}{P}\frac{dP}{di} &= -\frac{1}{P}\sum_{t=1}^{n}\frac{(-t)C_t}{(1+i)^{t+1}} \\
&= \frac{1}{P(1+i)}\sum_{t=1}^{n}\frac{tC_t}{(1+i)^t} \\
&= \frac{1}{1+i}\sum_{t=1}^{n}t\left[\frac{\mathrm{PV}(C_t)}{P}\right] \\
&= \frac{D}{1+i}.
\end{aligned}
\qquad (8.7)
$$

We define

$$
D^* = \frac{D}{1+i}, \qquad (8.8)
$$

and call it the **modified duration**, which is always positive and measures the percentage decrease of the value of the investment per unit increase in the rate of interest. Note that in (8.8) i is the rate of interest per payment period, while the Macaulay duration D can be in terms of years or number of payment periods.

Example 8.4: Calculate the modified duration of the bonds in Examples 8.1 and 8.2.

Solution: For Example 8.1, we have

$$
D^* = \frac{3.6761}{1.055} = 3.4845 \text{ years.}
$$

Thus, the bond drops in value by 3.4845% per 1 percentage point increase (*not* percentage increase) in interest rate. However, as the bond price and interest rate relationship is nonlinear, this statement is only correct approximately and applies to the current rate of interest of 5.5%. For Example 8.2, we have

$$
D^* = \frac{3.8830}{1.024} = 3.7920 \text{ half-years.}
$$

Thus, the bond drops in value by 3.7920% per 1 percentage point increase in the rate of interest per half-year.

To use the modified duration as a measure of the sensitivity of the price of the investment with respect to the rate of interest, note that if the modified duration is expressed in terms of the number of payment periods, then the interest rate quoted must also be per payment period. Thus, in the above example, the value of the bond drops by 3.7920% per 1 percentage point increase (*not* percentage increase) in the rate of interest per half-year. Alternatively, we can state that the bond drops by 1.896% in value per 1 percentage point increase in the rate of interest per year.

Excel provides the function **DURATION** to compute the Macaulay duration and the function **MDURATION** to compute the modified duration of a bond. The bond is assumed to be redeemable at par. The specifications of these functions are given as follows:

Excel functions: DURATION/MDURATION (smt,mty,crt,yld,frq,basis)

smt = settlement date
mty = maturity date
crt = coupon rate of interest per annum
yld = annualized bond yield
frq = number of coupon payments per year
basis = day count, 30/360 if omitted (or set to 0) and actual/actual if set to 1
Output = Macaulay/modified duration of the bond in years

Exhibit 8.1 illustrates the use of the **DURATION** and **MDURATION** functions to compute the answers for Examples 8.1 through 8.4. Note that we have arbitrarily fixed the settlement date as January 1, 2001, and the maturity date is then entered based on the given time to maturity of the bond.

Exhibit 8.1: Use of **DURATION** and **MDURATION**

	A	B	C	D
1	1/1/2001	1/1/2001		
2	1/1/2005	1/1/2003		
3	0.06	0.04		
4	0.055	0.048		
5	3.676	=duration(a1,a2,a3,a4,1)		
6	3.485	=mduration(a1,a2,a3,a4,1)		
7	1.941	=duration(b1,b2,b3,b4,2)		
8	1.896	=mduration(b1,b2,b3,b4,2)		
9				

File   Edit   View   Insert   Format   Tools   Da

E18

8.2   Duration for Price Correction

We now consider the use of the modified duration to approximate the price change of a bond when the rate of interest changes. We denote $P(i)$ as the price of a bond when the yield to maturity is i per coupon-payment period. When the rate of interest changes to $i + \Delta i$, the bond price is revised to $P(i + \Delta i)$. While the bond price can be re-calculated at the rate of interest $i + \Delta i$ using one of the pricing formulas in Chapter 6, an approximation is available using the modified duration or the Macaulay duration.

For a continuous function $f(x)$ with first- and second-order derivatives, the function evaluated at $x + \Delta x$, i.e., $f(x + \Delta x)$, can be approximated by Taylor's expansion as follows (see Appendix A.8):

$$f(x + \Delta x) \approx f(x) + \frac{df(x)}{dx}\Delta x + \frac{1}{2}\frac{d^2 f(x)}{dx^2}(\Delta x)^2. \qquad (8.9)$$

Thus, if we expand the bond price $P(i + \Delta i)$ using Taylor's expansion up to the first-order derivative, we obtain

$$
\begin{aligned}
P(i + \Delta i) &\approx P(i) + \frac{dP(i)}{di}\Delta i \\
&= P(i)\left[1 - \left(-\frac{1}{P(i)}\frac{dP(i)}{di}\right)\Delta i\right] \\
&= P(i)\left(1 - D^*\Delta i\right). \qquad (8.10)
\end{aligned}
$$

Hence, we can use the modified duration (D^*) to obtain a first-order linear approximation to the revised bond price with respect to a change in the rate of interest. Note that in (8.10), as i is per coupon-payment period, D^* and Δi should also be measured in coupon-payment period. However, we may also express D^* in years, in which case Δi is the change in the rate of interest per annum.

There is another first-order approximation to the revised bond price with respect to a change in the rate of interest, which is based on the Macaulay duration (D),

$$P(i + \Delta i) \approx P(i)\left[\frac{1 + i}{1 + i + \Delta i}\right]^D. \qquad (8.11)$$

It can be shown that, under certain general conditions, the approximation in (8.11) is at least as accurate as the linear modified duration approximation in (8.10).[1]

---

[1] See R. Alps, "Using Duration and Convexity to Approximate Change in Present Value", *SOA Financial Mathematics Study Note FM-24-17.*

Example 8.5: A 10-year semiannual coupon bond with coupon rate of 7% per year is selling to yield 6.5% per year compounded semiannually. What is the bond price if the yield changes to (i) 6%, and (ii) 6.7%, compounded semiannually? You should (a) use the exact method, (b) use the first-order linear approximation based on the modified duration, and (c) use the first-order approximation based on the Macaulay duration.

Solution: (a) We use the basic formula (6.1) with $r = 3.5\%$, $i = 3.25\%$ and $n = 20$, to obtain

$$P(0.0325) = 103.6348.$$

Similarly, we compute the bond price at the new rates of interest $i = 3\%$ and 3.35%, to obtain

$$P(0.03) = 107.4387$$

and

$$P(0.0335) = 102.1611.$$

Thus, the bond price increases by 3.8039 when the yield per half-year drops by 0.25 percentage point, and it decreases by 1.4737 when the yield per half-year increases by 0.1 percentage point.

At the rate of interest of 3.25% we have $(Ia)_{\overline{20}|} = 137.306$, so that from (8.6) the Macaulay duration is

$$
\begin{aligned}
D &= \frac{0.035 \times 137.306 + 20(1.0325)^{-20}}{1.036348} \\
&= 14.8166 \text{ half-years},
\end{aligned}
$$

and hence the modified duration is

$$D^* = \frac{14.8166}{1.0325} = 14.3502 \text{ half-years}.$$

(b) We approximate the price change using the modified duration. The annual yield rate decreases from 6.5% to 6% when $\Delta i = -0.0025$ (per half-year). Thus, from (8.10), we have

$$P(0.03) \approx 103.6348[1 - 14.3502(-0.0025)] = 107.3528 < 107.4387.$$

Similarly, if the annual yield rate increases from 6.5% to 6.7%, we have $\Delta i = 0.001$ (per half-year), so that

$$P(0.0335) \approx 103.6348[1 - 14.3502(0.001)] = 102.1476 < 102.1611.$$

(c) On the other hand, we may also approximate the price change using the Macaulay duration. From (8.11), we have

$$P(0.03) \approx 103.6348 \left[\frac{1.0325}{1.03} \right]^{14.8166} = 107.4249 < 107.4387.$$

and

$$P(0.0335) \approx 103.6348 \left[\frac{1.0325}{1.0335} \right]^{14.8166} = 102.1590 < 102.1611.$$

Results in (b) and (c) are quite close to the exact results obtained in (a), although it can be seen that the approximate values are less than the exact values in both cases. Thus, using (8.10) or (8.11), approximate values of the price of the bond can be computed with small changes in the interest rate without using the bond price formulas.

Figure 8.2 illustrates the application of (8.10). The relationship between the bond price and the rate of interest is given by the curve, which is *convex* to the origin. Equation (8.10) approximates the bond price using the straight line which is tangent to the point $(i, P(i))$ with a negative slope of $-P(i)D^*$. Note that due to the convexity of the relationship between the interest rate and the bond price, the correction based on the modified duration always under-approximates the exact price. This point is illustrated by Example 8.5(b). To improve the approximation, we may take into account the convexity of the relationship. This leads us to introduce the convexity measure in the next section. We do not discuss the correction to the approximation based on the Macaulay duration in this book. Interested readers may refer to the reference provided in the first footnote of this Chapter.

8.3 Convexity

To obtain a better approximation for the bond price, we apply Taylor's expansion in (8.9) to the second order, giving

$$P(i + \Delta i) \approx P(i) + \frac{dP(i)}{di} \Delta i + \frac{1}{2} \frac{d^2 P(i)}{di^2} (\Delta i)^2$$

$$= P(i) \left[1 - \left(-\frac{1}{P(i)} \frac{dP(i)}{di} \right) \Delta i + \frac{1}{2P(i)} \left(\frac{d^2 P(i)}{di^2} \right) (\Delta i)^2 \right]. \quad (8.12)$$

Now we define the **convexity of the bond** as

$$C = \frac{1}{P(i)} \times \frac{d^2 P(i)}{di^2}, \quad (8.13)$$

Figure 8.2: Bond-price approximation using modified duration

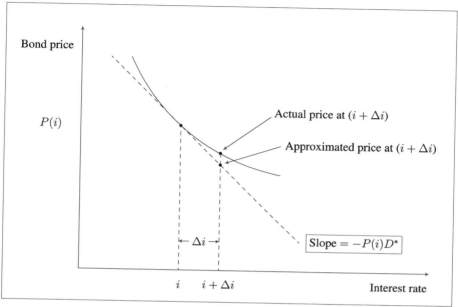

so that (8.12) becomes

$$P(i + \Delta i) \approx P(i) \left[1 - D^* \Delta i + \frac{1}{2} C(\Delta i)^2 \right].$$ (8.14)

For the investment with price given in (8.1) and (8.2), we have

$$\frac{d^2 P(i)}{di^2} = \sum_{t=1}^{n} \frac{(t+1)tC_t}{(1+i)^{t+2}},$$ (8.15)

so that the convexity is

$$
\begin{aligned}
C &= \frac{1}{P(i)} \times \frac{d^2 P(i)}{di^2} \\
&= \frac{1}{P(i)} \sum_{t=1}^{n} \frac{(t+1)tC_t}{(1+i)^{t+2}} \\
&= \frac{1}{P(i)(1+i)^2} \sum_{t=1}^{n} \frac{(t+1)tC_t}{(1+i)^t} \\
&= \frac{1}{P(i)(1+i)^2} \sum_{t=1}^{n} (t+1)t \, \text{PV}(C_t).
\end{aligned}
$$ (8.16)

For a bond investment, $C_t \geq 0$ for all t, so that $C > 0$, verifying the convexity relationship in Figure 8.2. Thus, the correction term $\frac{C(\Delta i)^2}{2}$ in (8.14) is always positive, which compensates for the under-approximation in (8.10).

Example 8.6: Revisit Example 8.5(b) and approximate the bond prices with convexity correction.

Solution: We calculate the convexity using (8.16) to obtain

$$C = \frac{1}{(103.6348)(1.0325)^2} \left[\frac{2 \times 1 \times 3.5}{1.0325} + \frac{3 \times 2 \times 3.5}{(1.0325)^2} + \cdots + \frac{21 \times 20 \times 103.5}{(1.0325)^{20}} \right]$$
$$= 260.9566.$$

Thus, the approximate bond prices are

$$P(0.03) \approx 107.3528 + (103.6348)(0.5)(260.9566)(-0.0025)^2 = 107.4373,$$

and

$$P(0.0335) \approx 102.1476 + (103.6348)(0.5)(260.9566)(0.001)^2 = 102.1612.$$

We can see that the approximation is now further improved.

8.4 Some Rules for Duration

Duration measures the price sensitivity of a bond (or the present value of a stream of cash flows) with respect to interest rate. It is a very important tool for bond or asset-liability management. In this section, we summarize some useful rules for duration.

Rule 1: *The Macaulay duration D of a bond is always less than or equal to its time to maturity n. Equality holds only for a zero-coupon bond.*

This rule is quite obvious as D is a weighted average of the time of occurrences of cash flows, each of which is less than or equal to n, with equality only for the cash flow of a zero-coupon bond.

Rule 2: *Holding the time to maturity n of a bond constant, when the coupon rate of interest r decreases, the Macaulay duration D increases.*

This rule can be understood from Figure 8.1. The Macaulay duration measures the distance from the origin to the *center of gravity* of the bars. When r is lower, the bars representing the present values of the coupons will be shorter while that representing the face value remains unchanged. This shifts the center of gravity to the right, resulting in a higher duration D.

Rule 3: *Other things being equal, when the yield to maturity i decreases, the Macaulay duration D increases.*

Again from Figure 8.1, lower i raises the height of the bars. The effect on the face value dominates and thus shifts the duration to the right.

Rule 4: *For a level perpetuity-immediate, the modified duration D* is equal to $\frac{1}{i}$.*

Consider a level perpetuity of unit amount. The price of the perpetuity is $\frac{1}{i}$ (see (2.9)), so that $\frac{dP(i)}{di} = -\frac{1}{i^2}$ and

$$D^* = i \times \frac{1}{i^2} = \frac{1}{i}.$$

Rule 5: *For a level annuity-immediate of n payments, the modified duration is*

$$D^* = \frac{1}{i} - \frac{n}{(1+i)\left[(1+i)^n - 1\right]}. \tag{8.17}$$

This rule can be proved by direct differentiation of the price of the annuity (assuming unit payment), which is

$$P(i) = a_{\overline{n}|} = \frac{1 - v^n}{i}.$$

Rule 6: *The modified duration D* of a coupon bond with coupon rate of r per payment, n payments to maturity and yield to maturity of i per coupon-payment period is*

$$D^* = \frac{1}{i} - \frac{(1+i) + n(r-i)}{(1+i)\left[((1+i)^n - 1)\, r + i\right]}. \tag{8.18}$$

The readers are invited to prove this rule by directly differentiating the basic price formula (6.1).

Rule 7: *For a coupon bond selling at par, the modified duration is*

$$D^* = \frac{1}{i}\left[1 - \frac{1}{(1+i)^n}\right]. \tag{8.19}$$

This can be obtained from (8.18) by setting $r = i$.

Rule 8: *Holding other things constant, a bond's duration D usually increases with its time to maturity n.*

Figure 8.3:   Macaulay duration versus time to maturity

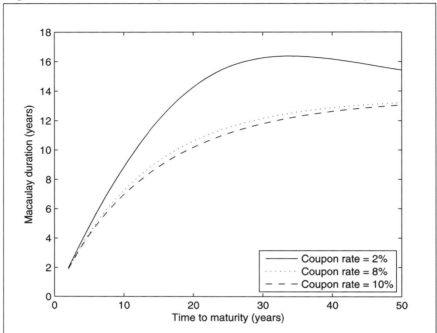

For premium and par bonds, the relationship is monotonic so that D *always* increases with n. For deep-discount bonds, however, D may increase with n for bonds with short maturity and then decreases with further increases in maturity. Figure 8.3 illustrates this phenomenon. We assume the yield curve is flat at 8% per annum, and consider three annual coupon bonds with coupon rates of 2%, 8% and 10% per annum. Thus, the bond with 2% coupon rate is in deep discount, the 8% coupon bond is at par and the 10% coupon bond is at a premium. Figure 8.3 plots the Macaulay duration against the time to maturity of the bond. For the 2% coupon bond, the Macaulay duration increases with the time to maturity until the maturity reaches 34 years, from which onwards the Macaulay duration decreases when the time to maturity increases further. In contrast, however, for the par and premium bonds the Macaulay duration increases monotonically with the time to maturity.

Suppose a portfolio of bonds is constructed from M bonds, with durations $D_1, \cdots, D_M$. Let the bond values be $P_1, \cdots, P_M$, so that their total value is $P = \sum_{j=1}^{M} P_j$. Define $w_j = \frac{P_j}{P}$ as the weight of Bond j in the portfolio, then the duration D_P of the portfolio is the weighted average of the bond durations, i.e.,

$$D_P = \sum_{j=1}^{M} w_j D_j. \tag{8.20}$$

This result is very useful for bond portfolio management when a portfolio with a certain duration is required. Readers are invited to prove (8.20).

Example 8.7: A bond manager has a choice of two bonds, A and B. Bond A is a 4-year annual coupon bond with coupon rate of 6%. Bond B is a 2-year annual coupon bond with coupon rate of 4%. The current yield to maturity in the market is 5.5% per annum for all maturities. How does the manager construct a portfolio of $100 million, consisting of bonds A and B, with a Macaulay duration of 2.5 years?

Solution: From Example 8.1, we know that Bond A has a Macaulay duration of 3.6761 years. We compute the Macaulay duration of Bond B as 1.9610 years. Let w be the proportion of investment in Bond A. Thus, from (8.20) we require

$$3.6761w + 1.9610(1 - w) = 2.5,$$

so that

$$w = \frac{2.5 - 1.9610}{3.6761 - 1.9610} = 31.43\%.$$

Hence the portfolio should consist of $31.43 million of Bond A and $68.57 million of Bond B.

8.5 Immunization Strategies

Financial institutions are often faced with the problem of meeting a liability of a given amount some time in the future. For example, a corporation may be required to make a lump sum payment to its retirees one year later. To fix ideas, we consider a liability of amount V to be paid T periods later. A simple strategy to meet this obligation is to purchase a zero-coupon bond with face value V, maturing at time T. This strategy is called **cash-flow matching**. When cash-flow matching is adopted, the obligation is always met, even if there is fluctuation in the rate of interest.

However, zero-coupon bonds of the required maturity may not be available in the market. Institutions often fund their liabilities with coupon bonds, with a current market value higher than or equal to the present value of their liabilities. However, when interest rate changes, the value of the bond will change, as well as the accumulation of the interest of the coupon payments. Consequently, the accumulated fund may not be able to meet the targeted liabilities.

Immunization is a strategy of managing a portfolio of assets such that the business is *immune* to interest-rate fluctuations. For the simple situation above, the **target-date immunization** strategy may be adopted. This involves holding a portfolio of bonds that will accumulate in value to V at time T at the current market rate of interest. The portfolio, however, should be constructed in such a way that its Macaulay duration D is equal to the targeted date of the liability T. Specifically, suppose the current yield rate is i, the current value of the portfolio of bonds, denoted by $P(i)$, must be

$$P(i) = \frac{V}{(1+i)^T}. \tag{8.21}$$

Now if interest rate remains unchanged until time T, this bond portfolio will accumulate in value to V at the maturity date of the liability. If interest rate increases, the bond portfolio will drop in value. However, the coupon payments will generate higher interest and compensate for this. On the other hand, if interest rate drops, the bond portfolio value goes up, with subsequent slow-down in accumulation of interest. Under either situation, as we shall see, the bond portfolio value will finally accumulate to V at time T, provided the portfolio's Macaulay duration D is equal to T and there is only a one-time change in the rate of interest of a small amount.

We consider the bond value for a *one-time small change* in the rate of interest. If interest rate changes to $i + \Delta i$ immediately after the purchase of the bond, the bond price becomes $P(i + \Delta i)$ which, at time T, accumulates to $P(i + \Delta i)(1 + i + \Delta i)^T$ if the rate of interest remains at $i + \Delta i$. We approximate $(1 + i + \Delta i)^T$ to the first order in Δi to obtain (apply Taylor's expansion to $f(i) = (1 + i)^T$)

$$(1 + i + \Delta i)^T \approx (1 + i)^T + T(1 + i)^{T-1}\Delta i. \tag{8.22}$$

Using (8.10) and (8.22) we have

$$P(i + \Delta i)(1 + i + \Delta i)^T \approx P(i)(1 - D^*\Delta i)\left[(1 + i)^T + T(1 + i)^{T-1}\Delta i\right].$$

However, as $D^* = \frac{D}{(1+i)}$ and $T = D$, the above equation becomes

$$\begin{aligned}
P(i + \Delta i)(1 + i + \Delta i)^T &\approx P(i)\left[(1 + i)^D - D^*\Delta i(1 + i)^D + D(1 + i)^{D-1}\Delta i\right] \\
&= P(i)(1 + i)^D \\
&= V.
\end{aligned} \tag{8.23}$$

Thus, for a small one-time change in interest rate, the bond accumulates to V at time T after the interest-rate change so that the business is immunized against interest-rate fluctuations.

Example 8.8: A company has to pay $100 million 3.6761 years from now. The current market rate of interest is 5.5%. Demonstrate the funding strategy the company should adopt with the 6% annual coupon bond in Example 8.1. Consider the scenarios when there is an immediate one-time change in interest rate to (a) 5%, and (b) 6%.

Solution: From equation (8.21), the current value of the bond should be

$$\frac{100}{(1.055)^{3.6761}} = \$82.1338 \text{ million.}$$

From Example 8.1, the bond price is 101.7526% of the face value and the Macaulay duration is 3.6761 years, which is the target date for the payment. Hence, the bond purchased should have a face value of

$$\frac{82.13375}{1.017526} = \$80.7191 \text{ million.}$$

At the end of year 3, the accumulated value of the coupon payments is

$$80.7191 \times 0.06 s_{\overline{3}|0.055} = \$15.3432 \text{ million,}$$

and the bond price is (the bond will mature in 1 year with a 6% coupon payment and redemption payment of 80.7191)

$$\frac{80.7191 \times 0.06 + 80.7191}{1.055} = \$81.1017 \text{ million.}$$

Thus, the bond price plus the accumulated coupon values at time 3.6761 years is

$$(81.1017 + 15.3432)(1.055)^{0.6761} = \$100 \text{ million.}$$

Suppose interest rate drops to 5% immediately after the purchase of the bond, the accumulated coupon value 3 years later is

$$80.7191 \times 0.06 s_{\overline{3}|0.05} = \$15.2680 \text{ million,}$$

and the bond price at year 3 is

$$\frac{80.7191(1.06)}{1.05} = \$81.4879 \text{ million.}$$

The total of the bond value and the accumulated coupon payments at time 3.6761 years is

$$(81.4879 + 15.2680)(1.05)^{0.6761} = \$100 \text{ million.}$$

On the other hand, if interest rate increases to 6% immediately after the purchase of the bond, the accumulated coupon value 3 years later is

$$80.7191 \times 0.06s_{\overline{3}|0.06} = \$15.4186 \text{ million,}$$

and the bond price at year 3 is 80.7191 (this is a par bond with yield rate equal to coupon rate). Thus, the total of the bond value and the accumulated coupon payments at time 3.6761 years is

$$(80.7191 + 15.4186)(1.06)^{0.6761} = \$100 \text{ million.}$$

Thus, for an immediate one-time small change in interest rate, the bond accumulates to the targeted value of $100 million at 3.6761 years, and the business is immunized.

Example 8.9: A company has to pay $100 million 4 years from now. The current market rate of interest is 5.5%. The company uses the 6% annual coupon bond in Example 8.1 to fund this liability. Is the bond sufficient to meet the liability when there is an immediate one-time change in interest rate to (a) 5%, and (b) 6%?

Solution: As the target date of the liability is 4 years and the Macaulay duration of the bond is 3.6761 years, there is a mismatch in the durations and the business is not immunized. To fund the liability in 4 years, the value of the bond purchased at time 0 is

$$\frac{100}{(1.055)^4} = \$80.7217 \text{ million,}$$

and the face value of the bond is

$$\frac{80.7217}{1.017526} = \$79.3313 \text{ million.}$$

If interest rate drops to 5%, the asset value at year 4 is

$$79.3313 \times 0.06s_{\overline{4}|0.05} + 79.3313 = \$99.8470 \text{ million,}$$

so that the liability is under-funded. On the other hand, if interest rate increases to 6%, the asset value at year 4 is

$$79.3313 \times 0.06s_{\overline{4}|0.06} + 79.3313 = \$100.1539 \text{ million,}$$

so that the liability is over-funded.

Figure 8.4: Illustration of target-date immunization

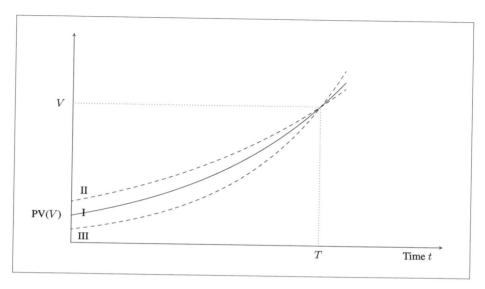

Figure 8.4 describes the working of the target-date immunization strategy. The liability to be funded at time T is of amount V. At current rate of interest i, a bond of Macaulay duration $D = T$ and value of PV(V) is purchased. Suppose interest rate remains unchanged, the bond increases in value through Path I to V at time T. If interest rate drops, the value of the bond increases to above PV(V), but then increases in value at a slower rate and accumulates in value through Path II to V at time T. On the other hand, if interest rate increases, the value of the bond drops below PV(V), but will then increase in value at a faster rate through Path III, until it reaches V at time T.

If a financial institution has multiple liability obligations to meet, the manager may adopt cash-flow matching to each obligation. This is a **dedication strategy** in which the manager selects a portfolio of bonds (zero-coupon or coupon bonds) to provide total cash flows in each period to match the required obligations. While this approach can eliminate interest-rate risk, it may be expensive to implement, or simply infeasible due to the constraints imposed on the selection of bonds. Alternatively, the manager may adopt target-date immunization for each liability obligation, matching the maturity date of the obligation with a bond (or portfolio of bonds) with the required duration and value.

The manager may also consider the liability obligations as a whole and construct a portfolio to fund these obligations, with the objective of controlling for the interest-rate risk. A commonly adopted strategy is **duration matching**. To fix ideas, we assume a financial institution has a stream of liabilities $L_1, L_2, \cdots, L_N$

to be paid out at various times in the future. It will fund these liabilities with assets $A_1, A_2, \cdots, A_M$ generating cash flows at various times in the future. For example, an insurance company may expect to pay claims or policy redemptions of amounts $L_1, L_2, \cdots, L_N$, and will receive policy premiums and bond incomes of amounts $A_1, A_2, \cdots, A_M$. Also, a pension fund may expect to pay retirees pensions of various amounts at various times, and will fund these with a portfolio of bonds providing coupon payments and redemption values at various times. We assume that the rate of interest i is flat for cash flows of all maturities and applies to both assets and liabilities.

We denote

$$\text{PV(assets)} = \sum_{j=1}^{M} \text{PV}(A_j) = V_A, \qquad (8.24)$$

and

$$\text{PV(liabilities)} = \sum_{j=1}^{N} \text{PV}(L_j) = V_L. \qquad (8.25)$$

Although the financial institution may initially have a portfolio of assets such that $V_A > V_L$, the values of the assets and liabilities may change differently when interest rate changes. Specifically, if interest rate increases and the drop in value in V_A is more than that in V_L, the liabilities may not be sufficiently funded. Duration matching is the technique of matching assets with liabilities to neutralize the interest-rate risk.

We denote the Macaulay durations of the assets and liabilities by D_A and D_L, respectively. The duration matching strategy involves constructing a portfolio of assets such that the following conditions hold:

1. $V_A \geq V_L$
2. $D_A = D_L$.

The first condition ensures that the liabilities are initially sufficiently funded. It is the second condition that gives this strategy its name. Note that the net worth of the financial institution is $V_A - V_L$, which will be denoted by S. Condition 2 ensures that, to the first-order approximation, the asset-liability ratio $\frac{V_A}{V_L}$ remains unchanged when interest rate changes. This result can be deduced as follows:

$$
\begin{aligned}
\frac{d}{di}\left(\frac{V_A}{V_L}\right) &= \frac{V_L \dfrac{dV_A}{di} - V_A \dfrac{dV_L}{di}}{V_L^2} \\
&= \frac{V_A}{V_L}\left(\frac{1}{V_A}\frac{dV_A}{di} - \frac{1}{V_L}\frac{dV_L}{di}\right) \\
&= \frac{V_A}{V_L(1+i)}(D_L - D_A) \\
&= 0. \qquad (8.26)
\end{aligned}
$$

Example 8.10: A financial institution has to pay $1,000 after 2 years and $2,000 after 4 years. The current market interest rate is 10%, and the yield curve is assumed to be flat at any time. The institution wishes to immunize the interest rate risk by purchasing zero-coupon bonds which mature after 1, 3 and 5 years. One member in the risk management team of the institution, Alan, devised the following strategy:

- Purchase a 1-year zero-coupon bond with a face value of $44.74,

- Purchase a 3-year zero-coupon bond with a face value of $2,450.83,

- Purchase a 5-year zero-coupon bond with a face value of $500.00.

(a) Find the present value of the liability. (b) Show that Alan's portfolio satisfies the conditions of the duration matching strategy. (c) Define surplus $S = V_A - V_L$, calculate S when there is an immediate one-time change of interest rate from 10% to (i) 9%, (ii) 11%, (iii) 15%, (iv) 30% and (v) 80%. (d) Find the convexity of the portfolio of assets and the portfolio of liabilities at $i = 10\%$.

Solution: (a) The present value of the liabilities is

$$V_L = 1,000\,(1.1)^{-2} + 2,000\,(1.1)^{-4} = \$2,192.47.$$

For (b), the present value of Alan's asset portfolio is

$$V_A = 44.74\,(1.1)^{-1} + 2,450.83\,(1.1)^{-3} + 500.00\,(1.1)^{-5} = \$2,192.47.$$

The Macaulay duration of the assets and liabilities can be calculated using equation (8.3) to give

$$
\begin{aligned}
D_A &= \frac{1 \times 44.74\,(1.1)^{-1} + 3 \times 2,450.83\,(1.1)^{-3} + 5 \times 500.00\,(1.1)^{-5}}{2,192.47} \\
&= 3.2461 \text{ years},
\end{aligned}
$$

$$
\begin{aligned}
D_L &= \frac{2 \times 1,000\,(1.1)^{-2} + 4 \times 2,000\,(1.1)^{-4}}{2,192.47} \\
&= 3.2461 \text{ years}.
\end{aligned}
$$

Since $V_A = V_L$ and $D_A = D_L$, the conditions of the duration matching strategy are met for Alan's portfolio.

For (c), when there is an immediate one-time shift in interest rate from 10% to 9%, using equation (8.2), we have

$$
\begin{aligned}
V_A &= 44.74\,(1.09)^{-1} + 2,450.83\,(1.09)^{-3} + 500.00\,(1.09)^{-5} = \$2,258.50, \\
V_L &= 1,000\,(1.09)^{-2} + 2,000\,(1.09)^{-4} = \$2,258.53, \\
S &= 2,258.50 - 2,258.53 = -\$0.03.
\end{aligned}
$$

We repeat the above calculations for interest rate of 11%, 15%, 30% and 80%. The results are summarized as follows:

Table 8.3: Results of Example 8.10

i	V_A	V_L	S
0.09	2,258.50	2,258.53	−0.03
0.10	2,192.47	2,192.47	0.00
0.11	2,129.05	2,129.08	−0.03
0.15	1,898.95	1,899.65	−0.70
0.30	1,284.61	1,291.97	−7.36
0.80	471.55	499.16	−27.61

For (d), using equation (8.16), the convexity of the assets is

$$C_A = \frac{2\times1\times44.74\,(1.1)^{-1} + 4\times3\times2{,}450.83\,(1.1)^{-3} + 6\times5\times500.00\,(1.1)^{-5}}{(1.1)^2 \times 2{,}192.47}$$

$$= 11.8706,$$

and the convexity of the liabilities is

$$C_L = \frac{3 \times 2 \times 1{,}000\,(1.1)^{-2} + 5 \times 4 \times 2{,}000\,(1.1)^{-4}}{(1.1)^2 \times 2{,}192.47}$$

$$= 12.1676.$$

Under duration matching, when there is an immediate one-time small shift in interest rate, the surplus ($S = V_A - V_L$) should be preserved (i.e., non-negative). In Example 8.10, we notice that the values of assets and liabilities are matched at $i = 10\%$ with $V_A = V_L = \$2{,}192.47$. When there is an immediate one-time interest rate change, both asset and liability values move in the same direction. However, the rate of change of the value in the asset portfolio is slightly lower than that of the liability portfolio, always resulting in a deficit position. For example, when interest rate drops from 10% to 9%, the asset and liability values increase to $2,258.50 and $ 2,258.53, respectively. On the other hand, when interest rate shifts up to 15%, the asset and liability values decrease to $1,898.95 and $1,899.65, respectively, with a deficit position of $S = -\$0.70$.

It should be noted that the duration matching strategy is based on the first-order approximation. To improve the strategy, we may take into account the convexity of the asset and liability portfolios. Using second-order approximation, we re-consider the rate of change of the asset-liability ratio in equation (8.26) to obtain

$$\frac{d}{di}\left(\frac{V_A}{V_L}\right) = \frac{V_A}{V_L}\left(\frac{1}{V_A}\frac{dV_A}{di} - \frac{1}{V_L}\frac{dV_L}{di}\right)$$

$$= \frac{V_A}{V_L(1+i)}(D_L - D_A) + \frac{V_A}{V_L}\cdot\frac{1}{2}(C_A - C_L), \quad (8.27)$$

where C_A and C_L are the convexity of the assets and liabilities, respectively. To protect the asset-liability ratio from dropping when interest rate changes, the **Redington immunization** strategy, named after the British actuary Frank Redington, imposes the following three conditions for constructing a portfolio of assets:

1. $V_A \geq V_L$
2. $D_A = D_L$
3. $C_A > C_L$.

These three conditions ensure that the right-hand side of equation (8.27) is greater than or equal to zero under the second-order approximation. In Example 8.10, the convexity measures of the assets and the liabilities are $C_A = 11.87$ and $C_L = 12.17$, respectively. Since $C_A < C_L$, Alan's portfolio does not meet the conditions of the Redington immunization strategy.

Example 8.11: For the financial institution in Example 8.10, a risk consultant, Alfred, recommended the following strategy:

- Purchase a 1-year zero-coupon bond with a face value of $154.16,
- Purchase a 3-year zero-coupon bond with a face value of $2,186.04,
- Purchase a 5-year zero-coupon bond with a face value of $660.18.

(a) Show that Alfred's portfolio satisfies the three conditions of the Redington immunization strategy. (b) Define surplus $S = V_A - V_L$, calculate S when there is an immediate one-time change of interest rate from 10% to (i) 9%, (ii) 11%, (iii) 15%, (iv) 30% and (v) 80%.

Solution: (a) The present value of Alfred's asset portfolio is

$$V_A = 154.16\,(1.1)^{-1} + 2,186.04\,(1.1)^{-3} + 660.18\,(1.1)^{-5} = \$2,192.47.$$

The Macaulay duration of the assets and liabilities can be calculated using equation (8.3) to give

$$D_A = \frac{1 \times 154.16\ (1.1)^{-1} + 3 \times 2{,}186.04\ (1.1)^{-3} + 5 \times 660.18\ (1.1)^{-5}}{2{,}192.47}$$

$$= 3.2461 \text{ years,}$$

$$D_L = \frac{2 \times 1{,}000\ (1.1)^{-2} + 4 \times 2{,}000\ (1.1)^{-4}}{2{,}192.47}$$

$$= 3.2461 \text{ years.}$$

Furthermore, using equation (8.16), we get

$$C_A = \frac{2{\times}1{\times}154.16\ (1.1)^{-1} + 4{\times}3{\times}2{,}186.04\ (1.1)^{-3} + 6{\times}5{\times}660.18\ (1.1)^{-5}}{(1.1)^2 \times 2{,}192.47}$$

$$= 12.1704,$$

$$C_L = \frac{3 \times 2 \times 1{,}000\ (1.1)^{-2} + 5 \times 4 \times 2{,}000\ (1.1)^{-4}}{(1.1)^2 \times 2{,}192.47}$$

$$= 12.1676.$$

Since $V_A = V_L$, $D_A = D_L$ and $C_A > C_L$, the conditions of the Redington immunization strategy are met for Alfred's strategy.

For (b), when there is an immediate one-time shift in interest rate from 10% to 9%, using equation (8.2), we have

$$V_A = 154.16\ (1.09)^{-1} + 2{,}186.04\ (1.09)^{-3} + 660.18\ (1.09)^{-5} = \$2{,}258.53,$$
$$V_L = 1{,}000\ (1.09)^{-2} + 2{,}000\ (1.09)^{-4} = \$2{,}258.53,$$
$$S = 2{,}258.53 - 2{,}258.53 = 0.$$

We repeat the above calculations for interest rate of 11%, 15%, 30% and 80%. The results are summarized as follows:

Table 8.4: Results of Example 8.11

i	V_A	V_L	S
0.09	2,258.53	2,258.53	0.00
0.10	2,192.47	2,192.47	0.00
0.11	2,129.08	2,129.08	0.00
0.15	1,899.64	1,899.65	−0.02
0.30	1,291.40	1,291.97	−0.57
0.80	495.42	499.16	−3.74

Figure 8.5: Illustration of cash flows in a full immunization strategy

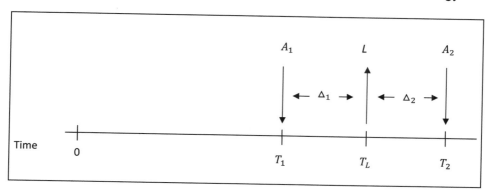

The Redington immunization strategy works well for a one-time *small* shift in interest rate. It protects the net-worth position of the financial institution. However, for a *radical* change of interest rate, the net-worth position might not be immunized under the Redington strategy. In Example 8.11, the financial institution would experience a deficit of $3.74 if the rate of interest had a big jump from 10% to 80%.

Under certain conditions, it is possible to construct a portfolio of assets such that the net-worth position of the financial institution is guaranteed to be non-negative in any positive interest rate environment. A **full immunization** strategy is said to be achieved if under any one-time shift of interest rate from i_0 to i,

$$S(i) = V_A(i) - V_L(i) \geq 0, \quad \text{for } i > 0.$$

We consider the example of a single liability of amount L to be paid T_L periods later. Full immunization strategy involves funding the liability by a portfolio of assets which will produce two cash inflows. The first inflow of amount A_1 is located at time T_1, which is Δ_1 periods *before* time T_L. The second inflow of amount A_2 is at time T_2, which is Δ_2 periods *after* time T_L. Figure 8.5 illustrates these three cashflows. It should be noted that all the values of $i_0, i, A_1, A_2, L, \Delta_1, \Delta_2, T_L, T_1$ and T_2 are positive, and Δ_1 is not necessarily equal to Δ_2. However, it should be noted that when $\Delta_1 = \Delta_2 = 0$, the full immunization strategy is reduced to the cash-flow matching strategy.

In this particular example, the conditions for constructing a portfolio of assets under the full immunization strategy are:

1. $V_A = V_L$
2. $D_A = D_L$.

The above conditions can be rewritten as

1. $A_1(1+i_0)^{-T_1} + A_2(1+i_0)^{-T_2} = L(1+i_0)^{-T_L}$
2. $T_1A_1(1+i_0)^{-T_1} + T_2A_2(1+i_0)^{-T_2} = T_L L(1+i_0)^{-T_L}$.

The proof of full immunization (i.e., $S(i) \geq 0$, for $i > 0$) under the above two conditions are demonstrated in Exercise 8.41 at the end of this Chapter.

The full immunization strategy can be applied to financial institutions with multiple liabilities. We can simply deal with the liabilities one by one, and construct a pair of assets to immunize each of them.

Example 8.12: For the financial institution in Examples 8.10 and 8.11, an actuary, Albert, constructed the following strategy:

- Purchase a 1-year zero-coupon bond with a face value of $454.55,
- Purchase a 3-year zero-coupon bond with a face value of $1,459.09,
- Purchase a 5-year zero-coupon bond with a face value of $1,100.00.

(a) Show that Albert's portfolio satisfies the conditions of the full immunization strategy. (b) Define surplus $S = V_A - V_L$, calculate S when there is an immediate one-time change of interest rate from 10% to (i) 9%, (ii) 11%, (iii) 15%, (iv) 30% and (v) 80%.

Solution: (a) The present value of Albert's asset portfolio is

$$V_A = 454.55\,(1.1)^{-1} + 1,459.09\,(1.1)^{-3} + 1,100.00\,(1.1)^{-5} = \$2,192.47.$$

Let A_1 and A_2 be the amount of 1-year and 3-year zero-coupon bonds that are needed to fully immunize the first liability of $L = 1,000$. Note that $T_1 = 1, T_L = 2$ and $T_2 = 3$. The two conditions for the full immunization strategy require

$$
\begin{aligned}
A_1(1.1)^{-1} + A_2(1.1)^{-3} &= 1,000(1.1)^{-2} \\
(1)A_1(1.1)^{-1} + (3)A_2(1.1)^{-3} &= (2)1,000(1.1)^{-2}.
\end{aligned}
$$

Solving the above system of equations, we get $A_1 = 454.55$ and $A_2 = 550.00$. Next, let A_1^* and A_2^* be the amounts of 3-year and 5-year zero-coupon bonds that would be needed to fully immunize the second liability $L = 2,000$. Note that now $T_1 = 3, T_L = 4$ and $T_2 = 5$. The two conditions for the full immunization strategy require

$$
\begin{aligned}
A_1^*(1.1)^{-3} + A_2^*(1.1)^{-5} &= 2,000(1.1)^{-4} \\
(3)A_1^*(1.1)^{-3} + (5)A_2^*(1.1)^{-5} &= (4)1,000(1.1)^{-4}.
\end{aligned}
$$

Solving the above system of equations, we get $A_1^* = 909.09$ and $A_2^* = 1,100.00$. The combined asset portfolio consists of a 1-year zero-coupon bond with a face value of \$454.55, a 3-year zero-coupon bond with a face value of (\$550.00 + \$909.09) = \$1,459.09 and a 5-year zero-coupon bond with a face value of \$1,100.00. This is indeed Albert's asset portfolio, which satisfies the full immunization conditions.

For (b), when there is an immediate one-time shift in interest rate from 10% to 9%, using equation (8.2), we have

$$
\begin{aligned}
V_A &= 454.55\,(1.09)^{-1} + 1,459.09\,(1.09)^{-3} + 1,100.00\,(1.09)^{-5} = \$2,258.62, \\
V_L &= 1,000\,(1.09)^{-2} + 2,000\,(1.09)^{-4} = \$2,258.53, \\
S &= 2,258.62 - 2,258.53 = 0.09.
\end{aligned}
$$

We repeat the above calculations for interest rate of 11%, 15%, 30% and 80%. The results are summarized as follows:

Table 8.5: Results of Example 8.12

i	V_A	V_L	S
0.09	2,258.62	2,258.53	0.09
0.10	2,192.47	2,192.47	0.00
0.11	2,129.17	2,129.08	0.09
0.15	1,901.53	1,899.65	1.88
0.30	1,310.04	1,291.97	18.07
0.80	560.93	499.16	61.76

To compare the duration matching, Redington and full immunization strategies, the results of Examples 8.10, 8.11 and 8.12 are plotted in Figure 8.6. The Redington strategy is an improved version of the duration matching method, and it ensures a relatively stable net-worth position when there is an immediate one-time small shift of the rate of interest. The full immunization strategy guarantees a non-negative surplus position regardless the size of the interest rate change. However, the surplus after the shift could be highly volatile. The cost of implementation of the immunization strategy, the availability of the required assets and the objectives of surplus management are the main factors for a financial institution to select an appropriate immunization strategy for its business. We also stress that the success of the immunization strategies discussed in this section depends on the assumption that the term structure is flat, and that the yield curve shift is parallel.

Figure 8.6:   Surplus positions under various immunization strategies

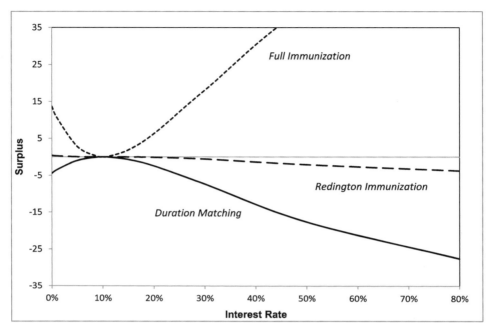

Finally, it should be noted that there might be numerous ways to design an asset portfolio to immunize a given liability portfolio against interest rate risk under each of the immunization strategies discussed in this subsection. For example, instead of employing 1-year and 3-year zero-coupon bonds to immunize the first liability in Example 8.12, one may use 1-year and 5-year bonds. It will lead to an alternative asset portfolio that also satisfies the full immunization conditions. In addition, while we have stated the duration matching, Redington immunization and full immunization conditions in terms of Macaulay durations, these conditions can be equivalently stated in terms of modified durations.

8.6   Some Shortcomings of Duration Matching

The technique of cash-flow matching and dedication was first suggested in 1942 by the Nobel laureate in Economics, Tjalling Koopmans, who proposed the use of linear programming algorithms in cash-flow matching. The British actuary Frank Redington introduced the notion of immunization in 1952. While the technique of matching the durations of assets and liabilities is easy to understand and apply, it is based on some simple assumptions, which may limit its validity. We now discuss some of the limitations of duration matching.

First, in classical duration matching, the term structure is assumed to be flat. That is, the same rate of interest is used to discount all cash flows, irrespective of their time of occurrence. This limitation can be relaxed to allow for a term structure that is nonflat, resulting in a more general definition of duration. Furthermore, we may consider different changes in the interest rate depending on the maturity of the cash flow. In other words, we may allow the shift in the term structure to be non-parallel. These extensions overcome the original assumption of duration matching, which considers only parallel shift in a flat term structure. The extension, however, has to be assessed in relation to the complexity it introduces and the benefits it brings about. In the next section, we shall discuss duration measure under a nonflat term structure.

Second, the characteristics of the assets and liabilities change over time. Even if the prevailing rate of interest remains unchanged, the durations of the assets and liabilities change over time due to time decay. Thus, the portfolio has to be re-balanced periodically to keep the durations matched. The frequency of re-balancing is an important question. The manager has to consider the cost of re-balancing the portfolio versus the benefits it achieves.

Third, we have assumed that the cash flows of the assets and liabilities are *fixed*, and there is no uncertainty in their timing and value. In some cases, however, cash flows may be contingent on some events. For example, the cash flows of a callable bond may depend on whether the issuer calls the bond. When interest rate drops, the price of the bond goes up. If the interest rate drops to a very low level, the likelihood of the bond being called may be substantial. This may put a check on the increase in the bond price, resulting in *price compression*. Indeed, we often observe *negative convexity* for a callable bond when the rate of interest is very low. Thus, for cash flows that are contingent on some uncertain events, the traditional duration measure will not be applicable. Improved methods such as the **option-adjusted duration** (also called **effective duration** or **stochastic duration**) should be considered. Conceptually, the effective duration is defined as the percentage drop in the price of the asset per unit increase in the rate of interest, i.e., $-\frac{dP}{di}\frac{1}{P}$. When the cash flows are contingent on some random events, however, equation (8.7) cannot be used. The effective duration can be numerically estimated using the formula

$$-\left[\frac{P(i+\Delta i) - P(i-\Delta i)}{2(\Delta i)P(i)}\right], \tag{8.28}$$

where the prices at perturbed interest rates $i + \Delta i$ and $i - \Delta i$ are calculated numerically taking account of the embedded options of the asset.

8.7   Duration under a Nonflat Term Structure

We consider a nonflat term structure defined by the sequence of spot rates i_t^S, for $t = 1, \cdots, n$. Denoting $i = (i_1^S, \cdots, i_n^S)'$ as the vector of the spot rates and $P(i)$ as the price of the asset under the prevailing term structure i, we have

$$P(i) = \sum_{t=1}^{n} \frac{C_t}{\left(1 + i_t^S\right)^t}. \tag{8.29}$$

Let $\Delta = (\Delta_1, \cdots, \Delta_n)'$ denote the vector of shifts in the spot rates so that the new term structure is

$$i + \Delta = (i_1^S + \Delta_1, \cdots, i_n^S + \Delta_n)', \tag{8.30}$$

and the price of the asset under the new term structure is

$$P(i + \Delta) = \sum_{t=1}^{n} \frac{C_t}{\left(1 + i_t^S + \Delta_t\right)^t}. \tag{8.31}$$

If, however, $\Delta_t = \Delta$ for $t = 1, \cdots, n$, then the term structure has a *parallel shift*, and (8.31) becomes

$$P(i + \Delta) = \sum_{t=1}^{n} \frac{C_t}{\left(1 + i_t^S + \Delta\right)^t}. \tag{8.32}$$

Using the first-order approximation in Taylor's expansion

$$\frac{1}{\left(1 + i_t^S + \Delta\right)^t} \approx \frac{1}{\left(1 + i_t^S\right)^t} - \frac{t\Delta}{\left(1 + i_t^S\right)^{t+1}},$$

we re-write (8.32) as

$$P(i + \Delta) \approx \sum_{t=1}^{n} \frac{C_t}{\left(1 + i_t^S\right)^t} - \Delta \sum_{t=1}^{n} \frac{t C_t}{\left(1 + i_t^S\right)^{t+1}},$$

which implies

$$P(i + \Delta) - P(i) \approx -\Delta \sum_{t=1}^{n} \frac{t C_t}{\left(1 + i_t^S\right)^{t+1}}$$

$$= -\Delta \sum_{t=1}^{n} \left[\frac{t}{1 + i_t^S} \right] \text{PV}(C_t), \tag{8.33}$$

where

$$\text{PV}(C_t) = \frac{C_t}{(1 + i_t^S)^t}.$$ (8.34)

Thus, we conclude

$$-\frac{1}{P(i)} \lim_{\Delta \to 0} \left[\frac{P(i + \Delta) - P(i)}{\Delta} \right] = \sum_{t=1}^{n} \frac{t}{1 + i_t^S} \left[\frac{\text{PV}(C_t)}{P(i)} \right]$$

$$= \sum_{t=1}^{n} W_t,$$ (8.35)

where

$$W_t = \frac{t}{1 + i_t^S} \left[\frac{\text{PV}(C_t)}{P(i)} \right].$$

The **Fisher-Weil duration**, denoted by D_F, is defined as

$$D_F = \sum_{t=1}^{n} t \left[\frac{\text{PV}(C_t)}{P(i)} \right] = \sum_{t=1}^{n} tw_t,$$ (8.36)

where

$$w_t = \frac{\text{PV}(C_t)}{P(i)}.$$

Note that Fisher-Weil duration is a generalization of Macaulay duration, with the present values of cash flows computed using a nonflat term structure. Similarly, the expression in equation (8.35) is a generalization of the modified duration of equation (8.7) to the case of a nonflat term structure with parallel shift. In particular, it measures the percentage change in the price of the asset when there is a parallel shift to the prevailing term structure. The duration-matching strategy discussed in Section 8.5 can be extended to the case of a nonflat term structure subject to parallel shift, with Macaulay duration replaced by Fisher-Weil duration.[2]

Equation (8.20) states that the Macaulay duration (modified duration) of a portfolio of bonds is equal to the weighted average of the Macaulay durations (modified durations) of the component bonds. This result also applies to the Fisher-Weil duration. However, it does not apply to the expression in equation (8.36).

---

[2]See E.S.W. Shiu, "On the Fisher-Weil immunization theorem", *Insurance: Mathematics and Economics* 6, 1987, 259 – 266, for more details and further extensions of nonparallel shifts.

Example 8.13: Bond A is a 2-year annual coupon bond with coupon rate of 3%. Bond B is a 5-year annual coupon bond with coupon rate of 5.5%. You are given that $i_t^S = 4.2\%$, 4.2%, 4.5%, 4.7% and 4.8%, for $t = 1, \cdots, 5$, respectively. Compute the Fisher-Weil duration of the two bonds, as well as the price sensitivity measure in (8.35). Also, calculate the Fisher-Weil duration of a portfolio with equal weights in the two bonds.

Solution: For Bond A, we have $C_1 = 3$ and $C_2 = 103$. Using the given term structure, we obtain $\text{PV}(C_1) = 2.879$ and $\text{PV}(C_2) = 94.864$, so that the price of Bond A is 2.879 + 94.864 = 97.743. Consequently, we obtain $W_1 = 0.028$ and $W_2 = 1.863$, so that the price sensitivity measure of Bond A as given in equation (8.35) is 1.891 (i.e., Bond A drops in value by 1.891% per 1 percentage point parallel increase in the term structure). Similarly, the Fisher-Weil duration of the bond is computed as 1.971 years.

Similar calculations can be performed for Bond B, and the results are shown in Table 8.3, with a Fisher-Weil duration of 4.510 years and a price sensitivity of 4.305 (i.e., Bond B drops in value by 4.305% per 1 percentage point parallel increase in the term structure). To compute the Fisher-Weil duration of the portfolio, we take the weighted average of the Fisher-Weil durations of the bonds to obtain 0.5(1.971 + 4.510) = 3.241 years.

Table 8.6: Results of Example 8.13

t	$\text{PV}(C_t)$	W_t	tw_t	$\text{PV}(C_t)$	W_t	tw_t
	A			B		
1	2.879	0.028	0.029	5.278	0.049	0.051
2	94.864	1.863	1.941	5.066	0.094	0.098
3				4.820	0.134	0.140
4				4.577	0.169	0.177
5				83.454	3.858	4.044
Sum	97.743	1.891	1.971	103.194	4.305	4.510

Example 8.14: Compute the prices of the bonds in Example 8.13 under the following term structures (with the years to maturity of the bonds remaining unchanged):

t	1	2	3	4	5
i_t^S of Case 1	4.6%	4.8%	5.5%	6.1%	6.4%
i_t^S of Case 2	3.7%	3.7%	4.0%	4.2%	4.3%

Comment on the use of equation (8.35) for the price changes of these bonds.

Solution: We note that the spot rate of interest i_t^S in Case 1 increases by the amount of 0.004, 0.006, 0.01, 0.014 and 0.016, for $t = 1, 2, \cdots, 5$, respectively. Thus, the shift in the term structure is not parallel, but the average increase is 1 percentage point. Using equation (6.10), the computed prices of Bonds A and B are, respectively, 96.649 and 96.655. Thus, the price of Bond A drops by 1.119% and that of Bond B drops by 6.337%. These figures contrast the values of 1.891% and 4.305%, respectively, predicted by equation (8.35). The discrepancy exists due to the fact that the shift in the term structure is not parallel.

Case 2 represents a parallel shift in the spot rates of -0.5 percentage point for all time to maturity. Using equation (6.10), the prices of Bonds A and B are found to be 98.674 and 105.447, respectively. Thus, Bonds A and B increase in value by 0.952% and 2.183%, respectively. These values are quite close to the changes predicted by equation (8.35) (i.e., half of the tabulated values, namely, 0.946% and 2.153%, respectively).

8.8   Passive versus Active Bond Management

From the asset management perspective, a bond fund may adopt a passive or active strategy. A passive strategy typically adopts a nonexpectational approach, without emphasis on the likely movements of the market conditions. Immunization is a form of passive strategy, in which the manager defensively attempts to protect the net worth of the portfolio against interest-rate risk. Indexing and buy-and-hold are other forms of passive bond management strategies. The **indexing strategy** attempts to replicate the performance of a benchmark, such as the return of a specific class of bonds. A fund managed under such a strategy is called an **index fund**. The theoretical underpinning of an index fund is that the market is efficient and fund managers cannot consistently outperform the market. An index fund would state the benchmark index it attempts to replicate. Depending on the investors' risk appetites, they may select funds that benchmark an aggressive or conservative market. The discrepancy between the fund's performance and the benchmark index is called the *tracking error*. Managers will attempt to reduce the tracking errors using quantitative techniques that minimize the error variance. Thus, the focus is on reducing the tracking errors at low costs without worrying about active asset selection and buy-sell timing.

On the other hand, an active bond management strategy may involve some form of interest-rate forecasting. The fund manager would consider different scenarios of interest-rate movements in the future and predict the holding-period yield for different bonds accordingly. As bonds with different characteristics may be affected by interest-rate changes differently, the holding-period yield discussed in Section 7.4 under various scenarios will generally be different. The manager will then choose the bond with the highest holding-period yield under the most likely scenario. If the manager's forecast for the interest-rate movement is correct, she will be able to outperform the benchmark return. Example 7.6 illustrates the use of horizon analysis to enhance the performance of a fund.

A broader active management framework would take a quantitative approach in assessing the value of a bond, taking into account all embedded options and structures of the bond. A proper application of relative-value analysis includes assessment of the sector of the bond issuer and its credit profile.

8.9 Summary

1. The Macaulay duration of a bond measures the average period of the investment. The modified duration is the Macaulay duration divided by 1 plus the yield rate per payment period. When measured in terms of the number of payment periods, the modified duration is the percentage increase in the bond price per one percentage point decrease in the yield per payment period.

2. The modified duration and the Macaulay duration can be used to approximate the change in the bond price for small changes in interest rate. If higher accuracy is desired, the convexity may also be incorporated in the bond price correction.

3. Duration varies with the coupon rate of interest, the yield to maturity and the time to maturity of a bond. The duration of a portfolio of bonds is the weighted average of the individual bonds in the portfolio.

4. Cash-flow matching and dedication strategy are methods of funding liability obligations by matching them with specific payments generated from a portfolio of bonds. These strategies are not subject to interest-rate risk.

5. Immunization is the technique to neutralize the interest-rate risk of a business. Target-date immunization is used when an obligation with a known amount at a fixed date is to be met. Duration-matching immunization neutralizes the interest-rate risk of a series of liabilities by a portfolio of bonds. Redington immunization requires the asset convexity to be larger than the liability convexity. Full immunization ensures net-worth to be non-negative under any flat term structure.

6. Traditional duration matching has drawbacks in that it assumes (a) the term structure is flat, (b) the term structure shifts in a parallel manner, and (c) the cash flows are fixed.

7. Fisher-Weil duration is a generalization of Macaulay duration. Immunization strategy assuming parallel shifts to a nonflat term structure may be based on matching the Fisher-Weil duration.

8. When an asset involves cash flows that are contingent on some random events, the effective duration may be estimated numerically by evaluating the asset prices at perturbed interest rates. The computed asset prices should take account of the embedded options in the asset.

9. Passive bond investment involves tracking the performance of a bond index. Managers may attempt to achieve higher returns than the index using horizon analysis, which involves comparing the holding-period yield of the bond under different forecasts of interest-rate movements.

Exercises

8.1 Calculate the modified duration and convexity of the cash-flow stream as shown below. Use $i = 6\%$.

t	C_t
1	0
2	2
3	0
4	4
5	0
6	6

8.2 Calculate the Macaulay duration and convexity of the cash-flow stream as shown below. Use $i = 4\%$.

t	C_t
1	3
2	0
3	7
4	2
5	5
6	6

8.3 Show that the Macaulay duration of a n-year level annuity immediate with annual payments is

$$\frac{(Ia)_{\overline{n}|i}}{a_{\overline{n}|i}}.$$

Hence verify Rule 5 in Section 8.4.

8.4 Use the Excel function **DURATION** to calculate the Macaulay duration of the three bonds plotted in Figure 8.3.

8.5 A preferred stock pays dividend annually in the form of a level perpetuity immediate. Find the Macaulay duration of the preferred stock at $i = 5\%$.

8.6 Show, by definition, that the modified duration of a coupon bond with annual modified coupon rate of g per annum and n years to mature is

$$D^* = \frac{g(Ia)_{\overline{n}|i} + nv^n}{(1+i)(ga_{\overline{n}|i} + v^n)}.$$

Hence verify Rule 6 in Section 8.4.

8.7 Use the Excel function **DURATION** to calculate the Macaulay duration of the semiannual coupon bonds in the following table. The bonds are redeemable at par and are yielding 8% compounded semiannually. What can you observe?

Time to	Coupon rate			
maturity	1%	3%	6%	10%
1				
2				
5				
10				
20				
50				
100				
∞				

8.8 Consider a bond with m coupons per year of rate r per annum. Show that when the time to maturity tends to infinity, its duration tends to

$$\frac{1 + \dfrac{i}{m}}{i}$$

(in years) where i is compounded m times per year. Note that the duration limit is independent of the coupon rate r, and is decreasing in i.

8.9 The interest-rate risk of a non-callable bond is higher for

(1) higher coupons,
(2) longer maturities,
(3) higher interest rates.

A. (2) only
B. (3) only
C. (1) and (2) only
D. (1) and (3) only

8.10 You want to construct a bond portfolio to immunize the interest-rate risk of a liability of $2,000 after 10 years. You have the choice of three bonds with the following information:

	Bond 1	Bond 2	Bond 3
Coupon rate	0%	3%	5%
Face value	$100	$1,000	$1,000
Macaulay duration	12 years	8 years	9 years

Which bonds can you choose to form the bond portfolio?

A. Bond 3

B. A mix of Bonds 1 and 2

C. A mix of Bonds 2 and 3

D. None of the above.

8.11 Calculate the Macaulay duration of a 12-year mortgage with quarterly installments. Interest rate is 12% compounded quarterly.

8.12 Show that

$$\sum_{t=1}^{n} t^2 v^t = \frac{1}{i} \left[2(Ia)_{\overline{n}|} + a_{\overline{n}|} + 1 - (n+1)^2 v^n \right].$$

[**Hint**: Write t^2 as $(t+1)^2 - 2t - 1$ and you can see why $2(Ia)_{\overline{n}|} + a_{\overline{n}|}$ appears. The same trick can be applied to obtain $\sum_{t=1}^{n} t^m v^t$ for any positive m.]

8.13 Using (8.16) and Exercise 8.12, or otherwise, show that

(a) the convexity of a level annuity-immediate of n payments is

$$\frac{v^2}{(1-v^n)} \left[2(Ia)_{\overline{n}|} + 2\ddot{a}_{\overline{n}|} - n(n+3)v^n \right],$$

(b) the convexity of a level perpetuity-immediate is $\dfrac{2}{i^2}$.

8.14 Consider the 12-year mortgage with quarterly installments in Exercise 8.11. Calculate the percentage change in the sum of the present values of the installments if interest rate drops from 12% to 11.4% (i.e., a drop of 60 basis points) by

(a) using the modified duration approximation,

(b) an exact calculation.

Compare the answers obtained in (a) and (b). Can the discrepancy be reduced by a convexity correction?

8.15 Using Exercise 8.12 or otherwise, show that

(a) the convexity of a n-year coupon bond with annual modified coupon rate of g is

$$\frac{v^2}{(ga_{\overline{n}|} + v^n)} \left\{ \frac{g}{i} \left[2(Ia)_{\overline{n}|} + 2\ddot{a}_{\overline{n}|} - n(n+3)v^n \right] + n(n+1)v^n \right\},$$

(b) the convexity of a n-year coupon bond with annual coupons, redeemable and priced at par, is $2v(Ia)_{\overline{n}|}$.

8.16 Use Exercise 8.15 to calculate the convexity in Example 8.6.

8.17 If the cash-flow stream C_t do not have a regular structure, to compute the present value, the Macaulay duration and the convexity of the cash flows we may set up a table similar to Table 8.2 using Excel. The following format may be considered:

Time t	C_t	PV(C_t)	$t \times$PV(C_t)	$(t^2 + t) \times$PV(C_t)
1				
2				
$\vdots$				
n				
Total				

After setting up the table, P, D, D^* and C can be found using the appropriate column sums.

(a) Using Excel, calculate the present value, modified duration and convexity of a decreasing annuity that pays 50 at time 1, 47 at time 2, 44 at time 3, $\cdots$, 2 at time 17 at $i = 4\%$.

(b) Using the results in (a), approximate the present value of the annuity if i increases by 0.5%. Compare the answer with the exact value.

8.18 Harry is the owner of a small grocery store and he has only one employee, Dick. Dick is going to retire after 4 years and Harry promises to pay Dick $7,000 once a year for a 5-year period, the first payment starting 5 years from now. Assume that Dick will be alive for at least 10 more years, that the yield curve is flat and that the prevailing interest rate is 4% effective.

(a) Calculate the present value, Macaulay duration and convexity of the retirement benefit entitled to Dick.

(b) Harry wants to use a $100 par value 5-year coupon bond with annual coupon rate of 4% and a $100 par value 10-year bond with annual coupon rate of 5% to construct an immunized portfolio. Find the face value of each of the two bonds.

8.19 You have a choice of two bonds X and Y. Bond X is a $1,000 par value 30-year 8% semiannual coupon government bond selling at $920. Bond Y is a $1,000 par value 20-year 10% semiannual coupon corporate bond selling at $1,057. You believe that the yield curve for government securities will be flat after 5 years at 7.5% compounded semiannually, while that for the corporate bond Y will be 8.5% compounded semiannually after 5 years. If you can re-invest coupons at 3.5% per half-year in the coming 5 years, what bond would you choose over an investment horizon of 5 years?

8.20 Consider a portfolio of m fixed-income securities, the yield rate of each is the same. Let w_k, $D^{*(k)}$, and $C^{(k)}$ be the proportion of the value, the modified duration, and the convexity of the kth security. Show that the modified duration and convexity of the portfolio are

$$\sum_{k=1}^{m} w_k D^{*(k)} \quad \text{and} \quad \sum_{k=1}^{m} w_k C^{(k)},$$

respectively.

8.21 You have a liability of $10,000 due in 10 years and you want to construct a portfolio using two bonds, X and Y, to meet the obligation. The following table shows the information of X and Y:

	X	Y
Semiannual coupon rate	6%	0%
Face value	$100	$100
Redemption value	$104	$100
Time to maturity	7 years	14 years

The prevailing yield to maturity in the market is 9% compounded semiannually for all maturities. How much should you invest in Bonds X and Y if you employ a target-date immunization strategy?

8.22 Revisit Exercise 8.21 and assume that the target-date immunization strategy derived in the question was employed at $t = 0$. Suppose interest rate stayed the same at 9% compounded semiannually for all maturities after 1 year.

(a) Calculate the weight of bond X in the portfolio of assets at $t = 1$ year, assuming a buy-and-hold strategy in the first year and that the coupons are reinvested in the same bond.

(b) Calculate the Macaulay durations of the liability and the portfolio of assets at $t = 1$ year, assuming a buy-and-hold strategy in the first year and that the coupons earned in the first year are reinvested in the same bond. Are these durations still the same?

(c) In (b) is there a mismatch between the duration of the asset and liability at $t = 1$? If yes, how do you re-balance the portfolio?

8.23 You are given the following forward rates observed in the market: $i_1^F = 4\%$, $i_2^F = i_3^F = 5\%$ and $i_4^F = 5.5\%$. If you believe that the yield curve will be flat after 2 years at 6% and your investment horizon is 3 years, which of the following two bonds would you purchase (assume the bonds are default-free and non-callable)?

Bond M: *3-year bond with 4% annual coupon, redeemable at 103%,*
Bond N: *4-year bond with 4.5% annual coupons, redeemable at par.*

8.24 A company needs to pay a yearly cash-flow stream as pension to a group of beneficiaries for 20 years. The first payment is $100 due 1 year from now, and subsequent payments increase by 3% per year. The company has to its choice two bonds: A and B. Bond A is a 12-year semiannual coupon bond with coupon rate of 6%. Bond B is a 20-year semiannual coupon bond with coupon rate of 4%. The current yield rate in the market is 5.5% compounded semiannually for all maturities.

(a) Calculate the Macaulay duration and convexity of the liability and the two bonds, using half-year as one period. [**Hint:** Use the spreadsheet developed in Exercise 8.17 for the liability.]

(b) Construct the cheapest portfolio consisting of Bonds A and B such that the Macaulay durations of the asset and liability are equal. Can such a portfolio minimize interest rate risk?

8.25 Let D_S be the Macaulay duration of the surplus S, which is defined by

$$D_S = \sum_{t=1}^{n} t \frac{\text{PV}(C_t)}{S},$$

where C_t is the net cash flow at time t and $S \neq 0$. Show that

$$D_S = D_A - \frac{V_L}{S}(D_L - D_A).$$

Hence, show that if $D_A = D_L$ then $D_A = D_L = D_S$.

8.26 Corporation X has an obligation to pay \$5,000 at the end of each year for 4 years. Given the following 4 non-callable and default-free bonds, construct a dedicated bond portfolio that eliminates interest-rate risk. Determine the face value of each of the following bonds purchased:

Bond E: 1-year bond with 4% annual coupon, redeemable at 103%,
Bond F: 2-year zero-coupon bond, redeemable at par,
Bond G: 3-year bond with 5% annual coupon, redeemable at par,
Bond H: 4-year bond with 5.5% annual coupons, redeemable at par.

8.27 The dividend discount model (DDM) for a stock assumes that the owner of a stock can expect to receive periodic dividends. The constant-growth model assumes that dividends grow at a constant rate g. The intrinsic value P of the stock is the present value of all future dividends. Assume that the current dividend is D_0 and that the yield curve is flat at $i > g$.

(a) Prove the Gordon formula

$$P = \frac{D_0(1+g)}{i-g}.$$

(b) Find the modified duration and the convexity of all the future dividends in terms of i and g. [**Hint**: Use Exercise 8.12.]

8.28 A company has to pay \$100,000 5 years from now. The current market rate of interest is 6%. The company uses a 8.6% annual coupon bond redeemable at par after 6 years to fund this liability.

(a) Calculate the face value and the Macaulay duration of the bond.

(b) Is the bond sufficient to meet the liability when there is a one-time change in interest rate to 5.5% after 2 years?

8.29 Suppose you have bought a 5-year non-callable default-free coupon bond with annual coupon rate of 4% at a yield to maturity of 5% effective per annum. Immediately after you bought the bond, the prevailing market interest rate jumps to 7% so that the coupons can be reinvested at 7%.

(a) Calculate your n-year holding-period yield for $n = 1, 2$ and 5.

(b) We know that bond price decreases with yield to maturity. What about the return on the bond investment as a whole?

8.30 Let D_A and D_L be the Macaulay duration of the assets and liabilities, respectively. Show that

$$D_A = D_L \quad \text{if and only if} \quad \frac{d}{di}\left(\frac{V_A}{V_L}\right) = 0.$$

What is the significance of this equivalence?

8.31 Show that the Macaulay duration can be calculated as

$$D = -\frac{d \ln P}{d\delta} = \frac{d \ln P}{d \ln v},$$

where δ is the force of interest. This result says that the Macaulay duration is the *elasticity* of the price with respect to the discount factor.

8.32 Which of the following statements about immunization is/are correct?

(a) Immunization is a method to structure the liability in order to reduce interest-rate risk.

(b) Immunization requires re-balancing only because interest rate fluctuates.

(c) Immunization may not work if the yield curve is not flat.

8.33 Discuss why dedication strategy is an effective but largely impractical method of eliminating interest-rate risk.

8.34 A bond-fund manager wants to mimic the performance of the Merrill Lynch Domestic Master Index, a bond index in the US market comprising of more than 5,000 investment-grade bonds. Discuss two difficulties in replicating the bond portfolio of the index.

8.35 You owe Mr Lauder $2,000 in tuition expenses due at the end of the year and you want to set up a fund to meet the obligation. The investment vehicle available to you is a 2-year zero-coupon bond earning 8.5% effective. You can also use your savings in your bank account, which offers you *no* interest because the principal is too small. Assume that the effective rate of interest is 8.5%.

(a) You plan to construct a fund consisting of the zero-coupon bond and bank deposit. At the time of the construction of the fund the surplus of you position is zero. How much should you invest in the zero-coupon bond to minimize the interest-rate risk?

(b) Calculate the present value of your portfolio if the effective rate of interest goes up or down by 50 basis points immediately after you start up the portfolio and compare it with the present value of the liability.

8.36 Assume that at yield rate i, the cash-flow stream of the asset is structured in a way such that $V_A(i) = V_L(i) = V$. Show that for small Δi,

$$S(i + \Delta i) \approx V\left[-(1+i)^{-1}(D_A - D_L)\Delta i + \frac{1}{2}(C_A - C_L)(\Delta i)^2\right],$$

where the durations and convexities are all calculated based on a yield to maturity of i. Hence, comment on the outcome of the duration-matching strategy. [**Hint**: Study the derivation of equation (8.12) in Section 8.3.]

8.37 Bond A is a 3-year annual coupon bond with coupon rate of 4%. Bond B is a 5-year annual coupon bond with coupon rate of 8%. You are given the current spot-rate curve i_t^S as follows:

t	1	2	3	4	5
i_t^S	6.1%	6.2%	6.3%	6.4%	6.5%

(a) Compute the Fisher-Weil duration of the two bonds, as well as the price sensitivity measure in equation (8.35).

(b) Compute the prices of the bonds under the following term structure (with the years to maturity of the bonds remaining unchanged). Comment on the use of equation (8.35) for the price changes of these two bonds.

t	1	2	3	4	5
i_t^S	6.8%	6.9%	7.0%	7.1%	7.2%

(c) Calculate the new Fisher-Weil duration of the two bonds immediately after the spot-rate curve shift in (b). Compare this with your results in (a).

Advanced Problems

8.38 Find the Macaulay duration and convexity of the following cash-flow stream using a yield rate of 5%:

$$
C_t = \begin{cases} 1 & \text{at } t = 1, 4, 7, \cdots, \\ 2 & \text{at } t = 2, 5, 8, \cdots, \\ 3 & \text{at } t = 3, 6, 9, \cdots. \end{cases}
$$

8.39 You have to pay $1,000 at the end of year 1, 2 and 4 from now. The only investments available to you are 1-, 3-, and 4-year zero-coupon bonds.

(a) Can a dedicated bond portfolio be constructed using the three zero-coupon bonds?

(b) Assuming that the yields to maturity of all bonds are 8%, find the cheapest bond portfolio that can immunize interest-rate risk according to the duration matching strategy in Section 8.5. Calculate the face values of the three zero-coupon bonds in this portfolio. [**Hint:** There are infinitely many immunization strategies which have the same price at 8%. You are only asked to find one.]

8.40 In this exercise we use a probabilistic argument to show Rule 3 in Section 8.4 that Macaulay duration decreases when i increases. Recall that (8.3) states that D is a weighted average of $1, 2, \cdots, n$ using weights $w_1, w_2, \cdots, w_n$. Since $w_t \geq 0$ for all t and they sum up to 1, we can treat them as probabilities.

(a) Let T be a random variable taking values in $1, 2, \cdots, n$ with probabilities $w_1, w_2, \cdots, w_n$. Find $E(T)$, the expectation of T.

(b) Show that the variance of T is $\text{Var}(T) = \sum_{t=1}^{n} t^2 w_t - D^2$. In financial economics, $\text{Var}(T)$ is called the M^2 of the cash-flow stream C_t. What does M^2 measure?

(c) Show that

$$
\frac{dD}{di} = -v \text{Var}(T)
$$

and complete the proof of Rule 3.

8.41 Consider the full immunization conditions and the corresponding cash-flow diagram in Figure 8.5.

(a) Show that the two full immunization conditions can be expressed as:

$$A_1(1+i_0)^{-T_1} + A_2(1+i_0)^{-T_2} = L(1+i_0)^{-T_L}$$
$$T_1 A_1(1+i_0)^{-T_1} + T_2 A_2(1+i_0)^{-T_2} = T_L L(1+i_0)^{-T_L}$$

(b) Based on the system of equations in (a), show that

$$A_1 = \left(\frac{\Delta_2}{\Delta_1}\right) A_2 (1+i_0)^{-(\Delta_1+\Delta_2)}$$

(c) Substitute the result in (b) into the first condition in (a), show that

$$L = A_2(1+i_0)^{-\Delta_2}\left(\frac{\Delta_2}{\Delta_1} + 1\right)$$

(d) Let $S(i) = V_A - V_L$, at interest rate i, show that

$$S(i) = C(i) \times \eta(i)$$

where $C(i)$ is a positive function of i, and

$$\eta(i) = \left[\left(\frac{\Delta_2}{\Delta_1}\right)\left(\frac{1+i}{1+i_0}\right)^{\Delta_1} + \left(\frac{1+i}{1+i_0}\right)^{-\Delta_2} - \left(\frac{\Delta_2}{\Delta_1} + 1\right)\right]$$

(e) Show that

$$\eta'(i) = \frac{d\eta(i)}{di} = \frac{\Delta_2}{1+i}\left[\left(\frac{1+i}{1+i_0}\right)^{\Delta_1} - \left(\frac{1+i}{1+i_0}\right)^{-\Delta_2}\right]$$

(f) When $0 < i < i_0$, show that $\eta(i)$ decreases when i increases. When $i > i_0 > 0$, show that $\eta(i)$ increases when i increases.

(g) Show that $\eta(i)$ achieves an absolute minimum at $i = i_0$ and $\eta(i_0) = 0$.

(h) Given the conditions in (a) and by combining the results from (b) to (g), show that $S(i) = V_A - V_L \geq 0$, for all $i > 0$.

9   Interest Rates and Financial Securities

In this chapter we outline the determination of rates of interest from an economic view point. We discuss the yields on various financial securities, including Treasury bonds. We examine the role of the government in setting interest rate targets and policies. Our discussion will focus mainly on the U.S. economy, which is the largest in the world and whose policies have major impact on other economies.

9.1 Interest Rate Determination

Given an accumulation function, the present value of a single payment or stream of payments can be computed using (2.17). When the term structure is flat, Sections 2.1 through 2.3 provide formulas for the computation of the present values of various annuities. The calculation of the future value of an annuity, however, requires assumption about how future payments accumulate in value. Under a fixed interest rate environment with a flat term structure this problem is easy to resolve, as all payments earn the same effective rate of interest i over any period. In practice, interest rates vary over time and we must be careful with our assumption about how future payments accumulate in value. In Section 1.7 we consider the assumption of future payments earning the current spot rates (i.e., the current term structure remains unchanged over time), whereas in Section 3.3 we introduce the assumption that future payments earn the (implicit) forward rates of interest. It must be emphasized that these assumptions are made *ex ante*. As interest rates are in practice time varying, both assumptions will generally be wrong *ex post*. It is thus important to understand how interest rates are determined in practice.

Depending on the type of financial security, the rate of interest (yield) earned may be explicit (e.g., a savings account) or imputed from the security prices (e.g., Treasury bonds). In Chapter 7, we describe methods to determine the spot rates of interest (and hence the term structure) from Treasury securities. Note that the term structure is *estimated* from the market prices of Treasury securities and is not directly observable. As the prices of Treasury securities are dependent on their supply and demand, the Central Bank can influence their prices by varying their supply. To the extent that interest rates affect the demand of capital investment and expenses on consumption goods, they have effects on the real economy. For an open economy with external trade, interest rates also affect the currency exchange rates with other countries, and hence imports and exports. In sum, interest rate is an important policy variable for the government to manage its economy.

Interest rate can be viewed as the *price* or *cost* of borrowing or acquiring capital. Like the price of any goods, its value depends on the demand and supply of the goods, namely, capital. On the demand side, capital is needed when there is opportunity to invest. Hence, we would expect the demand for capital to be high when the economy is expanding or there is new technology to be explored to make profit. On the other hand, the supply of capital may depend on the following factors:

- the time preference of consumers (willingness to give up current consumption for higher future consumption),

- the risk appetite of lenders (willingness to take risk),

- the expected rate of inflation (possible loss of purchasing power when consumption is deferred), and

- the characteristics of the financial securities.

Note that the first three factors are economy wide, while the last factor depends on the specific type of capital (financial asset). As short-term Treasury securities (say, 90-day Treasury bill) are risk-free and highly liquid, we use the yield on these securities as the benchmark for determining the yields on other securities.

The rate of return on short-term Treasury bill is called the **nominal risk-free rate of interest**. The term "nominal" refers to the fact that the rate of interest does not take into account inflation. It is also called the **money risk-free rate of interest** or **quoted risk-free rate of interest**. The frequency of compounding (and hence the notion of effective rate of interest) has no bearing on its meaning here.

Inflation refers to the increase in the general price level of goods and services. The **rate of inflation** is usually measured by the rate of increase of a general price index, such as the consumer price index (CPI), whole-sale price index or gross domestic product deflator. Inflation reduces the purchasing power of money. While money invested earns interest, the purchasing power of the principal plus interest is eroded due to inflation. We define the **real rate of interest** as the interest earned by an investment after taking account of the erosion of purchasing power due to inflation. We denote r_I as the inflation rate, and r_N as the nominal rate of interest. The real rate of interest r_R is then defined by the equation

$$1 + r_R = \frac{1 + r_N}{1 + r_I},$$ (9.1)

from which we obtain

$$r_R = \frac{1 + r_N}{1 + r_I} - 1 = \frac{r_N - r_I}{1 + r_I}. \tag{9.2}$$

If the rate of inflation r_I is low, we can write (9.2) as

$$r_R \approx r_N - r_I, \tag{9.3}$$

which says that the real rate of interest is approximately equal to the nominal rate of interest minus the rate of inflation.

Note that (9.1) and (9.3) are *ex post* relationships. They hold empirically and do not refer to any theoretical relationship between the three quantities r_N, r_I and r_R. On the other hand, the economist Irving Fisher (1867 – 1947) argued that the nominal rate of interest ought to increase one for one with the *expected* rate of inflation. The so-called *Fisher equation* states that

$$r_N = r_R + \mathrm{E}(r_I), \tag{9.4}$$

where $\mathrm{E}(r_I)$ is the expected rate of inflation over the term of the financial asset, also called the **inflation premium**. This equation implies that if the real rate of interest is stable, a higher nominal rate of interest predicts a higher expected rate of inflation. In contrast to (9.3), the Fisher equation is an *ex ante* prediction. Applying the Fisher equation to short-term Treasury bill, we have

Nominal risk-free rate of interest = real risk-free rate of interest +

inflation premium. (9.5)

It should be emphasized that inflation premium is time varying. It depends on the market participants' expectation of the future rate of inflation. Typically this premium rises when the experienced rate of inflation is on the rise.

An asset which is not subject to inflation risk is the U.S. inflation-indexed Treasury bond. This bond adjusts the principal based on the rate of inflation as measured by the CPI. As the principal rises with the rate of inflation, so does the coupon payments. Investors are thus protected against inflation. Hence, the nominal rate of interest of the indexed bond is also its real rate of interest.

Example 9.1: A stock will pay a dividend of $0.50 two months from now and the annual dividend is expected to grow at a rate of 4% per annum indefinitely. If the stock is traded at $7.5 and inflation is expected to be 2% per annum, what is the expected effective annual real rate of return for an investor who purchases the stock?

Solution: Let $v = \frac{1}{1+r_N}$, where r_N is the nominal rate of return prior to adjustment for inflation. The dividends are $0.5, 1.04(0.5), 1.04^2(0.5), \cdots$ at time of 2 months, 14 months, 26 months, $\cdots$, respectively, from now. Thus, the equation of value is

$$
\begin{aligned}
7.5 &= 0.5v^{\frac{1}{6}} + 1.04(0.5)v^{\frac{14}{12}} + 1.04^2(0.5)v^{\frac{26}{12}} + \cdots \\
&= 0.5v^{\frac{1}{6}}\left[1 + 1.04v + (1.04v)^2 + \cdots\right] \\
&= \frac{0.5v^{\frac{1}{6}}}{1 - 1.04v}.
\end{aligned}
$$

The above equation has no analytic solution, and we solve it using Excel to obtain $v = 0.898568$ and $r_N = \frac{1}{0.898568} - 1 = 0.112882$. Thus, the real rate of return is

$$
r_R = \frac{1+r_N}{1+r_I} - 1 = \frac{1.112882}{1.02} - 1 = 9.1061\%.
$$

While Treasury securities are risk free, other financial assets may be subject to default. Hence, investors may demand higher returns to compensate for the risk, and the rate of interest of the security would incorporate a **default risk premium**. For a corporate bond, the default risk can be measured by the bond's rating. A corporate bond with a higher rating will have a lower risk of default. Thus, its rate of interest will generally be lower.

The liquidity of an asset also influences its interest rate. If the asset may not be bought or sold easily due to lack of liquidity, investors will demand compensation for this, creating a spread called the **liquidity premium**. As U.S. short-term Treasury securities are highly liquid, investors do not demand a liquidity premium.

Finally, long-term securities may also trade with a premium due to the uncertainty inherent to a longer maturity and holding period, called the **maturity risk premium** or **term premium**. The term premium is generally higher the longer the time to maturity of the asset. This premium varies over time and usually rises when interest rates are more volatile.

In sum, the nominal rate of interest of a financial asset incorporates all the aforementioned risk components, which must be added to the nominal risk-free rate of interest of a liquid short-term Treasure security. Hence, the nominal rate of interest of a financial asset may be generally written as follows:

Nominal rate of interest = real risk-free rate of interest + inflation premium +

default risk premium + liquidity premium + term premium. (9.6)

9.2 Financial Securities

Having delineated the determination of the yield of a financial asset, we now consider the yields of different types of securities traded in the financial markets. Yield (or interest rate) data can be obtained from various sources. They can be found in the websites of the Central Banks, such as the **Board of Governors of the Federal Reserve System** (the Fed), Bank of England, Bank of Canada and European Central Bank. Major financial media such as the *Wall Street Journal, The Financial Times*, Thomson Reuters and Bloomberg publish extensive data on interest rates. In addition, specific data can be found in the websites of exchanges and trade organizations such as the Intercontinental Exchange (ICE) and the International Swaps and Derivatives Association (ISDA).

Table 9.1 presents a sample of yields of different financial assets. They are taken from the Fed's website, covering some securities from the U.S. market, and the ICE, covering some securities from the London market. It can be seen that the yields of these securities may be quite different, which is the result of the interaction of the different risk premium components discussed in the last section. In what follows, we take a closer look at each of the selected securities.

The first two instruments in the U.S. market, the Federal funds and Discount Window credit, are the main policy instruments through which the Fed manages its monetary policy. Federal funds are the reserve balances that private banks keep at their local Federal Reserve Bank. Private banks lend Federal funds to each other to meet temporary shortages in liquidity. While the Fed cannot dictate the interest rate banks charge each other for such borrowing, it regularly announces its target rate to let market participants know about its policy direction. In December 2015, the Fed raised the target range of the Federal funds interest rate to 0.25% to 0.5%, indicating its intention to tighten the credit market.

The Fed tries to keep the Federal funds rate within the target range by trading short-term securities. When the Fed wants to increase reserves (and lower the Federal funds rate), it buys Treasury securities. On the other hand, when the Fed wants to reduce reserves (and raise the Federal funds rate) it sells Treasury securities. The short-term transactions the Fed uses for this purpose are called **repurchase agreements** or **repos**.[1] The Federal funds (effective) rate reported in Table 9.1 is the daily rate computed as a weighted average of rates quoted on brokered trades. It can be seen that its value of 0.38% is within the targeted range announced by the Fed.

The **Discount Window** is an instrument that allows eligible institutions and banks to borrow money directly from the Fed on a short-term basis to meet temporary shortage of liquidity. Unlike the Federal funds rate, the Fed has direct control

---

[1]See the forthcoming discussions on repurchase agreements.

over the interest rate charged at the Discount Window. There are different levels of rates charged: primary credit rate, secondary credit rate and seasonal credit rate, depending on the credit rating of the borrower. The Discount Window rate is typically higher than the Federal funds rate, and this is indeed found to be true from the table (Discount Window primary credit rate is 1%). Finally, it should be noted that both the Federal funds and Discount Window credit are not discount instruments as defined in Section 1.5: their quoted values are interest rates, not discount rates.

Table 9.1 shows two groups of U.S. government security yields: Treasury bills and Treasury constant maturity. The Treasury bill rates are annualized on a discount basis using a 360-day year count. The **Treasury constant maturity** (CMT) yields are based on the most recently auctioned (on-the-run) Treasury securities (bills of less than 1-year maturity, notes of 2- up to 10-year maturity, as well as 30-year bonds). The yield curve is derived using a quasi-cubic hermite spline function, based on the knots at selected maturities. As on-the-run securities typically trade close to par, the smoothed yield curve can be considered as a par curve. We can see that the sampled yield curve is upward sloping, increasing from 0.53% for 1-year yield to 2.39% for 30-year yield. Thus, the term premium increases with the time-to-maturity.

The swap rates are the ICE mid-market par swap rates. They are the rates for a Fixed Rate Payer in a vanilla interest rate swap in return for the 3-month LIBOR.[2] These rates are computed as the averages of the volume-weighted bid and ask quotes of swaps of various tenors and currencies (the rates quoted in Table 9.1 are for U.S. dollar). Theoretically these rates would render the present value of the fixed payments equal to the present value of the floating payments. Using the bootstrap method discussed in Section 7.5, the swap rates can be used to estimate the **swap zero curve** similar to the spot-rate curve computed using Treasury securities.

The **state and local bonds** yield is an index for the average yield of municipal bonds. A municipal bond is a bond security issued by local governments (states or cities) and their agencies for the purpose of financing infrastructure needs and other expenses. The figure in Table 9.1 is the Bond Buyer (a daily newspaper covering the municipal bond market) Index based on 20 general obligation municipal bonds with maturity in 20 years. It can be seen that the quoted yield of the index of 3.18% is higher than the Treasury constant maturity yield with 20-year maturity of 1.96%. This is due to the positive default risk premium of the municipal bonds over Treasury securities, despite their backing by the local governments.

Commercial paper is a security issued by large corporations to raise funds to meet short-term financial needs. It is typically backed by a bank or the issuing corporation itself without any collateral. Hence, only firms with good credit rating are able to sell commercial papers. The figure in Table 9.1 is on a discount basis

---

[2]See the forthcoming discussions on the LIBOR.

annualized using 360-day year for commercial papers maturing in three months. Its quoted value of 0.49% is higher than the 3-month Treasury bill rate of 0.27%, due to its positive risk premium.[3]

The **bank prime loan** rate is one of several base rates used by banks to price short-term commercial loans. The quoted figure in Table 9.1 is based on rates issued by the top 25 insured U.S.-chartered commercial banks.

The **corporate bond** yields are the average yields of Moody's seasoned Aaa and Baa bonds, which are the ratings for "prime" and "lower medium" grade bonds, respectively. It can be seen that the yield ranking is in the decreasing order of Baa, Aaa and Treasury constant maturities, due to the differences in default risk premium.

The conventional mortgage rate is the average of contract interest rates on 30-year fixed-rate first mortgages. This rate is based on the Primary Mortgage Market Survey provided by Freddie Mac.

As the most important trading currency in the world, the U.S. dollar is widely traded globally. **Eurodollars** are time deposits in U.S. dollar in banks outside the U.S., and they are thus not under the jurisdiction of the Fed. While this term is originally coined for U.S. dollars deposited in European banks, it has since been expanded to include deposits in other markets, such as Tokyo. Consequently this term has no connection with the Euro currency or the Euro zone. Indeed, the prefix *Euro* is now used to indicate any currency held in a country in which it is not the official currency, such as **Euroyen** or even **Euroeuro**.

London is currently the most important global market for trading currencies worldwide. The **London Interbank Offered Rate** (LIBOR) is the interest rate offered by leading banks in London that they would charge to other borrowing banks. It is the primary benchmark for short-term interest rates around the world. Since 2014, the ICE has taken over the administration of the LIBOR. It calculates and publishes LIBOR every business day for five currencies (U.S. dollar, Euro, British pound, Japanese yen and Swiss franc) for seven maturities (1 day, 1 week, 1-, 2-, 3-, 6- and 12-month). Table 9.1 shows the overnight (1-day) LIBOR for three currencies.

In March 2016, the European Central Bank announced some stimulus measures aimed at boosting recovery in the European region. It cut its main refinancing rate to zero percent and its deposit rate to –0.4%. This measure caused a drop in the LIBOR for the Euro. As can be seen from Table 9.1, the Euro LIBOR overnight rate is in the negative territory.

---

[3]Note that these two figures are both on a discount basis.

Table 9.1: Selected interest rates of the U.S. and London markets

Securities	Annualized yield (%)
U.S. market	
Federal funds (effective)	0.38
Discount Window primary credit	1.00
U.S. government securities	
Treasury bills	
3-month	0.27
1-year	0.50
Treasury constant maturities	
1-year	0.53
5-year	1.10
10-year	1.57
20-year	1.96
30-year	2.39
Swap rates	
1-year	0.78
5-year	1.10
10-year	1.47
State and local bonds	3.18
Commercial paper (3-month)	0.49
Bank prime loan	3.50
Corporate bonds (Moody's seasoned)	
Aaa	3.43
Baa	4.47
Conventional mortgages	3.54
London market	
U.S. dollar LIBOR overnight	0.3855
Euro LIBOR overnight	−0.3950
British pound LIBOR overnight	0.4813

Notes: The U.S. data are from the Federal Reserve Bank (www.federalreserve.gov). The LIBOR data are from the Intercontinental Exchange (ICE) (www.theice.com). All data are at mid June 2016.

Another important primary benchmark for short-term interest rate not shown in Table 9.1 is the **Euro Interbank Offered Rate** (Euribor), which is a daily reference rate published by the European Money Markets Institute. This is the average interest rate at which Eurozone banks charge other banks for borrowing.[4]

9.3   Inflation and Central Bank Policy

The Federal Reserve System (the Fed) is the central banking system of the U.S. The **Federal Reserve Act** mandates the Fed with three duties: Sustain maximum employment, maintain stable prices and moderate long-term interest rates.

The Fed has seven governors, who are appointed by the U.S. President. It is comprised of twelve regional Federal Reserve Banks.[5] An important committee in the Fed is the **Federal Open Market Committee** (FOMC), which consists of the seven governors of the Fed, as well as the twelve presidents of the regional Federal Reserve Banks. The FOMC is in charge of carrying out the monetary policies of the Fed. However, only the seven governors and five Federal Reserve Bank presidents vote at any given time.[6]

The Fed influences the rate of interest (and hence the rate of inflation) through controlling the amount of reserves commercial banks are required to hold. They have the following three instruments to use in carrying out their mandate: Reserve ratio, Discount Window lending and open market operation.

The **reserve ratio** is the fractional reserve requirement that a depository institution needs to hold in the Federal Reserve Banks. By changing the reserve ratio, the Fed can affect the money supply and hence the rate of interest. For example, increasing the reserve ratio causes a contraction in the money supply and thus an increase in the rate of interest. However, changing the reserve ratio is a very blunt measure and it is rarely used.[7]

The Fed has its own lending facility, namely, the Discount Window, through which they lend directly to the commercial banks that need to boost their reserve to meet short-term regulatory requirements. The Fed sets the rate of interest for such borrowing. This rate has generally been about 100 basis points above the target Federal funds rate. Commercial banks usually seek alternative borrowing from other banks before using the Discount Window.

The Fed engages in **open market operations** through repurchase agreements (repos). Under a repo the Fed buys U.S. Treasury securities, U.S. agency securities

---

[4]Note that Euro LIBOR and Euribor are both interbank rates for borrowing euro. While the former is based on banks in London, the latter is based on a panel of European banks.

[5]Nationally chartered banks are required to hold stocks in the Federal Reserve Bank of their region.

[6]The president of the New York Fed and four other presidents rotate through 1-year terms.

[7]Many countries, such as Canada and the U.K., have no reserve requirements.

or mortgage-backed securities from a primary dealer, who would buy them back when the agreement matures. This operation increases reserves and injects liquidity into the market, thus lowering the rate of interest.

Inflation is usually caused by an excessively loose monetary policy when the monetary base expands too fast, resulting in "too much money chasing too few goods". Low and steady inflation is necessary for companies to plan for their investment and production. The rate of interest is inversely related to the rate of inflation, and the task of maintaining an appropriate interest rate level is thus an important mandate of the monetary authority.

9.4   Macroeconomic Management

Governments have the important mandate to sustain economic growth and maintain full employment. They can fulfill these goals by managing the aggregate demand in the economy. When the economy is weak, the government can increase aggregate demand by directly spending on public projects. Through the so called **multiplier effect**, an increase of one billion dollar in public expenditure will increase the aggregate demand by more than one billion dollar. Alternatively, the government can leave the potential to spend to the private sector by cutting taxes. If tax cut is not done concurrently with a cut in public spending it will have an effect in increasing the aggregate demand. Changing government expenditure or taxation is referred to as **fiscal policy**. An expansionary fiscal policy involves increasing government expenditure or reducing tax, or both. A contractional fiscal policy is the reverse: reducing government expenditure or increasing tax, or both.

In some countries, increasing public expenditure may require congressional or parliamentary approval. Fiscal policy directly affects aggregate demand and may effect higher growth and employment within a shorter period of time. However, a government that accumulates big deficits by overspending may bring about slower growth in the economy in the future. In addition, the government assumes the role in deciding how to spend to stimulate the economy. The decision and the process in arriving at such decision may be controversial. It may benefit one group of people more than others, depending on the bargaining and political power of the people or region concerned. Many economists and politicians advocate small governments for fear of indiscriminate public spending. This puts limitations on the use of fiscal policy in managing the economy.

Aggregate demand can also be managed through the use of **monetary policy**. Central banks can increase money supply by purchasing treasury bonds or other securities in their open market operations, as discussed in the last section. The increase in money supply injects liquidity into the economy and drives down the rate of interest. This stimulates consumers to spend and companies to invest.

Unlike fiscal policy, monetary policy usually has broader effects on the economy. As monetary policy is not directly targeting certain sectors of the economy, its impacts are usually spread across the economy. Nonetheless, sectors that are more interest-rate sensitive may have to adjust to monetary policy more aggressively. Finally, as monetary policy usually does not require congressional or parliamentary approval, it can be implemented relatively quickly.

9.5   Rate of Interest in an Open Economy

We have so far discussed interest rate changes in a single economy. As a country trades in the international markets, the prices of its goods and services are influenced by global demand and supply. Likewise, the interest rate of a country is influenced by the global demand and supply of capital. This is particularly true if a country has a policy of free capital mobility, by which it does not restrict the free flow of capital.

During the global financial crisis of 2008, which originated from the U.S. economy, the Fed implemented **quantitative easying**. It injected a large amount of liquidity into the U.S. economy, driving the rate of interest to unprecedentedly low level. The effects of quantitative easying, however, does not stay only in the U.S. economy. Much of the liquidity leaks out of the U.S., partly to chase higher returns elsewhere. This caused the rate of interest to be globally depressed.

In sum, in a globally open economy, interest rates are not just influenced by its own conditions and government policies. It is also dependent on how inter-related it is with respect to other countries, as well as what policies other countries are implementing.

9.6   Summary

1. The rate of interest of a risk-free asset is a benchmark for the rate of interest of other securities.

2. The nominal risk-free rate of interest is the sum of the real risk-free rate of interest and the expected rate of inflation.

3. For a security in general, its rate of interest consists of premiums due to liquidity, default risk and maturity risk.

4. Two important tools for the Fed to manage the supply of money are the reserve ratio and interest rate charged at the Discount Window.

5. The Federal funds rate is the interest rate commercial banks charge each other for borrowing Federal funds.

6. From time to time the Fed sets the target Federal funds rate and tries to meet the target through open-market operations.

7. Governments implement fiscal policy through changes in government spending and taxes.

8. Central banks are in charge of setting and implementing monetary policies, through which they influence liquidity and the rates of interest.

9. Interest rates in different countries are inter-related as countries trade against each other and capital can move around globally.

Exercises

9.1 You put your money into a savings account yielding 8% effective for 4 years, while inflation rate is 7% in the first year, and increases to a "double digit" of 10% in the next three years. Find the percentage loss of the purchasing power.

9.2 It is given that $r_N = 4\%$ and $r_I = 4.5\%$ over the next four years. For an investment of $100, find the value of the investment after four years in real terms (that is, in the monetary unit that has the same purchasing power as at $t = 0$).

9.3 It is given that $r_N = 4\%$ and $r_I = 3\%$ over the last year. Find the real rate of interest over the last year.

9.4 It is given that $r_N = 4\%$ and $r_I = 4.5\%$ over the next 4 years. For an investment of $100 at the beginning of every year for 4 years, find the value of the investment after 4 years in real terms.

9.5 A company has to pay a plaintiff ten annual payments after a lawsuit. The first payment is $20,000 due today and subsequent payments are inflation-adjusted. Under the assumption that the anticipated inflation is 4% per year and that the nominal rate of interest is 6% per year, find the present value of the obligation of the company.

10 Stochastic Interest Rates

In previous chapters we have assumed the rate of interest to be constant through time, or varying through time in a deterministic manner. A well-known deterministic set of interest rate scenarios is the collection of seven prescribed interest rate movements required by the U.S. 1990 Standard Valuation Law for cash-flow testing. These scenarios are similar to those used in the New York Regulation 126 and they are now commonly known as the NY7 model.

In reality interest rates are determined by many forces in the economy and they are hardly constant nor deterministic. In this chapter we discuss several stochastic approaches to modeling interest rates. First, we consider the random-scenario approach, in which the modeler specifies the probability distribution of some interest rate scenarios. Second, we discuss the lognormal approach, which assumes that the 1-period future spot interest rates are independent random variables following a lognormal distribution. Third, we outline the autoregressive model, which assumes a dynamic structure of the interest-rate variables through time, while maintaining the lognormal distribution assumption. Fourth, we briefly discuss the dynamic term structure model, which can simultaneously characterize both the shape of the term structure of interest rates and its evolution. Finally, we apply the stochastic interest rate approach to study the cost of a guaranteed income fund.

Learning Objectives

- *Deterministic scenarios of interest rates*
- *Random-scenario model*
- *Independent lognormal model*
- *Autoregressive lognormal model*
- *Dynamic term structure model*
- *Illustration of stochastic interest rate approach via an application*

10.1   Deterministic Scenarios of Interest Rates

Recall the concepts of the **spot rate of interest**, i_t^S, and the **forward rate of interest**, i_t^F, in Section 3.1. These two rates are related by equation (3.5). Some interest rate models characterize the spot rates, while others model the forward rates. Given a set of spot rates, the forward rates can be determined, and vice versa. It should be noted that i_t^S is the (annualized) t-period rate applicable from time 0 to time t, while i_t^F is a 1-period rate determined at time 0 and applicable from time $t - 1$ to time t. In this chapter we denote i_t, for $t = 2, 3, \cdots$, as the 1-period future spot rate applicable from time $t - 1$ to time t (for completeness we denote $i_1 = i_1^S$, which is known at time 0). Unlike the forward rates i_t^F, which are determined by the current term structure through (3.5), i_t for $t > 1$ is unknown at time 0. However, scenarios may be constructed to model the possible values of i_t.

A deterministic interest rate scenario is a sequence of pre-specified 1-period rates i_t applicable in the future. There are many financial and actuarial applications of the deterministic scenario approach. For example, the U.S. 1990 Standard Valuation Law requires cash-flow testing under seven prescribed interest rate scenarios. These scenarios are similar to those used in the New York Regulation 126 and they are now commonly known as the NY7 scenarios. A brief description of the NY7 interest rate scenarios is given in Table 10.1.

Table 10.1: The NY7 interest rate scenarios

	Scenario	Interest rate movement
1	Base scenario	Level
2	Gradual increase	Uniformly increasing over 10 years at 0.5% per year, and then level
3	Up-down	Uniformly increasing over 5 years at 1% per year, then uniformly decreasing over 5 years at 1% per year to the original level at the end of 10 years, and then level
4	Pop-up	An immediate increase of 3%, and then level
5	Gradual decrease	Uniformly decreasing over 10 years at 0.5% per year, and then level
6	Down-up	Uniformly decreasing over 5 years at 1% per year, then uniformly increasing over 5 years at 1% per year to the original level at the end of 10 years, and then level
7	Pop-down	An immediate decrease of 3%, and then level

Example 10.1: Given that the current 1-year spot rate is 6%, (a) find i_t for $t = 1, \cdots, 12$ under the "up-down" scenario of NY7, and (b) compute $a_{\overline{12}|}$ under this interest rate scenario.

Solution: (a) The interest rates under the "up-down" scenario are given in the following table:

t	1	2	3	4	5	6	7	8	9	10	11	12
i_t	6%	7%	8%	9%	10%	11%	10%	9%	8%	7%	6%	6%

(b) Using equation (3.12) (with i_t^F replaced by i_t) and the above interest rate scenario, we obtain $a_{\overline{12}|} = 7.48$.

There have been growing research interests in interest-rate modeling, and many stochastic models have been developed in the literature recently. In what follows we discuss several stochastic approaches to modeling interest rates.[1]

10.2 Random-Scenario Model

In previous chapters we have assumed the rate of interest to be constant through time, or varying through time in a deterministic manner. In reality interest rates

---

[1]For a comprehensive account of stochastic interest rate models, readers may refer to Cairns, A.J.G, *Interest Rate Models: An Introduction*, Princeton University Press, 2004.

are determined by many forces in the economy and they are hardly constant nor deterministic.

A random-scenario model is a collection of specified plausible interest rate scenarios. The modeler, however, needs to state the probability distribution of these scenarios. Both the choice of scenarios and the corresponding probability assignment require personal judgement, which should reflect the modeler's view on the future interest-rate environment of the economy.

Example 10.2: Consider the following random interest rate scenario model.

Scenario	Probability	i_1	i_2	i_3	i_4	i_5
1	0.1	3.0%	2.0%	2.0%	1.5%	1.0%
2	0.6	3.0%	3.0%	3.0%	3.5%	4.0%
3	0.3	3.0%	4.0%	5.0%	5.0%	5.0%

Find the mean, the variance and the standard deviation of $a(5)$, $\frac{1}{a(5)}$, $a_{\overline{5}|}$, $\ddot{a}_{\overline{5}|}$, $s_{\overline{5}|}$ and $\ddot{s}_{\overline{5}|}$ under this model.

Solution: Note that

$$\ddot{a}_{\overline{n}|} = \sum_{t=0}^{n-1} \frac{1}{a(t)}$$

$$= 1 + \sum_{t=1}^{n-1} \frac{1}{a(t)}$$

$$= 1 + \sum_{t=1}^{n-1} \frac{1}{\prod_{j=1}^{t}(1+i_j)}. \tag{10.1}$$

Using (3.10), (3.11), (3.12), (10.1), (3.14) and (3.15) (with i_t^F replaced by i_t), we can compute the values of $a(5)$, $\frac{1}{a(5)}$, $a_{\overline{5}|}$, $\ddot{a}_{\overline{5}|}$, $s_{\overline{5}|}$ and $\ddot{s}_{\overline{5}|}$ under each scenario. For example, under the first scenario, we have

$$a(5) = (1.03)(1.02)(1.02)(1.015)(1.01) = 1.0986,$$

$$\frac{1}{a(5)} = \frac{1}{1.0986} = 0.9103,$$

$$a_{\overline{5}|} = \frac{1}{(1.03)} + \frac{1}{(1.03)(1.02)} + \cdots + \frac{1}{(1.03)(1.02)(1.02)(1.015)(1.01)} = 4.6855,$$

$$\ddot{a}_{\overline{5}|} = 1 + \frac{1}{(1.03)} + \cdots + \frac{1}{(1.03)(1.02)(1.02)(1.015)} = 4.7753,$$

$$s_{\overline{5}|} = 1 + (1.01) + \cdots + (1.01)(1.015)(1.02)(1.02) = 5.1474,$$

and

$$\ddot{s}_{\overline{5}|} = (1.01) + (1.01)(1.015) + \cdots + (1.01)(1.015)(1.02)(1.02)(1.03) = 5.2459.$$

We repeat the calculations for the other two scenarios and summarize the results in the following table.

Scenario	Probability	$a(5)$	$\frac{1}{a(5)}$	$a_{\overline{5}|}$	$\ddot{a}_{\overline{5}|}$	$s_{\overline{5}|}$	$\ddot{s}_{\overline{5}|}$
1	0.1	1.0986	0.9103	4.6855	4.7753	5.1474	5.2459
2	0.6	1.1762	0.8502	4.5630	4.7128	5.3670	5.5433
3	0.3	1.2400	0.8064	4.4466	4.6402	5.5141	5.7541

Therefore,

$$E\left[\frac{1}{a(5)}\right] = (0.1 \times 0.9103) + (0.6 \times 0.8502) + (0.3 \times 0.8064) = 0.8431,$$

and

$$
\begin{aligned}
\text{Var}\left[\frac{1}{a(5)}\right] &= 0.1 \times (0.9103 - 0.8431)^2 + 0.6 \times (0.8502 - 0.8431) \\
&\quad + 0.3 \times (0.8064 - 0.8431)^2 \\
&= 0.00089.
\end{aligned}
$$

The mean, the variance and the standard deviation of other variables can be computed similarly. The results are given in the following table.

	$a(5)$	$\frac{1}{a(5)}$	$a_{\overline{5}|}$	$\ddot{a}_{\overline{5}|}$	$s_{\overline{5}|}$	$\ddot{s}_{\overline{5}|}$
Mean	1.1876	0.8431	4.5403	4.6973	5.3892	5.5768
Variance	0.00170	0.00089	0.00505	0.00173	0.01082	0.02105
Std Dev	0.0412	0.0298	0.0711	0.0416	0.1040	0.1451

10.3   Independent Lognormal Model

The **Independent Lognormal Model** assumes that $1 + i_t$ are independently lognormally distributed with parameters μ and σ^2. In other words, $\ln(1 + i_t)$ follows a normal distribution with mean μ and variance σ^2, i.e., (see Appendix A.14)

$$\ln(1 + i_t) \sim N(\mu, \sigma^2). \tag{10.2}$$

The mean and variance of the lognormal random variable $(1 + i_t)$ are

$$\mathrm{E}\,(1 + i_t) = e^{\mu + \frac{1}{2}\sigma^2}, \tag{10.3}$$

and

$$\mathrm{Var}(1 + i_t) = \left(e^{2\mu + \sigma^2}\right)\left(e^{\sigma^2} - 1\right), \tag{10.4}$$

respectively.[2]

We now discuss the mean and variance of $a(n)$, $\frac{1}{a(n)}$, $\ddot{s}_{\overline{n}|}$, $a_{\overline{n}|}$, $s_{\overline{n}|}$ and $\ddot{a}_{\overline{n}|}$ under the independent lognormal interest rate model. Note that we shall assume all 1-period spot rates to be random, including the rate for the first period i_1. Apart from theoretical convenience, there are also practical justifications for this assumption (see Section 10.6 for an empirical example).

First, from (3.10), we have

$$a(n) = \prod_{t=1}^{n}(1 + i_t).$$

Thus,

$$\ln\left[a(n)\right] = \sum_{t=1}^{n}\ln(1 + i_t). \tag{10.5}$$

From (10.2), we conclude that the right-hand side of (10.5) is a sum of n independent normal random variables, each with mean μ and variance σ^2. Therefore, $\ln\left[a(n)\right]$ is normal with mean $n\mu$ and variance $n\sigma^2$. This implies $a(n)$ is lognormal with parameters $n\mu$ and $n\sigma^2$. Using (10.3) and (10.4), we have

$$\mathrm{E}\left[a(n)\right] = e^{n\mu + \frac{n}{2}\sigma^2}, \tag{10.6}$$

and

$$\mathrm{Var}\left[a(n)\right] = \left(e^{2n\mu + n\sigma^2}\right)\left(e^{n\sigma^2} - 1\right). \tag{10.7}$$

---

[2]Other statistical properties of the lognormal model can be found in Klugman, S.A., Panjer, H.H. and Willmot, G.E., *Loss Models: From Data to Decisions*, 4th Edition, John Wiley & Sons, 2012.

Next, we examine the distribution of $(1 + i_t)^{-1}$ under the lognormal model. Note that

$$\ln\left[(1 + i_t)^{-1}\right] = -\ln(1 + i_t).$$

Thus, from (10.2), we have

$$\ln\left[(1 + i_t)^{-1}\right] \sim N(-\mu, \sigma^2), \tag{10.8}$$

and $(1 + i_t)^{-1}$ follows a lognormal distribution with parameters $-\mu$ and σ^2. From (3.11), we have

$$\frac{1}{a(n)} = \prod_{t=1}^{n}(1 + i_t)^{-1}.$$

Using a similar argument as in (10.6) and (10.7), we obtain

$$E\left[\frac{1}{a(n)}\right] = e^{-n\mu + \frac{n}{2}\sigma^2}, \tag{10.9}$$

and

$$\text{Var}\left[\frac{1}{a(n)}\right] = \left(e^{-2n\mu + n\sigma^2}\right)\left(e^{n\sigma^2} - 1\right). \tag{10.10}$$

The statistical properties of annuities (say, $\ddot{s}_{\overline{n}|}$, $a_{\overline{n}|}$, $s_{\overline{n}|}$ and $\ddot{a}_{\overline{n}|}$) under the lognormal interest rate assumption are fairly complex. We shall present and discuss some applications of their mean and variance formulas without going through the proof.[3]

We begin with $\ddot{s}_{\overline{n}|}$. Let us define r_s such that

$$1 + r_s = E(1 + i_t) = e^{\mu + \frac{1}{2}\sigma^2}.$$

This implies

$$r_s = e^{\mu + \frac{1}{2}\sigma^2} - 1. \tag{10.11}$$

Furthermore, let

$$j_s = 2r_s + r_s^2 + v_s^2, \tag{10.12}$$

where

$$v_s^2 = \text{Var}(1 + i_t) = \left(e^{2\mu + \sigma^2}\right)\left(e^{\sigma^2} - 1\right). \tag{10.13}$$

---

[3]For the theoretical details, interested readers may refer to Kellison, S.G., *The Theory of Interest*, 3rd Edition, McGraw-Hill, 2008.

The mean of $\ddot{s}_{\overline{n}|}$ is

$$
\begin{aligned}
\mathrm{E}\left(\ddot{s}_{\overline{n}|}\right) &= \mathrm{E}\left[\sum_{t=1}^{n}\prod_{j=1}^{t}(1+i_{n-j+1})\right] \\
&= \sum_{t=1}^{n}\prod_{j=1}^{t}\mathrm{E}(1+i_{n-j+1}) \\
&= \sum_{t=1}^{n}(1+r_s)^t \\
&= \ddot{s}_{\overline{n}|r_s},
\end{aligned}
\tag{10.14}
$$

where $\ddot{s}_{\overline{n}|r_s}$ is $\ddot{s}_{\overline{n}|}$ evaluated at the rate r_s. Without providing the details of the proof we state the variance of $\ddot{s}_{\overline{n}|}$ as

$$
\mathrm{Var}\left(\ddot{s}_{\overline{n}|}\right) = \left(\frac{j_s+r_s+2}{j_s-r_s}\right)\ddot{s}_{\overline{n}|j_s} - \left(\frac{2j_s+2}{j_s-r_s}\right)\ddot{s}_{\overline{n}|r_s} - \left(\ddot{s}_{\overline{n}|r_s}\right)^2.
\tag{10.15}
$$

Next, we consider $a_{\overline{n}|}$. Let us define r_a such that

$$
(1+r_a)^{-1} = \mathrm{E}(1+i_t)^{-1} = e^{-\mu+\frac{1}{2}\sigma^2}.
$$

This implies

$$
r_a = e^{\mu-\frac{1}{2}\sigma^2} - 1.
\tag{10.16}
$$

Furthermore, let

$$
j_a = e^{2(\mu-\sigma^2)} - 1.
\tag{10.17}
$$

Similar to (10.14), we can show that the mean of $a_{\overline{n}|}$ is

$$
\mathrm{E}\left(a_{\overline{n}|}\right) = a_{\overline{n}|r_a}.
\tag{10.18}
$$

Along the same argument as in (10.15), the variance of $a_{\overline{n}|}$ is

$$
\mathrm{Var}\left(a_{\overline{n}|}\right) = \left(\frac{j_a+r_a+2}{r_a-j_a}\right)a_{\overline{n}|j_a} - \left(\frac{2r_a+2}{r_a-j_a}\right)a_{\overline{n}|r_a} - \left(a_{\overline{n}|r_a}\right)^2.
\tag{10.19}
$$

For $\ddot{a}_{\overline{n}|}$ and $s_{\overline{n}|}$, from (2.7) and (2.8), we have

$$
\ddot{a}_{\overline{n}|} = 1 + a_{\overline{n-1}|},
$$

and

$$
s_{\overline{n}|} = 1 + \ddot{s}_{\overline{n-1}|}.
$$

Therefore,

$$E\left(\ddot{a}_{\overline{n}|}\right) = 1 + E\left(a_{\overline{n-1}|}\right), \tag{10.20}$$

and

$$E\left(s_{\overline{n}|}\right) = 1 + E\left(\ddot{s}_{\overline{n-1}|}\right). \tag{10.21}$$

Furthermore,

$$\text{Var}\left(\ddot{a}_{\overline{n}|}\right) = \text{Var}\left(a_{\overline{n-1}|}\right), \tag{10.22}$$

and

$$\text{Var}\left(s_{\overline{n}|}\right) = \text{Var}\left(\ddot{s}_{\overline{n-1}|}\right). \tag{10.23}$$

Example 10.3: Consider a lognormal interest rate model with parameters $\mu = 0.04$ and $\sigma^2 = 0.016$. Find the mean and variance of $a(5)$, $\frac{1}{a(5)}$, $\ddot{s}_{\overline{5}|}$, $a_{\overline{5}|}$, $s_{\overline{5}|}$ and $\ddot{a}_{\overline{5}|}$ under this model.

Solution: We directly apply equations (10.6), (10.7), (10.9) and (10.10) to obtain

$$
\begin{aligned}
E\left[a(5)\right] &= 1.27125, \\
\text{Var}\left[a(5)\right] &= 0.13460, \\
E\left[\frac{1}{a(5)}\right] &= 0.85214, \\
\text{Var}\left[\frac{1}{a(5)}\right] &= 0.06058.
\end{aligned}
$$

For $\ddot{s}_{\overline{5}|}$, using expressions (10.11) to (10.13), we have

$$
\begin{aligned}
r_s &= e^{0.04+\frac{1}{2}(0.016)} - 1 = 0.04917, \\
v_s^2 &= \left(e^{2(0.04)+0.016}\right)\left(e^{0.016} - 1\right) = 0.01775, \\
j_s &= 2r_s + r_s^2 + v_s^2 = 0.11851, \\
\ddot{s}_{\overline{5}|r_s} &= 5.78773, \\
\ddot{s}_{\overline{5}|j_s} &= 7.08477.
\end{aligned}
$$

Applying equations (10.14) and (10.15), we obtain

$$
\begin{aligned}
E\left(\ddot{s}_{\overline{5}|}\right) &= 5.78773, \\
\text{Var}\left(\ddot{s}_{\overline{5}|}\right) &= 1.26076.
\end{aligned}
$$

For $a_{\overline{5}|}$, using expressions (10.16) and (10.17), we have

$$
\begin{aligned}
r_a &= e^{0.04-\frac{1}{2}(0.016)} - 1 = 0.03252, \\
j_a &= e^{2(0.04-0.016)} - 1 = 0.04917, \\
a_{\overline{5}|r_a} &= 4.54697, \\
a_{\overline{5}|j_a} &= 4.33942.
\end{aligned}
$$

Applying equations (10.18) and (10.19), we obtain

$$
\begin{aligned}
\mathrm{E}\left(a_{\overline{5}|}\right) &= 4.54697, \\
\mathrm{Var}\left(a_{\overline{5}|}\right) &= 0.72268.
\end{aligned}
$$

Finally, employing formulas (10.20) to (10.23), we obtain

$$
\begin{aligned}
\mathrm{E}\left(\ddot{a}_{\overline{5}|}\right) &= 1 + \mathrm{E}\left(a_{\overline{4}|}\right) = 1 + 3.69483 = 4.69483, \\
\mathrm{Var}\left(\ddot{a}_{\overline{5}|}\right) &= \mathrm{Var}\left(a_{\overline{4}|}\right) = 0.40836, \\
\mathrm{E}\left(s_{\overline{5}|}\right) &= 1 + \mathrm{E}\left(\ddot{s}_{\overline{4}|}\right) = 1 + 4.51648 = 5.51648, \\
\mathrm{Var}\left(s_{\overline{5}|}\right) &= \mathrm{Var}\left(\ddot{s}_{\overline{4}|}\right) = 0.64414.
\end{aligned}
$$

10.4   Autoregressive Model

Let $Y_t = \ln(1 + i_t)$. Under the independent lognormal model, we have

$$
Y_t = \ln(1 + i_t) \sim N(\mu, \sigma^2), \tag{10.24}
$$

where there are no correlations between Y_t and Y_{t-k} for all $k \geq 1$. In this section we consider interest rate models that allow some dependence among Y_t's, say,

$$
\mathrm{Corr}(Y_t, Y_{t-k}) \neq 0, \quad \text{for some } k \geq 1, \tag{10.25}
$$

while maintaining the lognormal assumption in (10.24).

In the literature of statistical time series analysis there are many classes of discrete time series models which may be applied to characterize the dependence among Y_t's.[4] As an introductory illustration of the basic idea we consider the class of first-order autoregressive models, denoted by AR(1). The AR(1) model has the form

$$
Y_t = c + \phi Y_{t-1} + e_t, \tag{10.26}
$$

where c is the intercept and ϕ is the autoregressive parameter and e_t are independently and identically distributed normal random variates each with mean zero and variance σ^2. For $|\phi| < 1$, the correlation structure of the interest-rate process $\{Y_t\}$ is

$$
\mathrm{Corr}(Y_t, Y_{t-k}) = \phi^k, \quad \text{for } k = 1, 2, \cdots, \tag{10.27}
$$

---

[4]For example, see Wei, W.W.S., *Time Series Analysis: Univariate and Multivariate Methods*, 2nd Edition, Pearson Addison Wesley, 2006.

which does not vary with t. There are empirical justifications for using the autoregressive assumption in stochastic interest rate modeling.[5]

The mean and variance expressions of $a(n)$, $\frac{1}{a(n)}$, $a_{\overline{n}|}$, $\ddot{a}_{\overline{n}|}$, $s_{\overline{n}|}$ and $\ddot{s}_{\overline{n}|}$ under an AR(1) interest rate model are very complex. Thus, we consider a stochastic simulation approach to obtain the empirical distributions (and hence the numerical values of the means and variances) of these functions. As an illustration we outline the simulation steps for the $a_{\overline{n}|}$ function in Table 10.2. Procedures for calculating other annuity functions are similar.

Table 10.2: A simulation procedure of $a_{\overline{n}|}$ for the AR(1) process

Step	Procedure
1	Using historical interest rate data, estimate the parameters (c, ϕ, σ^2) in the AR(1) model.
2	Draw random normal numbers $e_1, e_2, \cdots, e_n$ (with mean zero and variance σ^2) from a random number generator.
3	Compute $Y_1, Y_2, \cdots, Y_n$ using the AR(1) equation (10.26) and setting the initial value $Y_0 = \overline{Y}$, where $\overline{Y}$ is the sample average of the observed data.
4	Convert Y_t's to an interest rate path $(i_1, i_2, \cdots, i_n)$ using the relationship $i_t = e^{Y_t} - 1$.
5	Compute the $a_{\overline{n}|}$ function under the simulated interest rate path in Step 4.
6	Repeat Steps 2 to 4 m times. Note that the random normal variates in Step 2 are redrawn each time and we have a different simulated interest rate path in each replication.

From the simulation procedure in Table 10.2, we obtain m numerical realizations of $a_{\overline{n}|}$ under the AR(1) interest rate model. Statistical properties of the distribution of $a_{\overline{n}|}$, therefore, can be evaluated empirically.

Example 10.4: Consider an AR(1) interest-rate model with parameters $c = 0.03$, $\phi = 0.6$ and $\sigma^2 = 0.001$. Using the stochastic simulation method described in Table 10.2 (with $m = 1,000$ and $Y_0 = 0.06$), find the mean and variance of $a(10)$, $\frac{1}{a(10)}$, $a_{\overline{10}|}$, $\ddot{a}_{\overline{10}|}$, $s_{\overline{10}|}$ and $\ddot{s}_{\overline{10}|}$ under this model.

Solution: We follow the simulation steps in Table 10.2 and obtain the empirical distributions (histograms) of the six functions, which are plotted in Figure 10.1.

---

[5]See Panjer, H.H. and Bellhouse, D.R. (1980), "Stochastic Modelling of Interest Rates with Applications to Life Contingencies", *Journal of Risk and Insurance* 47, 91–110.

The empirical means and variances are as follows:

Figure 10.1: Histograms of simulated results in Example 10.4

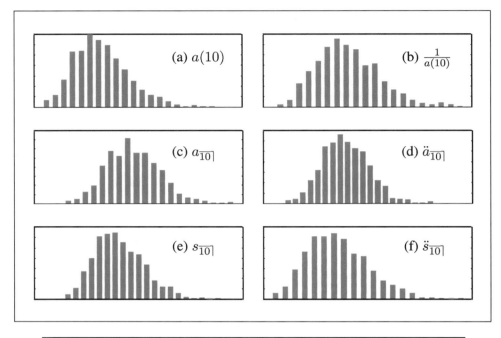

	$a(10)$	$\frac{1}{a(10)}$	$a_{\overline{10}|}$	$\ddot{a}_{\overline{10}|}$	$s_{\overline{10}|}$	$\ddot{s}_{\overline{10}|}$
Mean	2.1656	0.4836	6.8382	7.3546	14.5018	15.6674
Variance	0.2224	0.0110	0.5678	0.4383	3.5101	5.3524

10.5   Dynamic Term Structure Model

Each yield curve shown in Figure 3.4 is for a particular date. If we examine the yield curve on another date, the shape of the curve may be different. Figures 7.3 and 7.4 plot the UK and US yield curves in the period January 2002 to December 2015, respectively.

In Section 7.7 we discuss some static term structure models which explain the shape of the spot-rate curve (i.e., the term structure of interest rates) at a fixed date. In the literature there are some advanced models that can characterize the shape of the term structure as well as its evolution simultaneously. In other words, these approaches try to model the dynamics of the observed yield curves (i.e., the whole surface area of yield curves as in Figure 7.3 or Figure 7.4).

There are two popular approaches to model the term structure. The **no-arbitrage approach** focuses on perfectly fitting the term structure at a point in time to ensure that no arbitrage opportunities exist in the financial markets. This approach is important for pricing derivatives. On the other hand, the **equilibrium modeling approach** focuses on modeling the instantaneous spot rate of interest, called the **short rate**, and use **affine models** to derive the yields at other maturities under various assumptions of the risk premium. These models are at a mathematical and probability level beyond the scope of this book. Interested readers may refer to a paper by Yong Yao and the references therein.[6]

10.6 An Application: Guaranteed Investment Income

We consider a hypothetical **guaranteed income fund** offered by a bank with the following features:

- It is a **closed-end** fund. The bank sells only a fixed number of units (say, 10,000 units with $1,000 face amount per unit) in the initial public offering (IPO). No more units will be issued by the bank after the IPO. Redemption prior to the maturity date is not allowed.

- Investment period is 9 years.

- At maturity, the bank will return 100% of the face amount to the investors.

- At the end of each of the nine years, earnings from the fund will be distributed to investors. In addition, the bank provides a guarantee on the minimum rate of return each year according to a fixed schedule:

At the end of	Guaranteed rate (as % of initial investment)
Year 1	3%
Year 2	4%
Year 3	4%
Year 4	5%
Year 5	5%
Year 6	5%
Year 7	5%
Year 8	5%
Year 9	5%

[6]Yao, Y. (2004), "Efficient Factor Models for Yield Curve Dynamics", *North American Actuarial Journal* 8, 90–105.

In other words, if the fund earns less than the guaranteed rate in any year, the bank has to top up the difference.

Example 10.5: Consider the above guaranteed income fund. Assume that the rates of return for the fund in the next nine years are: 2%, 3%, 4%, 5%, 6%, 5%, 4%, 3%, 2%, respectively. Compute the cost of the guarantee to the bank (i.e., the present value of the top-up amounts).

Solution: Let G_t be the guaranteed rate for year t offered by the bank, i_t be the rate of return earned by the fund for year t, and U_t be the top-up amount (per $1,000 face amount) by the bank to honor the guarantee payable at the end of year t. Note that

$$U_t = \begin{cases} 0, & \text{if } i_t \geq G_t, \\ 1,000(G_t - i_t), & \text{if } i_t < G_t. \end{cases} \tag{10.28}$$

Using equation (10.28), we compute U_t for each year. The results are given as follows.

t	1	2	3	4	5	6	7	8	9
i_t	2%	3%	4%	5%	6%	5%	4%	3%	2%
G_t	3%	4%	4%	5%	5%	5%	5%	5%	5%
U_t	10	10	0	0	0	0	10	20	30

The cost of the guarantee C is the present value of the U_t's. Thus,

$$
\begin{aligned}
C &= \sum_{t=1}^{9} \frac{U_t}{\prod_{j=1}^{t}(1 + i_j)} \tag{10.29} \\
&= \frac{10}{1.02} + \frac{10}{(1.02)(1.03)} + \frac{0}{(1.02)(1.03)(1.04)} + \cdots \\
&= 62.98.
\end{aligned}
$$

The bank needs to charge an up-front premium to cover the cost of the guarantee. We now apply the stochastic interest rate approach to examine the distribution of C. This information is useful to the bank's management for setting the premium.

For illustration, we assume that the fund invests only in government bonds and the returns of the fund follow an independent lognormal interest rate model with parameters $\mu = 0.06$ and $\sigma^2 = 0.0009$, i.e.,

$$\ln(1 + i_t) \sim N(0.06, 0.0009). \tag{10.30}$$

We use stochastic simulation to produce a series of future interest rate movements. For each of the simulated path, using equations (10.28) through (10.30), a realization of C can be computed. We repeat the simulation experiment m times (say, $m = 5,000$) and the empirical distribution (histogram) of C can be obtained.

The time lag between the bank's filing of the required fund documents to the regulator for approval and the actual IPO is often lengthy. The bank has to determine the premium rate well before the IPO date. Therefore, in the simulation, the first-period rate of return i_1 is not known at time 0. Thus, we treat i_1 as a random variable following the lognormal model as in (10.30).

The simulation study is carried out and the empirical distribution (histogram) of C is plotted in Figure 10.2.

There are many approaches for setting the premium to cover the cost of the guarantee. For example, the bank management may set the premium as the expected value of C. This can be computed as the sample average from the data in Figure 10.2, the result of which is $42.30 per $1,000 face value. On the other hand, the bank management may set the premium such that it is adequate to cover the cost with a probability of 95%. In this case, we can estimate the target premium by computing the 95th percentile of the data, the result of which is $99.32.

Figure 10.2: Empirical distribution (histogram) of the cost of the guarantee (C)

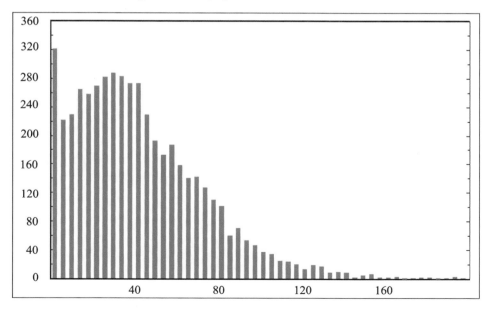

10.7 Summary

1. A deterministic interest rate scenario is a sequence of pre-specified 1-period interest rates applicable in the future. We describe the NY7 interest rate scenarios which are seven prescribed interest rate paths required by the U.S. 1990 Standard Valuation Law for cash flow testing.

2. A random-scenario model is a collection of specified plausible interest rate scenarios. The modeler needs to state the probability distribution of these scenarios. Both the choice of scenarios and the corresponding probability assignment require personal judgement, which should reflect the modeler's view of the future interest rate environment of the economy.

3. The lognormal model assumes that the random 1-period future spot interest rate variable follows an independent lognormal distribution. The mean and variance expressions for the $a(n)$, $\frac{1}{a(n)}$, $a_{\overline{n}|}$, $\ddot{a}_{\overline{n}|}$, $s_{\overline{n}|}$ and $\ddot{s}_{\overline{n}|}$ functions under the lognormal model can be obtained analytically.

4. The autoregressive model allows a dependent structure among the interest rate variables while maintaining the lognormal distribution assumption. The mean and variance expressions of the accumulation and annuity functions under an AR(1) interest rate model are very complex. However, we can employ the stochastic simulation approach to obtain the empirical distributions (and hence the numerical values of means and variances) of these functions.

5. Some dynamic term structure models can characterize both the shape of the term structure of interest rates and its evolution simultaneously.

Exercises

10.1 A zero-coupon $100 par-value 1-year government bond is traded at a price of $96, while a 2-year $1,000, 7% annual coupon government bond is traded at a price of $1,021. Find i_2^F.

10.2 Given that the current 1-year spot rate is $i_1 = 5\%$,

  (a) compute $s_{\overline{5}|}$ under the "gradual decrease" (i.e., $i_2 = 4.5\%$, etc.) and "pop-up" (i.e., $i_2 = 8\%$, etc.) scenarios of NY7,

  (b) compute the mean and standard deviation of $s_{\overline{5}|}$ if the "base", "gradual decrease" and "pop-up" scenarios of NY7 occur with probability 0.3, 0.55 and 0.15, respectively.

10.3 Write a spreadsheet program to implement the NY7 random scenario model for the present value of a cash-flow stream. The spreadsheet should have two worksheets named "Input" and "Calculation".

(a) In worksheet "Input", set up the following: i_1; cash flows at $t = 0, 1, \cdots, 20$; and the probability of occurrence for each of the scenarios.

(b) In worksheet "Calculation", set up the seven interest rate scenarios as in Example 10.2. It would be convenient to insert a row for $(1 + i_1)(1 + i_2) \cdots (1 + i_t)$ for each scenario. Calculate the present value of the cash-flow stream in "Input" using the spot rates of interest under each scenario.

(c) Finally, copy the seven present values in "Calculation" to "Input" and compute the mean and standard deviation of the present value of the cash-flow stream.

Use the spreadsheet to verify the results in Example 10.1.

10.4 Calculate the mean and variance of $\ddot{a}_{\overline{10}|}$ under the NY7 random scenario model using $i_1 = 7\%$. Assume that the seven scenarios are equally probable to occur.

10.5 For a bond portfolio, which of the seven NY7 scenarios is the worst scenario?

10.6 Consider the following random interest rate scenario model:

Scenario	Probability	i_1	i_2	i_3	i_4
1	0.15	4%	4%	4%	4%
2	0.60	4%	3%	2%	3%
3	0.25	4%	5%	5%	3%

Find the mean and standard deviation of the present value of $3 payable at the end of 4 years.

10.7 Consider the following random interest rate scenario model:

Scenario	Probability	i_1	i_2	i_3	i_4
1	0.20	4%	5%	4%	3%
2	0.45	4%	2%	2%	3%
3	0.35	4%	7%	6%	4%

Find the mean and variance of $(Is)_{\overline{4}|}$.

10.8 Give two shortcomings of the random interest rate scenario approach.

10.9 The random walk model (in particular, the binomial-tree model) is widely used in financial engineering. In essence, the random walk model gives a convenient way to construct random scenarios. Let $i_1 = 3\%$. The 1-period spot rate over the next period is 105% of the previous 1-period spot rate with probability 0.55, and is 95% of the previous 1-period spot rate with probability 0.45.

(a) Construct all scenarios for the 1-period spot rates over the next 3 years and give the corresponding probability for each scenario.

(b) Find the mean and standard deviation of the accumulated value of $1 after 3 years.

10.10 Assume that $i_1, i_2, \cdots, i_n$ are independently and identically distributed interest rate random variables with mean $\mu = 0.05$ and variance $\sigma^2 = 0.0001$. Following (3.10), we define

$$a(n) = \prod_{j=1}^{n}(1 + i_j).$$

Find the mean and standard deviation of $a(10)$.

10.11 Assume that $i_1, i_2, \cdots, i_n$ are independently and identically distributed interest rate random variables with mean $\mu = 0.10$ and variance $\sigma^2 = 0.0004$. Following (3.15), we define

$$\ddot{s}_{\overline{n}|} = \sum_{t=0}^{n-1}\left(\prod_{j=t+1}^{n}(1 + i_j)\right).$$

Find the mean and standard deviation of $\ddot{s}_{\overline{8}|}$.

10.12 Assume that $i_1, i_2, \cdots, i_n$ are independently and identically distributed interest rate random variables uniformly distributed on the interval $[0.06, 0.08]$. Following (3.15), we define

$$\ddot{s}_{\overline{n}|} = \sum_{t=0}^{n-1}\left(\prod_{j=t+1}^{n}(1 + i_j)\right).$$

Find the mean and standard deviation of $\ddot{s}_{\overline{n}|}$, for $n = 11, 12, \cdots, 20$.

10.13 Suggest a reason why it is not appropriate to use an independent normal model for forward interest rates.

10.14 It is given that $1 + i_t$ follows an independent lognormal distribution with $\mu = 0.06$ and $\sigma^2 = 0.03$ for $t = 1, 2, \cdots$.

    (a) Find $E(i_t)$.

    (b) Find $E\left[\dfrac{1}{a(5)}\right]$, and $\dfrac{1}{a(5)}$ calculated at rate $E(i_t)$. Are they the same?

10.15 It is given that $1 + i_t$ follow independent lognormal distributions with $\mu = 0.04$ and $\sigma^2 = 0.02$ for $t = 1, 2, \cdots$. Find the mean and variance of

    (a) the accumulated value of \$1 at $t = 4$,

    (b) the present value of \$1 payable at $t = 4$.

10.16 It is given that $1 + i_t$ follow lognormal distributions with $\mu = 0.04$ and $\sigma^2 = 0.02$ for $t = 1, 2$ and 3, and with $\mu = 0.03$ and $\sigma^2 = 0.03$ for $t = 4$ and 5. Furthermore, i_t are independent. Find the mean and variance of

    (a) the accumulated value of \$1 at $t = 5$,

    (b) the present value of \$1 payable at $t = 5$.

10.17 Given that $1 + i_t$ follow independent lognormal distributions with $\mu = 0.04$ and $\sigma^2 = 0.02$ for $t = 1, 2, \cdots$, find the mean and variance of

    (a) $a_{\overline{7}|}$,

    (b) $\ddot{a}_{\overline{7}|}$.

10.18 Given that $1 + i_t$ follow independent lognormal distributions with $\mu = 0.01$ and $\sigma^2 = 0.03$ for $t = 1, 2, \cdots$, find the mean and variance of

    (a) $s_{\overline{7}|}$,

    (b) $\ddot{s}_{\overline{7}|}$.

10.19 Given that $1 + i_t$ follow independent lognormal distributions with $\mu = 0.05$ and $\sigma^2 = 0.005$ for $t = 1, 2, \cdots$, find the 95% confidence interval of the present value of \$3 payable at the end of 4 years.

10.20 Describe how the mean and variance of $(Ia)_{\overline{n}|}$ can be simulated under the independent lognormal model.

10.21 In this exercise, we illustrate some properties of the AR(1) model numerically. Consider the following AR(1) model for $\{Y_t\}$:

$$Y_t = c + \phi Y_{t-1} + e_t,$$

where $\{e_t\}$ are independently and identically $N(0, \sigma^2)$ distributed.

(a) Let $c = 0.04$, $\phi = 0.5$, $\sigma = 0.03$ and $Y_0 = 0.02$. Simulate three sample paths for $\{Y_t\}$ for $t = 1$ to $t = 1,000$. Do the three sample paths oscillate around 0.08 as t approaches 1,000? Repeat with different values of Y_0. What do you observe? [**Hint**: A convenient way to simulate a $N(\mu, \sigma^2)$ random variable using the inverse transformation with Excel is as follows. First, generate a uniform random variable (say, u) in the interval $[0, 1]$ using the function **RAND**(), then use **NORMINV**(u, μ, σ) to obtain the normal random variable.]

(b) Let $c = 0.04$, $\phi = 1.2$, $\sigma = 0.03$ and $Y_0 = 0.02$. Simulate three sample paths for $\{Y_t\}$ for $t = 1$ to $t = 1,000$. Do the three sample paths oscillate around a long-term mean? Repeat with different values of Y_0. What can you observe? Repeat with $\phi = -1.2$.

(c) Comment on the constraint $|\phi| < 1$ when modeling interest rates.

10.22 Consider the following AR(1) model for $\{Y_t\}$:

$$Y_t = 0.05 + 0.7 Y_{t-1} + 0.05 e_t,$$

where $\{e_t\}$ are independently and identically $N(0, 1)$ distributed. The 1-period spot rates of interest are obtained from $Y_t = \ln(1 + i_t)$. Six random numbers are generated from the standard normal distribution:

$$-1.41644, \quad 0.07851, \quad 0.05061, \quad -0.22096, \quad 1.29722, \quad -1.28000$$

Using a starting value of $Y_0 = -0.026$, calculate the interest rate path $(i_1, \cdots, i_6)$.

10.23 You are given the following AR(1) model for $\{Y_t\}$:

$$Y_t = 0.03 + 0.5 Y_{t-1} + e_t,$$

where $\{e_t\}$ are independently and identically $N(0, 0.005)$ distributed. The forward interest rates are obtained from $Y_t = \ln(1 + i_t)$. Conditional on the current observed spot rate i_1^S of 3.4%, calculate the mean and standard deviation of i_3.

10.24 Consider the AR(1) model

$$Y_t = 0.02 + 0.8Y_{t-1} + e_t,$$

where $\{e_t\}$ are independently and identically normally distributed with mean 0 and standard deviation 0.063. The 1-period spot rates of interest are obtained from $Y_t = \ln(1 + i_t)$. Using 25,000 simulations with $Y_0 = 0.05$, estimate the mean and standard deviation of $\ddot{s}_{\overline{10|}}$ and $(Ia)_{\overline{10|}}$.

10.25 Consider the hypothetical guaranteed income fund described in Section 10.6 with the assumption that the returns of the fund follow an independent lognormal interest rate model in (10.30). Estimate the probability that the bank does not need to top up any amount for the guarantee (i.e., $U_t \equiv 0$ for $t = 1, \cdots, 9$) using the stochastic simulation approach.

10.26 Consider Exercise 10.25 again. Suppose that the bank is considering a 10% increase in the guaranteed rates, i.e., the new rates are:

At the end of	Guaranteed rate (as % of initial investment)
Year 1	3.3%
Year 2	4.4%
Year 3	4.4%
Year 4	5.5%
Year 5	5.5%
Year 6	5.5%
Year 7	5.5%
Year 8	5.5%
Year 9	5.5%

Using the stochastic simulation approach, estimate

(a) the decrease for the probability in Exercise 10.25,

(b) the increase for the expected cost of the guarantee.

APPENDIX A
Review of Mathematics and Statistics

A.1 Exponential function

The exponential function $e^x = \exp(x)$ is defined as the limit of the following expansion

$$e^x = \sum_{n=0}^{\infty} \frac{x^n}{n!}.$$

Hence, putting $x = 1$, we have

$$e = \sum_{n=0}^{\infty} \frac{1}{n!}.$$

For any constant c,

$$\lim_{m \to \infty} \left[1 + \frac{c}{m} \right]^m = e^c.$$

Hence,

$$\lim_{m \to \infty} \left[1 + \frac{c}{m} \right]^{mt} = \left(\lim_{m \to \infty} \left[1 + \frac{c}{m} \right]^m \right)^t = e^{ct}.$$

A.2 Logarithmic function

If $y = b^x$, where $b > 0$ and $b \neq 1$, we define $\log_b y = x$, and say that x is the logarithm of y to the base b. Note that $y > 0$ is defined for all values of x on the real line, provided $b > 0$. As $b^0 = 1$, we have $\log_b 1 = 0$ for all $b > 0$ and not equal to 1. For $b = e$, we write $x = \ln y = \log_e y$, i.e., x is the logarithm of y to the base e, called the natural logarithm. Note that $\log_b b = 1$, and

$$\log_b(y^a) = a \log_b y, \qquad y > 0.$$

$$\log_b(yz) = \log_b y + \log_b z, \qquad y, z > 0.$$

A.3 Roots of a quadratic equation

The following quadratic equation in x

$$ax^2 + bx + c = 0$$

has the following two roots

$$\frac{-b \pm \sqrt{b^2 - 4ac}}{2a}.$$

If $b^2 - 4ac < 0$, the equation has two complex roots.

A.4 Arithmetic progression

Consider the sum of the following arithmetic progression with n terms

$$S = a + (a + d) + (a + 2d) + \cdots + (a + (n - 1)d),$$

with initial value a and common difference d. The value of S is

$$na + \frac{n(n - 1)}{2}d.$$

A.5 Geometric progression

Consider the sum of the following geometric progression with n terms

$$S = a + ar + ar^2 + \cdots + ar^{n-1},$$

with initial value a and common ratio r. The value of S is

$$\frac{a(1 - r^n)}{1 - r}.$$

If $|r| < 1$, then $r^n \to 0$ as $n \to \infty$, so that $S \to a/(1 - r)$ as $n \to \infty$.

A.6 Some derivatives

$$\frac{dx^n}{dx} = nx^{n-1},$$

$$\frac{da^x}{dx} = a^x \ln a,$$

$$\frac{d \ln x}{dx} = \frac{1}{x}.$$

A.7 Integration by part

If $u(x)$ and $v(x)$ are functions of x, then

$$\int u(x)\, dv\,(x) = u(x)v(x) - \int v(x)\, du(x).$$

This result applies to definite as well as indefinite integrals. Now if $u(x) \equiv 1$, we have (as $\int v(x)\, du(x) = 0$)

$$\int_a^b dv(x) = v(b) - v(a).$$

A.8 Taylor series expansion

For a function $y = f(x)$, the expansion of $f(x + \Delta x)$ around x for a small value of Δx is, to the first order approximation, given by

$$f(x + \Delta x) = f(x) + \frac{df(x)}{dx}(\Delta x) + o(\Delta x),$$

where

$$\frac{o(\Delta x)}{\Delta x} \to 0$$

as $\Delta x \to 0$. The expansion to the second order approximation is

$$f(x + \Delta x) = f(x) + \frac{df(x)}{dx}(\Delta x) + \frac{d^2 f(x)}{dx^2}(\Delta x)^2 + o((\Delta x)^2),$$

where

$$\frac{o((\Delta x)^2)}{(\Delta x)^2} \to 0$$

as $\Delta x \to 0$.

A.9 Binomial expansion

For a positive integer n,

$$(x + y)^n = \sum_{i=0}^{n} \binom{n}{i} x^i y^{n-i},$$

where

$$\binom{n}{i} = \frac{n!}{i!(n-i)!}.$$

A.10 Expected value and variance of a random variable

The mean (also called expected value or expectation) of a continuous random variable X, which can take values in the range (a, b), is denoted by $E(X)$ and is defined as

$$E(X) = \int_a^b x \, dF_X(x) = \int_a^b x f_X(x) \, dx,$$

where $F_X(x)$ and $f_X(x)$ are, respectively, the distribution function and density function of X. The variance of X, denoted by $\mathrm{Var}(X)$, is defined as

$$\mathrm{Var}(X) = \int_a^b (x - E(X))^2 \, dF_X(x) = \int_a^b (x - E(X))^2 f_X(x) \, dx.$$

A.11 Mean and variance of sum of random variables

Consider a set of random variables $X_1, X_2, \cdots, X_n$ with mean $E(X_i)$ and variance $\mathrm{Var}(X_i)$ for $i = 1, 2, \cdots, n$; and let the covariance of X_i and X_j be $\mathrm{Cov}(X_i, X_j)$. Let $w_1, w_2, \cdots, w_n$ be a set of constants. Then

$$E\left(\sum_{i=1}^n w_i X_i\right) = \sum_{i=1}^n w_i E(X_i),$$

$$\mathrm{Var}\left(\sum_{i=1}^n w_i X_i\right) = \sum_{i=1}^n w_i^2 \mathrm{Var}(X_i) + \underbrace{\sum_{i=1}^n \sum_{j=1}^n w_i w_j \mathrm{Cov}(X_i, X_j)}_{i \neq j}.$$

For $n = 2$, we have

$$\mathrm{Var}(w_1 X_1 \pm w_2 X_2) = w_1^2 \mathrm{Var}(X_1) + w_2^2 \mathrm{Var}(X_2) \pm 2 w_1 w_2 \mathrm{Cov}(X_1, X_2).$$

If the correlation coefficient between X_i and X_j is denoted by ρ_{ij}, then

$$\mathrm{Cov}(X_i, X_j) = \rho_{ij} \sqrt{\mathrm{Var}(X_1) \mathrm{Var}(X_2)}.$$

A.12 Uniform distribution

X is said to have a uniform distribution in the interval (a, b) if the density function of X is $f_X(x) = \frac{1}{b-a}$ for $x \in (a, b)$ and zero otherwise. The mean and variance of X are $\frac{a+b}{2}$ and $\frac{(b-a)^2}{12}$, respectively.

A.13 Normal distribution

Let X be a continuous random variable which can take values on the real line. X is said to follow a normal distribution with mean μ and variance σ^2, denoted by $X \sim N(\mu, \sigma^2)$, if the density function of X is

$$f_X(x) = \frac{1}{\sqrt{2\pi}\sigma} \exp\left(-\frac{(x - \mu)^2}{2\sigma^2}\right).$$

X is said to be a standard normal random variable if it is normally distributed with mean 0 and variance 1, denoted by Z, so that $Z \sim N(0, 1)$. If $X \sim N(\mu, \sigma^2)$, then $\frac{X-\mu}{\sigma} \sim Z$.

The distribution function $F_Z(z) = \Pr(Z \leq z) = d$ of Z can be computed using the Excel function **NORMSDIST**(z), e.g., **NORMSDIST**(1.2816) returns the value 0.9. Similarly, the inverse of the distribution function $F_Z^{-1}(d) = z$ of Z can be computed using the Excel function **NORMSINV**(d), e.g., **NORMSINV**(0.9) returns the value 1.2816.

If X_1 and X_2 are independent random variables with $X_i \sim N(\mu_i, \sigma_i^2)$ for $i = 1, 2$, and w_1 and w_2 are constants, then $w_1 X_1 + w_2 X_2$ is normally distributed with mean $w_1\mu_1 + w_2\mu_2$ and variance $w_1^2\sigma_1^2 + w_2^2\sigma_2^2$. In general, linear combinations of normally distributed random variables (not necessarily independent) are normally distributed.

A.14 Lognormal distribution

Suppose X is a continuous positive random variable. If $\ln X$ follows a normal distribution with mean μ and variance σ^2, then X is said to follow a lognormal distribution with parameters μ and σ^2. The mean and variance of X are

$$\mathrm{E}(X) = e^{\mu + \frac{1}{2}\sigma^2},$$

$$\mathrm{Var}(X) = \left(e^{2\mu + \sigma^2}\right)\left(e^{\sigma^2} - 1\right).$$

If X_1 and X_2 are independently distributed lognormal random variables with $\ln X_i \sim N(\mu_i, \sigma_i^2)$ for $i = 1, 2$, and w_1 and w_2 are constants, then $Y = X_1^{w_1} X_2^{w_2}$ is lognormally distributed with parameters $w_1\mu_1 + w_2\mu_2$ and $w_1^2\sigma_1^2 + w_2^2\sigma_2^2$. This result holds as

$$\begin{aligned}
\ln Y &= \ln X_1^{w_1} X_2^{w_2} \\
&= w_1 \ln X_1 + w_2 \ln X_2 \\
&\sim N(w_1\mu_1 + w_2\mu_2, w_1^2\sigma_1^2 + w_2^2\sigma_2^2).
\end{aligned}$$

In general, products of powers of lognormally distributed random variables (not necessarily independent) are lognormally distributed.

APPENDIX B

Answers to Selected Exercises

Chapter 1

1.1 $27,456.15

1.3 $I(5) = 300$, $A(6) = 2,040$

1.4 $A(3) = 321$, $i(4) = 4.36\%$

1.5   (a) $1,315.79   (b) $1,240.00   (c) $1,262.48
       (d) $1,268.99   (e) $1,272.01   (f) $1,271.25

1.6   (a) $i(2) = 32.34\%$, $i(3) = 26.85\%$ (b) $I(3) = \$519.76$

1.7   (b) $9.597

1.8   Only (c)

1.9   (a) 10.488%   (b) 9.729%   (c) 10.098%   (d) 9.973%   (e) $(1.104876)^t$

1.10   7.39%

1.12 $1,740.20, $240.20

1.13   (a) $25   (b) $312.6

1.14   18 years, 17.67 years

1.15   (a) $434.83   (b) $434.06   (c) $455.84   (d) $443.73

1.16   8%

1.17   Lender A

1.18   15%

1.19   Present value = 2,366.28, future value = 2,612.56

1.20   (b) $2,902

1.21   (a) 0.05, 0.04762, 0.04545 (b) Simple interest at 5%

1.22   (a) $441.18 (b) $438.71

1.23 $3,999.30

1.24   (b) $i = 18.73\%$ or 1.07%

1.25   15.1029 years

1.26   15.0984 years

1.27   All but the upper right-hand figure

1.28   2.422%

1.29   4%

1.30   (a) $8,500 (b) $4,545.05

1.31   4

1.32   1.2144%

1.33   (b) Simple rate of discount of 1% per year for 100 years

1.34   0.3077

1.35   Only (a)

1.36   0.064

1.37   (a) 4.3000 (b) 4.3076 (c) 4.3283

1.38   (a) 1.8682 (b) 0.125

1.39   131.45

1.40   Option (b)

1.42 $t = 8.87$

1.43   (a) $\delta = \ln(1 + i)$ (b) $\delta = -\ln(1 - d)$

Chapter 2

2.1 (a) 12.5779   (b) 4.5460   (c) 30.9822   (d) 22.0185   (e) 20

2.2 (a) 1.9505   (b) 4.1757   (c) 10.6624

2.5 (a) $6,910.67   (b) $3,387.58   (c) $6,432.77

2.6 $4,716.35

2.7 14.47%

2.8 $612.97

2.9 (a) 5.4920   (b) 6.16, No

2.10 $1,000 $\left[\dfrac{1+i}{i} - \dfrac{(1+i)^2}{(1+i)^4 - 1} \right]$

2.11 $74.90

2.12 $7,351.40

2.13 $92.91

2.14 $9.0021

2.16 $808.61

2.17 2.081 years

2.18 $50,811.18

2.19 $528.59

2.22 $\ddot{s}_{\overline{m}|}$ at the interest rate i_k, where $i_k = (1+i)^k - 1$

2.23 $\dfrac{d^{(12)}}{r^{(52)}}$

2.24 44 months

2.26 $97.81

2.27 (a) $i(Ia)_{\overline{n}|}$ (b) The principal is n

2.28 $2,000(\ddot{s}_{\overline{7}|}^{(4)} - \ddot{s}_{\overline{2}|}^{(4)})$

2.29 $1,000(\ddot{s}_{\overline{12}|} + \ddot{s}_{\overline{8}|} + \ddot{s}_{\overline{4}|})$

2.30 (a) $\dfrac{2}{t+2}$ (b) 1.5667

2.31 $1,789.31

2.32 $n - \dfrac{n(n-1)d}{2}$

2.34 (a) $\dfrac{a_{\overline{60}|}}{s_{\overline{4}|}}$ (b) $\dfrac{s_{\overline{23}|} - s_{\overline{5}|}}{s_{\overline{3}|}}$

2.36 $21,154.84

2.37 $(Ia)_{\overline{n}|} + v^n (Da)_{\overline{n}|}$

2.38 (a) $138.87   (b) $370.30

2.39 $\dfrac{n(n+1)}{2} + \left[\dfrac{n(n+1)(2n+1)}{6}\right] i$

2.40 $688.123

2.41 $20,748.23

2.43 $177.5960

2.44 $297.26 at $t = 18$ or $315.37 at $t = 20$ or $299.05 at $t = 18.2$

2.45 35

2.46 $57.83

2.47 (a) 5.7905%   (b) 6.6563%   (c) 4.9494%   (d) 4.4778%

2.48 $2\ln(1+t)$

2.50 (a) $1,361.23   (b) $10,429.65   (c) $1,553.93

2.51 (a) $n = 10$, $1,369.73
     (b) $2,630.27 at $t = 11$; $4,000 at $t = 12, \cdots, 28$; $44.95 at $t = 29$

2.53 $x^2 \left[\left(\dfrac{y-x}{x}\right)^k - 1\right] \left[\dfrac{1}{y-2x}\right]$

Chapter 3

3.1 (a) Yes

3.2 (a) $i_1^F = 3.0\%$, $i_2^F = 4.002\%$, $i_3^F = 3.500\%$, $i_4^F = 4.504\%$
(b) $a_{\overline{4}|} = 3.669$, $s_{\overline{3}|} = 3.111$

3.3 (a) $i_1^S = 6.000\%$, $i_2^S = 6.100\%$, $i_3^S = 6.233\%$, $i_4^S = 6.424\%$
(b) $a_{\overline{4}|} = 3.445$, $s_{\overline{4}|} = 4.420$

3.4 (a) $i_1^F = 2.100\%$, $i_2^S = 2.350\%$, $i_3^F = 4.617\%$, $i_4^S = 3.225\%$
(b) $\ddot{a}_{\overline{4}|} = 3.847$, $\ddot{s}_{\overline{4}|} = 4.367$

3.5 (a) 4.386%   (b) $(Ia)_{\overline{4}|} = 8.7536$, $(Da)_{\overline{4}|} = 9.1913$

3.6 $8,756.90

3.7 $i_2^S = 1.005\%$, $i_3^F = 2.530\%$

3.8 (a) $334.45   (b) 7.56%

3.9 i_j^F for $j = 2, \cdots, 6$ are: 4.00%, 4.20%, 5.00%, 4.50% and 5.50%

3.12 (a) i_j^F for $j = 1, \cdots, 5$, are 4%; $i_6^F = 10.15\%$; i_j^F
for $j = 7, \cdots, 10$, are 5%
(b) $784.41   (c) $1,277.72   (d) $1,277.72   (e) $1,240.90
(f) $1,240.90

3.13 (a) $i_1^S = 5.000\%$, $i_2^S = 4.881\%$, $i_{2.5}^S = 4.824\%$
(b) $a_2(1) = 1.0455$, $a_2(2) = 1.0909$, $a_2(2.5) = 1.1136$
(c) $i_{2,1}^F = 4.55\%$, $i_{2,2}^F = 4.45\%$, $i_{2,2.5}^F = 4.40\%$

3.14 (a) $a_5(t) = \exp\left[\dfrac{30t + t^2}{400}\right]$ (b) $i_{5,1}^F = 8.06\%$, $i_{5,2}^F = 8.33\%$

3.16 $3,104.04

3.17 (a) $59.48854k$ (b) 12.9744   (c) 12.9744

3.18 (a) 3.4522%   (b) 4.6120%   (c) 2.5433%
(d) −$26,622   (e) −$88,737.04   (f) 4.1995%

3.20 (a) 20.0583
(b) i_j^F for $j = 1, \cdots, 6$, are: 4.00%, 4.40%, 4.80%, 5.20%, 5.60%
and 6.01%

3.21 1,483.10

Chapter 4

4.1   13.7%

4.2 -53.2% or 28.2%

4.3   (a) \$25.4895   (b) \$25.3050

4.4   (a) \$116.95   (b) \$135.85

4.5   4.623%

4.6   (a) 14.5%

4.8   (a) -8.629% (b) \$1,158.33   (c) -8.633%

4.9 -8.33%

4.10   DWRR = 3.91%, TWRR = 14.13%

4.11   AM = 5.81%, GM = 4.98%

4.12   AM = 30.32%, GM = 21.31%

4.13   AM = 12.97%, GM = 12.40%

4.14   Exact = 2.93%, approximate = 2.90%

4.15   TWRR = 6.9685%, DWRR = 6.6298%

4.16   5% or 12%

4.17   The internal rate of return is not a real number

4.18   16.2103% (effective rate)

4.19   (a) 7.503%   (b) 6.398%

4.20   6.154%

4.21   (a) 3   (b) 17.33%

4.22   (a) TWRR = -23.61%, DWRR = 3.11%

4.23   Expected return = 18.05%, standard deviation = 19.5179%

4.24   4.65%

4.25 (a) -0.508 (b) Weight = 0.2085, expected return = 12.117%

4.26 (a) Expected return = 14.4%, standard deviation = 21.72%
     (b) Expected return = 9.6%, standard deviation = 10.92%

4.29 (a) $95.38 (b) -9.1%

4.30 (a) $67 (b) $70.6

4.31 20%

4.32 (a) 22% (b) 20% (c) 16%

4.33 $X = 8.0157\%$, $Y = 5.6054\%$

4.34 The investment-year rates are $i_1^{2008} = 6.7\%$, $i_2^{2007} = 6.3\%$ and $i_3^{2006} = 6.0\%$
     The portfolio rate is $i^{2008} = 6.2\%$

4.35 $108.48

4.36 5.725%

4.37 $3.3634

4.38 5.54%

4.39 $153.55

4.40 $-$129.28

4.41 $28.3896, not acceptable

4.46 $-$85.8223, profitable

4.47 Pay cash

4.48 15.48%

4.49 (a) 7.863% (b) 7.570%

4.50 (a) 32.25% (b) $1,727.82

4.51 (a) 11.5% (b) $20.20

Chapter 5

5.2   (a) $8,982.59   (b) $8,982.59

5.3 $2,118.68

5.4   (a) $2,855.44   (b) $2,855.44

5.5   (a) 7%, $1,552.17

5.6   (a) $1,584.72   (b) $2,523.38

5.7 $3,489

5.10   The effective annual rate is 4.04%.

5.13 $3,880.96

5.14 $461.88

5.15   (a) $8,956.30   (b) $8,956.30,
       The interest portion in the 7th annual payment is $537.38.

5.16   (a) $9,670.26   (b) $878.25

5.17 $62,004.60

5.18 $18,852.50

5.19   (a) $1,170.45   (b) $1,077.20

5.20 $361.16

5.21   (a) $254.163   (b) 4.91%

5.22   (a) $13,507.98   (b) $13,523.61

5.26   The first level instalment is $1,250, other results follow

5.27   The first level instalment is $1,750, other results follow

5.28   The first level instalment is $1,200, other results follow

5.30 $500i$

5.31 $P = \$176.55$

5.32   32 months, $93.09

5.33   (a) $153.25   (b) $26,540.96   (c) $42,976.50

5.34   (c) $1,049.47

5.35 $17.09

5.36   8.76%

5.37   3.37%

5.38 $12,092.96

5.39   The sinking fund deposit is $1,153.68

5.40   (a) $873.28   (b) 3.944%

5.41   (a) 50   (b) 39th period

5.43   (a) 7%   (b) 8.52%

5.44   The sinking fund deposit is $272.63, other results follow

5.45   (a) $3,202.45

5.46   The sinking fund deposit is $434.73, other results follow

5.47   The sinking fund deposit is $443.49, other results follow

5.48   The sinking fund deposit is $443.99, other results follow

5.49 $730.88

5.50   7

5.51   (a) $1,131.16   (b) $3,920.29   (c) $101.59

5.52 $56.64

5.53   (a) $1,039.52   (b) $5,111.65

5.54   (a) $2,235.44   (b) $2,183.90

5.55 $3,101.47

5.56   9.06%

5.57   (a) $121.33   (b) $118.44   (c) $118.65

5.58   (a) 8.3%   (b) 7.7%   (c) 7.8%

5.59   (a) 12.68%   (b) 11.77%

5.60   11.25%, 11.85%

5.61   Yes

5.63   Option (c)

5.64   Option (b)

5.65   Option (a) is most attractive, Option (b) is most costly

5.66   (a) $3,600   (b) $3,684.67

5.67 $(1 - i)^9 (1 - 2i)^{10} L$

5.68   (a) $n + 1$

Chapter 6

6.2   136.27, 129.60, 123.34, 117.47, 111.95, 106.77, 101.89, 97.30, 92.98, 88.91

6.4   (d)

6.5   (a) only

6.8   Purchase price = $97.9288, accrued interest = $1.7255, quoted price = $96.203

6.9   2.02% per annum

6.10

Bond	$i = 7\%$	$i = 5\%$
A	973.757	1,027.232
B	929.764	1,077.217

Bond B is more sensitive.

6.11 $1,000

6.14   Book value $B_7 = \$105.4916$, other results follow

6.15 $998.32

6.16   (a) $92.56   (b) $102.97

6.17 $7.4785 discount

6.18   3.6%

6.19   (a) At maturity   (b) At the end of the 6th year

6.20 $P(1+i)^t - t(Fr)$

6.21   Book value $B_3 = \$102.0129$, other results follow

6.22 $1.2578 write-up

6.24 $1,045

6.26 $102.1220

6.27 $36.67

6.28 $3.83 discount

6.29   (a) $99.9399   (b) $104.2941

6.30   (a) At issue: $107.1062, after 7 months: $94.3933   (b) 16.3%

6.32 $1,610.50

Chapter 7

7.1   (a) 8.52% convertible semiannually   (b) 7.41% convertible semiannually
     (c) $1,036.51

7.2 $1,053.89, 8.30% convertible semiannually

7.3   11.12% convertible semiannually

7.4   (a) 7.40% convertible semiannually   (b) $1,067

7.5   (a) 9.746%   (b) 9.833%   (c) 9.654%; all compounded semiannually

7.6   3.962%

7.7   (a) $\exp(0.03t)$ for $t \le 5$ and $\exp[0.06 + 0.0025(1+t)^2]$ for $t > 5$
     (b) $135.9413   (c) 3.142% compounded semiannually

7.8   4.44%

7.11   7.3678%

7.12 (a) 3.0205%   (b) 100

7.13 (a) 5.0% convertible semiannually   (b) 4.0%
      (c) 8.23% convertible annually

7.14 (a) 3.78%   (b) 4.01%

7.15 (a) 7.073%   (b) 6.801%

7.16 i_H for Bond A over 3 years are 5.3222% (Scenario Up) and 5.8077% (Down),

      i_H for Bond B over 3 years are 5.1974% (Scenario Up) and 5.1769% (Down).

7.17 4.0816%, 5.1957%, 6.8937%, 7.7320%

7.18 2.0408%, 2.5978%, 5.6145%, 7.1794%

7.21 3.0393%

7.22 4.0816%, 5.5723%, 5.0000%, 5.9589%, 6.3708%, 6.7790%

7.23 8.0811%, 8.2078%, 8.3582%, 8.6505%

Chapter 8

8.1 $D^* = 4.2772, C = 24.4070$

8.2 $D = 3.9346, C = 20.5458$

8.5   21 years

8.9   Statement A

8.10 Statement B

8.11 4.752 years

8.14 (a) +2.768%   (b) +2.828%

8.16 260.9566

8.17 (a) $P = 350.409, D^* = 5.4045$ years, $C = 48.0435$
      (b) Approximate value = 341.151, true value = 341.147

8.18 (a) $P = \$26,\!638.05$, $D = 6.9216$ years, $C = 52.5392$

(b) $\$9,\!495$, $\$15,\!857$

8.19 Bond X

8.21 Bond X: $\$2,\!004.682$, Bond Y: $\$2,\!141.747$

8.22 (a) 48.3472%　(b) Liability: 9 years, Assets: 9.167 years

8.23 Bond M

8.24 (a) Liability: $D = 19.3642$, $C = 497.9611$

　　　Bond A: $D = 17.6013$, $C = 371.0864$

　　　Bond B: $D = 26.4562$, $C = 879.9213$

(b) $\$1,\!212.11$ in Bond A and $\$301.31$ in Bond B

8.26 $E : \$4,\!218.3680$, $F : \$4,\!513.6538$, $G : \$4,\!513.6538$, $H : \$4,\!739.3365$

8.27 (b) $D^* = (i - g)^{-1}$, $C = 2(i - g)^{-2}$

8.28 (a) $\$66,\!255.08$, 5 years　(b) Yes

8.29 (a) -1.92%, 2.45%, 5.15% for $n = 1, 2$ and 5, respectively

8.32 Statement (c) only

8.35 (a) $\$921.659$　(b) Up: $\$1,\!834.88$, Down: $\$1,\!851.87$

8.37 (a) $D_F = 2.882$ years for Bond A and 4.332 years for Bond B

　　　$\sum W_t = 2.711$ years (A) and 4.069 years (B)

(b) Actual price changes: -1.873% (A) and -2.796% (B)

　　　Predicted price changes: -1.898% (A) and -2.848% (B)

(c) $D_F = 2.881$ years (A) and 4.322 years (B)

8.38 21.3384, 813.2149

8.39 (a) No　(b) 1,617.20 (1-year bond), 0 (3-year bond), 1,388.60 (4-year bond)

8.40 (a) $\mathrm{E}(T) = D$

Chapter 9

9.1   4.5%

9.2 $98.10

9.3   0.97%

9.4 $395.24

9.5 $183,845.68

Chapter 10

10.1   7.7%

10.2   (a) 5.3633, 5.8666   (b) 5.4875, 0.1746

10.4   7.5544, 0.2565

10.5   "Pop-up" scenario

10.6   2.6191, 0.0575

10.7   10.3662, 0.0115

10.9   (b) 1.0932, 0.003552

10.10   1.6289, 0.0491

10.11   12.5795, 0.4406

10.12   21.55, 0.2809 for $n = 13$; 36.38, 0.5699 for $n = 18$

10.14   (a) 7.7884%   (b) 0.7985, 0.6873

10.15   (a) 1.2214, 0.1243   (b) 0.8869, 0.0655

10.16   (a) 1.2713, 0.2064   (b) 0.8869, 0.1003

10.17   (a) 6.2196, 2.1994   (b) 6.4090, 1.4758

10.18   (a) 7.5546, 3.5302   (b) 7.7459, 5.6514

10.19   (1.8616, 3.2407)

10.22 $(-3.83\%,\ 2.70\%,\ 7.38\%,\ 9.28\%,\ 19.36\%,\ 11.62\%)$

10.23 $5.8109\%,\ 8.3782\%$

10.24   (a) $\ddot{s}_{\overline{10}|}$: $19.1062,\ 9.9410$ (b) $(Ia)_{\overline{10}|}$: $36.4177,\ 16.9342$

Index